The Schwenkfelders in Silesia

by

Horst Weigelt

Pennsburg, PA
Schwenkfelder Library
1985

translated from Horst Weigelt, *Spiritualistische Tradition im Protestantismus: Die Geschichte des Schwenckfeldertums in Schlesien* (Berlin: Walter de Gruyter, 1973) by Peter C. Erb

ISBN 0-935980-04-0

In Memory of
Selina Gerhard Schultz

Table of Contents

Preface

Spiritualistische Tradition im Protestantismus: Die Geschichte des Schwenckfeldertums in Schlesien by Professor Horst Weigelt of the Institute for Protestant Theology at the University of Bamberg, was published in 1973 by Walter de Gruyter in Berlin. It was immediately clear that the work made major contributions to the history of Christianity, many of particular interest to the Schwenkfelders in America and students of their history. To reach a wider American audience the Directors of Schwenkfelder Library requested that I prepare this English version.

By treating the whole expanse of Silesian Schwenkfelder history from Schwenckfeld's first steps in reform in the early 1520s through to the death of the last European Schwenkfelder in the early nineteenth century, Professor Weigelt's study allows one to view developments in the movement as never before. First, it offers insight into the early period of Schwenckfeld's thought until his self-exile from his homeland in 1529, pointing particularly to the significant role played by his colleague Valentin Crautwald in shaping distinctive Schwenkfeldian doctrines, and outlining initial contacts between those holding to Schwenckfeld's position and the Lutherans, the reformed churches in Switzerland and South Germany, and the Anabaptists. In addition, the volume casts light on the period of Schwenkfelder history between the death of Schwenckfeld in 1561 and the arrival of the Jesuit Mission in Harpersdorf in 1719. Little was known concerning this period prior to the publication of Professor Weigelt's study, although there had long been a serious interest in it. Especially important in his treatment of this so-called "dark ages" is his discussion of the change which occurred in Schwenkfelder thought during it, namely of the movement from Schwenckfeld's primarily christological concerns to later Schwenkfelder interest in soteriology, the doctrine of salvation and its operation in human life. Third, for students of the Reformation in general and the Radical Reformation in particular, Professor Weigelt's book opens new areas for consideration in its detailed descriptions of the relationships between radical and magisterial reformation groups and the significance of humanism in the development of Reformation principles.

Finally, as is made clear in the title of the original, the volume is of importance as a contribution to the study of "spiritualism" in Protestantism. English readers must take special care in interpreting the words "spiritualism" and "spiritualist" as they are used throughout this book and elsewhere in Schwenckfeld studies. The terms do not in this case refer to an interest in speaking with departed souls through mediums. Rather they are used to describe a theological approach which places emphasis on the spiritual as opposed to the corporeal aspects of religious life, on the spirit as set over against the body, the spiritual participation in the sacrament as opposed to the physical eating and drinking, the spiritual significance of the words of the Scripture as opposed to the literal text.

A number of people assisted in the preparation of this text and deserve special thanks. Professor Weigelt, Dr. Hans Schwartz and Mr. Timothy Steward worked carefully over successive drafts and made valuable suggestions for improving the translation. Alice Croft displayed her usual patient accuracy in checking draft after draft. Dave Kroeker was responsible for preparing coded electronic copy and for extensive stylistic suggestions. Hart Bezner and the staff of the Computing Centre at Wilfrid Laurier University, Waterloo, Ontario, Canada were as always most helpful. Some of the initial costs were covered with a grant from Wilfrid Laurier. Above all, I wish personally to thank the members of the Board of Schwenkfelder Library, for their encouragement and financial support of this project and many others undertaken over the past decade. Their leadership under President Claude A. Schultz, Jr., and Vice-President W. Kyrel Meschter has resulted directly in a growing interest in Schwenkfelder studies, the results of which are of value not only for members of the Schwenkfelder community itself, but also for the many persons working on broader issues in Reformation and Post-Reformation thought.

Peter C. Erb
Associate Director
Schwenkfelder Library

Author's Preface

The present volume is a translation of a shortened version of my Habilitationsschrift presented to the Lutheran theological faculty of the University of Erlangen-Nürnberg. Sources which were discovered before its publication in book form in 1973 and significant secondary literature which appeared during that time have been added. A complete inclusion of the latest results of research as well as the listing of any new literature in this translation has not been possible due to a lack of time and for economic reasons. Regarding the recent literature on this behalf I especially draw attention to the two forthcoming volumes of papers, which will be edited by Peter C. Erb, Associate Director of Schwenkfelder Library, in connection with the Colloquium on Schwenckfeld and Schwenkfelders.

Throughout the years in which I have studied the history of the Schwenkfelders in Silesia, a movement in which the spiritualist tradition in Protestantism is particularly evident, I have received encouragement and constructive criticism from many sides. For this I thank all those persons—Protestant and Catholic, German and non-German—who have spoken with me regarding the project.

My thanks go as well to the Deutsche Forschungsgemeinschaft for a stipend which made possible trips to Poland and to the United States where I was twice the guest of the Schwenkfelder Library. Mr. Andrew Berky, then director of the Library made its extensive collection available to me and offered me every possible help. In addition I have received extensive aid from German, Dutch, Italian, Austrian, Polish and Czecheslovakian libraries and archives, and the University Library of Erlangen-Nürnberg.

The German edition of this book first appeared as number 43 in the series (Arbeiten zur Kirchengeschichte) and I wish to thank the editors of that series, Professors Kurt Aland, Carl Andresen and Gerhard Müler, as well as the publisher Walter de Gruyter for accepting the volume for the series; the publication was made possible by a subvention from the Deutsche Forschungsgemeinschaft. I am especially thankful to Professor Gerhard Müler who carefully oversaw the publication of the German original.

I dedicate my special thanks to Dr. Peter C. Erb, who translated the manuscript with enormous sacrifice of time and energy, never ceasing patience and great persistence. For carefully reviewing the translation I thank Prof. Dr. Hans Schwarz and Mr. Timothy Stewart. Finally I thank the staff of the Schwenkfelder Library for seeing the project through to its completion.

This English edition of my book is dedicated in memory of Dr. Selina Gerhard Schultz, who many years ago followed the first steps of my studies with intense attention and gave them encouraging support.

Horst Weigelt

Abbreviations

ADB	*Allgemeine Deutsche Biographie.* Herausgegeben durch die Historische Kommission bei der Bayerischen Akademie der Wissenschaften. 55 Bde. und 1 Reg.-Bd. München und Leipzig 1875-1912.
AGP	*Arbeiten zur Geschichte des Pietismus.*
Allen	*Opus epistolarum Des. Erasmi Roterodami.* Denuo recognitum et acutum per P. S. Allen, H. M. Allen and H. W. Garrod. 12 vols. Oxford 1960-1958.
ARG	*Archiv für Reformationsgeschichte.*
ArSKG	*Archiv für schlesische Kirchengeschichte.*
AThANT	*Abhandlungen zur Theologie des Alten und Neuen Testaments.*
AZTh	*Arbeiten zur Theologie.*
BBKG	*Beiträge zur bayerischen Kirchengeschichte.*
BHTh	*Beiträge zur historischen Theologie.*
Bl-Debr	*F. Blass—A. Debrunner, Grammatik des neutestamentlichen Griechisch.* 9. Auflage. Göttingen 1954.
Bll.württ.KG	*Blätter für württembergische Kirchengeschichte.*
ChH	*Church History.*
ChW	*Die christliche Welt.*
Correspondenz-Blatt	*Correspondenzblatt des Vereins für Geschichte der Evangelischen Kirche Schlesiens.*
CR	*Corpus Reformatorum.*
CS	*Corpus Schwenckfeldianorum.*
CSEL	*Corpus scriptorum ecclesiasticorum Latinorum.*
Denz.	H. Denzinger, *Enchiridion Symbolorum, Definitionum et Declarationum de rebus fidei et morum.* 31. Auflage. Freiburg i. Br. 1960.
End	*Dr. Martin Luthers Briefwechsel.* Bearbeitet von Dr. Ernst Ludwig Enders. 19 Bde. Frankfurt a. Main 1884-1932.
FKGG	*Forschungen zur Kirchen- und Geistesgeschichte.*
Friedlaender	E. Friedlaender, *Aeltere Universitäts-Matrikeln. I. Universität Frankfurt a. O.* Aus der Originalhandschrift unter Mitwirkung von Georg Liebe und Emil Theuner herausgegeben von Ernst Friedlaender. Bd. I (1506-1648.) Leipzig 1887.
JGPrO	*Jahrbuch der Gesellschaft für die Geschichte des Protestantismus in Osterreich.*

Jöcher	*Allgemeines Gelehrten-Lexicon.* Herausgegeben von Ch. G. Jöcher. 4 Teile. Leipzig 1950-51.
Jöcher-Adelung	*Fortsetzung und Ergänzungen zu Jöcher's Allgemeinem Gelehrten-Lexicon.* Bd. 1-2 (v. J. Ch. Adelung). Leipzig 1784-1787. Bd. 3-6 (v. H. W. Rotermund). Delmenhorst und Bremen 1810-1822. Bd. 7 (v. O. Günther). Leipzig 1897.
JSchlKG	*Jahrbuch für Schlesische Kirchengeschichte.*
Le Clerc	*Desiderii Erasmi Roterodami Opera omnia emendatiora et auctiora, ad optimas editiones, praecipue quas ipse Erasmus postremo curavit, summa fide exacta, doctorum virorum notis illustrata.* Recognovit Joannes Clericus. 10 vols. Lugduni Batavorum 1703-1706.
LW	*Luther's Works,* edited by J. Pelikan. 55 vols. St. Louis, MO, 1958-1967
ME	*Mennonite Encyclopedia.* 4 vols. Scottdale 1955-1959.
MGP	*Monumenta Germaniae Paedagogica.*
ML	*Mennonitisches Lexikon.* 4 Bde. Frankfurt a. Main—Karlsruhe 1913-1967.
MPG	*Patrologiae cursus completus, series Graeca.* edited by J. P. Migne. 161 vols. Paris 1857-1866.
MPL	*Patrologiae cursus completus, series Latina.* edited by J. P. Migne. 217 vols. Paris 1878-1890.
NKZ	*Neue Kirchliche Zeitschrift.*
QFRG	*Quellen und Forschungen zur Reformationsgeschichte.*
RE	*Realencyklopädie für protestantische Theologie und Kirche.* Begründet v. J. J. Herzog, herausgegeben v. A. Hauck. 3. Auflage. 24 Bde. Leipzig 1896-1913.
RGG	*Die Religion in Geschichte und Gegenwart.* 3. Auflage. 6 Bde. Tübingen 1956-1962.
Schl	*Bibliographie zur deutschen Geschichte im Zeitalter der Glaubensspaltung 1517-85.* Herausgegeben von K. Schottenloher. 7 Bde. Stuttgart 1956-1966.
Schultz	Selina Gerhard Schultz, *Caspar Schwenckfeld von Ossig* Pennsburg, 1946
Sehling	*Die evangelischen Kirchenordnungen des XVI. Jahrhunderts. Herausgegeben von Emil Sehling. Bd. III. Die Mark Brandenburg.—Die Markgrafenthümer Ober-*

	Lausitz und Nieder-Lausitz.—Schlesien. Leipzig 1909.
SGV	*Sammlung gemeinverständlicher Vorträge und Schriften aus dem Gebiet der Theologie und Religionsgeschichte.*
Sommervogel	*Bibliothèque de la Compagnie de Jésus. Nouvelle édition par C. Sommervogel. Vol. V. and VI. Brussels-Paris 1895-1896.*
Suppl. Mel.	*Supplementa Melanchthoniana. Werke Philipp Melanchthons, die im Corpus Reformatorum vermisst werden.* Leipzig 1910 ff.
SVRG	*Schriften des Vereins für Reformationsgeschichte.*
TA Elsass I	*Quellen zur Geschichte der Täufer. Bd. VII. Elsass, I. Teil Stadt Strassburg 1522-1532.* Bearbeitet von Manfred Krebs und Hans Georg Rott. Gütersloh 1959.
TA Elsass II	*Quellen zur Geschichte der Täufer. Bd. VII. Elsass, II. Teil Stadt Strassburg 1533-1535.* Bearbeitet von Manfred Krebs und Hans Georg Rott. Gütersloh 1960.
ThEx	*Theologische Existenz heute.*
ThJB	*Theologischer Jahresbericht.*
ThLZ	*Theologische Literaturzeitung.*
ThStKr	*Theologische Studien und Kritiken.*
ThZ	*Theologische Zeitschrift.*
Unschuldige Nachrichten	*Unschuldige Nachrichten von Alten und Neuen Theologischen Sachen.*
W[1]	*Luthers Werke.* Herausgegeben von Joh. G. Walch. 1. Auflage.
WA	*Luthers Werke. Kritische Gesamtausgabe.*
WAB	*Luthers Werke. Kritische Gesamtausgabe. Briefwechsel.*
WA Bibl	*Luthers Werke. Kritische Gesamtausgabe. Die Deutsche Bibel.*
WAT	*Luthers Werke. Kritische Gesamtausgabe. Tischreden.*
ZBG	*Zeitschrift für Brüdergeschichte.*
ZBKG	*Zeitschrift für bayerische Kirchengeschichte.*
ZDPV	*Zeitschrift des Deutschen Palästinavereins.*
ZHTh	*Zeitschrift für die historische Theologie.*
ZKG	*Zeitschrift für Kirchengeschichte.*
ZRGG	*Zeitschrift für Religions- und Geistesgeschichte.*
ZVG Schles.	*Zeitschrift des Vereins für Geschichte Schlesiens.*
ZWL	*Zeitschrift für kirchliche Wissenschaft und kirchliches Leben.*

INTRODUCTION

Although research into Anabaptism has progressed without interruption since the middle of the last century, the study of sixteenth-century mystical spiritualism has been unduly neglected. In particular, there exist few descriptions dealing with the groups within this tributary of the Reformation. Mystical spiritualism is without doubt characterized by a tendency to individualism, but certain of its members did unite in communities. Among these, the most significant theologically and historically were the Schwenkfelders in Silesia who survived into the first thirty years of the nineteenth century. Their history, little studied until now, is the subject of this monograph. Three questions are specifically treated. First, where are the roots of the movement to be found? Do they lie in late medieval mysticism, in humanism, or in the theology of the young Luther? Secondly, how did Schwenckfeld and his followers set themselves apart from the Reformation? Were they influenced by Reformation theology and if so, how? Finally, what is the relationship of later Schwenkfeldianism to other theological and spiritual movements, in particular to the mystical spiritualism of the seventeenth century, to Pietism, and to the Enlightenment. The result serves as a contribution to studies of the spiritualist tradition in Protestantism.

The study which follows is based on the Schwenkfeldian and anti-Schwenkfeldian sources indicated in the text. The description of early Schwenkfeldianism is drawn from materials printed in the *Corpus Schwenckfeldianorum* as well as from the works of Crautwald, which have survived nearly completely. His personal library, the volumes of which are filled with marginalia and citations, has been investigated. In addition, manuscripts and books of the most significant Schwenkfelder theologians, above all Johann Sigismund Werner and Fabian Eckel, were consulted. The *Acta Capituli Wratislaviensis* also offered valuable insights. The research on later Schwenkfeldianism was made possible, above all, because of the archives of the Schwenkfelder Library in Pennsburg, Pennsylvania. These stem, primarily, from the collections brought by the Schwenkfelders who emigrated to America in 1734, taking with them not only devotional materials but letters and treatises as well. In Pennsburg as well is preserved the extensive correspondence which they continued with their fellow believers who remained behind in their homeland. In addition to this material are numerous Schwenkfeldian pieces, copied or purchased by the *Corpus* editors. The archives of German, Dutch, Polish, and Czechoslovakian libraries have served to complete the unique collection housed in the Schwenkfelder Library.

Since these sources are widely scattered and are in part not easily accessible, they have been quoted extensively. This will at the same time allow readers to form their own judgments regarding the material.

I The Beginnings of Schwenkfeldianism and its Criticism of Luther's Doctrine of Justification

1. Origins and Early Growth

Sometime after 1523 there existed in Silesia a relatively unified religious body which initially saw itself as part of the Wittenberg movement. By 1525, however, with the beginning of the controversy over the Lord's Supper, it separated itself more and more from Wittenberg, and by 1528, in disagreement over the means by which grace is communicated to the believer, it developed into an independent movement. Its founder and initial advocate, Caspar Schwenckfeld von Ossig,[1] was born in 1489 on his parental estate of Ossig near Lüben in the principality of Liegnitz.[2] Hans von Schwenckfeld, his father, descended from a noble family whose roots went back to thirteenth century Silesia, and his mother, Barbara, nee von Kreckwitz, stemmed from long-established Croatian nobility. As a youth, Schwenckfeld likely attended one of the three schools in Liegnitz.[3]

In his sixteenth year, according to his own testimony, he went to the University of Cologne,[4] at that time a stronghold of the *via antiqua*, and in 1507, a year after the humanist Ulrich von Hutten, he traveled to Frankfurt on the Oder,[5] where in 1506 Elector Joachim I had established a state university, the Viadrina, for Brandenburg. At this *alma mater*, a base for humanism, many noted scholars taught, among whom were Johann Rhagius Aesticampianus, a friend of Conrad Celtis, and Publicus Vigilantius Bacillaris Axungia, the first dean of the philosophy faculty. Whether he studied at other universities as he claimed cannot be documented.[6] His letters and other writings make no mention of the disciplines he studied, but in addition to the liberal arts he probably concerned himself with canon law. He received no academic degree.

By March, 1511 at the latest, he entered the service of Duke Karl I of Münsterberg-Oels.[7] The duke was the grandson of the excommunicated Bohemian king, Georg von Podiebrad, who was sympathetic to the Hussite cause, and had, therefore, together with his next three generations been excommunicated. Schwenckfeld, however, could hardly have been exposed to Hussite ideas there. A landed noble, Schwenckfeld later went to the court of the easy-going ruler, Duke Georg I of Brieg,[8] who died May 30, 1521 "corrupted by excessive drinking and other passions."[9] According to Schwenckfeld's own testimony, as a "courtier" he had not "concerned himself much with the Scriptures at the time."[10] During his stay in Brieg, the controversy over Reuchlin occurred. It caused particular agitation in Silesia but whether or not Schwenckfeld took part is not known. If he did, it is possible he was a Reuchlinist like Johann Hess, one of his closest friends.[11]

In all likelihood at the end of 1519,[12] either during his residence in Brieg, or possibly during his court service at Liegnitz, Schwenckfeld experienced a religious awakening under the influence of Luther's writings, which were sold in Silesia soon after their publication[13] and in 1519 were being published in Breslau by Adam Dyon.[14] As he later told the Göppinger pastor Jacob Andreae, he studied the Wittenberg reformer's work with zeal. ''Without pride,'' he wrote, ''I can say I have read as many of Doctor Luther's books as you have, and (I wish to point out) that perhaps before you knew your ABCs, I had read many of his writings cover to cover with great energy, and in prayer according to Paul's rule: *Omnia probate*, search diligently and verify.''[15] As Emanuel Hirsch was first to demonstrate Luther's 1517 *Commentary on the Seven Penitential Psalms* was especially influential.[16] Since Schwenckfeld was indebted to Luther for his conversion, he felt himself inwardly obliged to the Wittenberg reformer when the final break came. Thus, for example, on September 10, 1533 he wrote, ''I am under debt to pray for Luther, for he was of much service in leading me and others to a knowledge of the truth.''[17] Even in 1546, after he had experienced Luther's vehement rejection,[18] he declared, ''Since Luther initially aided me in coming to a knowledge of the papacy and many points of truth, I do not believe it unreasonable to acknowledge my debt with gratitude and to pray to God for him.''[19]

Apparently after the death of his father and sometime before September 19, 1519,[20] perhaps on the occasion of the marriage of Duke Frederick II of Liegnitz on November 14, 1518 to Sophie, daughter of Count Frederick V of Brandenburg-Ansbach, Schwenckfeld entered royal service as the duke's counselor.[21] Thanks to his position of trust with Frederick II who, unlike his brother Georg I, was deeply religious, Schwenckfeld succeeded in a short time in initiating the reform movement in the city and principality of Liegnitz and in attracting numerous adherents.

To begin with he won Fabian Eckel to the cause. In 1522 Frederick II had called Eckel from Oels to his home town of Liegnitz, where the latter immediately associated himself with the Wittenberg reform.[22] It is likely that Schwenckfeld played a role in initiating the call. He had first wished that the vacancy at St. Mary's church be filled by Johann Hess,[23] but the latter refused the call, choosing rather to accept a call from Oels and to recommend Fabian Eckel. On June 8, 1522 Eckel, without the bishop's investiture, preached the first sermon in the new faith at St. Mary's, one of two pastorates in the city. In the same year, Jerome Wittich of Breslau was installed as a deacon in St. Mary's. Later superintendent of Brieg, Wittich would be one of the most determined opponents of the Schwenkfelders. In 1522 as well, the Franciscan Sebastian Schubart,[24] who according to tradition was born in Kulmbach,[25] preached the new faith at St. John's. He soon became a dedicated adherent of Schwenckfeld, a fact he later could not deny, although he anxiously attempted to conceal it.[26]

It was possibly at the end of 1523 that Schwenckfeld came to know Valentin Crautwald who was to have such great significance for the Schwenkfelder movement in Silesia. He is the one who gave Schwenkfeldianism its theological profile, a fact unrecognized in present research.

Crautwald was born of peasant stock[27] (which probably took its name from the place name Crautenwalde[28] in Neisse, a town which served as the Breslau bishop's residence in the sixteenth and seventeenth centuries) around 1490[29] and attended the Latin school there.[30] In the summer of 1506 he went to the University of Cracow, a highly reputable European university where humanism had made an early impact.[31] Initially a student of the liberal arts, he may later have studied canon law. Whether he attended other universities is not known. Around 1507 he became a teacher in his native town together with Johann Furenschild at the school of St. Jacob's, which was very famous at the beginning of the sixteenth century. A few years later he was appointed rector.[32] Here, where he "had earlier lived as a student and undergone many sorrows,"[33] one of his students was Franciscus Faber who was later to be counted among the most significant humanists in Silesia.[34]

By 1514 at the latest Johann V. Turzo, Bishop of Breslau, a Renaissance man and patron of humanist studies, had named Crautwald secretary in his chancellery; as such he was at the same time a public notary.[35] Three years later Turzo made him altarist in Neisse and at the cathedral in Breslau.[36] On September 4, 1520 he became a canon in Neisse and under Bishop Jacob von Salza, episcopal protonotary.[37]

During this period Crautwald, who possessed an extensive humanist education[38] and belonged to the Silesian Reuchlinists,[39] made friends with numerous humanists, among them Johann Hess, later a Breslau reformer, Caspar Ursinus Velius, later court historian to Ferdinand I and tutor to Emperor Maximilian II, the canon Stanislaus Sauer, the notary and Breslau chancellor Michael Wittiger, as well as with Ambrose Moibanus, moderator of the cathedral school in Breslau. Together they held Johann Reuchlin in great respect, paying careful attention to his quarrel with the University of Cologne and the Dominicans, but not becoming enmeshed in literary controversy themselves.[40] How enthusiastically Crautwald opened himself to humanism is manifested by his almost fully extant library which is both valuable and, considering his economic status, quite extensive.[41] It includes works of the ancients as well as writings of Italian and German humanists, in particular Erasmus.[42] Not only had he read and reread these, but for several he had even composed subject and word indexes.

Soon after the public emergence of the Wittenberg movement, at the latest in the spring of 1520, Crautwald and his friend Wittiger, possibly through the mediation of Johann Hess, established contacts in Wittenberg, in particular with Melanchthon,[43] and examined the question of the practice of the Lord's Supper there under discussion.[44] Because of this, C. Ursinus Velius, who remained firm in the old faith, did not make use in the second edition of his *Variorum Carminum* (1522)—as he had in the earlier 1517 edition—of a letter he had written to Crautwald from Rome. Unfortunately because of the paucity of sources it is not possible to outline in detail Crautwald's conversion to the new faith. It can only be said that he broke outwardly with humanism and, according to Adam Reisner, his first biographer, burned all his philosophical writings as well as his other compositions in prose and verse.[45]

In 1523, most likely at the instigation of Johann Hess, Crautwald was called as canon to the wealthy Liegnitz Cathedral of The Holy Sepulchre,[46] and on July 11, 1524 was invested by the duke, who possessed the right of investiture.[47] Here he assumed the endowed position of lecturer in theology.[48] Finding new freedom in his change of residence,[49] Crautwald seems to have begun his friendship with Schwenckfeld in Liegnitz very early after his arrival. This is attested to by the latter's remarks to Bucer in a letter of July 3, 1528: "In all things both Crautwald and I are united."[50]

At about the same time that Crautwald was called, Frederick II called Johann Sigismund Werner, who had earlier taught at the Latin school in his native Goldberg,[51] to be his court preacher.[52] He was also soon an enthusiastic follower of Crautwald and of Schwenckfeld, whom he had known since 1516. Later, through his effective preaching and his writings, Werner became one of the most important leaders of the Schwenkfelders in Silesia.

Finally, according to a reliable tradition, on Michaelmas, 1525 the Görlitz shoemaker's son, Valerius Rosenhayn who had earlier worked in the parish church at Schweidnitz, was called alongside the former Franciscan Wenzel Küchler,[53] as pastor to the church of Sts. Peter and Paul.[54] Since Küchler had early been a dedicated disciple of Schwenckfeld, this final pastorate in Liegnitz was also filled by a Schwenkfeldian.

Soon Schwenckfeld gained several more friends and disciples among the pastors of the principality of Wohlau. The city of Wohlau was a particularly important center. There Ambrose Kreusig of Breslau,[55] who had studied at Frankfurt in the summer of 1508,[56] and Bernhard Egetius [57] were active. Schwenckfeld often discussed with them "the gathering and edification of the church."[58] Since the end of 1522 or the beginning of 1523 he had remained primarily on his estate at Ossig near Wohlau. Because of increasing deafness, he had given up his position with Frederick II.[59] Nevertheless, as will become evident, up until his departure from Silesia in 1529, he remained the close confidant and counsel of his duke.[60] A second strong Schwenkfeldian center was Ossig itself, in the principality of Liegnitz, not far from Lüben. Scaurus[61] (a close friend of Schwenckfeld) was active here. Scaurus had been pastor since 1522 and with him the Silesian nobleman often discussed theological questions.

But Schwenckfeld did not have followers only among the pastors. The nobles also, among them Erhard vom Queis and Hans Magnus von Axleben, were drawn to him. Above all, this was possible because of the influence of Frederick II who, because of his extensive territorial control[62] was the most powerful prince in Silesia and, because of his far-flung family relationships[63] had great influence outside of Silesia. The grandson of Georg von Podiebrad, Frederick II had made a pilgrimage to the Holy Land in 1507[64] and was released thereby from the ban of excommunication placed on his family. According to his apology of 1527 he had early stood against the Reformation "with accusations and prohibitions."[65] He may also have feared that the reform movement would result in confusion and disorder similar to that which surrounded the Hussite reform. For this reason he sought counsel "among wise scholars and men of good conscience,"[66] likely with the canons at the Holy Sepulchre, Bartholomäus Ruersdorf and Master Johann Lange from Löwenberg, as well as the prince's own counselors, the chancellor Erhard vom Queis, Georg von Eicke, and Philipp von Poppschütz. It is, however, certain that it was mostly because of the influence of Schwenckfeld that by June 1522 at the latest, Frederick II had confessed the new faith.[67] Possibly the general tendency for reformation in Silesia had attracted him as well. In any case, as Sebastian Frank correctly noted, Frederick II was, by his early decision to join the Reformation, the first prince in Germany to affirm the new faith.

Through his letters and pastoral visits, Schwenckfeld so united this brotherhood of like-minded men, composed of both nobles and theologians, that the association was able to continue in part for decades even after his exile in 1529. This was possible for Schwenckfeld not only because of his influential position in the court but also because of his natural talent for gaining and nurturing friendships.

The question naturally arises whether or not these followers of Schwenckfeld were also bound together by a common spiritual tradition. Since we possess almost exclusively writings only by Schwenckfeld prior to 1524/25 and the Catholic background of his friends and disciples is known only in part, an answer to this question cannot be given. One can say, however, that humanism, at least, did provide a bond, since not only Crautwald, but Eckel and Werner as well, belonged to the Silesian humanist movement.

2. *The Attempts of the Schwenkfelders to Bring About the Reformation in Silesia*

Since Schwenckfeld and his friends understood themselves to be members of the reformation movement, they endeavored to work for its success in Silesia. For this reason they sought to encourage the Breslau bishop Jacob von Salza to undertake a diocesan reform. Unlike his Cathedral Chapter he was not opposed to the Reformation in principle, but maintained his predecessor's (Johann V. Turzo[1]) attitude of reserve towards Wittenberg. Like his brother Stanislaus, Bishop of Olmütz and influential leader of humanism in Moravia, Turzo was a man of letters and ranked among the most significant humanists in the Germano-Slavo-Hungarian area. He had studied the liberal arts at Cracow and canon law at a number of Italian universities. After his consecration as bishop on March 22, 1506, he gathered about himself as patron a circle of poets and scholars. Among these was the poet C. Ursinus Velius, episcopal secretary after 1517 and canon after 1520, Stephanus Taurinus, the minstrel of the Hungarian peasants' war, and Jerome Cingularius, the founder of the later important Goldberg school. As an admirer of Erasmus,[2] Turzo was sympathetic to the Wittenberg scholars and followed their reform ideas with interest. To Luther and Melanchthon he sent words of encouragement and friendly acknowledgement through the canon Dominicus Schleupner, who during his three-year tenure as a member of the Cathedral Chapter was in Wittenberg in 1519.[3] The reformers wrote him letters of consolation on July 30 and August 1, 1520 when he was lying gravely ill.[4] The two letters which Schleupner brought with him when he returned home did not reach the bishop, however, for he died on August 2, 1520. On receiving notice of his death, Luther wrote on November 15, 1520 to Georg Spalatin: "The bishop of Breslau died in the same faith; he was the best of all bishops of this century."[5] Possibly because of the influence of Schleupner, Luther overestimated Turzo's interest in the Reformation.

Jacob von Salza[6] was unanimously elected as Turzo's successor by the Cathedral Chapter on September 1, 1520,[7] but not until September 1, 1521, after protracted negotiations with Rome, was he consecrated by the suffragan bishop Heinrich von Füllstein in the presence of Gnesisch and Polish suffragans. Like Turzo, Jacob von Salza held to humanist reform principles. Consequently, he did not completely reject the Wittenberg movement.

The Breslau Cathedral Chapter, however, disturbed by the early influence of the Reformation in Silesia, particularly in Breslau, and robbed of its support by the indecisive attitude of Jacob von Salza, attempted to block any future advances of the reformation movement itself. It decided on November 18, 1522 to seek help from the pope, the college of cardinals, and certain powerful individual cardinals.[8] As a result Hadrian VI wrote three apostolic briefs to Jacob von Salza, Frederick II, and the Breslau municipal council.[9] In his decree to the municipal council of Breslau on July 23, 1523 the pope called for opposition to the new belief. Firm measures, he wrote, were to be brought against any "who profess, follow, praise, defend, preach or uphold that heresy and its founder Martin Luther and any of his followers who sell, buy, print, read, teach, hear, hold or have any books of the same Luther or Lutherans, and those who presume to perpetuate these teachings by word or deed, and whose favor and affection toward the aforesaid heresy or Lutheran sect is truly able to be argued. The penalties against those who are involved in such activity are to be firmly applied."[10]

At the same time the Cathedral Chapter also sought support from the secular authorities. For this reason they forgot their former principle of avoiding Polish influence in the Breslau bishopric and decided on February 6, 1523 to call for help through the chancellor Stanislaus Burg from Sigismund I of Poland[11] who was antagonistic to the Reformation. Sigismund I asked his nephew Ludwig II to oppose the Lutheran "pestilence"[12] since he had already issued a strong anti-Lutheran decree on December 24, 1521.[13] Ludwig followed the request from his uncle on April 16, 1523 since in the meantime the Cathedral Chapter had also contacted him directly on March 13, 1523.[14] In his edict, Ludwig forbade, under threat of confiscation of goods and exile, the propagation of Lutheran teaching in Silesia, the importation or sale of Lutheran books, or the introduction of any kind "of novelty against the practice of the Christian church and the laws of the holy councils and the church fathers."[15] Secondly, on July 19, 1523 Sigismund I and the Cathedral Chapter requested Frederick II, as the head of state, to protect Catholic clergymen against the Reformation.[16] Thirdly, King Sigismund of Poland in two letters of September 13 and October 10, made public to the Breslau municipal council his displeasure with the continued existence of the Lutheran heresy in the capital city and threatened to bring economic sanctions against Breslau to protect his own subjects against the new faith.[17] At this the Breslau municipal council declared in its response of September 22, 1523 that it suffered no heresy in its midst.[18] Frederick II, as well, on November 30, 1523 stated that he encouraged only "the Holy Gospel and pure word of God, without the additions of Luther or any other person."[19] All were particularly anxious to avoid the charge of being Luther's followers.

Schwenckfeld and his associates, who followed these events closely, felt the time had come to request Jacob von Salza to support the Reformation openly. They were rightly convinced that the bishopric of Breslau, and thus almost all of Silesia with the exception of some border areas[20] which were under other dioceses, would accept the new faith if the prince bishop, who was also responsible for the duchy of Grottkau and the principality of Neisse, would place himself at the forefront of the Reformation. Further advances for the Reformation in Silesia appeared otherwise unlikely to Schwenckfeld and his friends considering the anti-reformation attempts of the Cathedral Chapter.

For this reason, Schwenckfeld and his friend, the nobleman Hans Magnus von Axleben of Langenwaldau,[21] who belonged to a nobility that had been highly regarded for centuries, sent an epistle to Jacob von Salza on New Year's Day, 1524. It was printed in Breslau by Caspar Libisch under the title: *A Christian Exhortation for the Furtherance of the Word of God.*[22] In this lengthy composition they were particularly concerned that the Gospel be made known "without human additions,"[23] thereby taking up a central principle of the Wittenberg movement. They therefore requested the bishop to issue a decree that in his diocese "henceforth nothing but the pure Gospel of Christ according to the explication of the Holy Scriptures be allowed to be preached."[24] Thus they repudiated the claim that they were Lutherans, that they were opposed to the church's authority, or that they were introducing novel heretical principles.[25] Finally, they took up the question of ecclesiastical grievances, attacking externalization of worship,[26] the inadequate education of many clerics,[27] the decline of monasticism,[28] the papacy, and the cardinals at the Roman court.[29] They did not simply criticize but concluded with a list of concrete proposals for reform. They demanded, as Luther had done in his reformation writings since 1520, an intensification of preaching,[30] the use of German in the mass,[31] the rejection of private masses,[32] a lifting of the vow of celibacy,[33] and the use of the ban.[34] The epistle did not move Jacob to acknowledge the reformation movement. According to Schwenckfeld, the bishop replied in a letter, unfortunately not extant, that he had always ordered that the Gospel be preached and that, to his knowledge, this was being done.[35]

Having failed to win over the spiritual authorities into participating in a reformation, Schwenckfeld and his friends turned to the secular power, namely Frederick II, requesting him to issue a mandate on the matter. They hoped to achieve this since the diet opened at Grottkau on January 17, 1524, which had lasted approximately two weeks and was attended by representatives of the princes, nobles, and other estates in the presence of royal commissioners and the bishop's delegates, had unanimously demanded the free proclamation of the word of God without regard to tradition.[36]

Since no agreement was reached, a second diet was called for Breslau on April 11, 1524. To achieve a unified front at the outset, the bishop called together the abbots, canons, and senior clerics of the diocese to a meeting in Breslau on April 4.[37] Agreement was reached to hold to the traditional faith.

At the diet,[38] chaired by Jacob von Salza, the two points of view clashed violently. Whereas the delegates of the princes, estates, and towns, after passionate disagreement, demanded in writing "that the preaching of the Holy Gospel be allowed unhindered according to the meaning of the Holy Scriptures, and that these be followed without regard to human opinion,"[39] Jacob von Salza declared that he had seen to it that the Gospel was being proclaimed in its original sense and according to the understanding of the Church Fathers, but not according to the conclusions of certain preachers or false evangelists. He was referring to Luther and his followers. As a result, the laity threatened no longer to punish those who did not pay tithes and offerings to the church until the free proclamation of the Gospel was established.

On June 11, 1524, two months after the diet at Breslau and after a public disputation by Hess, which took place from April 20 until April 22,[40] Schwenckfeld published his *An Admonition to all the Brethren in Silesia.*[41] Dedicated to Frederick II,[42] the treatise had been composed, in all likelihood, at Frederick's request.[43] In it, Schwenckfeld wished to give his duke a legitimate reason to publish a Reformation decree. On June 24 the decree, no longer extant, was issued; in it, according to V. L. von Seckendorf, he ordered that, on the basis of his reform privilege, "that teaching be carried out on the basis of sacred Scripture as norm and rule without any human addition, even that of Luther."[44]

Schwenckfeld and his colleagues did not only endeavor to move the spiritual and secular authorities to undertake a reformation in Silesia, but themselves did all in their power for it. From the beginning they were deeply concerned that preaching be intensified as they had suggested in their epistle to Jacob von Salza and in their *Admonition to all the Brethren in Silesia.* It was for this reason as well that Schwenckfeld had worked as a lay preacher "for several years, before rulers, princes, and bishops, and large numbers of people."[45] (Wolfgang Knörrlich's assertion that this was already the case during Schwenckfeld's first years at Liegnitz is false.[46]) According to his own testimony, he first did this in 1522 or 1523.[47] Among those who heard him were Count Georg the Pious of Brandenburg-Ansbach and his brother Albrecht[48] who stayed at Liegnitz on many different occasions,[49] the sister-in-law of Duke Frederick II, the widowed duchess Anna von Brieg at whose castle in Lüben Schwenckfeld had preached,[50] and the nuns at the St. Magdalena convent at Naumburg am Queis, to whom he preached the word of God during a 1523 visit made at their request.[51] His vivid language in both sermons and treatises was not without effect. In 1524, for example, he described with obvious pride the moral improvement among the Ossig subjects under his control.[52] That he felt not only justified but also required to preach arose from his spiritualized understanding of vocation. Such a call to preach occurred, to his mind, in an unmediated fashion through the Spirit. Thus, in a letter to Johann Hess on June 13, 1522 he wrote: "According to my judgment, those men are called by the Spirit of God whom God incites with a hidden impulse of his Spirit to preach his word purely."[53] Luther encouraged him as lay evangelist. "I am glad to hear," wrote the reformer in a letter no longer extant, "that you have become a preacher. Go on preaching in God's name; may he give you much blessing and grace for his purpose."[54] At the beginning of December, 1525 Bugenhagen was still expressly commending the preaching activity of the Silesian nobleman.[55]

Not only Schwenckfeld but the Liegnitz pastors as well must have preached with great success. After a short time only a few people held to the old faith. Among these were the canons at the Collegiate Church of the Holy Sepulchre who, unlike the Observants who were driven out,[56] were able to continue their communal life unhindered. As late as 1537 Crautwald complained, "In the Collegiate Church things are regulated so that the mass and unseemly liturgy still remain."[57]

In Lent or Easter of 1524, the Lord's Supper began to be celebrated in both forms.[58] Possibly to avoid association with the Hussites, who had had a dreadful effect in Silesia, it was not done earlier. The first to serve communion under both forms was Sebastian Schubart at St. John's. He was followed by Johann Sigismund Werner who, as the court preacher for Frederick II, observed the Lord's Supper in the Protestant fashion during Lent, in all likelihood on March 26, 1524 in the court chapel. Fabian Eckel at St. Mary's followed the pattern set by his colleagues; thus the Liegnitz pastors in Silesia were the first to celebrate the Lord's Supper according to the rite of the new faith.[59] It is especially to be noted that Liegnitz was very conservative concerning liturgical reform. Up to 1525, the only change was the use of the German language in the liturgy.

In addition to the sermon, Schwenckfeld and, above all, Crautwald, following their humanist background, paid particular attention to catechetical instruction. They related the grave shortcomings of their contemporary Christianity directly to the lack of Christian education. As they wrote to Bishop Jacob von Salza: "Catechetical instruction has ceased. There are no longer any catechumens, that is students of the faith, who several years before were everywhere as can be seen from the missals. Nor are there any longer teachers of faith, that is catechists of the sacraments and other matters that Christians ought to know by which they are to be raised, nourished, and taught. It necessarily follows from this that there will be few Christians."[60] To remedy this shortcoming, Schwenckfeld and Crautwald held catechetical instruction for adults in Liegnitz on specific days of the week. A catechetical sermon on the articles of faith was preached, then discussed, and finally summarized.[61] In addition, the preachers answered questions that did not directly relate to the material under discussion.[62]

Ascribing so great an importance to catechetical instruction, Schwenckfeld and his friends applied themselves to the composition of useable instructional material. Already in the second half of 1525, the *Catechism of Liegnitz* had appeared[63] as the first catechism of the Reformation. It treated only baptism and the Lord's Supper and was presumably written by Schwenckfeld and the two former teachers, Crautwald and Werner.[64] It was probably in the same year that Crautwald wrote his *Catechism of Christ*[65] in which he treated topics earlier outlined as necessary for Christian study in his 1525 didactic and methodological manual, the *Catechism, that is, a Truly Full and Useful Institute of a Christian Man.*[66] At about the same time he also wrote his *Small Institute*[67] which sought to expand upon the sacramental teaching of the *Catechism of Christ.* Schwenckfeld wrote his *Catechism of the Word of the Cross*[68] in the fall of 1526 (although it was first printed in 1545), and in 1531 he prepared his *Catechism of the Principal Articles of the Christian Faith.*[69] Sometime before 1534[70] Johann Sigismund Werner wrote his *Catechism,*[71] This volume, as will be indicated later, was to be greatly admired by future Schwenkfelders; it laid the foundation for catechetical instruction for later generations. In their construction, these Schwenkfeldian catechisms are clearly distinguished from those German language catechisms of the late middle ages; whereas late medieval manuals contained expositions of the Decalogue, Creed, Lord's Prayer, and Sacraments, the Schwenkfeldian pieces followed the outline of salvation history: creation, fall, redemption, and eschatology. They are especially interested in the realization of the new man. In this they have much in common with the 1522 *Questions for Children* of the Bohemian Brethren. These centered, above all, on the pure Christian life and the new obedience.[72] Further dependence based on content cannot be established.

Crautwald also busied himself intensively with the question of didactics and methodology for catechetical instruction. In his 1525 *Catechism* he sought to base the necessity of catechetical instruction on the Holy Scriptures,[73] especially with regard to Acts, but he looked as well to the Christian tradition, namely to Ambrose, *On the Mysteries*, Augustine, *On Cathechetical Instruction*, John Gerson, *On Training Youth in Christian Faith,* and the sixth chapter of John Chrysostom's *Commentary on Hebrews.*[74] He then discussed methods[75] and topics of instruction,[76] concluding with a model catechism on the depravity of human nature[77] and a short catechism for children.[78] In 1534 he wrote a second didactic manual, *A Brief Guide to Catechetical Instruction.*[79]

Since Schwenckfeld and his colleagues did not feel capable of creating enough catechetical literature by themselves, they asked others to aid them in this undertaking. For example, Crautwald repeatedly encouraged Michael Wittiger to compose a catechism,[80] although he was perhaps already working on one.[81] With the same purpose Crautwald wrote Dominicus Schluepner[82] and Johann Hess.[83]

These common endeavors to bring about a complete reformation movement in the principality of Liegnitz drew Schwenckfeld and his friends together into a community. This is obvious in their production of a prayer book in the late 1520s which was reprinted in 1537 by Jobst Gutknecht in Nürnberg under the title, *The Confession of Sin with several Observations and practical Prayers*.[84] Although these prayers are very much directed to personal appropriation of salvation, it is false to designate them "completely one-sidedly" individualistic as Ferdinand Cohrs has done.[85] Paul Althaus Sr. earlier noted this and commented that they belong to the best and most significant Protestant prayer literature of the sixteenth century because of "their deep subjectivity and religious immediacy, their earnest concern with penance, and their striving for personal sanctification."[86] It is interesting and noteworthy that these prayers were soon made use of in Lutheran, Reformed, and Roman Catholic prayer books, although when this was done, their source was, with only one exception, hidden.[87]

3. The Liegnitz Brotherhood and Other Reformation Centers Within and Beyond Silesia

Schwenckfeld and his circle quickly became leading figures in the Silesian reformation movement because of their work, which first introduced the Reformation to the city and principality of Liegnitz. This was pointed out by the Breslau municipal secretary, Laurentius Corvinus, in his summary remarks at the disputation of April 22, 1524 over which Johann Hess presided: "It [the Reformation] entered Liegnitz with its high fortifications because of the trusting acceptance of the illustrious duke."[1] The first sermons in the new faith had, however, not been preached in Liegnitz but as early as 1518 at the castle of the Hussite supporter Georg von Zedlitz in Neukirch in the principality of Jauer by the former Augustinian Melchior Hoffmann, one of the students of Luther from Goldberg.[2] After 1522, Lutheran-influenced preachers were found in others places in Silesia as well. Valerius Rosenhayn in Freystadt[3] and Ambrose Creusig in Wohlau[4] are examples. Nevertheless, the town and principality of Liegnitz held priority since almost all the defenders of the Reformation joined ranks there and the first Protestant pastors were called and appointed there.

The second center for reform in Silesia was Breslau, which took no second place to the free imperial cities, since its municipal council held sovereignty over the whole region. The decisive breakthrough of the Reformation into this city occurred after the disputation held under Johann Hess at St. Dorthea's church from April 20-22, 1524. For him and his associates, Antonius Niger and Valentin Trotzendorf, the disputation was a complete success. Hess had been appointed by the municipal council to the pastorate at St. Magdalena's church on October 21, 1523 against the advice of the chancellery. Immediately after the disputation Hess began to initiate reform activity. In 1524 Adam Dyon published *The German Baptismal Book of Breslau* which, despite numerous alterations taken from Andreas Osiander's baptismal book of 1524[5] and perhaps from Breslau tradition, was based on Luther's baptismal book of 1523.[6] In 1525 the same printer published the oldest Protestant hymnal of Breslau which contained thirty-nine hymns and a communion prayer and is generally a reprint of Maler's *Enchiridion* of the same year.[7] These changes, which took place over a year's time, were described by the chronicler Nicolaus Pol in his narrative of the Breslau reformation under a single date: "On 23 April, Quasimodogeniti Sunday, the following activities were curtailed and forbidden without any trouble: the invocation and adoration of images, processions with the sacraments, vigils, masses for the dead, requiems, anniversaries, the use of relics, of holy water, incense, salt, and herbs. Baptisms began to be performed in German. All priests were allowed to marry, and still execute ecclesiastical positions and ceremonies. The people were allowed to eat meat on Friday and during Lent."[8]

Schwenckfeld and Crautwald became close friends with the Breslau associates of the Wittenberg movement, particularly with Johann Hess and Andreas Moibanus, and remained so until 1525. They had become personally acquainted in the service of Karl I of Münsterberg-Oels or during their work in the episcopal chancery. Once again it was above all humanism which brought them together; this was particularly true for the trilingual Crautwald. Their friendship was deepened by the occurrences at Wittenberg in which, as humanists, they naturally had a lively interest. The Silesians corresponded with one another on such matters as the adoration of the Eucharist,[9] notified one another of recent publications and discussed them among themselves. Thus, on October 14, 1521[10] Schwenckfeld asked Hess to advise him why he had expressed himself so disparagingly over a work of Ulrich von Hutten.[11]

After Schwenckfeld had openly committed himself to the Reformation, he urged Hess, concerning whose indecision Melanchthon also complained,[12] to follow his example. According to the extant sources, he did this first in his letter of October 14, 1521.[13] Since his request was unanswered, he wrote again on June 13, 1522, this time ironically commenting, "But I see that you await the voice of God demanding that you come forth in public."[14] Above all, he criticized Hess for accepting an invitation of Jacob von Salza "because of the bishop's unexpected clemency,"[15] although the bishop had at that time cast the Wohlau pastor of Creusig into the Ottmacher prison for opposing the 1521 anti-Reformation mandate of Ludwig II "because of his unexpected cruelty."[16] This letter must have impressed Hess, for shortly after receiving it he joined the Reformation. His decision was also aided by the cessation of the unrest in Wittenberg, concerning which Hess had received details in a letter on October 8, 1521[17] from Sebastian Helmann, later Breslau councilman, and which were certainly repulsive to him as a humanist. Therefore, it was undoubtedly because of Schwenckfeld's efforts that Breslau gradually became the second center of the Reformation in Silesia.

Schwenckfeld and Crautwald were also exchanging ideas with Wittenberg and with Königsberg, the center of the Prussian Reformation. Prior to his visit in Wittenberg at the beginning of December 1525 Schwenckfeld had certainly not met Luther and his colleagues personally. However, there is no indication in the sources that the Silesian nobleman was in Wittenberg between the end of 1518 or the beginning of 1519 and February of 1522, as is frequently stated.[18] Nor is it likely that the letter of Moibanus to Hess on December 8, 1521[19] can be interpreted to mean that Crautwald was in Wittenberg during the disturbances there. Neither can it be demonstrated that Crautwald and Justus Jonas studied in Erfurt at the same time.[20] Yet there was certainly correspondence from Wittenberg to Schwenckfeld and Crautwald. The Silesian nobleman cites once from a letter which Luther had sent to him,[21] and in a letter to Hess on April 17, 1520 Melanchthon mentions a letter in Hebrew which Matthäus Adrian had written to Wittiger and Crautwald.[22] Several times Melanchthon and Luther sent greetings to Crautwald through Hess and Wittiger.[23]

Schwenckfeld was also associated with the reformers in Prussia, particularly with Paul Speratus. The acquaintance probably went back to Albrecht von Brandenburg, the brother-in-law of Frederick II. The Grand Master of the German Order in all probability got to know Schwenckfeld in April of 1522 when on his journey into the German Empire he visited Liegnitz, from where he traveled with his sister Sophie's husband to Prague.[24] Following this, Schwenckfeld and Albrecht, who had subsequently frequently come to Liegnitz,[25] began corresponding.[26] Looking back, the Silesian nobleman described his relationship with Albrecht, later the duke of Prussia, to the royal counselor Johann Bachaleb: "The duke in Prussia is a pious and knowledgeable Christian; he is a prince experienced in the Scriptures. Concerning the matters of the kingdom of God he had conferred often with me orally and in writing."[27] That Schwenckfeld's nephew was in court service to the Duke of Prussia from ca. 1525 to his death in 1530 must have deepened the association,[28] and it is likely that when he appointed Speratus as court chaplain early in 1524, Albrecht encouraged him to correspond with Schwenckfeld. The bishop of Pomesania, Erhard vom Queis may have played the role of middleman[29] since he and Schwenckfeld had not only been friends during their youth and fellow students at the Viadrina[30] but had also served together as counselors to Frederick II.[31] When Schwenckfeld and Speratus first began corresponding is not known, but the first extant letter, an answer from Schwenckfeld, is dated June 23, 1525.[32]

4. The Liegnitz Brotherhood and the Left Wing of the Reformation

It has been common in recent research to ask whether Schwenckfeld and his followers had personal contact with leaders of the left wing of the Reformation during their early reforming activity. Conrad, for example, without any reference, asserts that Schwenckfeld was in Wittenberg between January 25 and March 6, 1522 and there met "Thomas Müntzer and established a close relation with Karlstadt."[1] As has been pointed out, however, it cannot be demonstrated that Schwenckfeld was in Wittenberg at this time and it is highly unlikely that Crautwald was there. It is possible, however, that Fabian Eckel met Müntzer during his student years since both were at the Viadrina during the winter semester of 1512.[2]

Schwenckfeld and his friends do not seem to have corresponded with other followers of the left wing of the Reformation either. At least there is no correspondence extant and there is no indication that any existed. Only much later, on May 15, 1528, did Karlstadt attempt to send a letter to the Liegnitz Brotherhood.[3] In it he said he had earlier written "many letters" but had to set them aside because "no messenger was appropriate" to carry them.[4] Even this letter did not reach its addressees. It was intercepted and given to Luther,[5] who then sent it to the chancellor Gregor Brück on September 24, 1528 to demonstrate that Karlstadt had, against his word, continued to conspire with the left wing reformers.[6]

Schwenckfeld and Crautwald certainly had read Karlstadt's writings, since at the Wittenberg colloquy of December, 1525 the Silesian nobleman displayed a good knowledge of Karlstadt's understanding of the Lord's Supper,[7] and Crautwald described Karlstadt in his 1525 tract *On the Meaning of the Words of the Lord's Supper* as, a "dear and fellow worker in the Lord."[8] Acquaintance with Karlstadt's writings was easily possible in Silesia since they were printed and disseminated there at a very early period.[9] For this reason Luther felt compelled to warn Hess against the opinions of Karlstadt on July 19, 1525.[10] Bugenhagen did likewise in his tract *Against the New Error Concerning the Sacrament of the Body and Blood*, which he published in 1525 and dedicated to Hess.[11]

5. Schwenckfeld's Criticism of the Reformation Doctrine of Justification

Beginning around 1522 a continually growing discomfort over the absence of the moral renewal, which he expected as a result of the Reformation, is reflected in Schwenckfeld's letters and treatises. The first indication of this is found in his letter of April 13, 1522 to Johann Hess, in which he declared that he would like to see the fruits of the Gospel.[1] His sorrow is expressed in a more concrete form in an epistle[2] dated January 1, 1524 which he directed to Bishop Jacob von Salza. In it he agreed tentatively[3] with the reproach of the common people that among the preachers who proclaimed the Gospel the loudest, one sensed the least moral improvement.[4] He was also opposed to the moral laxity of many Protestant pastors: "They mean to cover their unrighteousness with the Gospel. When they drink to excess and live in ribaldry, they call it brotherly love. They say it is love which leads them into illicit affairs. They also twist brotherly love if they take something from someone by saying that they are in need of it. They describe Christian freedom as being established if they eat meat on Friday and fish on Sunday."[5] They are deceived in their belief that they are "good evangelical people"[6] if they no longer fast, pray, and give alms, for which activities, however, they would rail at the pope and the clergy.[7] Schwenckfeld's impatience is most clearly evident in his *Admonition to all the Brethren in Silesia*, which was published in June of 1524. In it he lashed out against the evangelical preachers who fill all the taverns[8] and who insist exclusively on faith and issue polemics against works.[9] Finally, in a June 23, 1525 letter to Speratus, he urgently sought Speratus' intercession since there were many "who attached themselves to the Gospel with stone hearts and did no acts of love,"[10] justifying their position with the doctrine of the depravity of human nature.[11] Schwenckfeld's disappointment over the lack of renewal within Christendom was a major theme in his conversation with Luther at the beginning of December, 1525 in Wittenberg.[12]

It is interesting that at almost the same time in South Germany, the most important leaders of mystical spiritualism were discussing the same problem. Among them were Hans Denck and especially Sebastian Franck, whose life displays striking parallels to that of Schwenckfeld. This native of Donauworth had lived as a preacher and parish administrator in impoverished conditions since the beginning of 1525 in the Ansbach village of Büchenbach by Schwabach. Three years later as a curate for early masses in the small town of Gustenfelden, Franck was initially a follower of the Lutheran reformation.[13] However, when he saw no moral improvement in his congregation despite his dedication, he gave up his pastorate out of frustration in 1528 or at the latest 1529[14] and went to work as a writer in Nürnberg, the "eye and ear of Germany'' at the time. In a similar manner Denck separated himself from the Reformation after less than half a year at the St. Sebald school in Nürnberg to which the rector, on the recommendation of Oecolampadius, had called him. Upset over the lack of renewal and under the influence of Müntzer and Karlstadt, Denck finally chose the way to mystical spiritualism which seemed to him to be the only possible means of real reformation.[15]

In his paper ''On Understanding Schwenckfeld''[16] Emanuel Hirsch stated that Schwenckfeld's unease reflected an ''inner dilemma''[17] and that he was ''without a distinctive creative power to overcome it.''[18] This suggestion, as a careful analysis of the sources indicates, if true, is true for only the very earliest period. At the very beginning Schwenckfeld attempted to explain by means of the prevalent proclamation of the Word of God the manifold ethical shortcomings which were so obvious among those attached to the Reformation. Many Godless men, who in pre-Reformation times were ''held as pious to outward view,''[19] are now ''revealed and known''[20] to be hypocrites in the light of the Gospel. The Gospel, according to I Corinthians 14:25, has the power to reveal the inner man.[21] Because of this he could be satisfied temporarily, since, although there were numerous shortcomings, there were also many indications of ethical renewal. Thus he declared in his letter to Jacob von Salza that he knew ''many pious people who have been remarkably renewed through the Lutheran teaching.''[22] As a concrete example he pointed to his subjects in Ossig[23] and noted that Jesus had had no success during his three years of activity in and around Jerusalem either—in fact, the Jews had killed him and his disciples had fled.[24]

As Schwenckfeld and his followers became ever more convinced that the desired renewal of Christendom remained distant, they asked themselves if the cause might not perhaps be found in the Lutheran doctrine of justification itself. As a result of this questioning they came to the conclusion that this doctrine was indeed in part misleading and in part false. This conclusion was first made public by Schwenckfeld in his *Admonition to all Brethren in Silesia* of June 1524, published by Caspar Libisch in Breslau. With this treatise he addressed himself to all evangelically-minded persons in Silesia, warning them especially against the misinterpretations and errors in the Reformation doctrine of justification. ''I am compelled,'' he wrote at the beginning, ''by the honor of God and Christian love which I have for you all especially, to point out several principal articles of the Gospel, through which (as I know and see) many men fall, either through ignorance or immodest pretension under the guise of the Gospel, into carnal freedom and arrogance. But they do not know how to submit themselves, according to the Scriptures, thoroughly and with blessedness.''[25]

The absence of ethical improvement, according to Schwenckfeld, lay primarily in the misleading and misunderstood term "by faith alone." He wished, of course, to insist that "faith alone justifies us,"[26] but he criticized the suggestion that justification did not have any conditions. "They do not wish to hear or learn how or in what manner they might come into such a living faith through God."[27] According to Schwenckfeld the prerequisites for receiving grace are cross and suffering: the mortification of the flesh and withdrawal from the world.[28]

In the second place, he criticized the Reformation doctrine of justification because it totally denied the freedom of man's will.[29] Initially, as he wrote retrospectively in 1554, he had agreed with Melanchthon that post-lapsarian man had no free will either for good or evil.[30] But in this he was "deceived," making "pious, holy God a cause of sin."[31] However, he soon saw through this "horrid heathen error."[32] John 8:44 and I John 3:8 gave him certain knowledge that unbelief had its roots in the devil.[33] This conviction he must have reached, at the latest, by early 1524, for his earlier concept is no longer present in the *Admonition.* Above all he now pressed the idea that the believer regains the freedom to do good. The gift of the Spirit and freedom are identical according to Romans 8.[34] This regained freedom makes man morally responsible and makes it possible to admonish him. If the reborn man has no free will to do good, the result, in his opinion, will be "a carnal life and a decline of good deeds."[35]

In his criticism of the Reformation doctrine of the bondage of the will, Schwenckfeld was turning not so much against Luther as against Melanchthon,[36] although in his *Admonition* he nowhere quotes Melanchthon's *Loci* of 1521. In fact, in this first Protestant dogmatic handbook, Melanchthon held to an absolute determinism.[37] Thus, even earlier than the fall of 1524, when Erasmus' *Diatribe Concerning the Free Will* appeared and the controversy between him and Luther began on the question of free will, this question had become a major theological, and above all, pastoral problem for Schwenckfeld. The Silesian nobleman must have read Erasmus' tract later, since at the beginning of December, 1525 he spoke to Luther about Erasmus;[38] apparently, however, Luther's arguments were not about to dispel Schwenckfeld's questioning of the Reformation teaching on the bondage of the will. In any case, he first attacked it fiercely in February of 1528 in an epistle[39] to Johann Rurer, professor of rhetoric at Liegnitz. In this epistle he did not refrain from pointing to Melanchthon's changed position, which was caused by the controversy between Luther and Erasmus, as a comparison of his *Loci* of 1521 and the *Scholia on Colossians* of 1527 indicate.[40] A year later in his tract *On Faith in Christ,*[41] Schwenckfeld's view of free will had reached its final formulaic clarity: The old man has a free will for evil, the new man a free will for good.[42]

Thirdly, Schwenckfeld criticized the Reformation doctrine of justification in his *Admonition* because it completely eliminated the significance of works for justification.[43] Certainly Schwenckfeld agreed that the redemptive work of Christ was the only basis for receiving grace, but he did not believe that works were irrelevant for salvation. In this he distinguished between the works of the natural man and those of the reborn man. Insofar as the former are concerned, works are meaningless for justification. "Note that our work, that is *our* work, the work which is of our own power, provides nothing towards holiness."[44] It is completely different with the works which "proceed from a faithful and upright heart, since they are gifts of God."[45] These works God "will crown and graciously reward, not out of duty, but out of boundless mercy, after this life, as he has promised."[46] By no means must man be conscious of his works of love nor look for reward as the parable on the last judgment (Matthew 25:31-46) and the parable of the servants (Luke 17:7-10) point out.[47]

6. Schwenckfeld's Early Doctrine of Justification

Until the beginning of 1525 almost the only Liegnitz Reformation writings extant are Schwenckfeld's; for this reason, a description of the early doctrine of justification as held by the Liegnitz Brotherhood is not possible. Only in a single work, the epistle to Jacob von Salza is Hans Magnus von Axleben named as a co-editor with Schwenckfeld.[1] Yet it is unlikely that he was closely involved with the composition. Besides this there exists only a German translation of a Latin *ars moriendi* (art of dying) from the pen of Crautwald.[2] This translation, the source of which is unknown, Crautwald finished in 1524 on the wish of his friend Georg Jeschko,[3] vicar at the Church of the Holy Cross in Breslau.[4] Entitled *A Useful, Noble Book on the Preparation for Death,* it is dedicated to the Breslau merchant and landowner Erasmus Heyland,[5] Crautwald's financial supporter.[6] This book of consolation intends to show how Satan's temptations may be overcome at the hour of death. It belongs not to the genre of literature concerned with proper living, made popular by humanism, but to the medieval *ars moriendi* genre. Yet, several formal aspects are missing, such as interrogations and orations, a fact which probably testifies to the Reformation influence.

Schwenckfeld described justification briefly and occasionally as a forensic act. According to him we, who are "by nature children of wrath (Ephesians 2:3),"[7] are placed in a new relationship with God through faith in Jesus Christ. We become "children of God and co-heirs of the eternal fatherland (Romans 8:16-17)."[8] Yet in his early writings Schwenckfeld says little concerning the new relationship between God and man since he was much more concerned with the imputed justification for "post-lapsarian" man. Further investigation will also show that his theological interest was concerned almost totally with the birth and reality of the new man.

This understanding of justification as sanctifying was rooted first in his conception of the Reformation as a renewal of Christendom. Secondly, it was personally motivated. As has been pointed out, Schwenckfeld seemed to have met with extreme moral licentiousness (which was even greater than common at the time) during his early life at the court of Georg I of Brieg. His experience was completely different from Luther's. The latter came from the narrow world of the cloister with its fasts, vigils, and prayers; the former, from the worldly court with feasting, gaming, and dancing. A comparison of their autobiographical comments makes the difference especially clear. In 1548 while convalescing in Wildbad from a complex arm fracture,[9] Schwenckfeld wrote, "I have neglected many things during my recent illness, but a thousand times more in my sinful youth. I was an evil wretch, serving the world rather than God."[10] Luther, on the other hand, wrote, "Although I was a great, complete, and wretched sinner and spent my youth damnably and wastefully, yet my greatest sins were that I was such a "holy" monk, and with so many masses, horribly angered, martyred, and tortured my beloved Lord for more than fifteen years."[11] If one wishes then to understand fully Schwenckfeld's insistence on the manifestation of the new man, one must study carefully his social-cultural milieu, so completely different from that in which Luther experienced his religious awakening.

Schwenckfeld was, therefore, convinced that one gained imputed justification only through grace and not by works.[12] To prove this he first quoted Scripture (e.g., Romans 1:17).[13] Secondly, he used a syllogism to demonstrate that without grace the new man could not arise. He pointed to those "who wished to bring about their righteousness by their own power through external works and human obedience,"[14] who "never became better" but ever "remained in their arrogance, pride, impurity, and wrath."[15] This imputed justification occurred, according to his understanding, not in a single act but in a continuing process.

There are three stages to be distinguished, which stand in an external connection. At the beginning of imputed justification is repentance which purifies the human heart, "filled with its egoism, arrogance, wrath, impurity, and tyranny,"[16] and prepares it for the reception of grace. Without this purification one is not able to receive grace, since "the Gospel is not a sermon for every man—it is an overly sweet sermon; it is of no use to a raw, dried-up heart but makes people only more insolent and frivolous."[17] According to Schwenckfeld, this purification does not come about through a meditative mysticism of the cross but through suffering and an ascetical life.[18] God, he declares, "ordained from eternity that the chosen who believe in his Son, Jesus Christ, could come to heavenly joy in no other way than the way Christ himself had gone, that is through the cross, persecution, and trouble."[19] The goal of this purification is the death of the ungodly "I" of man. "Only when the whole heart gives itself over to God, are all evil desires in it destroyed."[20] Unfortunately it is not possible to ascertain from the sources where Schwenckfeld borrowed his ideal of discipleship under the cross, which was an ideal common to scholasticism, German mysticism, and the *Devotio moderna*.[21] This process of purification is a necessary prerequisite, according to Schwenckfeld, for the granting of the Spirit.[22] Yet in his early writings he offered no specific suggestion as to how this occurs. It is very likely, however, that he believed it came about not through a medium of salvation, but unmediated through the influence of God.[23] This gift of the Spirit makes of a two-fold man a tripartite new man who, in addition to body and soul, now also possesses a spirit.[24] The spirit will be evident in a new life. "When such a new life is begun, the Spirit of God writes the commandments in our hearts; then the heart becomes joyous and unafraid, men can and do suffer all things which for God's will are to be endured and suffered."[25] He occasionally described the new existence with a terminology that approached perfectionism. Thus, in his *Admonition,* for example, he asserts that in the new man all evil desires are destroyed, for example "pride, impurity, covetousness, wrath, and envy toward neighbor, the great vice of greed, as well as all other desires of the flesh."[26] Nevertheless, it is not correct to describe Schwenckfeld as a perfectionist, as his opponent Matthias Flacius Illyricus later did in his anti-Schwenkfeldian tract of 1553, *On the Holy Scripture and its Power against Caspar Schwenckfeld*. Schwenckfeld would already clearly reject the claim that he taught that the Christian was without sin, in a circular letter to the Silesian followers of the Reformation,[27] and especially in connection with his altercation with Illyricus. In 1554 he wrote: "Illyricus criticizes me falsely and unjustly when he writes that I teach of the perfect, complete fullness of God and his whole divine being, as if one were able to receive this here fully or might keep God's law *perfectly* and had no longer any need to pray the Lord's prayer [cf. the fifth petition]."[28]

Characteristically, the socio-political aspect of the new man is almost completely lacking in Schwenckfeld's description, although he himself once regretted the apolitical stance of the Anabaptists. His own life, as well as his writings, point out that he did not concern himself with this matter by chance. He hardly took notice of the political and economic happenings of his day, much less involving himself, taking no position on the 1521 peace between Prussia and Poland in Thorn nor on the Peasants' War, which had not affected Silesia. Likewise, the sale of the principality of Wohlau in 1523, which must have interested him as a counselor to Frederick II, does not seem to have been a major issue for him; at least one does not find indications of this in his writings. Nevertheless, he was not blind to the social situation as it affected the common people and once commented satirically that eggs, cheese, and butter were proscribed during Lent and on Friday even though the people hardly had enough bread to eat.[29]

Imputed justification reached its conclusion in the deification of man. This aspect is incipient in the theology of the young Schwenckfeld.[30] It is only later, after the development of his teaching on the Lord's Supper and his Christology, that deification becomes central to the doctrine of justification in his work and in that of his disciples, especially of Crautwald and Werner. By the gift of the Spirit then, as has been pointed out, they understood an essential spiritual gift of the deified flesh of the glorified Christ. Thus, for example, Crautwald wrote in his 1530 *The New Man:* ''His flesh adds what is divine and recreates a spiritual and heavenly creature from carnal and earthly flesh. The new Christian man receives, I say, a grain of eternal seed. God enters the heart of man and by him man grows. From a youth he becomes a man in Christ. God makes the flesh a part of his divine nature by means of and because of Christ's flesh.''[31] Yet both Crautwald and Schwenckfeld took great care to disassociate themselves from the idea of an apotheosis of man. Thus, in the tract cited above Crautwald suggests: ''The new man remains nevertheless flesh, and the law of the members, the old inclinations, concupiscence, the instruments and offices of the senses remain.''[32]

7. The Theological and Spiritual Roots of Schwenckfeld's Early Doctrine of Justification

The question concerning the roots of Schwenckfeld's early theology has already been raised. This theology, as has been made clear, centered above all on the doctrine of justification. The first suggestion concerning the roots of Schwenckfeld's theology was therefore that they are to be found in the Lutheran Reformation and that the Silesian nobleman did not, at least essentially, differentiate himself from the Wittenberg reformer until 1525. In modern research this premise was first supported by Karl Ecke in a dissertation he did under Heinrich Boehmer in 1911. According to Ecke, the Silesian nobleman had a ''lasting, positive, personal relationship with Luther.''[1] A similar conclusion was reached by Emanuel Hirsch in his study ''On Understanding Schwenckfeld.'' He was of the opinion that Schwenckfeld must ''be seen . . . until 1525 as a follower and student of Luther who did not develop his own theological position.''[2] Reinhold Pietz in his dissertation on

Schwenckfeld's anthropology also took this position. However, mistakenly, he saw Schwenckfeld's close relationship to Luther as based on the biblicism at the root of the thought of both men.[3] Wolfgang Knörrlich likewise, in his historical study, *Caspar von Schwenckfeld and the Reformation in Silesia,* agreed that the Silesian nobleman "was essentially and without deviation in Luther's camp" until 1525 and that he proclaimed "his ideas."[4] Yet he added that from the beginning, that is from Schwenckfeld's letter to Jacob von Salza,[5] one can note a "growing spiritualism"[6] which in the beginning led to barely recognizable shifts in emphasis.

A second group of scholars has held that mysticism was the distinctive source of Schwenckfeld's theology. This thesis was first proposed by Heinrich Wilhelm Erbkam in 1848 in his *History of the Protestant Sects in the Time of the Reformation.* According to him, Schwenckfeld was an "intellectual mystic."[7] "In [Schwenckfeld]," Erbkam declared, "the mystical life broke forth in its full power; it was not based on the study of the older mysticism, and then mimicked; rather [Schwenckfeld's mysticism] was self-experienced, based on individual experience."[8] According to Erbkam, the Silesian nobleman did indeed support Luther in his battle against the papacy, but he went his own way as the mystics had indicated to him. Under the influence of mysticism "the inner experience of the divine life became the central point for Christian life."[9] Gottfried Maron in his study, *Individualism and Community in Caspar von Schwenckfeld,* also took up this position, modified and expanded it. The Silesian nobleman was for him a representative of a mysticism filled with Gnostic elements, who could understand only the "indwelling Christ, who, as such is a preaching Christ (semper et ipse). Thus, for Schwenckfeld no Reformation understanding of justification is possible: *the just shall live by faith* is not applicable."[10]

Thirdly, it has been suggested that the early theology of Schwenckfeld grew out of spiritualism. The leading proponent of this opinion was Erich Seeberg. In his 1929 study, *The Controversy between Zwingli, Schwenckfeld, and Luther,* he endeavored to indicate in a treatment of Schwenckfeld's doctrine on baptism that the center of his theology was an exclusive concern with the Spirit, and that this united him with Zwingli and the humanists but distinguished him from Luther. This understanding of the Spirit led the Silesian nobleman to another doctrine of justification. "A man becomes holy through the new birth, that is, through the indwelling Christ."[11] A similar judgment was reached by Richard Heinrich Grützmacher who emphasized however that the influence of the mystics was stronger than that of the spiritualists.[12] Against Grützmacher, Joachim Wach emphasized a purely spirtualist base in the theology of Schwenckfeld. His "theology is an attempt to unfold the basic conception of the work of the Holy Spirit, a conception which plays a determining role, even in his earliest writings.''[13]

In the face of this scholarly disagreement it is necessary to deal once again with the problem of the spiritual roots of Schwenckfeld's theology. A close analysis of Schwenckfeld's early writings demonstrates that he was not influenced by one, but rather by a number of theological and spiritual streams, namely: humanism, mysticism, and Lutheranism. But these worked with differing intensity on him. He had first been influenced, as has been shown, by humanism during his university years and his interest was deepened later through his personal acquaintance with humanists such as Hess and Crautwald. Moreover, Schwenckfeld had read other humanist literature, such as the works of Ulrich von Hutten.[14]

The second movement which influenced the theology of the young Schwenckfeld was German mysticism, but the significance of this for his thought must not be over-emphasized. Early in 1551 he wrote to a friend, Hans Wilhelm von Laubenberg, that he had with great profit ''studied Tauler in an old edition some twenty years ago.''[15] On the basis of these words, Ecke stated that the Silesian nobleman had read the Strassburg Dominican preacher ''first in 1531, only after he had already made certain of his own understanding based on Luther and the Scriptures.''[16] This conclusion is false. In his statement Schwenckfeld had only acknowledged that he had worked intensively with Tauler since 1532, but this does not mean he had not studied him earlier. In fact, it can be demonstrated that he had read the Strassburg mystic before 1532. Already on January 1, 1524 in his letter to Jacob von Salza, he had quoted a passage from Tauler's second sermon on the fourth Sunday after Trinity: ''All work of which God is not the beginning, middle, and end, he does not involve himself in for the breadth of a hair.''[17] Ecke stated that Schwenckfeld as ''an educated man and student of Luther''[18] could have known this passage without reading Tauler. As Hirsch pointed out, however, the passage is not found in Luther.[19] For this reason it may be held that the young Schwenckfeld was deeply versed in Tauler. The theological influence of Taulerian mysticism is evident, above all in Schwenckfeld's emphasis on serenity. With Tauler and Luther, Schwenckfeld emphasized total serenity. In the 1524 *Admonition,* for example, he writes: ''Yea, you must finally come to the point that you stand so completely serene in the will of God that it will not concern you if after this life God sends you to straight to hell or heaven.''[20] Moreover, Schwenckfeld's description of the process of salvation with its steps of purgation, illumination, and deification of man is influenced by Tauler, who, as is well known, developed and systematized the medieval doctrine of the three ways.[21] According to this, man must go through purgation before entering upon the illuminative and unitive ways. Although for Tauler the goal of the unitive way, the mystical union, resulted in the drawing of the soul into the Godhead, for Schwenckfeld and his associates the divinely formed man remained always in a sure relationship to God.

Along with the humanist and mystical influences, the impact of Luther on the early theology of Schwenckfeld can also be seen. After 1518 hardly a work of Luther's appeared which was not read by the Silesian nobleman. Although until 1525 he notes only one by title, Luther's *Exposition on the Seven Penitential Psalms,*[22] it has been demonstrated by Hirsch[23] that he read others, because it is possible to show that he cited them.[24] Through this reading Schwenckfeld learned essential elements for his own understanding of justification. There always remained for him a conviction that salvation was received by man from outside himself, and that there was and would continue to be a distinction between God and the deified man. On the other hand, he had no sense of the distinction between law and Gospel and, therefore, of the center of the Reformation's doctrine of justification.

II The Controversies over The Lord's Supper with the Lutherans, the Strassburgers, and the anti-Schwenkfeldian Mandate of Ferdinand I

Until the year 1525 Schwenckfeld and his followers understood themselves as part of the Wittenberg movement. Despite their criticism of the Lutheran doctrine of justification, they did not think of themselves as opponents. They first saw themselves in this role as the controversy surrounding the practice of the Lord's Supper developed. It is interesting to note that Luther in particular contributed significantly to this development.

1. Schwenckfeld's Doctrine of the Lord's Supper before 1525

Schwenckfeld's early understanding of the Lord's Supper can no longer be determined since the subject did not come to his attention until 1525. It is known, however, that after his conversion to the Reformation he wrote against the mass.[1] How much he borrowed from Luther's early thoughts on the subject is unknown, but in looking back on the situation, he was certainly referring to his early teaching on the sacraments when he wrote: "I was as good a Lutheran in this as any man might be."[2] Following the early summer of 1525, an initially hesitant but, nevertheless, continually growing criticism of Luther's doctrine of the Lord's Supper is found in Schwenckfeld's letters and treatises. His uncertainty here was the same as that which had troubled him over the question of justification; he felt he did not perceive the moral renewal among the communicants which he expected them to demonstrate after their reception of the sacrament. He acknowledged this to Luther indirectly on his visit to Wittenberg early in December of 1525,[3] but his first public expression of this concern was in the apology[4] written by himself and the Liegnitz Brotherhood on April 21, 1526. In this tract they confessed that they had seen "little improvement"[5] among many participants in the Lord's Supper, and thus came to the conclusion that even among the followers of the new faith the sacrament was not administered closely enough to the words of Christ and the Pauline account.[6]

In addition, Luther's controversies on the sacrament, which began about the same time with the Dutchman Cornelius Honius,[7] with Karlstadt,[8] and with the South Germans and the Swiss after 1525, stirred Schwenckfeld to concern himself with the Lutheran teaching on the subject. The Silesian nobleman followed these controversies carefully, as is evident from his correspondence at the time with Speratus[9] and from his dialogue with Luther and other reformers in Wittenberg in December 1525. He conceded candidly to Luther on December 2, 1525 that Zwingli's understanding "was also an occasion for further study of this article."[10]

Schwenckfeld's critical examination of Lutheran sacramental teaching was characteristically rooted in a concern with the practice of the Lord's Supper. He felt he had observed that to a large extent the Protestants were of the opinion that the simple acceptance of communion mediated salvation; in this he saw the danger of a new indulgence. "We also know," he complained on his visit in Wittenberg, "how much idolatry and what great abuse is connected with the sacrament. God grant that you may recognize it. I would counsel you to make inquiries about those who partake of the Supper. You will soon learn whether once again a work is being made of it."[11] This concern of Schwenckfeld's regarding a bare faith in the real presence of the body and blood of Christ in the elements of bread and wine is also found in Luther. He, too, stressed that a faith which knows only "that the body and blood is in the Lord's Supper"[12] was not merely simple and useless but also dangerous and corrupting. Such a faith was no saving faith but simply an historical faith.[13]

But Schwenckfeld, unlike Luther, could not be satisfied in the long run with warning against a false insistence upon the objectification of the sacrament. In the meantime he had become doubtful that each communicant received the body and blood in the sacrament as Luther taught. Did the traitor Judas, he asked himself, really partake of the body of Jesus and the blood of Christ at the Last Supper as the Lutherans maintained?[14] He felt he had to deny this Lutheran teaching since according to the discourse on the bread of life (John 6:54) each participant in the Lord's Supper had the actual life itself, whereas Judas, according to the Johannine account (John 13:21-30), came under the power of Satan.[15] He found support for this interpretation in II Corinthians 6:15 and in the summary of Hebrews 11.[16] The Johannine passage on the bread of life (although not the words of institution concerning the interpretation of which he intentionally did not initially concern himself[17]) was for him the key to an understanding of the sacrament. Christ Himself, not the elements in the Lord's Supper, is the bread of life. "When I discovered," he wrote in retrospect, "that the king of heaven certainly did not wish to be normal baked bread, nor to be in, with, or under the bread, but that he himself is the bread, celestial and truly divine, and food and drink for needy souls; the more I read in the sixth chapter of John, the clearer its meaning became to me."[18]

But how, according to Schwenckfeld's conception at the time, did the believer partake of the bread of life? Was he referring to a spiritual reception of the body of Christ which was in some mysterious way bound to the elements of the bread and wine or was the eating identical with faith? Or might not both be accepted in a certain sense? No definite answer can be given, since in his only commentary on the development of his sacramentology, Schwenckfeld makes no direct statement on these matters. Nevertheless, he seems at the time to have equated eating with believing.[19]

Following this discovery, Schwenckfeld made public his serious reservations about Luther's doctrine of the Lord's Supper in his *Twelve Questions or Arguments Against Impanation.*[20] He sent this work, unfortunately no longer extant,[21] to Wittenberg.[22] At the same time he sent copies to certain of his friends,[23] possibly to the pastors Johann Scaurus in Ossig and Bernhard Egetius in Wohlau, and to the Liegnitz theologians.[24] Although the Wittenbergers remained silent, all of Schwenckfeld's friends seemed to have answered.[25] In their letters, which are now lost, they may not have shared his opinion, but, as he noted, they were not able to overcome his reservations about Luther's teaching.[26]

Schwenckfeld attributed his early understanding of the Lord's Supper first and above all to divine revelation.[27] However, as he admitted in his conference with Luther,[28] he was doubtless influenced by the currents of his own day. First among these influences was that of Zwingli, with whose earlier writings he was acquainted, as a letter to Speratus on June 23, 1525[29] and the conversation in Wittenberg in December of the same year[30] make clear. He certainly had been attracted by Zwingli's tropological interpretation of the "is" in the words of institution and by his identification of believing and eating. In his letter to the Reutlinger pastor Matthäus Alber, Zwingli noted: "But how are we to be freed? Not by the eating of his body as a body is eaten . . . but by believing he died for us."[31] Zwingli had come to this conclusion in the early summer of 1524 under the influence of Cornelius Honius, who had been strongly influenced by Wessel Gansfort.[32] That theologically-interested Dutch lawyer had attempted to demonstrate[33] that it was legitimate to interpret the "is" as "signifies," since Jesus had referred to himself metaphorically as the door (John 10:7,9), the way (John 14:16), and the vine (John 15:1).[34] Nevertheless, he wished in no way that the Lord's Supper be understood simply as a human memorial, since Christ had promised in John 6 to give himself. This came through partaking of his flesh, which Zwingli held to be identical with faith. When one compares Schwenckfeld's and Zwingli's positions on the Lord's Supper, it is relatively certain that Walter Köhler's assumption that the Silesian nobleman "probably" originally held Zwingli's doctrine of the Lord's Supper is correct.[35] In any case, Zwingli's understanding prodded Schwenckfeld to work more intensively on the problem of the sacrament.[36]

Secondly, Schwenckfeld was probably influenced on this by the spiritualist position of the Bohemian Brethren, a position of which he was most certainly aware. He took their writings along as a gift on his trip to Wittenberg at the beginning of December, 1525[37] and presented them to Bugenhagen, who "received them with many thanks and asked that I send him more of the same kind of books."[38] It is probable that the book he brought was the 1508 Latin apology of the Bohemian Brethren, the *Defense of the Waldensian Brethren against two letters of Doctor Augustine.*[39] As Erhard Peschke has shown, this piece, composed at the time of Bishop Lucas of Prague, the most significant representative of the Unity of the Brethren, rejected the doctrine of trans-substantiation and taught a somewhat modified spiritualism.[40] It might reasonably be asserted that Schwenckfeld prized the basic understanding of this work and adopted spiritual elements from it. It was not a major influence, of course, since Schwenckfeld did not adopt the characteristic teaching of the Bohemian Brethren that the bread and wine figuratively represent the sacramental body and blood of Christ. Above all, unlike them, Schwenckfeld did not reject the interpretation of the words of institution on the basis of John 6 but rather emphasized them.[41]

On the other hand, Schwenckfeld's early understanding of the Lord's Supper was probably not influenced by Karlstadt, something that is often claimed.[42] There are certainly morphological parallels between the sacramental teaching of the two men, as Bugenhagen pointed out during the Wittenberg colloquy,[43] but no historical relationship can be demonstrated. Nevertheless, Schwenckfeld was acquainted with Karlstadt's sacramental teaching and possibly also with his writings concerning the Lord's Supper.[44]

2. *Crautwald's Doctrine of the Lord's Supper*

Sometime near the beginning of September 1525 Schwenckfeld talked about his new understanding of the Lord's Supper with Crautwald.[1] He turned to the trilingual scholar because he himself did not yet possess the necessary linguistic knowledge to be able to test his premises with the original text.[2] Crautwald immediately and decisively opposed him and counseled him not to lead the brothers astray, since "the words as they stand are crystal clear."[3] At this Schwenckfeld set forth his *Twelve Questions* and asked Crautwald to concern himself in prayer with the proper understanding of the most significant words in the synoptic descriptions of the Last Supper.[4] Crautwald was to help him bring his teaching on the Supper, based as it was on John 6, into agreement with the synoptic texts on the topic.

Fully resolved to work solely with the words of institution themselves and to understand them only literally, Crautwald undertook Schwenckfeld's request, praying all the time.[5] On the morning of September 17, 1525 a new understanding of the Lord's Supper was revealed to him, one which, as will become clear, did not differ essentially from Schwenckfeld's. Fourteen days later, at the request of Schwenckfeld,[6] Crautwald described the visionary experience through which he received the revelation in a detailed Latin report.[7] The description was later translated rather freely into German[8] and in 1570 appeared under the title *Concerning the Initial Divine Revelation for a Correct Understanding of the Words of the Lord at the Last Supper*[9] in the first collected edition of Schwenckfeld's writings. According to these autobiographical notes, Crautwald worked with more intensity than he had formerly on the subject of the Eucharist the entire day of Saturday, September 16, 1525.[10] Only in order to participate in a sacramental service did he briefly interrupt his study.[11] He concentrated not only on the New Testament accounts of the Lord's Supper but compared as well the understandings of Luther and Zwingli.[12] He came to doubt, as a result, whether Luther, Zwingli, or he himself had interpreted the texts correctly until then.[13] "Was there another sense of the words of Christ, more true, genuine, and germane to those men and also to you, I thought to myself."[14] In his desperation he reached for Cyprian's account of the subject,[15] but it too brought no clarity.[16] In the early morning of September 17 he experienced a vision in which he was granted a new understanding of the Supper, which will be discussed below. Because of the significance of this event, we cite Crautwald at length: "And behold, after a brief period of time, a certain power, miraculously efficacious and powerful came upon me. As if in darkness, light suddenly shone. A power absorbed me completely, and giving much wisdom, led me into a new knowledge of the Eucharist. It spread through my whole body, particularly my head, and all Scriptural passages on the Eucharist were seen as in a single glance of my eye and it explained to me the complete meaning of the Lord's meal. Then in the sweetest voice, much was declared to me."[17] Hardly had the words of the vision passed when he began to doubt if they had ever actually occurred or whether he had fallen prey to a dream or hallucination.[18] Still fully disconcerted, he again heard the voice which was commanding him to test this revelation of the Spirit on the basis of the Scriptures, in accordance with the admonition of I John 4:1.[19] He went once more into his study and immersed himself again in the synoptic as well as the Pauline versions of the Last Supper.[20] "I was obedient and I listened to one sweetly teaching. He left for me no other responsibility but to pore over the pages, and tears streamed down my face. This lecture lasted a long time. But after a while, because of the sweetness of the doctrine, the memory became dull and the lethargic mind shuddered before this great lecture."[21]

For almost ten days Crautwald kept his vision secret and only requested the prayers of two of his closest friends.[22] He himself continued to compare synoptic and Pauline texts[23] and worked especially[24] with the writings of the early Church Fathers,[25] finding primarily in Tertullian and Cyprian much that seemed to support the correctness of his new understanding of the Lord's Supper.[26] Encouraged thereby in his belief, he finally revealed his new sacramental understanding to the two pastors of St. Mary's Church, Fabian Eckel and Jerome Wittich.[27] They decided to spend a week together comparing it with Scripture and tradition.[28] These two Liegnitz pastors then went with their conclusions to their friend Bernhard Egetius, a colleague in Wohlau, whom they took into their confidence.[29] His judgment seems to have been positive.[30] Only then did Crautwald write to Schwenckfeld about his new understanding of the sacrament.[31] The Silesian nobleman, feeling that the account he had was not clear enough, requested him to present his sacramental understanding in more detail and to simplify it,[32] something he willingly did.[33] This understanding of the Lord's Supper must have greatly impressed and convinced Schwenckfeld; in any event, he made it so much his own that a few months later, in early December 1525, he defended it in Wittenberg as his own position. Likewise all the Liegnitz pastors with the exception of Wenzel Küchler, who possibly believed it to be only a variation of Zwinglianism, accepted Crautwald's reading.[34]

What was the basic structure of Crautwald's position on the Lord's Supper? To answer this question completely it is necessary not only to make use of his autobiographical accounts and early writings on the subject, but also to study thoroughly his other letters and writings prior to the spring of 1526, that is before his final rejection of Lutheranism.

Crautwald first separated himself from Luther's teaching on the real presence.[35] He was convinced that the body of Christ was to be found "neither in, with, or under the bread."[36] Nothing earthly is able, according to his belief, to offer "the heavenly bread of eternal life and daily sustenance of the children of God."[37] He opposed Zwingli as well,[38] who at this time supported a purely symbolic interpretation of the words of institution and by the real presence understood only a presence of Christ in the believing community. Crautwald held that the use of "signifies" for "is" was wrong, since in the Scriptures "*is* never ought or is able to be read as *signifies*."[39] He stated that the "is" is always "is" and cannot be accepted for "signifies."[40] Crautwald's concern in his early writings was not so much to disprove Luther's and Zwingli's understandings but to present completely and provide a firm foundation for his own teaching. In this he continually made use of John 6,[41] since by his vision he had come to know that this discourse was the correct guide to the order of the words of institution.[42] According to this passage, Christ himself is the spiritual, heavenly bread which the believer naturally cannot break with his teeth. "Do not be so foolish as to let yourself be deluded," he wrote, "that you are receiving this living bread of heaven from the hands or by means of men or that you are taking the elements into your mouth and thus bringing them to your soul.''[43] Rather, this reception takes place when the believer rises with the liturgical phrase ''Lift up your hearts'' to the glorified Christ. ''If you go begging to heaven, call God your Father in the spirit of faith and wish to seek first the kingdom of God and his righteousness, then you will be able by God's grace to send a small sack or basket with true faith toward heaven into the house of God where Christ is sitting at his right hand and will have your sack or basket soon filled with this bread.''[44] This spiritual heavenly bread the believer receives with the teeth of faith.[45] Thus, Crautwald was opposed to the idea that spiritual eating of the heavenly bread is simply identical with faith, as Schwenckfeld perhaps first understood it. Like Calvin after him, Crautwald felt that faith is concentrated in a much more significant way through the liturgical phrase ''Lift up your hearts.''

According to Crautwald this spiritual eating is possible not only in the Eucharistic service itself. Rather, the believer is continually able to enjoy the heavenly bread spiritually.[46] Christ instituted the practice of the Supper only to make men most certainly aware of the essence of heavenly bread by means of physical bread. ''How might he have done this more easily and more lovingly and yet more understandably? In that he introduced and portrayed bread for bread, drink for drink, eating for eating, drinking for drinking in a living, fresh action, deed, and work; thus one understands the one from the other. The heavenly and spiritual mode, manner, and treasure are understood in physical bread, wine, eating and drinking.''[47] The elements of the bread and wine are as all things creaturely ''pictures, portrayals, images''[48] of the body and blood of the glorified Christ. Although these elements are, after the consecration, nothing but bread and wine, there is, according to Crautwald, a special quality in them. This results from their function as a means of making present the heavenly bread. ''They are nevertheless more noble and in a certain way more holy when they are taken up in this ministry, not by their own being but because of the Lord's ministry for which they are intended. For the bread of the Lord's Supper is more noble than ordinary bread since it is now attached to the holy purposes of the Lord and serves the Lord. It is made unique for the Lord, it serves for the Lord's supper, and the remembrance of the Lord.''[49] What did Crautwald see as the fruit of spiritual eating? According to John 6, it was, above all else, the gift of immortality. ''Heavenly, spiritual bread feeds, strengthens, nourishes, and maintains our hungry soul so that it will neither die nor perish eternally, and that we also, through this nourishment's power, rise again on the Last Day and receive eternal life.''[50] The heavenly bread is therefore a medicine through which man participates in divinity even during his own lifetime.[51] This description of deification became even more central for Crautwald and his companions, especially after the development of their Christology. Spiritual eating of the heavenly bread also brings about forgiveness of sins,[52] although, remarkably enough, Crautwald treats this topic only occasionally and incidentally in his doctrine of the Lord's Supper.

Crautwald worked intensively to prove his new understanding of the Lord's Supper from Scripture, reason, and tradition. With the help of grammatical and philological exegesis, he sought first to prove that interpretation based on John 6 was in agreement with the texts of the New Testament relating to the Lord's Supper. According to his grammatically correct understanding, the "This" (*touto*) in "This is my body" cannot be the subject of the sentence but must be a predicate noun, since otherwise the Greek syntax would call for the omission of the article with "body" (*to soma*).[53] Therefore the sentence is to be read as "My body is this."[54] The same would be true, according to Crautwald, if one translated the words back into Hebrew.[55] According to the Hebrew syntax of a declarative sentence, the subject follows the predicate unless the predicate is to have special emphasis.[56] Moreover, the "this" (*touto*) cannot refer to the "bread" (*artos*), since "this" is neuter and "bread" is masculine.[57] Therefore he wished to construe the words of institution in the following way: "Christ received the bread, broke it, and gave blessing to his disciples saying: Take and eat. This, that is, this thing, is my body which is given for you."[58] The elements of the bread and wine present at the table were only to point to heavenly bread and heavenly drink.[59] He also based this understanding of the words of institution philologically on the contention that here, as often in the Old and New Testaments, one did not have metonymic but rather metaphoric language, since here there was no real participation of the real subject with the representative subject. Instead of using the term metaphor Crautwald used the concept of parable, particularly when he wished, in a generally intelligible fashion, to describe his doctrine of the Lord's Supper, as he did for example in a letter to Schwenckfeld in 1526.[60] He contended that Christ also used this rhetorical style at the Last Supper to explain most clearly to his disciples "what His body was, which was given and broken for them and also what his precious blood was, which was poured out for them."[61]

Secondly, Crautwald endeavored to show that the Church Fathers construed the words of institution in this way and that they too had interpreted them on the basis of John 6. For this he relied predominantly on Tertullian, according to whom, in his tract against Marcion, *This Is My Body, which is to say, The Figure of my Body,*[62] the bread makes the body of Christ present. Yet in a later letter, Crautwald correctly noted that Tertullian did not intend a pure symbolism but rather that he inferred from the bread as a portrayal of the body of Christ to the actual existence of the body of Christ as heavenly bread.

"Moreover it could not be an image, unless there was an actual body. Besides, a nonexistent thing cannot be represented because it is a phantasm."[63] Next to Tertullian, Crautwald liked to quote Cyprian, the bishop of Carthage, who had interpreted the order of the words on the bread in the same way[64] and who had also pointed out that the "this" is neuter and cannot be applied to "blood" or "cup."[65] He believed that among the Church Fathers, Hilary of Poitiers,[66] Ambrose,[67] and John Chrysostom[68] understood the synoptic accounts of the Lord's Supper on the basis of John 6.

Thirdly, Crautwald used a philosophic argument in defense of his position, an argument which differentiated between creature and spirit. Because of this metaphysical dualism, he believed it was impossible that the body and blood of the glorified Christ could be present in a visible thing, that is in bread and wine. The spiritual can never be bound to or mixed with the creaturely. Therefore, the believer always receives the body and blood of the ascended and glorified Christ immediately. Remarkably, this philosophical argument is used only occasionally and sparingly in Crautwald's early writings.[69] In his later writings it plays a more significant role. As time went on his dualism became stronger.

Crautwald himself emphatically based his understanding of the Lord's Supper on divine revelation.[70] His friends and colleagues, above all Schwenckfeld, were also convinced; in 1526 Schwenckfeld wrote that God had given them their doctrine of the Lord's Supper directly "through our beloved brother in Christ, Crautwald."[71] In this connection it can be noted that the Liegnitz Brotherhood often called upon divine revelation in support of its new doctrines. According to Sebastian Schubart this occurred in particular after Sebastian Eisenmann[72] came to Liegnitz in 1527[73] and served as Crautwald's servant.[74] Eisenmann had earlier studied at Erfurt,[75] Wittenberg, and perhaps elsewhere[76] and had held a parish.[77] These visions seemed to have impressed the Liegnitz Brotherhood greatly. In any case, under Eisenmann's leadership the people came together at the school of St. Mary's to fast, pray, and wait for divine revelations which Gregor Tag, the cantor, often wrote down.[78] These religious inspirations were soon expanded beyond their small circle, and in public. Sebastian Schubart provides an example of the result. "A young honorable virgin (who is still living) became involved in the wretched place (which I should call the school). An active, strong spirit possessed her, and one Sunday while Fabian Eckel was preaching this new teaching to a full church, she jumped from the bench and called out loudly that the cantor ought to be married to her."[79] Since such things seemingly occurred regularly thereafter,[80] many rumors regarding them were widespread within and beyond Silesia. Conrad Cordatus, who had been at Liegnitz University since the fall of 1526, helped to spread them. On November 28, 1528 Luther wrote to him, "You write of marvels in your Liegnitz where in one place and at the same time the spirit and the flesh are so powerful and dear. Some live only by the Spirit, others only by the flesh."[81] Although Schwenckfeld himself twice heard visionary voices, once on his departure from Silesia and again at his death,[82] he was probably not in direct contact with the Eisenmann circle. In any case there is no indication of this in Sebastian Schubart's history of Schwenkfeldianism or in the Liegnitz chronicles. Because of these occurrences in early Schwenkfeldianism the question must be raised whether or not there was a relationship between them and the visionary and ecstatic phenomena in the Hussite movement. It is remarkable that similar phenomena occurred among other religious groups which were in contact with the Hussites. The circle of the Zwickau prophets comes immediately to mind.[83]

Crautwald's claim that his understanding of the Lord's Supper was based on a heavenly vision is not satisfactory for the historian. Theological and spiritual influences which led him to his view of the Lord's Supper must be studied. As already mentioned, the sources indicate that his teaching was first shaped by his debates on the subject with Zwingli[84] and Oecolampadius.[85] Crautwald had in his library some of their books, which had been known and reprinted in Silesia,[86] and he had studied them carefully as his numerous marginal notes indicate.[87] It was most likely by them, despite his criticisms, that he was strengthened in his belief that John 6 was the foundation of the doctrine of the Lord's Supper and that the external reception of the sacrament did not aid salvation. Secondly, it may also be said that Erasmus' writings were influential. Crautwald also owned many of the Dutch humanist's books,[88] and as he had done with those of Zwingli, he also annotated these extensively. For example, in a letter to Schwenckfeld he cited Erasmus' *Paraphrases* of Matthew and John to bolster his assertion regarding the metaphoric language of the Holy Scripture.[89] It is striking, however, that later on he seldom cites Erasmus. Perhaps he recognized that the Dutch writer's teaching on the Lord's Supper was not purely symbolic but was at the same time realistic.[90] Thirdly, the Greek and Latin Fathers certainly helped form Crautwald's conception of the sacrament, even if they served him primarily as the means to legitimize his position from tradition. He must have read them carefully even before 1525, since during his first intensive study of the Lord's Supper he could turn with certainty to Cyprian, Tertullian, Hilary of Poitiers, and Chrysostom to find his support.[91] Later when he tried to show that his understanding of the Lord's Supper agreed with the tradition of the ancient church, he intensified his study of the Church Fathers, especially of those who seemingly held a symbolic interpretation of the Lord's Supper. Thus he wrote to Bernhard Egetius on December 10, 1525: "Read Hilary's *On the Trinity,* Books 8 and 10, question diligently, and you will find great light for our darkness."[92]

3. The Attempts of the Schwenkfelders to Win the Lutherans to their Position on the Lord's Supper

Schwenckfeld and Crautwald, as well as their friends, were convinced that Luther's position on the Supper was false. As a result, they felt themselves compelled to make their new understanding known, thereby hoping Luther and his followers would give up their view of the sacrament and accept the Liegnitz position.

(a) The Liegnitz Brotherhood and the Wittenbergers

The Schwenkfelders characteristically turned once again to Wittenberg although they had received no answer to the *Twelve Questions.*[1] They decided however, not to write but to carry their message personally. For this reason, Schwenckfeld went to Wittenberg at the end of November, 1525.[2] The public reason for the trip was given as diplomatic business.[3] It is likely that he was to discuss with Luther Frederick II's proposal to found a university in Liegnitz.[4] Schwenckfeld carried with him a volume with treatises on the Supper which the Liegnitz Brotherhood had composed from September to October.[5] These included Crautwald's October, 1525 Latin letter to Schwenckfeld,[6] a treatise on the Lord's Supper by Crautwald,[7] a Latin letter (since lost) to Justus Jonas on the same subject,[8] a copy of Schwenckfeld's *Twelve Questions,*[9] and a note by Bernhard Egetius.[10] It is not known if Schwenckfeld had other letters with him.[11]

A full account exists[12] of the discussions which Schwenckfeld had with Luther, Bugenhagen, and Justus Jonas on December 1-4. It was composed by the Silesian nobleman in 1540 at the request of Frederick von Walden from a diary he had kept at the time.[13] In contrast, Luther only made two fleeting comments on his meeting with Schwenckfeld in his *Table Talk.*[14]

The colloquy with Luther began December 2.[15] Luther, however, would not at first undertake a theological discussion[16] but only immersed himself in the writings of Crautwald and Egetius which Schwenckfeld had brought to him.[17] In all likelihood he saw Crautwald as the true inaugurator of the theory. When Luther later discussed the problem of the Lord's Supper with Schwenckfeld, the conversation was very friendly. Doubtless, this was a result of the afore-mentioned letter of Crautwald to Justus Jonas, who gave it to Luther to read.[18] In it Crautwald had complained that Luther was stubborn and obstinate,[19] something that troubled him greatly.[20] Bugenhagen, who had earlier written against the Liegnitz position (although not mentioning the Liegnitzers by name) in his *Letter Against the New Errors Concerning the Body and Blood of Our Lord Jesus Christ*, continued the dialogue in Luther's place. To him Schwenckfeld, decisively defending Crautwald's grammatical interpretation,[21] fully outlined his understanding of the Lord's Supper[22] and declared that the Liegnitz Brotherhood rejected both Luther's concept of the real presence and Zwingli's and Karlstadt's symbolic interpretation on the subject.[23] However, while Schwenckfeld's main concern was with the essence of the sacrament, Bugenhagen emphasized its gift. He said the words of institution were not the decisive factor but rather the promise of the forgiveness of sins which went with them. "Nevertheless we do not see the words which he spoke, *This is my body,* as anything other than a promise given for you."[24] Köhler has correctly pointed out that the doctrine of the Lord's Supper which Bugenhagen here put forth was essentially that which Luther taught in his *On the Misuse of the Mass* and *Against the Heavenly Prophets.*[25] Finally Bugenhagen gave to Schwenckfeld, on one sheet,[26] a short, succinct confession regarding the Lord's Supper which he had written not for this occasion but after his discussion with Gregor Casel, and which, on November 4, 1525 he had sent to Nicolaus Gerbel in Strassburg.[27] This cannot be regarded as the first Protestant confession on the Lord's Supper but neither as Bugenhagen's private writing since he was pastor in Wittenberg and had been commissioned to lead the discussion. After the confession was submitted, Schwenckfeld and Bugenhagen discussed the question once more[28] but reached no agreement. Between the discussions with Luther and Bugenhagen, Schwenckfeld also conversed with Justus Jonas who was "very friendly and open,"[29] but who apparently did not go extensively into the theological problems. Perhaps he, too, thought that the Liegnitz Brotherhood had not made its position entirely public, declaring "One must not treat matters of faith in the same way as one treats money matters, but uprightly, and should declare whatever one has in one's heart."[30] However, he gave assurance that he would give a hundred gold coins if the problem of the Lord's Supper could be solved.[31]

Schwenckfeld had been able to observe church life in Wittenberg carefully during his short stay;[32] he also discussed with Luther questions related to the structure of the believing community and the ban. He pressed seriously for the reinstatement of the ban so that one could "separate true Christians from false."[33] Otherwise no renewal of Christendom could be expected. Luther admitted that it troubled him "that no one was improving" but emphasized that he still had "seen nothing of the future church in his surroundings."[34] Moreover, he planned to set up a church register for those who wished to live full Christian lives, to pay attention to their practice, and to hold special worship services for them in the cloister; as for the rest, a chaplain would preach to them in the church.[35] Schwenckfeld still was not satisfied and insisted once again on the reinstatement of the ban[36] as well as on the establishment of a holy community, as described in Acts 4:32-34.[37] But Luther opposed him:

''Yes, dear Caspar, true Christians are not all too common and I would like to see two together, but I do not yet know of even one.''[38] For Luther, the true Christians were always a congregation of saints hidden under the body of the external church. Their community was marked by him only in their mission, that is in the proclamation of the Gospel in word and sacrament.[39] Against this, as G. Maron has convincingly shown,[40] Schwenckfeld wished to bring into being a communion of saints, at first by the excommunication of the unholy and later by the personal separation of the believers. Nevertheless, this discussion on the structure of the community was not without influence on Luther; in his *Preface to the German Mass,* on which he was working at the time and which appeared in print in late 1525 or early 1526, he took up the hope of Schwenckfeld to gather together all those who ''earnestly wished to be Christians.''[41] Yet, he added, this was not possible at present since there were ''not yet people or persons for this.''[42]

The discussions between Schwenckfeld and the Wittenbergers were by no means in vain, however, as one might suppose. Luther, as can be seen in his *Sermon on the Sacrament of the Body and Blood of Christ Against the Radical Spirits,*[43] recognized that he had to work more carefully in the future on the essence of the sacrament. On his side, Schwenckfeld realized that it was a senseless undertaking to attempt to win the Wittenbergers to his position if Luther and his followers could not be convinced that the words of institution were to be interpreted only on the basis of John 6. Concerning this, Luther had clearly said to the Silesian nobleman, ''Your position is correct when you prove that these two propositions are the same: ''This is my body'' and ''My body is truly food''.[44] On Schwenckfeld's return, therefore, the Liegnitz Brotherhood began immediately to compose treatises to give, as Bugenhagen had requested, ''further defense and foundation''[45] for their understanding of the sacrament. In these works[46] (the only ones of which are extant are Crautwald's[47]) an attempt was made to show that the words of institution must be understood according to John 6. Christ was the ''panis coelestis'' (heavenly bread) which was ''frangitur in ligno'' (broken on the tree), and through this bread ''not only are men raised to life from the dead, but with the same bread they find nourishment to eternal life.''[48] Through the physical bread and wine in the Lord's Supper, Christ wishes to show what function his body has.[49] The host is thus only an image[50] or type.[51] ''What physical bread is for the stomach, my body is for the world and for you, for whom it is given.''[52] This heavenly bread—Christ—can, however, as the early Church Fathers correctly acknowledged, be eaten only spiritually in the Supper.[53] These tracts were sent to Wittenberg at the beginning of 1526, in the hope of convincing Luther of the correctness of the Liegnitz doctrine. Before they reached him, however, Luther gave his judgment on the basis of manuscripts Schwenckfeld had left behind.[54] The judgment was negative, as is clear in his letters to Michael Stiefel,[55] to the Christians at Reutlingen,[56] to Johann Agricola,[57] and to Georg Spalatin.[58] In the middle of February, 1526 Luther returned the materials which he still had and, in a "sharp, heated letter,"[59] ordered the Liegnitzers to revise their doctrine. "We should," as Luther wrote according to Schwenckfeld, "stop leading the people astray; their blood will be on our heads'; and he concluded with the words: 'In short, either you or we must belong to the devil's party because we both value the word of God."[60] In the meantime, however, the new compositions arrived in Wittenberg and Luther and Bugenhagen felt obliged to answer once more. On April 13, 1526 Bugenhagen wrote to Crautwald and Schwenckfeld.[61] In a friendly but decisive way he declared that his conscience was bound to the word of Christ and therefore he could not share their teaching. However, he advised them: "If Christ reveals something, go silently; the Spirit of God will be triumphant and I will be nothing."[62] A day later Luther wrote a German letter to Schwenckfeld[63] and a Latin one to Crautwald.[64] In them he declared that in their writings the two of them had merely repeated their earlier claims and had not offered proof that the words of institution must be interpreted on the basis of John 6.[65] Therefore, he could not accept their sacramentology.[66] While he earnestly begged the Silesian nobleman to "leave your manifest error and do not be numbered among those who now lead the world so badly astray,"[67] he gave Crautwald the choice: "Farewell, and return to sanity or stop calling us brothers or communicating any words concerning Christ with us."[68] Luther was correct in his assumption that Crautwald was the initiator of the new doctrine on the sacrament.[69] Melanchthon and Justus Jonas wrote nothing to the Liegnitz Brotherhood, apparently because they had nothing to add to the judgments of Bugenhagen and Luther and because they wished to add nothing. Nevertheless, they warned the Breslau pastor Moibanus[70] concerning the Liegnitzers and on June 24, 1526 Jonas wrote to Bucer, "I have read some writings of Crautwald and Schwenckfeld and I see in them good and plausible thoughts, many of which are able to convince one, but I see nothing which, accepting the plain sense of the words, one is able to accept safely."[71]

(b) The Schwenkfelders and the Lutherans in Silesia and Prussia

From the beginning Schwenckfeld and Crautwald attempted to win not only the Wittenbergers but also their followers in Silesia to their doctrine of the Lord's Supper. For this reason, they sent more than two dozen letters (unfortunately only a few are extant) to the spiritual leaders in Breslau, Johann Hess[72] and A. Moibanus,[73] to the preacher of the order of Augustinians, Adam Adamus,[74] and to the pastor of St. Mary's, Matthias Funck in

Haynau,[75] as well as to Michael Wittiger, the notary and chancellor at the episcopal chancery in Breslau.[76] Lesser-known preachers, such as the Bunzlau pastor Jacob Süssenbach,[77] also seem to be among those who received their letters.[78] In this correspondence they emphasized once again that their understanding of the sacrament differed fundamentally not only from Luther's but also from Zwingli, that their interpretation of the texts on the basis of John 6 was the only legitimate one, and that only their grammatical rendering of the significant words was correct. In addition they pointed out that their position was in agreement with that of the Church Fathers. The Silesian Lutherans did not answer initially, obviously waiting for the decision from Wittenberg. Even when this was given, Moibanus and Hess still hesitated, although they were encouraged by Luther[79] and Melanchthon[80] to speak against Liegnitz. Presumably their silence was based chiefly on their long friendship with Schwenckfeld and Crautwald, but after the Liegnitz Brotherhood early in 1526 called for a *Stillstand,* that is a moratorium on celebrating the sacrament of the Lord's Supper, they finally distanced themselves from the Liegnitzers.

Schwenckfeld alone attempted to win the Prussian Lutherans. As has been noted, he had maintained a friendship with Duke Albrecht of Prussia as well as with Erhard vom Queis, bishop of Pomerania, and had corresponded with Paul Speratus, court preacher in Königsberg, to whom he had written on a number of occasions about the Lord's Supper, asking his opinion.[81] Just as the followers of Luther in Silesia had done, Speratus, along with the other leading Prussian theologians, Johann Briesmann and Johann Poliander, who had certainly been informed by Speratus,[82] delayed their response. Very likely they did so because they knew of the friendship between their duke and Schwenckfeld. Only after Liegnitz called for a moratorium on the sacrament did they, likely upon admonition from Wittenberg, feel called to make a public statement.

(c) The Suspension of the Supper in Liegnitz

After the discussions with the Wittenbergers had completely broken down, the Liegnitz Brotherhood, in agreement with their ruler, decided to forego the practice of the Supper for a time since Luther's current understanding of the sacrament had not led to a renewal of Christendom.[83] They said they had observed that communicants "wished to become evangelical men and good Christians"[84] simply by partaking of bread and wine. Their pattern of life indicated no moral improvement, however, which according to Galatians 5:6 was the decisive standard of judgment.[85] In areas where the Reformation had taken hold, the Lord's Supper had become the new indulgence which sanctioned moral laxity.[86] This misuse, they were convinced, could only be avoided if the Supper were offered only to those who wished to live a Christian life and held a correct understanding of the sacrament.[87] To attain this was essential,[88] but this was possible only by means of a catechumenate,[89] and thus Crautwald and Schwenckfeld busied themselves at this time in creating the necessary catechetical literature. The so-called *Stillstand* was therefore not in any sense thought to be a "test for the inner maturity and life of a Christian," as Hirsch surmised.[90]

As could have been expected, the Schwenkfelders were suspected both in and outside of Silesia of despising and rejecting the sacrament or at least of holding a different opinion than that "taught and described according to the correct, simple understanding and meaning of our Redeemer and Savior."[91] Thus, Georg of Brandenburg complained to his brother-in-law Frederick II on March 13, 1526 that he was tolerating despisers of the sacrament in Liegnitz.[92] Frederick replied immediately in a personal letter on March 27, 1526.[93] stating that he had never allowed this in his territories, and that there were various ideas concerning the Lord's Supper in other places besides Liegnitz. Moreover, the Schwenkfeldian teachings had been submitted "to the learned: Dr. Martin [Luther], Melanchthon, and others in Wittenberg as well as Doctor Hess and Doctor Moibanus as pastors in Breslau"[94] for a judgment. The Liegnitz Brotherhood likewise could not permit these charges to go unanswered, especially since they were increasing.[95] They thus wrote an apology[96] in which they defended the moratorium on the Supper against the charge of heresy. This defense, signed by the Liegnitz clergy as well as Crautwald and Schwenckfeld, was sent on April 21, 1526 to Duke Albrecht of Prussia,[97] to the Lutheran pastors in Breslau,[98] to the Wittenbergers,[99] and to Adamus,[100] among others. It was also publicized in other places—Breslau and Neisse, for example[101]—and one year later, in April 1527, at the Diet of the rulers at Grottkau.[102]

When it proved impossible to reach consensus with Wittenberg, it was of decisive importance for the Liegnitz Brotherhood to know how the Silesian and Prussian Lutherans would receive their defense. The Königsberg theologians answered first. Duke Albrecht had given the apology to Speratus, Johann Briesmann, and Johann Poliander and requested an evaluation. In their opinion, which was very short because of the press of time, they rejected the Liegnitz teaching.[103] With a friendly cover letter[104] from Speratus, the apology was sent on November 13, 1526 "to the servants of Jesus Christ, Valentin Crautwald and Caspar Schwenckfeld and to the brother preachers among the Liegnitz Christians for careful consideration."[105] A few days later, on November 29, 1526 the Breslau theologians also responded.[106] Without going into the details of the Crautwald-Schwenckfeld doctrine, they said it was far removed from the simple understanding of the words of institution and was incomprehensible to them. They added that they thought the appeal to direct revelation was in error and proceeded in a polemical manner: "The Lord give and abundantly pour upon all of us his grace that your sublimity might not despise our simplicity regarding the words of the Supper. We, as befits brothers in Christ, will most freely give thanks for your sublimity, if it is from Christ."[107] For a long time this letter was the last public discussion between the Silesian Lutherans and Schwenckfeld and his followers. From then on they followed the counsel which Melanchthon had given to his former student Moibanus on August 14, 1526: "But you will do by far the more correct thing if you do not quarrel with them and publicly shun this controversy as much as you are able; it leads to nothing"[108] With the negative judgment by the Prussian and Silesian Lutherans an important decision had been reached. Schwenckfeld and his followers had to acknowledge that they were no longer seen as members of the Lutheran reformation, neither by the Wittenbergers nor by those in Königsberg and Breslau. They immediately found themselves not only theologically, but also ecclesiastically, isolated. In light of the political development in Silesia, this necessitated their finding other allies to survive.

4. The Approach of the Schwenkfelders to the South Germans and Swiss

After the Liegnitz Brotherhood experienced the final break with Wittenberg in 1526, it moved slowly but resolutely closer to the South Germans and the Swiss.

(a) Beginnings and Development of the Friendship

Schwenckfeld and his colleagues had two main reasons for attempting to unite with the Swiss and South Germans.[1] In the first place, they became more aware that because of their spiritualism they stood theologically nearer to them than to Wittenberg. They were at one with the Swiss and South Germans, as will become clear, in that they saw no physical real presence of Christ in the bread and wine and believed such an assumption to be idolatry. To reach agreement with them on the Lord's Supper the Liegnitz Brotherhood had only to interpret more strongly the spiritual eating as faith and to emphasize, as they were doing, that the Lord's Supper was a memorial meal. Secondly, because of the changed political situation in Silesia, they saw themselves obliged to join with the Swiss and South Germans. After Ludwig II, king of Hungary and Bohemia, had been defeated and killed by Suleiman II, the Magnificent, at Mohacs on August 29, 1526, Archduke Ferdinand I of Austria, who had been married to Ludwig's sister Anna of Hungary since 1521, was elected to the throne of Bohemia on October 23, 1526.[2] As expected, the Silesian princes and estates acknowledged him as their lord paramount at the Diet of Leobschütz on December 5.[3] Although the confirmation of the existing rights and privileges (among them the right to reform) were made a prerequisite for his recognition,[4] the Silesian followers of the Reformation realized that this younger brother of Charles V would not leave the land alone as the weak Ludwig II had, but that he would attempt to recatholicize it. This was all the more possible since Silesia was not directly subject to the empire and could not carry its own cases directly to the diet. Moreover, large areas of Silesia, namely the significant principalities of Breslau, Schweidnitz, Jauer, and Gross-Glogau, had reverted to the Bohemian crown and its power after the death of their rulers, and were administered by royal deputies.[5]

The beginnings of the friendship between the South Germans and the Liegnitz Brotherhood go back to the spring of 1526 when Matthias Wickler[6] of Silesia traveled through Switzerland. He first visited Oecolampadius in Basel[7] and informed him of Luther's tyranny and the edict against the sale of Zwingli's writings in his homeland.[8] He then went to Zurich and told Zwingli[9] of the progress of the Reformation in Liegnitz and the new understanding of the Lord's Supper among the Liegnitz Brotherhood. He did not hide from him, however, that Liegnitz took offense at the purely symbolic understanding of the sacrament as held by the Swiss,[10] believing "that this word *signifies* was unworthy of Zwingli to use to explain the sacrament."[11] Zwingli rejoiced over the success of the Reformation in the territories of Frederick II, particularly because the foolish conception of the real presence had been abandoned there.[12] In a letter to Crautwald, Schwenckfeld, and the brethren in Silesia, which he sent back with Wickler, Zwingli attempted to set aside their hesitations over his purely symbolic position on the Supper.[13] In an attempt to appease them, he said he had only taken the inherently simple understanding of the Erasmian Lowlander Honius, because Honius' doctrine seemed to him to be the clearest exposition for everyone.[14] Moreover, the formulae "This bread represents my body" and "This bread is the symbol of my body" were not as clear and precise as the term "signifies."[15] Finally, he declared that none of the differences between them were of great importance so long as one did not insist on the physical real presence of Christ in the sacrament.[16] To underscore that this was his sole aim, he sent to the Liegnitz Brotherhood a tract[17] he had recently written on the subject for Theobald Billicanus and Urbanus Rhegius.[18] Nevertheless, prompted by a hint from Capito[19] he added some additional comments[20] in concession to the Schwenkfeldian-Crautwaldian exegesis. He agreed with them that it was precisely the promise, which Luther particularly stressed in those days, which spoke against a real presence of the body and blood of Christ in the Supper. Through this visit of Wickler, and Zwingli's answer a loose friendship was begun between the Swiss and the Liegnitzers, a friendship that would grow stronger in the following months. For their part, Schwenckfeld and his followers emphasized more and more that they stood with the Swiss in a common front against Luther's teaching on the real presence. "Thus it happens that in the present controversy over the sacrament, one side wishes to understand Christ's words about the eating of his body and drinking of his blood spiritually; namely, how the body and blood of Christ may be taken by no other means than in the living word, through living faith. The other side understands the words in a material manner; in that they wish to include the bread itself, they mix the heavenly food with the earthly and contend that the body of Christ is carried through the bread or in the bread."[21]

A good occasion for deepening the friendly relations with the Swiss and South Germans presented itself when Frederick II starting in 1525 followed through with his plan to found a state university in Liegnitz[22] to which, according to V. L. von Seckendorf,[23] he was to invite twenty-four lecturers. A great difficulty arose, however, in finding suitable instructors for this first Protestant university. Besides Crautwald there was only Valentin Trotzendorf, rector at the Goldberg Latin school, who was available to serve Frederick at this time. Consequently, in late August 1526 Frederick turned to Melanchthon with the request that he present him with the names of some scholars.[24] Melanchthon suggested the Hebraists Bernhard Ziegler and Conrad Cordatus, the latter a friend of Willibald Pirckheimer. Cordatus had translated several letters and works of Luther into Latin and had published them in 1525 under the title *Epistolarum Farrago.*[25] In addition, he especially recommended the versatile and learned humanist Antonius Niger of Breslau, who was then most likely active as a teacher in his native city.[26] He emphatically rejected as completely unfounded the rumor that he himself was thinking of coming to Liegnitz.[27] Of those suggested only Ziegler of Leipzig and Cordatus of Wittenberg could be persuaded to come. The university was opened in the fall of 1526, a year before the Philippina, the university at Marburg, was founded, in a very modest fashion since there is no mention of legal or medical studies. It was possibly housed in the Franciscan cloister which had been vacant since 1524 or in the also vacant Carthusian monastery.[28] Ziegler,[29] who remained true to Wittenberg, very probably taught Hebrew,[30] Cordatus, Luther's pupil, possibly lectured on the Old Testament, and Crautwald on the New Testament, Psalms, and the first chapters of Genesis.[31] Crautwald, according to his biographer Adam Reisner, "inflamed his hearers and he often wept with them."[32] Trotzendorf, a student of Melanchthon, first taught in Liegnitz in 1527.[33] Tense relations between Lutherans and Schwenkfelders, especially Crautwald, existed from the beginning. Shortly before November 28, 1526 Cordatus complained in a letter to Luther about the sacramentarians and expressed the wish to return immediately to Wittenberg. Luther at first counseled him to endure,[34] but as the situation became even more confused, he wrote on January 29, 1527 telling him to leave the opponents of Christ as soon as possible.[35] Cordatus thus left in April following the close of the winter semester. He was replaced in February by the Ansbach pastor Johann Rurer,[36] possibly at the suggestion of Duke Georg of Brandenberg-Ansbach, ruler of Jägerndorf.

After the antipathy between Schwenkfelders and Wittenbergers became even greater in the second half of 1526, Frederick II, who could thus expect no more support for the expansion of the university, set his hopes entirely on the Swiss. Early in 1527 he sent the former Goldberg teacher and now town clerk, Fabian Geppart, to the Swiss to hire teachers.[37] Geppart went first to Oecolampadius in Basel, to whom he delivered a letter (no longer extant) from Frederick II.[38] Since there were no suitable teachers there—except the unemployed Petrus Frabenberger (Gynoraeus) who, by chance, had just arrived[39]—he was directed to Zwingli,[40] who suggested Theodor Buchmann (Bibliander). The city council accepted the plan and released the youthful Bibliander for two years.[41] In May or early June this famous student of classical languages went to Basel and then to Strassburg from where he was to travel to Liegnitz with Bonifatius Wolfhart.[42] When this plan could not be carried out,[43] Bibliander traveled by himself to Liegnitz where he became a teacher of rhetoric.[44] Through him, later the successor of Zwingli as Old Testament professor in Zurich, a further bond was established between the Swiss and the Schwenkfelders.

The Swiss, especially Oecolampadius,[45] were particularly happy with this new bond since they had recently lost their dominating position in the north of Swabia where their doctrine on the Supper had been attacked in a book entitled *Syngramma Suevicum*[46] written against Zwingli's doctrine of the Lord's Supper.[47] This book was a reply to Oecolampadius' treatise *Concerning the Genuine Words of the Lord "This is My Body" exposited according to the Early Fathers*[48] which appeared in September 1525. In his tract Oecolampadius had rejected every realistic conception of the sacrament except its role as sacrifice and adopted a tropological interpretation of the Lord's Supper. He interpreted the words "This is my body" as "This is the figure of my body," and thereby, like Zwingli, supported a "transsubjective" character of the sacrament, since "figure" in distinction to "body" makes the conception of the Supper subjectively ambiguous. Yet his conception of the Supper, as G. Krodel correctly noted, was in no sense fully identical with Zwingli's since he taught that in the "union with Christ in faith" there also occurred an "eating of Christ's flesh and blood."[49] Oecolampadius thus held an Erasmian sacramental mysticism[50] which he defended as traditionally at one with the Fathers, exegetically in agreement with the metonymic use of the Holy Scriptures, philosophically in agreement with his understanding that the spiritual cannot be tied to the physical, and Christologically based on the session of Christ at the right hand of the Father. Johann Brenz, on the other hand, defended the physical real presence of Christ in his *Syngramma Suevicum.* He insisted that the doctrine of the *Syngramma* was taken from the Holy Scriptures[51] and not, as Oecolampadius apparently assumed,[52] from Book 4, Distinction 10, Chapter 1 of Peter Lombard's *Sentences.* The real presence of the body and blood of Christ did not come through magic but by the words of institution, whereby the words "bread" and "wine" guaranteed the objectivity of salvation.[53] Whereas Oecolampadius had confessed, "It must therefore be protested that the exemplar of things is in the two signs not in the things themselves,"[54] Brenz declared that the bread was "not only symbol and exemplar, but a symbol with the thing itself joined to it."[55] Since the Crautwaldian-Schwenkfeldian teaching with its emphasis on spiritual eating stood close to Oecolampadius, he and the Swiss were able to hope, not unreasonably, that the Schwenkfelders, especially Crautwald who was acquainted with both writings,[56] would become active in the continuing battle against Brenz and his followers.[57] They were disappointed in this since the Liegnitzers did not immediately join the debate. Schwenckfeld and Crautwald first entered the fray only when the disagreement between Luther and Zwingli had reached its height.

(b) The Alliance Between the Schwenkfelders and the Swiss

Soon after the Liegnitz Brotherhood had begun to ally itself with the Swiss and the South Germans, a literary controversy began over Luther's understanding of the sacrament. Luther delivered three sermons at the end of March, 1526 as preparation for the Easter communion. The sermons were probably published at the beginning of October in the same year under the title of *Sermon on the Sacrament of the Body and Blood of Christ Against the Sacramentarians.*[58] In the second sermon Luther wrote that until then he had not often dealt with the "object of faith, that is the work or thing which one believes or one should hold to,"[59] but only "with the other, the best,"[60] with "faith itself, or the use, as one believes, to which it should be put."[61] Now he felt constrained to treat the essence of the sacrament more closely because "it is claimed by many . . . that Christ's body and blood are not in the bread and wine."[62] In this sermon he criticized the positions of his opponents in such a way that it is clear he could distinguish their different positions quite well.[63] Yet at the same time he emphasized that no basic difference existed between them since they all rejected the physical real presence.[64]

Although he did not name them, Luther doubtless had Schwenckfeld and Crautwald in mind,[65] and thus they in turn felt compelled to defend their understanding of the sacrament. As a result, the Silesian nobleman in January or February of 1527 composed his very lengthy treatise on the Supper, *On the Ground and Cause concerning the Error and the Shortcoming in the Articles on the Sacrament of the Lord's Supper.*[66] Circulated in manuscript, it was not printed until 1570. In this work, in which he emphasized once more that the absence of a renewal of Christendom was the reason for his concern about the Supper,[67] Schwenckfeld firmly rejected Luther's teaching on the physical real presence of Christ in the Supper. He grounded his denial mainly on the argument that the spiritual can have nothing to do with the physical.[68] So as to make concessions to the Swiss and South Germans, he omitted the more characteristic marks of his understanding of the Lord's Supper. Spiritual eating he described not as the spiritual feeding on the body and blood of the ascended Lord, as he had earlier done, but rather as feeding on the Logos through which all believers are nourished in the sacrament and outside it.[69] By his use of this concept of the Logos, he enabled the spiritual eating to be interpreted in different ways. He himself, as Kohler has noted, continued to understand it as the spiritual enjoyment of the body and blood of the Ascended One.[70]

A copy of Schwenckfeld's treatise must have also reached Luther's hands, since he used it in his tract of March 1527 and discussed it in his work, *Confession Concerning Christ's Supper.* However, it is not possible to discover through whom Luther received the manuscript. It is unlikely that it was sent directly to him. Possibly Duke Albrecht of Prussia had it sent to him, as Schultz suggested.[71] Albrecht confirmed his receipt of a treatise on the sacrament in a letter to Schwenckfeld on May 9, 1527.[72] The treatise might have been the *Ground and Cause,* yet it is also possible that Luther received the treatise not from the duke but directly from Prussian theologians. At any rate, Erhard vom Queis, bishop of Pomesania, had obtained a tract on the Last Supper, since Schwenckfeld asked Speratus on March 20, 1527 to get some of the Liegnitz writings on the Lord's Supper from him.[73]

In March of 1527, about a month after Schwenckfeld's *Ground and Cause,* Luther's tract *That the Words of Christ "This is my body" still remain firm against the Radicals*[74] appeared. In it he wrote a few lines on the doctrine of Crautwald and Schwenckfeld[75] (he did mention either by name), in addition to discussing the teaching of Karlstadt, Zwingli, and Oecolampadius. While Schwenckfeld had declared that the spiritual could not be bound to the physical, Luther insisted that "the Spirit cannot be among us other than in physical things as in the word, in the water, in Christ's body, and in his saints on earth."[76] Albrecht of Prussia wrote on May 9, 1527 to the Silesian nobleman regarding Luther's treatise, requesting that he make a public statement if Luther's work did not appear to him to be correct.[77] Obviously the duke did not want the discussions between Luther and Schwenkfeld to break off, in the hope that an agreement might still be reached,[78] Schwenckfeld did in fact write his now lost *Chapters on Errors of the Books of Luther Against the Radicals*[79] during the summer months and sent it to Königsberg.[80] He urgently requested Speratus to examine it carefully on the basis of the Scriptures;[81] at the end of his letter he added in German that one must begin to solve the problem of the sacrament not with the words of institution but with Christology.[82] In marginalia to this Speratus wrote, "This faith comes not from the hearing of the word, but is a dream; the word would be changed, causing blindness."[83] On August 7, 1527 the duke thanked Schwenckfeld for the manuscript but said he found parts of it incomprehensible. He therefore asked Schwenckfeld to present his understanding of the sacrament more clearly in a new work which he would then send on to Wittenberg for judgment.[84] Schwenckfeld immediately complied with this request and wrote a treatise (this work too is lost), and sent it to Albrecht.[85] This composition in which Schwenckfeld summarized his criticism of Luther's tract of March, 1527 in twelve points appears to have been more understandable, for the duke now sent it on to Luther;[86] the Wittenberg reformer had not received it before the middle of November, however, assuming that the final remarks in his letter to Johann Hess, *Whether One may Flee from Death,* refer to this piece of Schwenckfeld's.[87]

(c) The Beginning of Ferdinand I's Persecution

Understandably, Ferdinand I also became aware of the controversy between Luther and Schwenckfeld over the Supper. In his answer to the presentation by Jacob von Salza, Duke Frederick II, and Margrave Georg regarding the Silesian election requirements and wishes in Vienna on January 11, 1527,[88] he talked evasively about the problem of the continuation of the ecclesiastical reform in Silesia,[89] but only three months later, in discussions with the Breslau deputation which had come to Prague for the coronation activities, it was clear that he intended to recatholicize his domains. On March 15, he indicated to the Breslau envoys through his chancellor Ulrich von Harrach that he would not tolerate arbitrary ecclesiastical reforms and that "the ceremonies and practices of all churches were to be reestablished and the presently Lutheran preachers expelled."[90] With this it must have been unmistakably clear to the followers of the Reformation that, following the homage that was supposed to be rendered the following May in Breslau, they could expect counter-Reformation measures.

Foreseeing such an event, Frederick II, who was suspected "in many places" by "nobles and commoners" of allowing "nothing but heresy, error and the deception of unchristian teaching to be preached in his lands and towns" and also willing to "encourage the same,"[91] wrote his first *Apology*[92] at the beginning of 1527. With this defense, in the writing of which Schwenckfeld certainly participated,[93] the duke wished to reject as unfounded the charge that he allowed heresy in his territories. In addition, he wanted to make it clear to the new lord paramount that he was not of a mind to give up his friendly attitude toward reformation. Finally, he wished to encourage the Protestant powers in Silesia, namely the municipal council of Breslau, Margrave Georg of Brandenburg-Ansbach, and Margrave Kasimar II of Teschen and Gross-Glogau, to continue supporting the Reformation. This would also explain why he did not treat the thorny problem of the sacrament in his *Apology*.

On May 1, 1527 Ferdinand I came to Breslau to receive the oath of allegiance from the princes and estates.[94] In his entourage was Johann Fabri[95] who had been court preacher and ecclesiastical advisor of the Hapsburgs since 1523 and coadjutor of Wiener Neustadt from 1524. Immediately seeing in Schwenkfeldianism the most serious danger to the old faith in Silesia, this blacksmith's son from Leutkirch became its vehement opponent, addressing complaints on behalf of the church against adherents of the new faith to Ferdinand I and the Cathedral Chapter.[95] He was likely also the instigator of the anti-reform mandate[97] published by the king on May 17 (i.e., after the homage was rendered and the tax for combatting the Turks was granted), in which the demand was made that "the whole religion be reestablished in its pristine state."[98] This both Duke Frederick II[99] and the Breslau municipal council[100] immediately rejected on May 18 as impossible. Ferdinand I did not sharply oppose these rejections but simply expressed the hope that his demand would be carried out at a suitable time.[101] On May 20, 1527 he left Breslau and went to Hungary where Johann Zapolya, Voivode of Transylvania, supported by the anti-German party and the Turks, had been elected king on November 11, 1526.

Before the king left Silesia, however, he demonstrated once again his firm resolution to reestablish the old faith. On May 20, 1527 in Schweidnitz, which belonged to his royal patrimonial lands, he had the preacher Johann Reichel of Striegau, also known as Eilfinger, taken captive and "hanged on a pear tree in the Jewish manner for denying the essential presence of the body of Christ in the bread of the sacrament."[102] It is not known if Reichel was a follower of Schwenckfeld,[103] but had this been the case, Schwenckfeld would probably have protested more energetically.[104] In addition, Ferdinand I soon moved against the followers of the Reformation with mandates and decrees.

In Braunau on his way to Hungary, he issued an edict against the followers of the new faith, according to the Chronicler Nicolaris Pol,[105] although this information is justifiably disputed.[106] Not in dispute are two other mandates, issued on June 28 in Vienna and on August 20 in Ofen. In them he did not attack the city of Breslau so much as Duke Frederick II.[107] At about the same time, Fabri's polemic treatise reached Liegnitz, provocatively dedicated to the Silesian duke. It was entitled *Confutation of New Things and of the Previously Unheard of Error Regarding the Eucharist, or An Assertion of the Truth Concerning the Presence of the Body and Blood of Our Lord Jesus Christ in the Sacrament of the Altar Against Caspar Schwenckfeld, a Silesian, to Frederick Duke of Liegnitz.* In it the confessor of Ferdinand I labeled the Schwenkfelders as followers of Zwingli and accused them of despising the sacrament.

In light of this ever more critical situation, Schwenckfeld, his followers, and their sovereign, were urgently constrained to defend themselves against these attacks. First Schwenckfeld and Crautwald wrote an emotional letter to Bishop Jacob von Salza in the middle of October 1527,[108] distancing themselves significantly from Luther's understanding of the Lord's Supper[109] and not hesitating to point out the difference between his earlier and later positions on the sacrament.[110] They also denied that their doctrine came from Zwingli, Oecolampadius, or anyone else,[111] and emphasized that their doctrine of the sacrament, on the contrary, was based on divine revelation.[112]

Meanwhile, Frederick II instructed his theologians—and probably Schwenckfeld as well—to compose a confession of faith.[113] In it[114] they returned to their original position on the Supper, more strongly interpreting the spiritual eating as partaking of the body and blood of the Logos.[115] They also still held to Zwingli's doctrine of the Supper as a memorial.[116] This confession of the Liegnitz pastors was published as a second apology by the Breslau printer Adam Dyon in November of 1527 with a foreword[117] by Frederick II, in which he denied the charge of despising the sacrament and with an afterword dated November 11, 1527[118] as a second apology.[119] Frederick sent it to the Breslau bishop, who passed it on to the Chapter with the request that they study it and advise him how to answer.[120] On November 26, 1527 the Chapter chose two of their own men, Dominicus von Prockendorf and Franz Preussner to give their expert opinion. There is no information in the record on their findings.

5. *The Final Position of the Liegnitz Brotherhood on the Sacrament and the Anti-Schwenkfeldian Measures of Ferdinand I*

At the end of 1527 or the beginning of 1528, Schwenckfeld wrote an epitome[1] of his *Ground and Cause*[2] in which he attempted to show that the doctrines of transsubstantiation and consubstantiation, between which he no longer distinguished, were false.[3] The six arguments contained in it[4] may be reduced to two. First, the doctrine of a real presence of Christ in the Lord's Supper cannot be found in the Holy Scriptures;[5] they describe rather the physical return of Christ only for the judgment, not in the bread.[6] Secondly, it was chiefly his dualism of Spirit and flesh, inner and outer, which caused him to reject every sense of a physical real presence of Christ in the sacrament.[7] He was convinced that God never came to men through external, manifest, and physical things, but only and always through the inner, unseen, and spiritual things. Consequently, he concluded that "our eternal treasure must not be in the bread on earth, but far above, namely, in heaven; and that, in the practice of the Supper, one ought not to direct faith to the bread or to the physical presence of Christ in the form of bread, but one's faith ought to be only in Christ in heaven, and, through Christ, in God where our life with Christ is now hidden."[8] By this he believed he held to the original Reformation position. In the treatise he endeavored, by the use of numerous single citations from his writings, to show that Luther had earlier taught the distinction between the Spirit and flesh although "he now wishes to procure faith from the Scripture and from the external word."[9] He contrasted Luther's *Two Sermons on Acts 15 and 16*[10] and *That the Words of Christ "This is my body, etc" still stand fast against the Radicals*[11] with the *Works on the Psalms,*[12] the *Church Postils,*[13] *Shunning Human Teaching and an Answer to the Passages Brought Forward to Strengthen Human Teaching,*[14] and *Preface to the Old Testament.*[15] This method of contrasting the later with the earlier Luther, although not first used by Schwenckfeld, was seldom used with such consequence by other leaders of the Radical Reformation.[16] In this work, Schwenckfeld did not describe his own position on the Lord's Supper, although he promised to do so in a later work[17] in which he wished to indicate how "the believer was fed and given drink through a true faith with the body and blood of Jesus Christ in the living word, and how the spiritual eating and breaking of bread and the memorial were to be distinguished."[18]

In January, 1528 Luther, at this time completing his last great treatise on the Supper, *Confession Concerning Christ's Supper,* received Schwenckfeld's epitome, although Schwenckfeld did not know it had been sent.[19] It is not known who sent the manuscript to Luther although perhaps it came via Albrecht of Prussia, whom Schwenckfeld met[20] between February 15 and

March 18 on an official journey from Ortelsberg to Memel.[21] The duke may have sent it to Wittenberg because Schwenckfeld had attempted to demonstrate in it that he, and not Luther, had held to the spiritual principle of the Reformation. In his last great treatise on the Supper, *Confession Concerning Christ's Supper,* written principally against Zwingli and Oecolampadius, Luther devoted a few pages to a fierce attack of Schwenckfeld's epitome[22] without mentioning the author. He recounted each of Schwenckfeld's six arguments[23] but did not refute them in detail, merely rejecting them summarily. He asked, for example, why the real presence of the body of Christ should be an offense against his dignity since it was not against his honor to be present in his divinity everywhere, even in hell.[24] Not the least of the reasons for his not dealing more thoroughly with Schwenckfeld's arguments was his belief that the Liegnitz Brotherhood's doctrine on the Supper was only a variant of Zwingli's.[25]

One month after Luther's great work on the sacrament appeared in March, 1528, Schwenckfeld sent his epitome to Bucer.[26] It is not known whether Schwenckfeld sent it on his own[27] or whether he was expressly requested to do so by the Strassburg theologians,[28] who had been working intensively with Luther's treatise since the beginning of April.[29] All that is certain is that Strassburg had expressed itself critically on Schwenckfeld's teaching because of Luther's attack and so had requested the Silesian to clarify it.[30] Whether or not they asked Schwenckfeld at the same time to send them a copy, as the title in the first complete edition of Schwenckfeld's letters states,[31] must remain an open question. Nevertheless, Schwenckfeld felt himself "compelled"[32] because of the Strassburgers' request to send a copy of his epitome to Strassburg, so that, if necessary, the theologians there might be able to correct him from the Holy Scriptures,[33] but also so that they might be able to make a more critical judgment.[34] Crautwald, in the name of the Liegnitzers, expressly asked Bucer, in an accompanying letter, to make certain that the manuscript not be published.[35] From Strassburg it was sent (since it was not expressly forbidden) to Oecolampadius in Basel[36] who, in turn, sent it to Zwingli on July 22, 1528. In an accompanying letter[37] Oecolampadius carefully made him aware that Luther had cited ("a little carelessly"[38]) the Silesian nobleman in his treatise *Confession Concerning Christ's Supper.*

On receiving Schwenckfeld's epitome, Zwingli was completing the last part of his attack on Luther's treatise, *On Martin Luther's Book Entitled Confession.* He dealt with Luther's criticism of Schwenckfeld, although he had earlier, without knowing the work, expressed the opinion that Luther had not understood the Silesian correctly.[39] On the basis of what he was now reading he was convinced of his earlier contention and now declared that Schwenckfeld had rightly emphasized that faith may never be directed to externals[40] and that it was totally opposed to faith to wish to gain forgiveness of sins by eating.[41] In this, the statements of the "pious Silesian" were "truly . . . more Christian and more thorough" than all "that Luther had ever written on this matter."[42] At the same time Zwingli reported that he wished to publish Schwenckfeld's epitome, so that it might be evident whether Luther had reported its contents correctly.[43] Whether he, in fact, did not know that its publication was against the express wish of Schwenckfeld is uncertain.[44] In any case, Oecolampadius' letter made no mention of this, but surely the Zurich reformer must have had the foresight to realize the difficulties in which publication would place the Silesian nobleman.

The promised edition appeared in Zurich from the Froschauer press between the end of August and the beginning of September. The foreword of Zwingli is dated August 24, 1528. In it he thanks Schwenckfeld for demonstrating that Luther's teaching on the real presence of the body of Christ is against Scripture and tradition.[45] He also approved of the grammatical construction of the words of institution[46] and stated that he and Schwenckfeld were in no way opposed, as Luther had said they were,[47] in their exegesis of the words of the Last Supper. Zwingli's own exposition included Schwenckfeld's.[48] This publication was, as will be seen, disastrous for Schwenckfeld and his friends; it forced him into exile and initiated decades of persecution.

During the summer of 1528 as Schwenckfeld's *Instruction* appeared in print, the Liegnitz Brotherhood was already separating itself from Zwingli.[49] This was first clear in a letter sent by Schwenckfeld to Albrecht of Prussia on March 22, 1528.[50] In it he attempted to show not only that the teaching of Luther was false, but that Zwingli's was as well.[51] While Luther emphasized the words of institution too much, Zwingli valued them too little.[52] The Zurich reformer understood them only as signifiers and held that the presence of the body of Christ in the Supper was only symbolic.[53] This separation of Schwenckfeld and his followers from the Zwinglian position in the first place had theological grounds. The Liegnitzers wished unconditionally to protect the idea of spiritual eating since "there were two breads and two drinks in the Supper, a spiritual and an earthly, an outer and an inner."[54] Zwingli had also affirmed a spiritual eating of the heavenly bread,[55] for example in the marginalia to his book *On Martin Luther's Book Entitled Confession,*[56] but he understood something quite different by it than had Schwenckfeld. For Zwingli spiritual eating was always and finally identical with faith. The Liegnitz Brotherhood, on the other hand, taught that the individual believer, through the lifting up of the heart, partook spiritually of the body and blood of the ascended Christ, of the Logos, and thus came to a real, dynamic, ontic union with Christ.[57] Certainly the Liegnitz Brotherhood's affirmation of a distinction between its own and Zwingli's doctrine of the Supper is not the result of their reading of Luther's sacramental writings. There Luther had demonstrated repeatedly that the Swiss, although speaking of spiritual eating, in fact denied every physical real presence of the body and blood of Christ in the Supper. Also in other matters the Schwenkfelders returned to their original position, thus defending firmly once again their characteristic grammatical construction of the words of institution[58] and their metonymic use of language.[59]

This break between the Swiss and the Liegnitz Brotherhood was also based on church politics. Through their friendly relations with the Swiss, the Liegnitzers had come under suspicion of being, like these, despisers of the sacrament. Two occurrences, in particular, led to this. In the first place, Oecolampadius had Schwenckfeld's letter to Cordatus, *On the Course of the Word of God*[60] published in 1527, although it was meant originally only as an epistle. Geppart, on his trip at the beginning of April, 1527,[61] which has previously been mentioned, brought, along with other things, a copy of the manuscript to Switzerland, where he had traveled in the service of Frederick II to gain lecturers for the university at Liegnitz. In Basel Geppart gave Oecolampadius not only a handwritten letter from his duke and a letter from Crautwald, but also the manuscript of *On the Course of the Word of God.*[62] Oecolampadius, in turn, without Schwenckfeld's knowledge or permission,[63] had Thomas Wolff publish the manuscript.[64] Oecolampadius undoubtedly wished to use it in support of his battle against his Swabian opponents and the Lutheran doctrine of the Supper. In a foreword dated May 31, 1527, which he added to the tract, Oecolampadius weakened Schwenckfeld's spiritualism by declaring that the learned and pious Silesian nobleman did not wish to lessen the uniqueness of the exterior word in any way, since the Holy Spirit was able to use it better and more fruitfully than any other tool.[65] What Schwenckfeld was concerned about was that all glory go to God alone,[66] and if this were the position of all other theologians, Oecolampadius added, the Holy Scripture would be interpreted "with greater faith, peace, and utility."[67] Finally, he expressed the desire that learned persons would endeavor to imitate Schwenckfeld's irenic attitude rather than criticize his teaching.[68] When Theodor Buchmann brought a copy of the work to Liegnitz,[69] Crautwald[70] and Schwenckfeld[71] were deeply disturbed. But Schwenckfeld finally accepted what had occurred, expressing the wish that "what had been done may bring glory to God although confusion to me."[72]

Secondly, the Liegnitz Brotherhood was possibly under suspicion of holding Swiss views of the Lord's Supper because Luther had repeatedly associated their doctrine, although not naming them, with that of the Swiss and had treated both as a theological unity. Both rejected the real presence of Christ in the sacrament; it must thus have appeared to readers, particularly Roman

Catholics, that they were also in agreement on their positive statements about the Lord's Supper.

From Prague on August 1, 1528 Ferdinand I issued a long mandate printed in Vienna[73] but only made public in Silesia on October 2. In it he especially opposed those who despised the sacrament,[74] since it was against the tradition of the church to deny the physical real presence of Christ in the sacrament.[75] All such blasphemers were henceforth to be executed.[76] Although Schwenckfeld and his colleagues were not designated by name, it was obvious that the mandate was intended for them. The Liegnitz Brotherhood and its protector Frederick II therefore felt it necessary to separate themselves, as quickly and ostentatiously as possible, from Zwingli. Indeed, the duke suggested that Schwenckfeld and his associates give up their theological position and unite with Luther. Schwenckfeld answered his prince on this in a letter at the beginning of October 1528,[77] stating that, in spite of Luther's obvious merit,[78] acceptance of his doctrine was not possible because no renewal of Christendom had occurred;[79] on the contrary, moral laxity and dissipation[80] existed everywhere among Protestants because they based their faith on the outer letter.[81] For this reason, he would rather be a papist than a Lutheran.[82] But since among the papists as well, conscience "was not left free,"[83] Schwenckfeld requested his lord to endure the present circumstances until "almighty God allows the words to be preached in his power that the congregations might be joined in Christian unity."[84]

In fact, Frederick II did at first accept Schwenckfeld's argument, and as the Breslau council had done,[85] protested[86] against the mandate to Ferdinand I through a letter of November 26, 1528 which he had delivered in Prague by his court marshal Philipp von Poppschütz.[87] In this protest he stated that a return to the old faith was not possible since the reforms could not be undone without bloodletting.[88] For this reason he asked that the status quo be maintained in his territories until the time of a general or national council.[89] At the same time he sent Ferdinand his two apologies, the *Cause, Foundation, and Excuse* as well as the *Instruction and Excuse,* in order to refute the charge that he tolerated despisers of the sacrament in his territories.[90] Before his letter reached Ferdinand, however, knowledge that Zwingli had published Schwenckfeld's epitome, *Instructions,* along with a preface recommending it became public. Thus Ferdinand I, counseled by his ecclesiastical advisor Fabri, felt it was demonstrated that there was no theological distinction between Liegnitz and the Swiss. He therefore immediately and sharply rejected Frederick's apology in a letter of December 15, 1528.[91] He emphasized that he knew from a reliable source that Frederick's "chief teacher and preacher"[92] spread his heresy not only verbally but also in writing. Thereby all Silesians in the empire and in other lands were under suspicion as well, although the charge applied only to the subjects of Frederick II;[93] consequently, Ferdinand reaffirmed his decision to move against those who despised the sacrament.[94]

At about the same time, Johann Fabri, for many years a fierce opponent of Zwingli,[95] was preparing an anti-Schwenkfeldian treatise which he published on February 8, 1529 in Vienna at the press of Johann Singriener under the title *Christian Rejection of the Frightful Error which Caspar Schwenckfeld in Silesia has Built up Against the Truth of the Most Praiseworthy Sacrament of the Body and Blood of Christ.* Dedicated to Frederick II, the treatise charges Schwenckfeld with despising the sacrament since, along with his "godless companions" Oecolampadius, Karlstadt, and others, he sees the sacrament as nothing more than baker's bread.[96] In his dedicatory preface, Fabri wrote that he directed it to the duke of Liegnitz so that "he, blinded by the Schwenkfelders until now, might have the scales fall from his eyes and that your princely grace might know how to protect yourself from the fiery serpents which come upon the common people."[97]

Because of the royal reply mentioned above, Frederick II had to decide whether to remain firm on the side of his former chief counselor and possibly lose both life and lands, or to separate himself from Schwenckfeld and possibly save the Schwenkfeldian movement in his territories. His decision was already slightly prejudiced, since the Silesian Lutheran opposition against Schwenckfeld, particularly among the nobility, had grown strong. According to the chronicler G. Thebesius, the influential Georg von Zedlitz had most emphatically recommended to the duke and the king that Schwenckfeld be exiled;[98] and in Liegnitz itself a significant opposition to Schwenckfeld and his colleagues could be noted since the fall of 1527.[99] Both verbally and in writing they were secretly and publicly attacked as "radicals, false spirits, new prophets, sectarians, dreamers, etc."[100] The chief leader of the opposition was Valentin Trotzendorf, who, except for B. Ziegler, was the only Lutheran still at the Liegnitz university. The student body had decreased significantly by this time because of the religious turmoil as well as because of the plague of 1527 and the threat of a Turkish invasion.[101] Untiringly and passionately Trotzendorf fought the *sponduloi* (Stinkfelders), as he called them in Greek.[102] Finally, according to tradition,[103] in the fall of 1529 he returned to Wittenberg with the last six students. Ziegler had left shortly before that.[104]

Schwenckfeld anticipated the decision of the duke by undertaking exile voluntarily, thereby making possible the continuation of the Schwenkfelder movement. On February 15, 1529 in a letter[105] delivered by his court marshal,[106] Duke Frederick II informed his lord paramount of Schwenckfeld's emigration[107] and correctly noted that his former court advisor had not sent his *Instructions* to Zwingli but to the Strassburg theologians with the urgent plea to keep it to themselves and in no case to have it published.[108] It was they who had sent it on to Zwingli, who had published the epitome.[109] In addition, Frederick II insisted that he tolerated no unchristian innovations[110] and that he had untiringly followed the royal mandate insofar as his conscience and that of his subjects allowed him.[111]

On Schwenckfeld's departure, Crautwald wrote a meditation on prayer,[112] dedicating it to the Silesian nobleman. Schwenckfeld then directed his steps to the imperial free city of Strassburg, arriving[113] before May 18, 1529.[114] He came not in poverty but as a relatively wealthy man, since he received yearly rent from his lands which he had left in the care of his younger brother Hans.[115] Two reasons must have led him to choose Strassburg as his temporary residence, the city where the most diverse religious groups and individuals had gathered. First, the theologians there were not only opposed, as he and his followers were, to the doctrine of the Lord's Supper of both Wittenberg and the Swiss, but in their *Comparison of Doctor Luther and his Opponents* they had also acknowledged a certain agreement between themselves and the Liegnitz Brotherhood in their understanding of the sacrament.[116] Secondly, as has been shown, it was the Strassburg theologians who had caused his exile by allowing the publication of his *Instruction.* Schwenckfeld could therefore count on the hospitality of Bucer, Capito, and others, plagued as they were by their consciences on the matter. Certainly he was warmly received in Strassburg, which had been prepared for his arrival by a letter from Crautwald.[117] Approvingly, Capito, at whose home he, as well as many other mystical spiritualists, found lodging, wrote to Zwingli on May 18, 1529 that Schwenckfeld was a "truly noble man. In his whole person, he breathes Christ."[118] In the same letter, it is suggested that there was an attempt to make amends in Strassburg.[119] This first became clearly evident in June 1529 when Capito wrote a foreword[120] to Schwenckfeld's *Apology,* recommending it.[121] In this composition the Silesian nobleman had rejected the premise that he despised the sacrament and insisted that Zwingli had published his *Instruction* against his will.

III The Golden Age of Moderate Schwenkfeldianism in the Territories of Frederick II

Following the voluntary exile of Schwenckfeld in February of 1529, a great blossoming of moderate Schwenkfeldianism began in the territories of Frederick II. It was to last almost a decade. This was caused in the first place by the Liegnitz Brotherhood's rejection of all Anabaptist influences as well as its thwarting the Anabaptists from taking a foothold in the prinicipality of Liegnitz. As a result, the Brotherhood was protected against the slightest suspicion that it sympathized with them. Secondly, after initial difficulties, Frederick II successfully suppressed the radical strain within the Schwenkfelder movement and thus decreased the differences from Lutheranism. Although both movements were almost parallel chronologically, the controversy of the Schwenkfeldians with the Anabaptists is treated first here, since it began somewhat earlier—indeed, before the exile of Schwenckfeld—and was concluded earlier as well.

1. The Controversy of the Liegnitz Brotherhood with the Anabaptists

During the controversy over the meaning of the external word, Schwenckfeld and Crautwald commented only sporadically and casually on baptism. The most complete discussion on the subject was by Crautwald in his *Judgment,*[1] which he wrote in a period of only a few days at the end of November 1528 at the urgent request of his friends.[2] It was in response to the anonymous Lutheran work,[3] *A Confession on the Kingdom of God, its Organization or the Control of His Kingdom,*[4] unfortunately no longer extant, which was sent only to places where the authors "hoped to clear up the situation and teach others."[5] This work was issued to counter the argument in Crautwald's important composition *On the Grace of God*[6] which was then circulating in manuscript form only. In the *Judgment*, in which Crautwald rejected the doctrine which derived baptism from circumcision,[8] he distinguished between a baptism of the heart[9] and a baptism of the external man.[10] The latter occurred with "water for the man"[11] and was no means for the forgiveness of sins.[12] Consequently, it was not necessary for salvation.[13] Christ had instituted it merely to symbolize the meaning of inner baptism[14] and to give man an opportunity openly to assert that he had received the Spirit.[15] Baptism of the heart occurred unmediated, directly from God, bringing about the new birth.[16] He who received the new birth[17] was, as John 13:10 pointed out, completely pure.[18] This understanding of baptism, behind which stood his conception of the flesh and the Spirit,[19] Crautwald attempted to prove by the baptismal doctrine and practice of the early church.[20] Of interest, however, is the fact that there is nothing here or in the other writings of Crautwald or Schwenckfeld before the year 1528 which gives any indication that they criticized the practice of infant baptism; in fact, they acknowledged it.[21]

The Liegnitz Brotherhood had no need to concern itself with the problem of adult baptism at this time, since there were no Anabaptists in the territories of Frederick II. However, in other areas of Silesia, Moravian and South German Anabaptist leaders seemed to have been preaching and establishing communities since 1526.[22] According to the chronicler Nicolaus Henel von Hennenfeld, by 1526 almost half of the population of the village of Stolz near Frankenstein in the principality of Münsterberg held Anabaptist convictions, prompting Karl I to issue an order of exile against them.[23] By the middle of 1527 at the latest, there existed an Anabaptist community in Breslau, as a January 27, 1528 letter from Luther to Johann Hess indicates.[24] Hess had asked Luther if the Anabaptists ought to be denounced to the Breslau magistracy. Luther opposed such an action since the Anabaptists would eventually reveal themselves and then be expelled anyhow. According to the testimony of Hans Hut, their leaders were a certain Oswald and Hess.[25] Indeed, the Breslau magistracy repeatedly forbade their residency and placed entertaining or accommodating them under heavy penalty.[26] Outside of these areas, Anabaptist communities were present especially in the principality of Glogau, where G. Ascherham apparently taught.[27]

(a) The Liegnitz Brotherhood and the Anabaptists in the Empire

Schwenckfeld stressed that it was from the Strassburg theologians that the Liegnitz Brotherhood received the impetus to concern itself with the practice of infant baptism.[28] In Strassburg, a center of heretical movements in the late Middle Ages, numerous Anabaptists gathered in the autumn of 1526; especially notable in their presence at nearly the same time were Martin Cellarius and such significant leaders of early Anabaptism as Michael Sattler, Ludwig Hätzer, and Hans Denck.[29] Although the city council had occasionally exiled some of them (Hans Denck, for example, on Christmas Day 1526[30]), the Anabaptists continued to crowd into the city as is clear from a letter of Capito to Zwingli on April 8, 1527.[31] Because of this and also the disturbing accounts of occurrences in nearby Worms,[32] Bucer felt it necessary to move against the Anabaptists. This was even more necessary for him since Capito had begun to sympathize more strongly with the Anabaptists, as indicated by his foreword[33] to the July 1527 Strassburg imprint *On the Works of God* by Martin Cellarius, his houseguest. Capito's reservations against the practice of infant baptism and his sympathy with the Anabaptists first became clear, however, only in his commentary on Hosea printed in Strassburg[34] between late March and early April of 1528. Bucer, who had taken note of Capito's turnabout, attempted to win him back to his own position. Thus in March of 1527 he made cursory comments against the Anabaptists in his commentary on Matthew[35] and then issued a condemning treatise[36] against Jacob Kautz, the Worms preacher. In his *Exposition of John,* which appeared in March 1528, he stubbornly defended infant baptism.[37]

To strengthen the front against Anabaptism, Bucer sought help from Zwingli as well as from Schwenckfeld and Crautwald. Unfortunately only the letter of April 15, 1528 to Zwingli is extant.[38] Those to the Liegnitz Brotherhood must be reconstructed from answers[39] and from other correspondence.[40] Since Crautwald's letters are theologically the most significant, they will be treated here in particular. He declared that salvation cannot be mediated by an external symbol.[41] For this reason he does not want to hasten to the external water but to him who is able by his blood to cleanse us from our sins.[42] Crautwald can affirm the practice of infant baptism provided that one insists on its cognitive character and, as often as possible, makes the baptized person aware that, even if he is immersed three times a day, he is not baptized until he is reborn through the Holy Spirit.[43] Such a teaching on baptism may best be taught by means of a catechism, such as Capito's 1527 *Instruction for Children.*[44] Crautwald is convinced that infant baptism cannot be justified either from the Scriptures or by reason.[45] Unlike Bucer—following Zwingli—in his *Commentary on John,* Crautwald refused to base infant baptism on circumcision as Colossians 2:11 might imply.[46] For him, discipleship (Matthew 28:19) is the greater basis for receiving baptism.[47] In this way, Crautwald strengthened Capito's reservations against infant baptism. Although suprisingly well informed about the persecution the "poor Anabaptists"[48] were experiencing,[49] in spite of the fact that they had no direct contact with them,[50] Schwenckfeld and Crautwald requested, as was expected, that Bucer proceed mildly.[51] These people had in fact, they wrote, a truer understanding of baptism than any others who were writing on the subject at the time.[52] In contrast to the Lutherans, they confessed that water baptism had no causative but only a cognitive meaning. In addition, Schwenckfeld and Crautwald attempted to convince Bucer not to incite the authorities to use force against the Anabaptists[53] but rather to oppose all such efforts; the Anabaptists could only be won back by instruction.[54] In this connection Schwenckfeld noted with obvious pride that he had thus far successfully prevented Frederick II of Liegnitz from issuing a mandate against the Anabaptists.[55]

Bucer's hopes for support from the Liegnitz Brotherhood in his defense of infant baptism were not fulfilled. This was made less serious, however, because Capito was won back to upholding the doctrine of infant baptism by a letter of Zwingli's written on June 17, 1528[56].

(b) The Liegnitz Brotherhood and the Anabaptists in the Principality of Liegnitz

Because of the concern of the Strassburg theologians on the issue, Schwenckfeld and Crautwald were compelled to rethink the basis of their understanding of baptism and their relation to the Anabaptists. This was soon to have immediate significance, since a short time later—in the spring of 1528—some important Anabaptist leaders arrived in the territories of Frederick II and made Liegnitz the center of their activity. They came by way of Nicolsburg, a small town at the foot of the Pollauer mountains, which had been regarded as the biblical Emmaus by South German Anabaptists since 1526.[57] To Nicolsburg and adjacent areas streamed those Anabaptists driven from Austria, Bavaria, Swabia, and Switzerland and, under the protection of Leonhard von Lichtenstein and his nephew, gradually established through missionary efforts a large community which is said to have numbered 6,000 members according to Kessler[58] and 12,000 according to Seckendorf, who based his estimate on Inquisition records.[59] Both estimates are clearly inflated. The main founder of the community which was said to have consisted almost exclusively of German-speaking Moravians[60] was Balthasar Hubmaier; he had found asylum in the area in July of 1526. Already in 1527 a serious crisis arose, because of a controversy between him and the Anabaptist leader Hans Hut, the latter having come to the town for a few weeks. The controversy centered superficially on the question of whether a Christian is compelled out of obedience to the authorities to go to war. Hubmaier insisted that he was and Hut, influenced by apocalyptic thought, denied it. The high point of this discussion was reached in the so-called Nicolsburg Colloquy of May 1527.[61] Oswald Glaidt, born in Cham in the upper Palatinate, took part in this debate according to the oldest Hutterian chronicle.[62] He had been associated with the Reformation since 1520 and thereafter was a preacher in several communities until he was won to the Anabaptist cause by Hubmaier in 1526 in Nicolsburg. When no agreement could be reached at the colloquy and Leonhard von Lichtenstein came to Hubmaier's and his followers' side—not without political reasons—Glaidt followed Hut to Vienna in May 1527, although he had still been a follower of Hubmaier in January of that year according to his *Apologia.* From Vienna he went to Regensburg, returned to Nicolsburg, and finally, in April 1528, to Liegnitz. He was probably attracted there because he knew of the tolerance of Frederick II, to whom Hubmaier in 1527 had dedicated his *Second Book on the Free Will of Man.*[63]

Simprecht Froschauer,[64] the printer who had printed sixteen works by Hubmaier[65] and Glaidt's *Apologia* in Nicolsburg, arrived in Liegnitz at about the same time. The von Lichtensteins could no longer protect him from the persecution of Ferdinand I which began in March 1528. Froschauer probably hoped to find religious tolerance in this city with its new university and also a new field of work. Unlike Glaidt he soon gave up his Anabaptist beliefs and joined Schwenckfeld. On September 17, 1528 he wrote to Zwingli from Frankfurt on the Main, where he attended a book fair, saying that the Liegnitz Brotherhood had requested him to bring personal greetings, but that since he was under pressure of time, he had to write rather than travel to Switzerland.[66] In Liegnitz, Froschauer printed three of the Silesian nobleman's treatises, in addition to a treatise for the peasants.[67]

Presumably in the same year as Glaidt, the learned Anabaptist leader Andreas Fischer[68] came to Liegnitz from Slovakia.[69] Probably born in 1480 in Cremnitz, this former Catholic priest had been a preacher among the Slovakian Anabaptists until forced to flee to Silesia.[70]

Glaidt and Fischer then began active work in the principality of Liegnitz. There, according to Crautwald, they worked not so much in the cities as in the villages[71] and "attracted some fat sheep, that is, rich constables and peasants, who had rich debt-free farms and hoards of money."[72] As was foreseeable, fierce controversy erupted between them and the Schwenkfelders on the validity of the Mosaic law. Infant baptism was a secondary matter. From this it is evident how much less concerned the Anabaptists were with adult baptism than they were with ethics.

In this controversy over the binding character of the Mosaic law, emphasis fell primarily on the problem of whether or not Christians ought to follow the Sabbath laws of the Old Testament. Glaidt and Fischer, whose teachings are known only through the attacks of their opponents, held that the Sabbath laws were binding on Christians since Exodus 31:16-17 (the conclusion of proclamation of the law) was an eternal covenant[73] and was not lifted by either Jesus or the disciples.[74] Further, they endeavored to prove that the early church also held this doctrine. According to Glaidt, the early church celebrated the Sabbath; Sunday worship was inaugurated by the papacy at a later date[75] The learned Fischer brought greater precision to this general argument, thanks to his greater knowledge of church history and patristics, by quoting from the Church Fathers, in particular Tertullian.[76] This early Christian apologist certainly[77] valued the Sabbath highly.[78] Glaidt and Schwenckfeld discussed the issue in Liegnitz.[79] Since they could not reach agreement, they began a literary controversy. The discussion was opened by Glaidt's tract, which is no longer extant and which Schwenckfeld tells us was called *On the Sabbath,*[80] In it Glaidt declared that keeping the Sabbath was a commandment of God and necessary for a Christian's salvation.[81] On the order of Frederick II, and at the manifold wish of his friends, Crautwald took up the challenge. He published a treatise,[82] no longer extant, in which, as he later notes, he discussed themes "on the Law of Moses, on Judaism, on the New Testament, on the freedom of the heathen, on those granted grace by Christ the Lord, on the Sabbath, on the fulfillment of the commandments and the will of God through Jesus Christ, etc.''[83] This retort was sent to Glaidt by those who requested it.[84] Although Glaidt did not himself reply,[85] it was answered at his request by Fischer[86] in a lost treatise titled *Sepastes Decalogi,*[87] a more lengthy work.[88] According to Crautwald, the piece enumerated sixteen reasons[89] for teaching that obedience to the Sabbath laws was a necessary practice for salvation. These could all be reduced to two lines of argument, however. In the first place, Fischer attempted exegetically to demonstrate that in all of the Old and New Testaments the Decalogue —and therefore implicitly the Sabbath law—was seen as binding and externally valid.[90] This was also clear in the statements of the early church concerning the Sabbath.[91] Secondly, he tried to demonstrate by quotations from the Church Fathers that in the first century the early church had worshipped on the Sabbath,[92] that Sunday was first established as the day of rest by Pope Victor I and that the state laws concerning the observance of Sunday were first enacted by Constantine.[93] Crautwald pointed out to Fischer that he depended, for the most part, on secondary sources, particularly Eusebius' *Ecclesiastical History* for his knowledge of the the Church Fathers.[94] It is striking that Fischer did not seem to base his argument on eschatological, chiliastic grounds, although this argument certainly was not totally lacking in either his work or Glaidt's. Schwenckfeld claimed that Glaidt wished, with the Jews and the chiliasts, to adhere to external observance of the Sabbath until the spiritual Sabbath would come with the millenium.[95] At that time, all the godless would be destroyed and the ''whole world would, in his opinion, be holy, pious, and righteous.''[96]

To refute Fischer, Crautwald composed his *Comment and Explanation, or How Without Skill or Good Understanding Andreas Fischer has Written Regarding the Sabbath,* once again ''at the request of certain lords and good friends.''[97] In this tract he stated that a distinction must be made between the law of Moses—which encompassed the natural and ceremonial law—and the law of Christ.[98] The Mosaic law was ceremonial—to it belonged the command for keeping the Sabbath—and no longer binding for Christians because it was external, temporal, and had been replaced by the law of Christ.[99] Its significance was now only in its typological portrayal of the law of Christ.[100] The Old Testament command to keep the Sabbath directs men to the eschatological Sabbath which is to be celebrated in the hearts of believers.[101] The law of Christ, on the other hand, was an ''eternal law, which was there before that of Moses and therefore continues and remains [effective] in its functions.''[102] It is therefore characterized not as a multitude of commands but as containing only one command, that of love of God and neighbor

(Mark 12:30-31).[103] Furthermore, Crautwald attempted to demonstrate historically that the Christian community had worshipped on Sunday, and not Saturday, since the apostolic period.[104] To support this, he referred in particular to Ignatius' letter to the Magnesians.[105] Crautwald believed that in the ninth chapter of the long version of this letter which had been printed in a Latin translation in 1498 and which was generally believed to be the authentic version, he had found a clear proof for the early Christian practice of worshipping on Sunday. Clearly the interpolated passage was intended to support the Christian practice of worshipping on Sunday rather than on Saturday as the day of Christ's resurrection.

Because of the zealous missionary work of Glaidt and Fischer, Crautwald also concerned himself with baptism, as indicated by a tract[106] which he sent to the exiled Schwenckfeld in Strassburg informing him about the situation in his homeland.[107] The Silesian nobleman, however, asked that he treat the problem of infant baptism directly, since he was arguing about this with the Anabaptists in Strassburg. In July 1529 Schwenckfeld had visited Jacob Kautz several times in prison, attempting to convert him from his Anabaptist beliefs.[108] In October he was permitted, together with Capito, to take Kautz home, in all likelihood for the purpose of continuing his attempt to convert him,[109] though without success.[110] At about the same time, he came to know the Anabaptist leaders Hans Bünderlin, who had been a preacher with Leonhard von Lichtenstein in Nicolsburg during 1527 and 1528, and Pilgram Marpeck, who had worked in Strassburg and environs since 1530. Especially with Marpeck, the former councilman and judge in the mining business of Rattenberg on the Inn, he had, "on the quiet,"[111] intense discussions.[112] It is also certain that he met Melchior Hoffmann, a furrier from Schwäbisch Hall, who had come to Strassburg for the first time at the end of 1529 and who had attached himself to the Anabaptists.[113] To prepare himself theologically for these discussions Schwenckfeld turned to his friend Crautwald.

Because of his own spiritualism, Crautwald had sharply criticized the Lutheran doctrine of baptism and the practice of infant baptism in his writings. He was convinced that the practice of infant baptism in apostolic times could not be demonstrated. According to his view there was clear evidence in the New Testament that only adults were baptized. To support this he cited the sequence of the baptismal commandment in Matthew 28:19; baptism followed discipleship.[114] Neither could it be shown that infant baptism was practiced during the patristic period, but rather "the testimonies and traces of the old practice"[115] always pointed to adult baptism. One must note, however, that the citations Crautwald used from Hilary,[116] Eusebius,[117] and Tertullian[118] merely indicated that adult baptism was practised as a consequence of the missionary activity of the early church. Whether or not it was the exclusive baptismal practice of the early church, cannot be demonstrated from these documents.[119]

In spite of his sharp criticism of the practice of infant baptism, Crautwald nowhere rejected it completely, as is often falsely asserted in the Silesian territorial histories.[120] Unlike the Anabaptists, he was not primarily concerned with the question of baptismal practice as such, since, as a spiritualist, he was convinced that "the external water does not reach the laziness and impurity of our hearts. It cannot make a new heart nor wash away our sin."[121] Therefore he wished above all to describe the baptism through which the new man arises.[122] According to his conviction, this certainly was not water baptism since it could "bring forth nothing new, that is nothing heavenly or eternal."[123] True baptism was rather the "living and heavenly water,"[124] the Logos, Jesus Christ. This baptism of the Spirit is not only believed but is also experienced in the heart. Its fruit is not only the forgiveness of sins but the deification of man as Lactantius had correctly taught in his *Divine Institutions.*[125] Yet Crautwald did not wish "in any way to take away from or minimize"[126] water baptism through this emphasis on the spiritual baptism. Rather, he tried always to demonstrate its significance. In his mind this significance was found first in the act of confession by the one being prepared[127] for baptism.[128] Through baptism the act of God which happens "in secluded instruction"[129] should be publicly manifested. This was the practice of the early church as shown in the book of Acts.[130] According to that book the believing catechumens "commonly"[131] were "brought together under the heavens and out in the open, set before the church where they were to confess the grace of Christ and the forgiveness of sins and call on and praise the name of the Father, Son, and Holy Spirit. Upon this they were counted among the people of God, acknowledged by them, and designated warriors of Christ."[132] Secondly, according to Crautwald, baptism had a symbolic character. It was to bring before the eyes of the external man the significance of the baptism of the heart. This point is made especially in Crautwald's catechism *Little Institute Concerning the Signs or Sacred Symbols and Sacraments,*[133] probably written in 1525. The washing of the body in running water was to symbolize the purification from sin, already completed.[134] Here Crautwald countered both Lutherans and Anabaptists. He rejected in principle their doctrine of baptism. "The Anabaptists," he declared, "do not understand the order of baptism nor do they know what baptism before God is."[135]

Schwenckfeld put great value on Crautwald's concept of baptism. This is evident in that decades later he still made use of excerpts from Crautwald's writings on the topic,[136] by sending them to his friend Solomon Mileus[137] when the latter was not satisfied[138] with the teaching he had given him.[139]

To what extent Schwenckfeld was directly influenced by Crautwald's teaching still needs to be studied.[140]

The discussion thus far has pointed out that Crautwald's and Schwenckfeld's understanding of baptism, insofar as it can be ascertained, was characterized by spiritualism, with its dualism of flesh and spirit, inner and outer. The question arises, nevertheless, if it was not also influenced by other traditions. Although no direct proof is available, in all probability the question can be answered in the affirmative. As Urner has correctly noted[141] there was a similar baptismal doctrine among the Bohemian Brethren, especially Peter Chelcicky and Lucas of Prague. Chelcicky, the free farmer from South Bohemia, for example, on the basis of the sequence in Matthew 28:18-20, sharply criticized the practice of infant baptism without completely rejecting it.[142] He strongly insisted that only those be baptized who believed and were able to agree intellectually with the truth of Christ.[143] For such persons baptism was unconditionally necessary because of the command of Christ.[144] Consequently he opposed those who held that the baptism of the Spirit alone was sufficient.[145] Similar statements may be found in Lucas of Prague, the spiritual leader of the Bohemian Brethren in the first three decades of the sixteenth century. He too insisted, with a spiritual concept of baptism, that baptism was never a medium of salvation but only a witness to an already present grace.[146] Hence it could properly be given only to adults who knowingly acknowledged Christ and who received baptism as assurance of the forgiveness of sins as well as of their reception into the covenant of God. Besides adult baptism, however, he also wished to continue the baptism of children whose parents belonged to the Unity of the Brethren. For these children, assurance was given that they would be reared and instructed by believing teachers until they finally made their own confession upon reaching the age of accountability.

The suggestion that Crautwald and Schwenckfeld were influenced by the Bohemian Brethren in their doctrine of baptism is strengthened when one notes that they knew of at least one of the Bohemian confessions of faith. Schwenckfeld had indeed, as has been pointed out, taken one of these, possibly the *Defense of the Waldensian Brothers Against Two Letters by the Augustinian Doctor Given to the King,* with him to Luther at Wittenberg.[147] Possibly by 1515/16, and certainly by 1519, Luther had known the views of the Bohemian Brethren through copies of the *Apology of Sacred Scripture* and the *Refutation of a Certain Apology of Sacred Scripture,* presented to him by the Leipzig theology professor and canon of Zeitz, Jerome Dungersheim of Ochsenfurt.[148] It was likely Schwenckfeld who suggested to his follower Catharine Zell that she republish the Bohemian Brethren hymnal (1531).[149] This hymnal was compiled by Michael Weisse and published in 1531 in Jung-

Bunzlau on the Georg Styrsa press. Weisse, like Crautwald born in Neisse, has based his version on a Czech songbook and a German collection of hymns which the elders of the Bohemian Brethren had compiled for non-Brethren visitors in the German congregations of Landskron and Fulnek.[150] Weisse's copy contained 157 hymns, some of which he merely collected, some of which he rewrote, and some of which he himself wrote; his contribution can longer be established.

(c) The Expulsion of the Anabaptists from Liegnitz

As noted earlier, Frederick II tolerated Anabaptists in his territories although since the August 1, 1528 mandate of Ferdinand I they had long been persecuted in other regions of Silesia. In the year of the mandate, for example, the Anabaptist Gabriel Ascherham with perhaps as many as 2,000 of his followers—who sold "land and goods for some 7,000 guilders and had entrusted their money to Gabriel and his helpers"[151]—were expelled from the duchy of Glogau. They went to Rossitz in Moravia where they found protection and help in the territories of Bohunka von Pernstein.

The end of the tolerance for Glaidt and Fischer and their followers in Liegnitz was thus only a matter of time. When Frederick began to suppress radical Schwenkfeldianism and to draw closer to Wittenberg, he was no longer able to tolerate the Anabaptists. Moreover, Ferdinand had ordered him on March 15, 1530[152] to track down and imprison all Anabaptists in his territory since they accepted no political authority but together with the Turks wished to set the whole land in upheaval so as to gain all worldly power for themselves. Moreover, Crautwald, the acknowledged authority of the Liegnitz Brotherhood, had issued emphatic warnings in his writing against Glaidt and Fischer, since he believed them to be secretly attached to Judaism and agents of the Synagogue.[153] On the authority of the early Fathers, Tertullian and Hilary, he was convinced that the God of the Jews had nothing to do with the Christian God.[154] "I say, however," he wrote, "that Christians do not believe in the same God as the Jews since the Jews do not believe in the great mystery of the Holy Trinity; they exclude Christ from the Godhead; he [Christ] purchased us in his flesh and today reigns in the power of God. This can be demonstrated by Jewish teaching, by the division and antagonism between Jews and Christians, and by the ancient Christian writers."[155] The Hebraist Crautwald[156] exhibited a completely different stance in relation to Judaism than the humanist Reuchlin, whom he otherwise so greatly revered.

Finally, after 1530 or perhaps even in 1529, Frederick II expelled the Anabaptists. Fischer went to Moravia and perhaps immediately thereafter to Nicolsburg, where he probably continued propagating the necessity of the observance of the Sabbath.[157] In the fall of 1531 Leonhard von Lichtenstein and his preacher, whose name is unknown to us, wrote to Capito for advice on the matter of observing the Sabbath,[158] sending along Glaidt's fundamental treatise *On the Sabbath,* then probably circulating in Nicolsburg, so that Capito might make a proper judgment. Capito was so busy that he only responded to Lichtenstein's pastor,[159] while Schwenckfeld wrote to Leonhard himself on January 1, 1532.[160] Unlike Fischer, it was widely assumed that Glaidt planned to go to Prussia.[161] On the way there, however, he met Anabaptist leaders Johann Mittermeyer, Oswald von Grieskirchen and Johann Wunderl [Hans Bünderlin], who had to leave Prussia because of Duke Albrecht's August 16, 1532 edict against Anabaptism. Glaidt thus went to Bohemia with them. In recent research it is assumed that Fischer went directly from Liegnitz to Bohemia.

2. The Suppression of Radical Schwenkfeldianism in the Territories of Frederick II

During the time the Liegnitz Brotherhood was expressly separating itself from the Anabaptists, Frederick II endeavored to suppress the radical forces of Schwenkfeldianism and to draw cautiously closer to the Lutheran camp. He felt obliged to do this for two essential reasons. In the first place, after the Diet of Speyer and during preparations for that at Augsburg, he found himself increasingly in danger of being isolated and exposed to the Counter Reformation measures of Ferdinand. Secondly, the Lutheran opposition to the Schwenkfelders in his territories had been increasing. Indicative of this were the occurrences arising from Eckel's substitution in the vacant post at Goldberg at the beginning of March 1529. On *Laetare* Sunday as he rose to preach there for the first time, numerous children, who according to old Silesian custom drove out death on that Sunday,[1] shouted "Mr. Eckel carries the Spirit in a sack."[2] They likely did this at the instigation of the Lutheran citizens who had the support of the mayor, Georg Helmrich Sr.[3] According to chronicler Nicolaus Pol, this incident "so troubled this Schwenkfeldian spirit so much that he left there"[4] and returned to Liegnitz.[5] The opposition of the Lutherans to the Schwenkfelders could increase so rapidly because Schwenckfeld's absence robbed his followers of their most important support. The Silesian nobleman continued to write to friends in his homeland but his influence over the movement he had begun rapidly waned. Nor were any of his followers able to gain a position of trust at the Liegnitz court similar to that which he had occupied.

To consolidate the religious situation in his territories Frederick II asked his brother-in-law Albrecht of Prussia to allow his chief official of the territory of Lötzen, Frederick von Heydeck, to come to Liegnitz for a time.[6] Heydeck had made himself very useful in introducing the Reformation in Prussia and was quite likely personally acquainted with the duke of Liegnitz.[7] The duke conveyed the request on March 12, 1529 asking him to comply with it since the duke owed much to Frederick, who was his brother-in-law.[8] Heydeck complied with the request of the duke and soon left for Liegnitz,[9] but because of severe illness after his arrival he was unable to undertake his duties immediately. By October he was well enough to make a zealous attempt to reestablish the observance of the Supper which had been "completely set aside"[10] in Liegnitz to the detriment and disadvantage of the people. Having obvious difficulties, he rode to Breslau to seek the advice of Hess;[11] the visit accomplished little towards clearing up the problem. Nevertheless, Frederick II decided to write Hess again on February 7, 1530 "as a servant and dispenser of the divine word and will."[12] He requested Hess, along with Moibanus and Peter Fontinus, to investigate how the observance of the Supper could be reinstituted in keeping with the teaching of Holy Scriptures and the tradition of the church and the Church Fathers. Their decisions, which they were to send him in strictest confidence, would be placed before the Liegnitz pastors and the opinions of these men would in turn be reported to Breslau. The request from Heydeck on the following day to Hess was similar. He asked him to indicate "the correct observance of the sacrament, and the closer to that of the early church the better" so that "the horror of the unchristian mass might be done away with along with whatever appertained to it."[13] Probably remembering the earlier counsel of Melanchthon to Moibanus not to immerse himself in this matter,[14] Hess did not answer these two letters, which were sent together.

It is likely that a letter from Hess would no longer have had any effect at all, for Heydeck was coming ever more strongly under the influence of the Liegnitz Brotherhood, as already indicated by his letter to the Breslau reformer. Late in 1530, he became a follower of Schwenckfeld. Consequently his continued residence in Liegnitz had become meaningless, and possibly at the end of 1530, he returned to his former position in Johannburg, taking the Schwenkfeldian doctrine with him and placing some Schwenkfeldian-oriented pastors mainly in pastorates in territory which belonged to his feudal estate.[15] With him came the preacher Peter Zenker, who was not especially theologically learned; he had come to Breslau to seek out the Liegnitz Brotherhood and had stayed to become an associate.[16] Four years later, in the summer of 1534, Heydeck, who remained to his death in 1536 a defender of the Schwenkfelders, was also able to convince Sebastian Schubart to take a pastoral position in Prussia.[17] Heydeck's defense of the Schwenkfelders was possible in the first place because of his relationship to Georg von Polentz, bishop of Samland. Near the end of 1527 the bishop had married Anna (his second wife), one of the two sisters of Heydeck.[18] Moreover, Heydeck had a friendly relationship with the Duke of Prussia, whom he was able increasingly to interest in Schwenkfeldianism.[19] One result of this was that the Altstaedt pastor Johann Poliander, highly respected by the ducal family, lost the favor of Albrecht and contemplated submitting his resignation.[20]

A few months after Heydeck's return, Speratus became aware of the danger that Schwenkfeldianism posed for South Prussia, that is Masuria.[21] As a dedicated Lutheran theologian, he immediately began to oppose the movement. Initially only Poliander was on his side. Poliander opened the controversy at the end of 1530 or the beginning of 1531 with a sermon,[22] which is no longer extant and in which he seems to have sharply attacked the Schwenkfeldian position on the Supper and the inner word. Heydeck probably sent a copy or a transcript to Liegnitz where Eckel penned a reply, also no longer extant.[23] Eckel's reply and Crautwald's lectures on I Corinthians 11,[24] in which he fully outlined his teaching on the Supper, were sent to Poliander.[25]

A short time later, Speratus entered the controversy directly. From his episcopal seat at Marienwerder in a May 13, 1531 letter to Pastor Zenker in Johannburg and Melchior Kranich in Lyck,[26] he ordered that the two men compose a confession on the Scriptures, the Supper, baptism, and original sin and defend this confession at the synod which was to meet June 8 and 9, 1531. Since Zenker apparently feared direct confrontation, he was satisfied with presenting his confession in writing.[27] Details of the Prussian controversy go beyond the scope of this study and are therefore not treated here.[28] All that needs to be said is that the differences between the Schwenkfelders and Lutherans in Prussia were not ended but rather reached their height at the end of 1531.

In this confused situation Heydeck was able to convince his duke to call a religious colloquy which was "not to be a disputation, but only a discussion."[29] Lutherans and Schwenkfelders were to discuss together "in the friendliest manner, the Lord's Supper, the body and blood of Christ, and the external preaching of the Word of God."[30] A number of Lutheran pastors took part in this discussion, which was held in Rastenburg December 29-30, 1531 at the parish home of the castle, and concerning which Speratus wrote a most thorough report.[31] In addition to the duke, who was accompanied by his chancellor, Johann Apel, and his personal physician, Laurentius Wild, those present included the two bishops, Speratus and Georg von Polentz, and the three Königsberg pastors, Johann Briesmann of Kneiphof, Johann Poliander of Alstaedt and Michael Meurer of Löbenicht. While the Lutherans were represented by their leading lights, the Schwenkfelders had only Heydeck, Zenker, and Eckel. Heydeck had insisted that Eckel join the

Schwenkfelder delegation so that he, instead of the theologically insignificant Zenker,[32] could be the delegation's spokesman.

Through this action, however, the Rastenburg Colloquy and the controversy which arose out of it, became from the start the true concern of the Liegnitz Brotherhood. After Duke Albrecht opened the proceedings, counseling conciliation,[33] he turned the chairmanship over to Speratus, an action which provided the Lutheran party with a significant advantage. The bishop initially asked Heydeck to refrain from the discussion and leave it up to Eckel. Then he stated the two points of discussion: the Supper and the external word. The Supper should be treated first because it was the most problematic topic.

After the texts relating to the Last Supper in Mark 14:22-25 and I Corinthians 11:23-25 were read in Greek by Wild, in Latin by Georg von Polentz, and in German by Speratus, Eckel explained his position on the sacrament by means of the words of institution. Speratus had earlier expressly rejected an interpretation of the Supper based on John 6 because the words concerning Jesus as the giver of the bread of life had nothing to do with the Last Supper.[34] Eckel proposed that the words of institution were not to be understood literally but "allegorically."[35] He supported this thesis, in the first place, by referring to the picturesque use of the language of Scripture which was intended as a didactic aid for the outer man.[36] To make his point he referred to the apothegm Matthew 16:6, to the metaphorical passages in John 10:11; 14:6; 15:1-17; the symbolic action in Ezekiel 5:1ff, and the vision in Ezekiel 37:1-14.[37] Secondly, he endeavored to support his understanding through grammar. On the authority of the Latin grammar, Priscianus' *On the Institution of Grammar (Book XVII)*, he argued that neither the Greek word "this" (*touto*) nor the Latin word *hoc* could refer to bread.[38] Because it was neuter and not masculine as the word "bread" is, it must be understood as an intellectual demonstration, "that is, a sign for the intellect, pointing not to an external thing, but leading man . . . beyond himself, so that he sees another thing and understands through it another story."[39] The words of institution are thus to be interpreted: my body is nourishment, just as bread is for the body. Speratus responded apodictically that he would not agree although he too knew grammar. Of the hermeneutical premise that the Scripture must be its own interpreter, he was convinced. Nevertheless, he felt that many passages, among which he included those referring to the Last Supper, do not need this kind of interpretation, but must be understood literally.[40] In the afternoon, the bishop of Pomesania requested that Poliander continue the discussion since he had already had a written debate with Eckel. Though he had a bad cold, he complied with the request. He, too, contended that the synoptic descriptions of the Last Supper "could in no way be allowed this parabolic and allegoric sense and exposition."[41] Unlike Speratus, he treated Eckel's grammatical argument in detail, attempting to weaken and refute it. He came to the conclusion that only Luther's exegesis was grammatically correct. In addition, he pointed out to Eckel that his understanding of the Supper was inevitably related to that of the Swiss since "they, too, considered this bread and wine as nothing more. . .than poor and common bread and wine."[42]

On Saturday, December 30, the hopelessly deadlocked discussion was suspended, and the second point, that relating to the external word, was taken up. Again Speratus demanded that Eckel discuss his position on the external, preached word in detail and explain whether or not that word was identical to the Word of God.[43] Eckel, who certainly knew Schwenckfeld's and Crautwald's writings on this point,[44] first declared evasively that Christ himself was the Word of God according to the prologue of John. This Logos did not only become flesh, but following his ascension, spoke to the hearts of the apostles.[45] The duty of the apostles and all preachers was and is that they must bear witness to this Logos for "what is spoken to the heart, that it be taken in and believed, that belongs alone to God."[46] Indignant with this evasive answer, Speratus was even more precise in his questions to force concrete answers from Eckel. Eckel then acknowledged openly his belief in a distinction between the internal and external word. The proclaimed word could on occasion be called the Word of God but was, in fact, only an image of the true, actual Word of God. While the external word could merely have cognitive significance for the external man, the inner word brought salvation. "This eternal, life-giving and equally almighty word," as Jeremiah 31:33 indicates, God wrote in the hearts of man through the Holy Spirit, and by it he gave Christ's "holy flesh and blood to all believers as food."[47] Here plainly Schwenkfeldian spiritualism with its rejection of a mediated reality of salvation appeared again. Against this Speratus, with a purely Lutheran emphasis, contended that the external word was and remained God's word, even if placed in the mouth of Balaam's ass (Numbers 22:28-30).[48] Without the external preached word one would not be able "to hear God with a physical voice."[49] In the afternoon, Poliander continued the discussion, setting forth the argument begun by Speratus, emphasizing once again the Lutheran point of view that it was God's will that the inner word be given through the outer.[50] Therefore God wished that "the preached word be considered as a certain means in and through which he himself might be heard, work, teach, illumine, draw, and convert the heart."[51] Nor did Poliander fail to note that Eckel's position in this regard was the same as that of the radicals. Moreover, Eckel believed that the spoken, preached word was only a witness of the Word of God.[52] That evening, after a concluding word by Speratus, Duke Albrecht ended the discussion.

The Rastenburg Colloquy had no obvious result other than to make clear the positions of the opposing sides. It merely served to clarify that for the Schwenkfelders the concept of a medium by which salvation was given to man was not acceptable and that they therefore rejected word and sacrament as means of grace. In their understanding no external object could bring salvation, that is create a new man, which was always their ultimate concern. Curiously enough, both Schwenkfelders and Prussian Lutherans were convinced that each had been victorious. The Schwenkfelders spread the rumor that the colloquy had been decided in their favor, causing Lutherans outside of Prussia to inquire with concern of their Prussian theologians who had been present, asking if this, in fact, was true.[53] In contrast, the duke's chancellor, Johann Apel, wrote to Hess on January 6, 1532 saying that the capable but heresy-infected Eckel had discussed the question with the Prussian bishops and pastors "without glory."[54]

Since the duke of Prussia had expressed the wish that the Rastenburg Colloquy might be further continued in writing,[55] Eckel, Heydeck, and Zenker composed their *Confession on the Last Supper of Jesus Christ,*[56] a piece written largely by Eckel. In the first part they described their understanding of the Supper, once again using John 6 to interpret it.[57] In John 6 Christ points "men from the physical eating to the spiritual, which occurs when man comes to Christ, drawn by the Father, and partakes of him through faith, eats his holy flesh and drinks his precious blood unto eternal life."[58] In the second part of the *Confession* they again asserted that the sermon and the Holy Scriptures only point to the Word of God but are, in no way, identical with it.[59] God gives the word directly through the Holy Ghost (Jeremiah 31:33).[60] With this word the believer receives at the same time the body and blood of Christ. In their *Confession* the Schwenkfelders were more open than they had been at Rastenburg, as Besch observes.[61] Apparently they no longer felt pressed by the presence of the Lutherans and were encouraged by the result of the colloquy.

In reply to the *Confession* Poliander wrote his *Refutation of Eckel's Confession,*[62] which in essence agreed with his arguments at Rastenburg. Somehow a copy came into the hands of the Liegnitz Brotherhood. It was answered by Crautwald in his *Transactions of the Silesians with the Prussian Preachers*[63] which he probably began in the spring of 1533 and which was supported by Eckel,[64] who returned to Liegnitz no later than March 18, 1532.[65] In this work Crautwald described the proceedings of the Rastenburg Colloquy and its result. Herewith he attempted to refute the position of Poliander and the other Lutherans that the body and blood of Christ were received with the elements of bread and wine, and that there was a double eating, a spiritual and a physical, in the Lord's Supper. This was impossible since God always dealt directly with men.[66] Secondly, at the request of his friends, Crautwald again discussed the exegesis of the words of institution, basing his argument on the metonymic rhetoric of the Holy Scriptures[67] and, grammatically, on the neuter case of the Greek word *touto* (this).[68] It is clear from this that Crautwald was clearly the most learned of the Liegnitzers.

Although Crautwald in his treatise had called upon Poliander and the Königsberg theologians to continue the discussion in oral debate or in writing,[69] they were not willing and perhaps not prepared to do so. In any case, they sent Crautwald's work to Wittenberg requesting a judgment.[70] Melanchthon, who knew Poliander's treatise,[71] met their request and wrote a short Latin reply, no longer extant.[72] He likely sent it to the Liegnitzers by way of Königsberg. At the end of 1533 or the beginning of 1534 Crautwald wrote a German tract on the Supper.[73] In the first complete edition of Schwenckfeld's works it was entitled *A Simple and Short Comment on Philipp Melanchthon's Letter on the Article of the Sacrament.* In it Crautwald again attempted systematically and grammatically to demonstrate his interpretation of the words of institution. The final treatise which is known to us in connection with the Rastenburg Colloquy was Eckel's refutation *On Poliander's Treatise.*[74] It must have been written after Crautwald's since Eckel referred in one instance to Crautwald's work. Only on November 15, 1537 does Crautwald write to Hans Christmann (Althansen) in Strassburg: "The Prussian discussion is finally over, partially carried on in person and then in writing, book after book, until the other side stopped and remained with Luther."[75] Throughout this long, drawn-out controversy, the Prussian Lutherans and Silesian Schwenkfelders also corresponded with one another. The correspondence between Eckel and Speratus[76] and between Schubart and Speratus[77] has survived.

While not directly germaine to this study, the development of Schwenkfeldianism in Prussia should be outlined briefly. Following the Rastenburg Colloquy, Schwenkfelder-oriented pastors were not only allowed to remain in their positions but additional pastorates were filled with their colleagues, so that the movement was able to grow. This was primarily due to Heydeck. According to the chronicler Johann Freiberg, Heydeck gained the sympathy of the nobility and even of the duke "for his seductive teaching."[78] This fact is supported by a report of Speratus from 1542.[79] Albrecht's strong attachment to Schwenkfeldianism is first marked in his reserved relationship with Luther, especially during 1532 and 1533. Luther was probably informed of these occurrences by the Königsberg theologians and was thus made aware of the danger which this posed for the Reformation. Since he felt he was responsible to write a letter to the duke on the relationship between the words of institution and John 6,[80] he used this occasion to engage in the controversy between the Schwenkfelders and the Prussian Lutherans. To demonstrate once again his complete break with these radicals, he not only wrote to Albrecht,[81] but also published it.[82] To affirm the physical real presence of Christ under the elements of bread and wine, Luther, in this short letter, called not only on the words of institution[83] but also on the church which he claimed had, since apostolic times, universally agreed with him.[84] The person who denied this doctrine denied his faith in the church and the promise of God: ''Behold, I will be with you every day to the end of the world.''[85] Luther justified the authority of the church here, as in all his writings, with Matthew 28:20 and the third article of the Apostles' Creed.[86] Thus, Tschackert's judgment that this epistle was ''the most conservative since 1517 to come from Luther's pen''[87] must be modified. In conclusion, Luther demanded that the duke expel the ''rebellious spirits,''[88] but his earnest counsel was initially almost completely ignored. Albrecht's only action was an August 16, 1532 order to the two bishops and the district official of Pomesania to ban the Anabaptists Johann Mittermeyer, Oswald von Grieskirchen, and Johann Wunderl [Hans Bünderlin].[89] It was not until June 11, 1533[90] that he answered Luther, declaring indignantly that he could not control the access of radicals into his territories because of the extent of his lands.[91] If he expelled every suspicious person he would also run the risk that in his sparsely populated territory vast areas would not be cultivated.[92] Luther was to be at peace, however, since the Lutherans Johann Briesmann and Johann Poliander remained in their offices, ''bravely carrying out their duties with warning and teaching, trusting fully in God that the Devil can do no harm.''[93] In addition, he stated that he had forbidden the sacramentarians to preach either publicly or secretly,[94] but beyond that he wished to protect the religious freedom of all his subjects since it was not fitting that people be forced to believe.[95] In conclusion he did not refrain from noting that there were many in Saxony who, even if silent, did not agree with Luther.[96]

Secondly, Duke Albrecht's sympathy for the Schwenkfelders is evident in his relationship at that time with leading Lutheran theologians. When they heard that the Schwenkfelders were spreading the rumor that they had defeated the Lutherans at Rastenburg, Speratus, despite his own serious illness, composed a report on the course of the colloquy, partly out of the protocols and partly from his memory. Before August 26, 1532 the bishops of Pomesania and Samland, Speratus and von Polentz, with the support of the Königsberg pastors, Poliander, Johann Briesmann, and M. Meurer, requested of their duke in an accompanying letter[97] that they be allowed to make the report public under his name, since he himself had called the colloquy and had taken part in it. They also pointed out that many people in the realm were waiting for a report. It seems that the duke did not agree, however, for the manuscript remained unpublished; it was not until the eighteenth and nineteenth centuries that the account was partially edited because of historical interest.[98] However, the more Albrecht sympathized with the Schwenkfelders, the more the Lutherans attempted to suppress them. Untiringly, Poliander in particular visited his congregations, which were scattered from Marienwerder to Lyck.[99] Out of concern for the congregations, he held visitations during the winter of 1534 in Moravia, the area most endangered by the Schwenkfelders. Moreover, the Lutheran theologians directly opposed Schwenkfelder-oriented pastors, in particular Sebastian Schubart, who was then pastor in Johannburg and Johann Knothe, who was successively pastor in Sold, Mohrungen, and Marienburg. It is possible to see that sometime after 1535 the duke's sympathies for Schwenkfeldianism waned. One reason for this change was undoubtedly the forceful exhortations of his Lutheran theologians, but the moral chaos and frightful events in the Anabaptist kingdom at Münster probably contributed to his waning sympathy as well. Albrecht had received detailed news about Münster on March 30, 1535 in a letter from Duke Johann Frederick of Saxony[100] and on August 1, a few weeks after the collapse of the Münsterite Anabaptists, he wrote to Speratus with an order that only Lutheran doctrine be tolerated in Pomesania.[101] This decree marks the turning point not only for Anabaptism but also for Schwenkfeldianism. The Schwenkfelder movement in Prussia died down quickly thereafter, since Heydeck, the tireless protector and proclaimer of Schwenkfeldianism, died unexpectedly on August 3, 1536. Sebastian Schubart, seeing no further possibility of propagating his ideas, returned to Liegnitz either freely or under duress. With these events the influence of the Liegnitz Brotherhood in Prussia came to an end.

It has been shown that the attempt of Frederick II of Liegnitz to suppress radical Schwenkfeldianism in his territories with the help of Frederick von Heydeck had failed by the end of 1513. Since he could not allow the ecclesiastical and religious status quo to remain because of the mandate of Ferdinand I, he was compelled to move against radical Schwenkfeldianism himself. He proceeded first against Valerius Rosenhayn, who, according to Ehrhardt had "among the Liegnitz pastors especially supported the Anabaptist error most strongly."[102] It is certain that Matthäus Albers is referring to this pastor at the Peter and Paul Church in Liegnitz when he writes, orthodox believer, "You befoul your mouth when you eat his body."[103] Because Rosenhayn evidently provocatively denied the real presence of Christ in the Lord's Supper and possibly sympathized with the Anabaptists, he was expelled from the city in 1530.[104] According to the municipal clerk, A. Baudis, Rosenhayn became pastor at Lauban in Lausitz.[105] Two years later, Frederick removed his court preacher, Johann Sigismund Werner, from his influential position and placed him at the Church of St. Peter and St. Paul. He did not banish him, probably because Werner knew how clearly to cover up his radical points of view. Not incorrectly , the syndic, G. Thebesius of Liegnitz, wrote regarding him, "He was not better but more secretive. This one could say when one compared Werner with Eckel."[106]

Sometime between October 1532 and the end of February 1533 Eckel was also banished.[107] What were the reasons for this? According to Sebastian Schubart, Eckel had criticized the practice of infant baptism as early as 1526. At that time he was supposed to have met with the Liegnitz Brotherhood in his study to ask of them "how one was to act in light of the fact that Christ's command did not support infant baptism; was it still necessary that water be sprinkled or should a basin be set in the middle so that each man might wash his own hands?"[108] Since there was no "already baptized" person present who "could administer such a mystery,"[109] he stayed away from the practice of adult baptism. After his return from Prussia, where he may have met the Anabaptist leader Bünderlin,[110] it appears that both he and others attacked and even rejected infant baptism openly. At least Thebesius gives this as the reason for his removal from office.[111] The suggestion is in one sense supported by a treatise of Melanchthon.[112] The Goldberg mayor G. Helmrich Sr. had turned to Melanchthon via pastor Johann Kresling for information on how to deal with the critics of infant baptism. Melanchthon answered that he had indeed warned against embittering the Anabaptists by openly naming them, but he felt now that one must proceed against them if they spread their erroneous teachings among the people. The Anabaptists were full of revolutionary ideas, against which one had to protect the country. It is not impossible that Frederick II knew of this letter. Moreover, Eckel's banishment was likely related to the results of the Rastenburg Colloquy, as Bahlow suspected.[113] Both during the colloquy and in the following controversy the Prussian Lutherans several times stated their charge that Eckel's doctrine of the sacrament and the external word was not based on Scripture. This charge must have deeply disturbed the duke of Liegnitz, since he had repeatedly stated in his letters to Bishop Jacob von Salza and King Ferdinand I that his theologians taught according to the Scriptures and could demonstrate this to all. Eckel emigrated to Neurode in the county of Glatz. His pastorate was taken over by Johann Wunschelt, a former Breslau Franciscan who had studied in Wittenberg and had earned the master's degree there on November 19, 1521. According to the financial reports of the church, Ambrose Leimbach seems to have left Liegnitz in the same year as Eckel. Since the 1520s, Leimbach had been chaplain at St. Mary's and an associate of the Liegnitz Brotherhood.[114]

How eager Frederick II was to keep all sectarian movements out of his territories in the future is evident in his highly sensitive reaction to an October

13, 1533 letter of the Breslau magistracy,[115] in which the duke was warned about an Anabaptist by the name of Clemens who made occasional missionary incursions into the duke's territory from Glatz.[116] Three days later the duke assured the magistracy in his reply[117] that he had captured this Anabaptist who "some time ago came into our land and began to teach rebaptism, unknown to us. . . . Furthermore, the people from two of our villages moved away with him."[118] He claimed that he had imprisoned him for several weeks in Wohlau and then banished him from the realm. In a mandate he had also forbidden every public and secret sermon and doctrine concerning rebaptism. In conclusion he declared that "be that as it may, we as the governing authority will strive with great diligence and as far as it is possible to see to it that all who might ferment unrest and disturbances be prevented and punished."[119]

3. Moderate Schwenkfeldianism

Unlike radical Schwenkfeldianism, the moderate wing of the movement experienced its last blossoming during these years in the territories of Frederick II. This is particularly evident in the lives and works of Crautwald and Werner. Crautwald, who had become the chief leader of the Liegnitz Brotherhood after Schwenckfeld's departure,[1] lived in a "handsome home" within the compound of the former St. John monastery, which had been secularized in 1528.[2] This monastery had been given to the canons for their use, since their Cathedral Chapter, which was located outside the city walls, had been demolished for strategic reasons in 1530. Since Crautwald's benefice was small, his way of life was modest;[3] for example, he once complained bitterly that he was not in a position to purchase some expensive and good books.[4] However, it would be wrong to assume that he was poor, since he was able to have a housekeeper and, after 1530 also an assistant, Sebastian Eisenmann.[5] In his position as financial manager of the seminary he had direct contact with the common people and had become familiar with their problems.[6] Moreover, it is clear from his treatises on Glaidt and Fischer that he was still called upon at times to act as theological advisor to Frederick II. However, Crautwald spent most of his time in scholarly pursuits and writing. Many hours were devoted to his extensive correspondence, the greater part of which unfortunately is no longer extant. He corresponded not only with Schwenckfeld but also with numerous of his followers in Silesia and in the empire. Often the Silesian nobleman directed his correspondents—the greater number of whom were women—to Crautwald for solutions to their theological problems.

While Crautwald lived reclusively in his study, Werner preached with astonishing results to the huge crowds which thronged from the city and the country to the Church of St. Peter and St. Paul.[7] This great fourteenth-century Gothic church could not hold the crowds. In a 1537 letter to M. Engelmann, Crautwald noted with evident pride that while Werner preached "even the doorways were so full—spilling over even to the marketplace—that often three people fainted during the sermon."[8] In the same letter he could not refrain from ironically noting that in contrast to Werner's sermons, the services of the Lutheran pastor Johann Wunschelt, who had just been the delegate to the 1536 assembly in Schmalcald, were rarely attended by more than ten old men or women, and even those came only to receive alms.[9]

During this period, that is between 1532 and 1536, Crautwald composed several of his catechetical and theological works, primarily on the problem of the external word and baptism. Only those which have not already been discussed in relation to the Rastenburg Colloquy and the subsequent controversy are discussed here. Werner, on the other hand, wrote only one catechism.

In 1534 Crautwald produced a culturally and historically interesting didactic and methodological guide intended for pastors.[10] In it he outlined the content and methodology of catechetical instruction and emphasized the use of various media; his pedagogical premises are strikingly modern. He insisted that attention be given to the socio-cultural environment of the student[11] and to the establishment of groups of various achievements within the same class.[12] Although he does not mention this fact, it may be stated with certainty that he wrote the work to assist the new religious conditions which Frederick II was intending to inaugurate in Liegnitz. The same purpose was to be served by Werner in his catechism, which was written earlier[13] and which Crautwald had recommended[14] along with works by Augustine (*De catechizandis rudibis*), Erasmus (*Symbolum sive Catechismus*), and Schwenckfeld's catechetical writings.[15] In this catechism, in which Werner treated the creed,[16] baptism,[17] and the Lord's Supper,[18] a definite spiritualism is to be noted, but neither baptism nor the sacrament of the altar are essentially rejected. Werner declares, for example, that in baptism it is not the earthly water through which one participates with Christ, but it is rather by the new birth that the Ascended One directly gives the Spirit.[19] Water baptism has only cognitive significance, serving as a reminder to the believer that he is already baptized inwardly.[20] Werner's catechism was probably first circulated in manuscript and then first printed with a commending foreword by Schwenckfeld[21] in 1546.[22] The Liegnitz Brotherhood had not been able to carry through its intention to make official use of the catechism in Liegnitz right after its completion because of the strenuous opposition of Valentin Trotzendorf.[23] This rector of the Goldberg school insisted that catechetical instruction should be performed only by pastors within the ecclesiastical setting. He was convinced that the essential character of the schools would be lost if catechetical education were removed, and he threatened to resign if the Schwenkfelder suggestion was accepted.[24] Frederick II obviously acceded to Trotzendorf, as witnessed by the latter's continued work in Goldberg.

Besides these catechetical works, Crautwald also wrote two significant theological pieces during this time. Probably in 1535 his Latin *Letter of Certain Ministers of the Word Concerning the Church, the Keys, the Sacraments and Truths, the Choice of Ministers of the Spirit,*[25] appeared in Ulm with an afterword by Sebastian Franck.[2627] The work was originally written about a year earlier as an epistle to Bonifacius Wolfhart in Augsburg.[28] In this letter, in which he also discussed the South German and Wittenberg Concord formulae, Crautwald rejected again the use of word and sacrament as distributive means of grace. Christ alone can give salvation, not the Scriptures and sacraments which have only cognitive significance.[29] Having treated the problem of the external word once again, Crautwald paid particular attention to baptism in his second work published by Schwenckfeld in 1538 under the title, *On the New Birth and Source of the Christian Man.*[30] In this work, he rejected any salvific significance in this sacrament. ''If it is true as we heard,'' he declared, ''that man needs for salvation a new and clean heart, . . . it follows that baptism or external water has no place in the new birth.''[31] The new birth occurs, only by means of the true baptismal water, namely the Logos, Christ himself.[32] Crautwald may have felt compelled to write this work because of the renewed incursions of the Anabaptists into Silesia. In spite of a law against accepting them, numerous Moravian Anabaptists had sought refuge there since 1535,[33] because they were forced to leave the Hapsburg territories on account of the mandate of the diet at Znaim (February 18, 1535).[34] They appeared particularly in the principalities of Glogau, Schweidnitz, and Jauer[35] as well as in Frederick II's territories.[36] Ferdinand I had insisted steadfastly in numerous mandates that they be sought out and punished.[37] Consequently, since approximately 1538, there were no Anabaptist communities to be found in Silesia—with the exception of Glatz—although a few scattered Anabaptists remained; repeated edicts were issued against them.

Except in the city of Liegnitz moderate Schwenkfeldianism flourished in Lüben, also located in the principality of Liegnitz. Here Duchess Anna von Brieg, who had been ''a great papist,''[38] had been won early to Schwenckfeld's ideas after she was widowed.[39] She succeeded, as Klose noted,[40] in gathering a circle of like-minded persons and gradually made Lüben and the villages belonging to it a center of Schwenkfeldianism. She was supported in this endeavor by the pastor Georg Hirsenberger who worked at the parish church.[41] That Anna of Brieg was able to do this was due primarily to her genuine piety and charity. Schwenckfeld praised her as the "true mother of the poor."[42] In 1549 when she lay very ill as the result of an accident, he expressed the wish that Christ would make her well and give her long life for the sake of the "many poor and needy."[43] Again and again he sent her his writings[44] and shared with her pastoral and theological advice in his letters. For example, she asked him for advice in 1538, when she wavered concerning whether or not she should again partake of the sacrament.[45]

A large circle of Schwenkfelders also existed in Wohlau which had come under Frederick II's jurisdiction in 1525. Among the most significant leaders of the movement here were B. Egetius, in whose parsonage Schwenckfeld had once held intensive Bible study, Scholastica von Kitlitz from Mallmitz, who had suddenly become blind during a court feast,[46] and Pastor Gregor Tag (Emeranus), who was a close friend of Crautwald and who possessed some of his manuscripts after his death.[47] Tag's great admiration for Crautwald is shown in that he considered him to be one of the two precursors of the Messiah prophesied in Revelation 11:3.[48] Schwenckfeld's followers could be found in other areas as well; for example, Balthasar Magnus von Dittersbach, who corresponded with the exiled Silesian nobleman, and Johann Scaurus, who had since 1534 been pastor in Steinau on the Oder.

It would be erroneous to suggest, however, that Schwenkfelders existed only in Frederick II's territories at the time. They were also present in other areas. For instance, the municipal clerk Blasius Pförtner of Neumarkt wrote in 1532 that "many people are led astray in the villages of Schweidnitz, Striegau, and Liegnitz."[49] Because of the scarcity of sources little can be said concerning these areas. Thanks to a letter of Crautwald's dated March 4, 1534[50] a few things are known about the significant Schwenkfelder circle in Breslau. The senior member of this circle was Michael Wittiger, who as notary public of the bishop had once been a colleague of Crautwald and was won over to Schwenkfeldianism by Crautwald in the spring of 1526 after a long controversy.[51] To this circle as well belonged the former Franciscan, Johann Schnabel, organist at St. Elisabeth's, Johann Hoffmann, who earlier lived in Brieg, and a certain Schorrdach. Their significant influence is founded in the fact that they were backed by the Breslau syndic Vispert Schwab and the two aldermen Ambrose Jenkwitz and Johann Metzler, who more or less publicly sympathized with Schwenkfeldianism.!

IV The Decline of Schwenkfeldianism in the Territories of Frederick II and the Schwenkfelder Communities in the County of Glatz

After Frederick II succeeded in suppressing radical Schwenkfeldianism in his territories, a certain coexistence was established between moderate Schwenkfeldianism and Lutherans. As time went on, however, this situation proved to be neither theologically or ecclesiastically satisfactory but demanded clarification. The duke, on grounds of personal faith as well as because of political motives, decided to draw closer to Wittenberg, an action which the Schwenkfelders strenuously opposed. In fact, theological vitality was once again evident among the Schwenkfelders, particularly in their disputes on the Christological problem to which they applied the full dimensions of their spiritualism. When Frederick II finally united with the Lutherans in 1529 and issued mandates against Schwenkfeldianism, he was successful, as we will see, in destroying Schwenkfeldianism in his territories, but transplanted it indirectly to Glatz and the Bober-Katzbach mountains. A number of Schwenkfelders fled to these places, adopted various Anabaptist ideals, and founded many small communities.

1. Frederick II's Approaches to the Lutherans

To settle the sacramental question in his territories, the duke of Liegnitz prepared an order of service, the text of which is no longer extant. It is quite likely that he sent this to Wittenberg for examination via his Brieg court pastor Jerome Wittich in the spring of 1533.[1] Melanchthon was pleased that Frederick II had decided to move against those who despised the sacrament.[2] He did not object to the order which played down the Lutheran doctrine of the Lord's Supper,[3] and agreed with plans for its publication in Wittenberg.[4] Following Wittich's departure, letters arrived from Lutherans, probably from Silesia, urgently warning against this Liegnitz emissary.[5] With this, "our scholars" decided that the "Silesian manuscript" would not be published.[6] Although Melanchthon had at the time still not found anything to criticize in the piece,[7] he accepted the advice of his Wittenberg colleagues and sent the order back to Wittich with the comment that it would be best for Wittich as well if it were not printed.[8]

The duke placed the order of service before the ecclesiastical leadership of Liegnitz, Goldberg, and Wohlau[9] at the beginning of 1534. When the Breslau Cathedral Chapter heard that a change was envisioned in the Roman rite of the mass, it decided on April 24, 1534 to lodge a complaint through an envoy to Bishop Jacob von Salza in Neisse so that he would protest to the king.[10] When the envoy returned a week later, on May 1, he brought with him not only a letter of reply but also a copy of the Brandenburg-Nürnberg church order of 1533. Clearly, the bishop wished to demonstrate to the Breslau canons that he was in no way as uninformed about what was going on in the church as they usually seemed to believe. From the fact that at this time Jacob von Salza already had a copy of the church order, it may be suggested that Count Georg von Brandenburg-Ansbach already had introduced it in 1533 in Jägerndorf where many Franckish craftsmen and civil servants had settled.[11] When Frederick II called together all the pastors of his duchy of Brieg to a general convention[12] on September 15 to exhort them to give an unambiguous confession for the new faith, he probably placed before them this same church order as the protocols of the Breslau chapter indicate.[13] But, as was the case in Liegnitz, the new Eucharistic order was not yet instituted; this was to happen only a year later.

In 1535 a commission of pastors in the territories of Frederick II met together to discuss "the divided doctrine and practice of the precious sacraments."[14] Whether or to what extent the recent order for the observance of the sacrament lay behind the talks is not known. The result of these discussions was the well-known Liegnitz church order of 1535[15] in which baptism and the Lord's Supper were liturgically and doctrinally defined. To determine the amount of possible Schwenckfelder influence, the relevant parts of the order will be briefly examined. The baptismal liturgy is fully independent; it does not rely on Luther's *Baptismal Book*[16] of 1526, nor on the baptismal rituals of the South Germans (which differed from Luther's), nor on that of Zwingli's baptismal ritual of 1525. In the Liegnitz baptismal order we find only the so-called "Flood prayer."[17] But here it is modified essentially along Schwenkfeldian lines. This prayer sees the new birth and not baptism (as did the Lutheran and Brandenburg-Nürnberg order) as prefigured in the flood and the escape of Israel through the Red Sea. As in the Brandenburg-Nürnberg church order, the Liegnitz liturgy[18] of the Lord's Supper follows initially the liturgy of the Sunday service, but the Liegnitz order omits the creed. In the sequence of the Eucharistic service, however, there are marked differences. The observance of the sacrament itself is introduced by the singing of the Lord's Prayer. It is followed by a reading of I Corinthians 2 or John 6 (here Schwenkfeldian influence is especially evident), the Credo, the call for repentance, the Confiteor, the prefatory, the Sanctus, the words of institution, and the dispensation of the sacrament. Following the communion, the hymn, "God be praised and blessed" was sung, and the collect read, followed by a congregational hymn such as Luther's first concluding hymn for Protestant services, "God will be merciful to us."

While Schwenkfeldian influence is only slightly noticeable in the baptismal and Eucharistic liturgy, the stamp of the Liegnitz Brotherhood is particularly clear in the respective doctrinal introductions. This is evident from the demand that God-fearing parents should choose pious Godparents who are later to concern themselves conscientiously with the child,[19] in the request that a catechumate should be established in every parish to which parents and Godparents might send their children[20] at the earliest possible age. Schwenkfeldian influence is especially evident in the doctrinal part of the teaching which is placed at the beginning of the communion service. There is not yet a purely significatory understanding of the elements, but the new birth is considered necessary for the efficacious reception of the sacrament. Such reception does not grant forgiveness of sins but eternal life.[21] This church order was accepted by all the pastors of the counties of Liegnitz and Brieg on November 12, 1535.[22] It was a compromise between Schwenkfeldian and Lutheran positions, although the latter took precedence because the physical real presence of Christ was taught.

In light of the fact that the Schwenkfeldian doctrine of the Lord's Supper was only partially adopted in the Liegnitz church order, it is interesting that Frederick II did not join the struggle for union among the South Germans and the Lutherans nor the later Wittenberg Concord, the position of which on sacramental unity would have suggested such a move. As will soon be evident, he did not do so because of the passionate Schwenkfeldian opposition.

Neither Bucer nor Capito had kept the Liegnitz Brotherhood informed about the movement toward a concord, something Bucer had been tirelessly working on since August 1530. The correspondence between Crautwald and the Strassburg theologians soon abated after Schwenckfeld's departure from Liegnitz. The primary reason for this was that Schwenckfeld, the Silesian refugee, was soon considered persona non grata by the Strassburgers. Initially Capito, Matthäus Zell, and Bucer as well, were friendly to Schwenckfeld, but theological disagreements arose within a few months. Finally, in August 1533 Schwenckfeld saw that it was necessary for him to leave Strassburg; he went to Augsburg, arriving there shortly before October 3.[23] Even the Swiss, who could have kept the Silesian informed about the discussions regarding a concord, could not have been the informants. Crautwald and Schwenckfeld had openly separated themselves from the Zwinglian position on the Supper after 1528 and a little later the sometimes close contact between Zurich, Basel, and Liegnitz was broken. It can be suggested that the Liegnitz Brotherhood was kept in touch regarding the attempts for unification between the South Germans and Wittenberg through Schwenckfeld, although no letter of Schwenckfeld's to Crautwald from this period is extant. This assumption is strengthened by a letter which Crautwald wrote in 1534 to Bonifacius

Wolfhart, pastor in Augsburg, where Schwenckfeld remained as a guest from October 1533 to June 1534. "I have heard that some are striving with great zeal to please others and are attempting to agree with them in dogmatic questions."[24]

Crautwald decisively opposed the attempts of the South Germans to join with Wittenberg, since this would spread the errors and increase Godlessness.[25] Clearly he was afraid that the South Germans would, under the influence of Wittenberg, give up their position on the non-mediated reception of salvation. Possibly he was also concerned about the future situation of the Schwenkfelders. If the concord talks were successful, the Schwenkfelders would inevitably be more and more isolated and would only find an open ear among spiritualists such as Sebastian Franck. This concern, however, Crautwald never made public.

Crautwald not only criticized the attempts to bring about a concord; he also attempted to point out his version of the only true way to real union.[26] He started with the initial assumption that the concord did not need to be between the reformed churches but between men and Christ.[27] This ought to be striven for by all and the learned, the pastors, and the common people must hold to it.[28] The means to achieve such a union included prayer[29] and the study of the Holy Scriptures, which the Spirit himself must interpret.[30] When the concord between the Exalted One and the believer is concluded, Christ will do away with all error, will allow the truth to be seen clearly everywhere, and will bless his sacraments with heavenly gifts.[31] Although Crautwald's criticism of the attempts at concord, as well as his own proposal for a concord, was in line with his spiritualism, one cannot avoid the impression that one is here dealing with an ivory tower scholar who, in spite of his vast correspondence, had no real insights—and perhaps did not wish to have any—into the political intrigues of German Protestantism of the time.

As everybody knows, on May 23, 1536 after long and tiresome negotiations between Wittenberg and the South Germans, a *Formula of Concord between Luther and Bucer* was reached by Bucer moving forward and Luther and Bugenhagen withdrawing on certain points.[32] The formula as outlined (sacramental unity between the bread and the body of Christ as well as the reception of the unworthy) could be variously interpreted. While Luther saw from the beginning that the formula would not solve all the differences, he allowed it to be accepted since it otherwise protected the objectivity of the real presence.[33] Barely two months later Schwenckfeld, in three short tracts, outlined his position on the concord.[34] Crautwald wrote only one, albeit an extensive work, on the topic.[35] According to him it was no concord but only "discordant seeds,"[36] self-contradictory and open to various interpretations.[37] After this declaration, he dealt critically with its treatment of the real presence, the dispensation and reception, and of the communion of the unworthy. He rejected decisively the notion that "the body and blood of Christ are truly and essentially present in the bread and wine and that they might be offered and received in them."[38] Not only the Scriptures but the axiom *similia similibus* was opposed to this belief. The sacrament of the altar was, on the contrary, a memorial[39] and the elements of the Supper symbols of heavenly food: "The flesh therefore has bread for a sign by which the soul is admonished."[40] Secondly, he was opposed to the concord because it postulated a third group, the unworthy, between believers and the ungodly. According to I Corinthians 11 there were only two classes of people—the worthy and the unworthy, who were the ungodly.[41] Schwenckfeld held on to this strict division to the end; in his treatise, *Argument of a Layman,* he wrote referring to Matthew 12:33, Mark 16:16, and Luke 11:23, saying, "Christ separates all people into two camps—the good and the bad, the faithful and the unfaithful....Of the indifferent and the halfway the Scriptures know nothing."[42]

Crautwald's decisive rejection of the Wittenberg Concord must assuredly have played a role in the decision not to implement it in the territories of Frederick II. This decision, however, robbed Frederick of the possibility of immediately joining the Schmalcald League, as the Protestants in South Germany did.

2. The Christological Controversies of the Schwenkfelders with the South Germans and the Lutherans

No sooner had the controversies over the Wittenberg Concord been essentially concluded, than, starting in 1537/38 new controversies on Christology arose between Schwenckfeld and the Swiss, South Germans, and later Wittenberg.[1] The discussion was carried on almost totally by Schwenckfeld although his Silesian friends, namely Crautwald, Werner, and Eckel did support him. Their part will be taken into consideration here. Schwenckfeld's Christological battles will only be treated insofar as they affected his followers in Silesia.

To understand properly the later form of Schwenkfeldian Christology and the antagonisms concerning it, it is necessary here to sketch briefly its early form. Two phases of the early development of the Christological doctrine may be noted; the first extends to 1528, the second from 1528 to the beginning of 1537.

In the writings of Schwenckfeld and Crautwald, the first Christological comments are found at the time when they were developing their views of the sacraments. As we have seen, they rejected oral communion and that of the unworthy and advocated a spiritual eating of the body of Christ, through which the believer participated in and was deified by the essence of Christ (II Peter 1:4).[2] They believed salvation depended on the humanity of Christ alone. This humanity he had taken with him to heaven.[3] It was therefore necessary that Schwenckfeld and Crautwald concerned themselves, above all, with the human nature of the ascended Christ.

In agreement with church tradition they taught that the preexistent Logos had come "in this earthly essence, that is in the flesh."[4] Such a doctrine conflicted directly with the spiritualist basis of their theology, according to which everything earthly, material, and creaturely, although not identical with sin,[5] fell within the region of sinfulness and could never be a part of heavenly, spiritual, and divine things. How could one envision then that the Logos, which belonged to the sphere of the spiritual, became flesh? To overcome this difficulty when they touched upon the incarnation, they made an exception to the rule that between Creator and creature an irreconcilable differentiation existed. Once and only once, in Christ's incarnation, did an "essential union of God and creature take place."[6] Although in the state of humiliation the humanity of Christ was "still weak, mortal, corporeal,"[7] in the state of glorification it was deified.[8] Thus Crautwald wrote in his 1527 lecture on II Corinthians 13:4, "Today Christ is and reigns in the glory of the Father. He was infirm for us, but that infirmity has ceased. There is nothing today in him but the power and strength of God. Divine power eliminated in the humanity of Christ all that was weak for our sakes."[9] By this idea that the humanity of the Exalted One had undergone deification, Crautwald and Schwenckfeld intended to make clear rationally how men might "become partakers of Christ's essence"[10] by spiritually eating the body of Christ, and by drinking "of his rose-red deified blood" "receive the divine power in their soul"[11] Yet, until the end of 1528, neither of them state clearly whether the divinization of Christ's humanity had begun while he was on earth and then progressively developed or whether it came immediately with his entering a state of glorification. Very likely they held to the latter notion. In 1527 Schwenckfeld had stressed in his large treatise on the Lord's Supper that the flesh of Christ first became "a cause of eternal holiness"[12] after the crucifixion, referring to John 12:24 and Hebrews 5:9.[13] In any case, Maier is correct in his somewhat vague observation that already before 1528 there are indications that Schwenckfeld was pointing to "the necessity of knowing the divine glory of Christ's exalted flesh."[14]

Since 1528, not since 1533 as Hirsch falsely stated,[15] Schwenckfeld and

Crautwald had begun to develop their doctrine that the deification of the humanity of Christ began in his state of humiliation on earth. Their teaching in this regard was necessitated by the controversy concerning the Lord's Supper[16] It is significant to note that the most important impulse came from Crautwald and not from Schwenckfeld, a fact earlier overlooked.[17] Both men now developed the belief that the flesh of Christ which had partially dwelt in the Logos, as in a "shell and box,"[18] was not identical with that of other men.[19] It belonged not to the realm of creation but to the redemption, since it had a "different origin."[20][21] On this matter they referred particularly to I Corinthians 15:45-49.[22] Nevertheless, they remained firm in their belief that Christ was a true man in his "state of humiliation" on earth.[23] The flesh of Christ, which they still designated as creaturely,[24] was further and further purified by the Logos. The process began with his birth and reached its culmination in his passion and crucifixion.[25] "The man in Christ," Crautwald wrote on September 30 to Jacob Held von Tieffenau, "became better and better, came nearer to God, was led ever higher through the indwelling of the word of God. That word of God in Christ drew the man to itself, yet not *vice versa.* The perfect remained perfect and helped the man in Christ."[26] This progressive deification was already evident in the earthly life of Jesus as revealed by the transfiguration (Matthew 17:2).[27] Following the completion of the divinization with the resurrection and ascension[28] the ascended Christ still had his human nature but its creatureliness was completely eradicated;[29] because of its complete penetration by the Logos (not because of a communication of idioms, as the Lutherans taught), it now possessed the same glory as the divine nature. While the divine nature of Christ enjoys ubiquity, his human nature, which "now at the right hand of God in the divine being had received all strength, glory, government and honor through the might of the right hand of God," because of its humanity "did not extend as far as the divine essence itself."[30] The humanity of Christ was thus localized in heaven at the right hand of the Father, but Crautwald made no further reference concerning topography.[31] Because of the successive deificiation of the flesh of Christ, man might eat of it spiritually and by this gain substantial participation in the divine nature.[32] As an illustration Crautwald pointed to physical food which must be prepared and cooked before it can be eaten.[33]

Although soteriology was without doubt the starting point in Crautwald's and Schwenckfeld's development of the doctrine of deification, it was their understanding of the Spirit that was the principal reason for their rejection of the assumption that the humanity of Jesus retained something of the creaturely even in the state of exaltation. In developing this thought they were influenced especially by the Church Fathers. They used the Fathers particularly to legitimize their Christological premises from tradition. The first citations—from Tertullian's anti-docetian *On the Flesh of Christ* and Hilary's main work, *On the Trinity* are found in Crautwald's *Judicum,*[34] written near the end of 1528. In this tract he stated that these Fathers had taught that the human nature of Christ had a quality different from that of other people.[35] Crautwald was right in pointing to Hilary of Poitiers, who served more and more as the chief witness for his Christology. Hilary had indeed held the opinion that Christ had a "caeleste corpus" (celestial flesh).[36] Later, Schwenckfeld too made greater use of the Fathers to demonstrate the correctness of his Christology,[37] citing not only those which Crautwald had earlier referred to, but —particularly after his exile from Silesia—pointing to others as well.[38]

Until the middle of the 1530s, the doctrine of deification and the rejection of the word "creature" to describe the humanity of Christ in its exalted state was probably not broadly criticized, because Schwenckfeld and Crautwald referred to it only sporadically in their writings and made more extensive mention of it only in the tracts to their friends. It is certainly not a mistake even to designate this early phase of Christological development as secret.[39] Thus the first public criticism came at the Tübingen Colloquy on May 28, 1535 at which, on the order of Duke Ulrich of Württemberg, Schwenckfeld, Bucer, Ambrose Blaurer and Martin Frecht debated. There Frecht accused Schwenckfeld of denying that Christ was a creature in the state of his exaltation and of teaching the doctrine of its deification.[40] Schwenckfeld did not deny the charge[41] but expressly added that he believed in the humanity of the Exalted One.[42] To demonstrate the correctness of his teaching, Schwenckfeld observed, not without some justification,[43] that not only Luther but Brenz and Erhard Schnepf as well had held similar views.[44] No other attack followed this first one immediately, but the signal had been given.

Further controversy between the South Germans, the Swiss, and later the Lutherans with Schwenckfeld continued only after he had further developed his Christology. Crautwald played an essential role in this development particularly in formulating the two central aspects of the doctrine on which the later controversy was concentrated: the theopassionate concept that Christ, in the state of humiliation, had also suffered in his divine nature, and the Eutychian principle that the humanity of Christ in the state of humiliation was not a creature at all.

Crautwald deeply regretted that Christology was initially not discussed among the Schwenkfelders. Around 1537 the Strassburg Schwenkfelder Margarete Engelmann accepted Zwingli's doctrine that the divine nature of Christ was not capable of suffering.[45] Informed of this by Schwenckfeld, Crautwald initially agreed with her, but he did so only to open the dialogue;

for he hardly had done this but he firmly defended the passion of the divinity of Christ. He insisted that Christ in his state of humiliation had suffered not only in his humanity but also in his divinity. "Jesus Christ, true God and man," he insisted, "suffered, was completely enveloped into suffering; he suffered completely, not separated in his natures, but as the whole person of Christ."[46] He was convinced, in fact, that the divine nature had suffered more than the human nature. He referred to Scripture, especially to the passion story, and he cited Hebrews 5:7.[47] He also referred to Ambrosian literature[48] and to Jerome,[49] where he found the idea that Christ suffered according to both natures. Crautwald placed so much emphasis on this doctrine of the passion of the divinity of Christ, because for him it was the criterion whether the unity of the two natures be accepted on the basis of the penetration of the humanity of Christ by the Logos, or by reason of the "communication of idioms,"[50] which Schwenckfeld, however, considered Nestorian. Since Crautwald foresaw that this doctrine would be attacked as Patripassianism, he emphasized that only the Son of God suffered. God himself could not and did not suffer.

While this Christological understanding was particularly offensive to the Swiss and to the South Germans and Frecht,[51] Bullinger,[52] Joachim Vadian,[53] and Sebastian Coccius[54] wrote against it, the assertion that Christ's humanity in the state of humiliation was not creaturely called the Lutherans into action as well. This denial of Christ as "creature" was merely the ultimate consequence of Schwenckfeld's and Crautwald's spiritualism and it was first outlined by Schwenckfeld in August, 1538.[55] Crautwald did not immediately accept the premise, but in a September 30, 1539 letter to Katharine Streicher,[56] he cited Hilary's *On the Trinity,* pointing out that the humanity of Christ in the state of humiliation could be referred to by the term "new creature."[57] Two days later, however, in a long postscript to this letter,[58] he abandoned the term "creature" because it could lead to misunderstanding and in the future only the majestic Christological titles of the Old and New Testament were to be used. "It would be good if one called Christ by the names which were given him by God, his Father, the angels, the apostles, and the evangelists, that is, the Son of God, Jesus Christ; if one wished to address him according to the prophets it might be done with good reason. He was Emmanuel etc., according to Isaiah, our righteousness, and according to Jeremiah, our righteous God."[59] Yet Crautwald, like Schwenckfeld,[60] wished to hold firm to the true humanity of Christ. He separated himself decisively from the doctrine that Christ brought his humanity with him from heaven. This Valentinian Christology was represented especially by Melchior Hoffmann and the Hoffmannites. In contrast to them—"who had fallen into the ancient errors regarding the flesh of Christ"[61]—Crautwald emphasized that the Logos did not have a preexistent humanity, but that God "the Holy Ghost had created in and of the hallowed flesh of Mary as it was united with him and formed his human essence to be housed in the Tabernacle of Mary as new, true flesh."[62] With this declaration Crautwald and Schwenckfeld believed they had clearly explained why the human nature of Christ could not be described as creaturely and yet why Christ was a true man. Nevertheless many, including Luther, soon branded this teaching, not incorrectly, as Eutychianism. It is true that Schwenkfeldian Christology is not identical in all its points with Eutychianism, but the basic intention of the two is the same.

While Crautwald's role in the development of Schwenckfeld's Christology is not to be underestimated, the exact influence can no longer be ascertained since a significant amount of the correspondence is no longer extant. Other members of the Liegnitz Brotherhood might also have played a part. Similar Christological descriptions can be noted in the writings of Werner and Eckel, although their interest is concentrated more on soteriology than on Christology.[63]

3. *The Suppression of Schwenkfeldianism in the Territories of Frederick II*

When Frederick II heard that a convention in Schmalcald had been called for February 7, 1537, he expressed the desire to be invited.[1] Quite probably he hoped thereby to demonstrate his complete turn to the Lutheran confession, which can be dated in 1536. Political motives may also have prompted his seeking contact with the Schmalcaldic League. This assumption is suggested by the geographic location of his territories. They lay at the periphery of the empire, and were also under the direct jurisdiction of Ferdinand I and therefore vulnerable. Because of his age[2] and probably from political caution, Frederick II did not take part personally in the Schmalcaldic convention; he was represented by his senechal Phillip von Poppschütz[3] and his theologians Johann Wunschelt and Bernhard Egetius.[4] Precisely what role Frederick's emissaries played in the Schmalcaldic discussions is not known. The reason why they did not sign Melanchthon's *Treatise on the Power and Primacy of the Pope* along with the other thirty-three theologians is probably not to be found in their premature departure, as Volz supposed,[5] but in the fact that the earlier Augsburg Confession had not yet been accepted in their territories.[6] On the other hand, we know that Philipp von Poppschütz, through whom Frederick II gave assurance that he was fully in agreement with the Schmalcaldians in his belief,[7] discussed the right of the princes to resist with Duke Johann Frederick.[8] The Liegnitz senechal questioned whether it was correct to defend the faith with force of arms against an emperor or king, citing Luther in his argument.[9] On March 31, on the conclusion of the convention, the Saxon prince wrote to Frederick II[10] admitting that he too was initially in doubt because of Luther's objection but that now, after listening to the arguments of the jurists with whom the Wittenberg theologians had in the meantime come to agreement, he was convinced that the princes had the right to resist. So that Frederick could satisfy himself on this, the Elector sent his report to him[11] and finally asked Frederick, the duke of Liegnitz, to join the Schmalcaldic League. Frederick did not do so, however, since, as he explained in July through his senechal once again in Weimar, he was not an elector of the empire; moreover, his territories were surrounded by Catholic nobles and peoples.[12] Nevertheless, he gave firm assurances that he would hold fast to the reforms he had initiated in his territories.[13] Although Frederick II did not join the Schmalcaldic League, he was considered part of it by the other members. This was evident at the Frankfurt debates of April, 1539 where they included him expressly in the defensive alliance.[14] The political advantage of Frederick's decision was made clear ten years later after the defeat of the alliance in the Schmalcaldic War of 1546/47. Unlike many members of the League, Frederick was not punished especially since he had promised troops—albeit under pressure—to assist Ferdinand I in the wars with the protestants.[15]

Following his conclusive affiliation with the Lutheran cause, Frederick II began fully to suppress Schwenkfeldianism in his lands, urged on as well by the Silesian Lutherans Trotzendorf, Wittich, and Moibanus. In 1537 for example, Moibanus wrote an exposition of Mark 16:14-20 in a tract *On the Glorious Command of Our Lord and Savior Jesus Christ*[16] and dedicated it to Frederick II. In this tract, in which he admonished the duke to move against the followers of Crautwald[17] for the sake of his own subjects, he attacked the idea of salvific reality brought about directly by the Spirit and emphasized the need for the external word and the sacrament as a means of dispensing grace. "Take the Gospel and baptism away," he wrote, "and we become the poorest and most wretched of men, suffering the ostracism and the wrath of God."[18] To this baptismal tract Luther wrote a foreword[19] in which he defended the necessity of a medium of salvation, underlining the well-known words: "Who does not attend to the Word of God does not attend to God, be it the true or false God since God does not deal with man except through his word and aside from his word he is not known to us as God and is no God. Therefore those who do not attend to the Gospel or to the pope's teaching have no God, whether true or false, but are fat pigs and lazy dogs who care nothing for future life."[20]

Besides the Silesian Lutherans, Frederick II was probably urged by Ferdinand I, who, on the occasion of his second journey to Silesia, had spent time in Liegnitz, to fight the Schwenkfeldian heresy. In any case, the king commanded the Breslau council on June 16, 1538 to take heed "that the frightful error of the Anabaptists and radicals be avoided."[21] The duke then moved against Werner, the last influential Schwenkfeldian pastor in his territories. Most of the other Schwenkfeldian pastors in Wohlau—Egetius, Scaurus, Creusig, and Tag—once faithful supporters of Schwenckfeld, were gradually won over to Lutheranism by 1536/37, mainly because of a now lost letter of Schwenckfeld's to his friend from youth, Balthazar Magnus von Axleben,[22] in which he rejected every possible function the word and sacrament might have for salvation.[23] Because of this letter, the pastors believed that Schwenckfeld and the Liegnitz Brotherhood were completely laying aside worship and preaching, an action which Schwenckfeld and Crautwald vehemently denied.[24] Nevertheless, Schwenkfeldianism did not die completely in Wohlau, but continued to have followers among both the common people and the nobility.[25]

The removal from office of Werner, the beloved pastor of the Church of St. Peter and St. Paul, dragged on for some time. The decisive moment came, according to tradition,[26] when he was charged with heresy by a colleague, Johann Wunschelt. He answered the charge, most probably in 1539, with his *Confession and Apology of the Chief Articles in the Service of the Gospel,*[27] perhaps at the instigation of Frederick II. This work, however, was received negatively not only by Jerome Wittich,[28] but also by Johann Brenz, and "learned men in the empire" to whom it had been sent for examination.[29] Nevertheless, Frederick II hesitated at first to remove his former court preacher since he felt himself particularly obliged to him.[30] In any case, in 1539 he paid Werner's way to Wittenberg "to Phillip Melanchthon, and not to Martin, since the latter was somewhat hot-headed" to "come to an understanding with learned and peaceable men."[31] Since Melancthon did not consider Werner's ideas in agreement with the Holy Scripture, and could not cause him to give in,[32] Werner was finally removed in the summer of 1539.

As a result of these actions not only did part of the populace stay away from the worship services out of protest but some individual Lutherans were prompted to question their convictions. In any case, Georg Bock von Polach, Frederick II's chancellor, once a declared opponent of Schwenckfeld's, now turned to him concerning the Lord's Supper.[33] As a result there arose a correspondence between the two men[34] concerning the external word and the sacrament, Christology, and ecclesiology.

Frederick II wanted to place a Lutheran in the vacant pastorate of Sts. Peter and Paul who would be able to fashion ecclesiastical polity in his territories after the character of the *Augsburg Confession* and *Apology.*[35] Consequently, on October 25, 1539 he requested the duke of Saxony to give him Georg Major for three years.[36] In a letter Johann Frederick had asked Luther for his opinion.[37] When Luther felt that Major could not be spared,[38] the duke withdrew his earlier permission[39] and suggested Martin Tectander instead.[40] Eventually, it was not Tectander but the court preacher of the duke of Mecklenburg, Aegidius Faber[41] from Schwerin, who came to Sts. Peter and Paul in Liegnitz. This was probably as a result of dynastic ties between the courts of Schwerin and Liegnitz. On March 3, 1538 Frederick III, the eldest son of Frederick II, married Katharina, the youngest daughter of Heinrich III von Mecklenburg.

It was astonishing that Crautwald was not affected by the anti-Schwenkfeldian mandates. He saw this as the gracious providence of God.[42] This was probably because his learning was still highly respected by the court[43] and because he was completely withdrawn from the world. He was led to this by his quiet, learned disposition, and also by his poor health. Already in 1534 he no longer dared to visit his circle of friends in Breslau because of his health.[44] Since his frailty continually increased,[45] he resigned by 1537 at the latest from the duties as financial manager of the monastery. He had always carried out these duties with great distaste since they interfered with his personal study. Besides reading the Bible, he zealously pursued his study of the Church Fathers and attentively read newly-published books. For example, he must have seen the theses *On the Divinity and Humanity of Christ*[46] shortly after Luther debated on them on February 29, 1540 since on November 11 he wrote to Jacob von Tieffenau, "I have received Doctor Luther's statements and have marveled over and consoled myself with them; it is his nature to scold and decry, although now he is still. The theses have been known here for a long time but the Lutherans have not boasted about them or found consolation in them. They are full of scholastic logic and sophistry."[47] Crautwald also spent much time on an extensive correspondence. He wrote not only his own friends in Silesia, but also followers of Schwenckfeld in South and West Germany with whom Schwenckfeld had put him in contact. His correspondents, among whom—reminiscent of late medieval mystics—there were many women, included Bonifacius Wolfhart from Augsburg, Catharine Streicher and Barbara Kurenbach from Ulm, Ursula Thumb von Stetten, Johann Bader from Landau, Jacob Held von Tieffenau, Margarete Engelmann, Elisabeth Pfersfelder, and Alexander Berner and Hans Christmann from Strassburg. He discussed primarily theological problems with them. Occasionally through provocative formulations he helped them clarify their own positions. The letters also contained much pastoral counsel and consolation and some practical help as well; for example, he sent a Hungarian guilder through Schwenckfeld to Andreas Neff from Cannstatt "to treat himself to something."[48] Neff had been imprisoned in 1543 for distributing Schwenkfeldian works and being unwilling to change his mind.[49]

A growing pessimistic note is observable in the works written by Crautwald during the last years of his life, possibly because of the continuous decline of the Liegnitz Brotherhood. In July, 1545, a month and a half before his death on September 5, he prophesied that the papacy would rise again and persecute the community of Christ because the anti-Christ would seek expanded power. The preachers would, however, not notice this and would continue in their overbearing attitude.[50]

After Frederick II had removed all the Schwenkfeldian pastors, at least in the territories of Liegnitz and Brieg, and replaced them with Lutherans, he issued a new church order[51]—on April 26 for the principality of Liegnitz and on October 7, 1542 for the principality of Brieg. In it, all pastors were ordered to observe the Lord's Supper and baptism and other "religious matters"[52] in accordance with the *Augsburg Confession* and *Apology.*[53] The remaining "secret followers"[54] of the expelled Schwenkfelder leaders were threatened with punishment for public and secret preaching and forbidden to visit the sick.[55] To further church life, Frederick II decreed in this order that senior pastors be placed over the pastors of the local parishes and a superintendent above them for each of the principalities of Liegnitz and Brieg.[56] The superintendents were to have disciplinary powers, that is, only with their agreement could future pastors presented by the lords of the manors because of their right of patronage, be placed in office or removed.[57] Furthermore, the seniors were to conduct local synods four times a year.[58] Finally, the landlords were ordered to fill vacant pastorates within three months and to return illegally confiscated church property or lose their patronage.[59] To ensure compliance, Frederick II as the "chief bishop" announced visitations "as soon as possible."[60] According to the protocols this was carried out in Brieg in that same year.[61] One was also held in Liegnitz,[62] according to a fragment of the visitation article of April 26, 1542, discovered by E. Sehling.[63]

In spite of this edict the secret Schwenkfeldianism mentioned in the church order could evidently not be rooted out,[64] since on January 20, 1545 Frederick II published his first anti-Schwenkfeldian mandate.[65] In it he threatened Schwenkfelders with exile if they did not accept the Lutheran Confession. How seriously the duke intended his threat is clear from his order of April 22, 1547 that two Schwenkfeldian citizens and a widow, after two warnings, had to sell their possessions and leave Liegnitz within four weeks.[66] This edict seems to have had results. Attendance at the sermons and at the Eucharistic services in the two Liegnitz churches of St. Mary's and Sts. Peter and Paul increased so much that a second vicar had to be installed at each of them.[67] Nevertheless, some Schwenkfelders obviously remained in Liegnitz and Brieg since Frederick III of Liegnitz and Georg II of Brieg and Wohlau, the two sons of Frederick II (who died September 17, 1547), took repeated actions against them. The Liegnitz magistracy, for instance, published an edict of Frederick III's on June 4, 1550 in which he ordered that the observance of word and sacrament be held frequently and that they avoid all heresies or leave the land.[68] Furthermore, under threat of serious punishment, an order was given to turn over all works of Schwenckfeld, Crautwald, and Werner to the authorities.[69] Nevertheless, Lutheran pastors[70] and laymen[71] continued to complain about the numerous Schwenkfelders. Consequently, Trotzendorf, still there, decided to go to Wittenberg in the spring of 1555 to "gain counsel and help to ascertain how and in what way, by means of divine grace, the crass corruption and error could be opposed for the consolation of a great number of souls."[72] In the same year, the Liegnitz superintendents, Heinrich Dietrich and Georg Seiler, requested that Duke Georg II renew the anti-Schwenkfeldian mandate of his father since "the Schwenkfeldian radicalism, like a great flood, is breaking in most parts of the principality and is being preached in various out-of-the-way places."[73] When "painstaking" investigations of "suspicious people"[74] were held at Liegnitz, it came to light that "some had not received the sacrament for 30, 40, 50, or 60 years, some for a shorter period, and some had never received it."[75] Despite these actions by religious and secular leaders,[76] Schwenkfelders remained among the notable citizens into the next decades; for example, Hans Heinrich served as a court juror.[77] When he died in "Schwenkfeldian heresy"[78] in 1585, he was "buried without the sound of bells, without the company of the pupils and the pastors, outside of the city of Liegnitz in the cemetery of St. Nicolaus."[79]

Unlike all the other districts in the principality of Liegnitz, the city and district of Lüben had not been affected by Frederick's edict. The duke respected the sovereign rights of his sister-in-law Anna who had controlled this territory in 1521 as a tenure for life and who had made this a center for Schwenkfeldianism, as has been mentioned already. His son, Frederick III, who was not like his father, broke into this enclave however and, laying aside the rights of his aunt, attempted in 1548 to imprison pastor Georg Hirsenberger, a sympathizer with the Schwenkfelders; Hirsenberger escaped, however.[80] He was replaced—likely in the same year—by Valentin Tilgner, a strong opponent of the Schwenkfelders.[81] Tilgner's strict Lutheranism, which emerged especially after the death of the duchess on April 25, 1550, put him into sharp contrast with the council and people of Lüben. He did, however, maintain the support of Frederick III, who moved firmly against the Schwenkfelders after one of them preached openly in the Lüben marketplace, apparently calling for rebellion against the political authorities. Tilgner died in 1551, the same year that Frederick III was suspended from power by

Ferdinand I because of the former's illegal visit to France. As a result, the Schwenkfelders in Lüben and surrounding areas gained a reprieve. According to a contemporary chronicler "whole villages,"[82] such as Ossig, supposedly became "purely Schwenkfeldian"[83] and had Schwenkfeldian pastors who preached with great success, drawing people all the way from Lüben.[84]

Not until the fall of 1558 did the Schwenkfelders once again find a bitter opponent in the energetic pastor Franciskus Rosentritt.[85] As this pastor in the parish of Lüben stressed, he tirelessly used the office to "beseech, pray, and earnestly admonish them to turn from their error."[86] He also threatened not to visit them "in sickness, either with the Lord's Supper (which they so denigrated in their lives), nor with the service of Christian visitation"[87] if they did not "in their healthy days convert and attend the holy sacrament as did other Christians."[88] In fact, he did refuse them the sacrament on their death beds and a Christian burial.[89] Because of this there was growing opposition to him by some Schwenkfelders.[90] According to a moderate estimate the Schwenkfelders made up only fifteen percent of the population but they had strong influence among important families as well as among the guilds—particularly among the weavers and council members.[91] On December 9, 1570 Rosentritt finally had to leave Lüben, particularly because neighboring pastors were suspicious that, as a former enthusiastic student of Melanchthon, he was a Philippist. Thus Schwenkfelders could be found in Lüben until the end of the sixteenth century.

4. Schwenkfeldianism in the County of Glatz

Lutheranism had gained footing shortly before 1525 in Glatz,[1] which from May 1, 1501 to 1525 was in the possession of Count Ulrich of Hardegg and Machland and thereafter until 1534 of his brother Hans.[2] When Schwenkfeldianism arrived can no longer be ascertained. The continued assertion that Schwenckfeld stayed in Glatz early in 1529—after his voluntary exile from the territories of Frederick II—is certainly wrong.[3] It is historically ascertainable that Schwenkfeldianism began here in 1538 with the arrival of numerous Schwenkfelders who were forced to flee from the principality of Liegnitz. A year earlier the territory of Glatz, which had been sold by Count Hans to Archduke Ferdinand of Austria,[4] came under the possession of Johann von Bernstein,[5] who evidently did not only tolerate the Schwenkfelders but may even have favored them.[6] A prominent Glatz citizen at the time was the influential Schwenkfelder Martin Strauch. A master in the weavers' guild and the head of the municipal council, he had emigrated from

Liegnitz.[7] According to Aelurius, he not only eagerly propagated his conviction among the citizens, but also "enticed, encouraged, and attracted numerous fellow believers to Glatz."[8]

The most important representative of the first Schwenkfelders in the area, however, was undoubtedly Fabian Eckel.[9] With the agreement of the Order of St. John of Jerusalem, which held the right of patronage, he was called to Glatz as pastor and installed in this office on April 19, 1538. It can be attributed to his preaching and evidently to the influence of Strauch, that not only the majority of the population but even eleven of the twelve aldermen professed their Schwenkfeldian beliefs that same year.[10] Although neither the Catholics nor the Lutherans opposed Eckel, the Anabaptists did. The latter must have been particularly numerous, especially in Habelschwerdt where in 1545, according to the oldest chronicles, almost the whole population was Anabaptist.[11] In a partially extant letter from Schwenckfeld,[12] Eckel discussed with them questions of Christology and the millenium. Having suffered apoplexy in the pulpit on Ascencion Sunday June 3, 1546,[13] he died two days later and was succeeded by Sebastian Eisenmann, long-time attendant and associate of Crautwald.[14]

In the same year Eckel was installed at Glatz, Valerius Rosenhayn came as pastor to Neurode,[15] which then belonged to Heinrich Stillfried Sr. of Ratienitz in Mittelsteine. A squire at the court at Liegnitz, Stillfried had early embraced the Reformation and had likely become acquainted with the Schwenkfelders there as well. Virtually nothing is known of Rosenhayn's work in Neurode. According to Schubart, who, however, says Rengersdorf in Glatz was his place of activity, he suffered apoplexy, was paralyzed, and could no longer preach.[16] Apparently he left Neurode (or Rengersdorf) in 1540; in any case, he died in Liegnitz in his own home.[17]

In 1540, two years after Eckel and Rosenhayn arrived, a third Schwenkfelder, Johann Sigismund Werner, came to Glatz.[18] He was called to Rengersdorf,[19] which then belonged to Jörg von Pannwitz; his sister Elizabeth was married to Heinrich Stillfried in 1540[20] These ties between the two patrons of Neurode and Rengersdorf and also Eckel's recommendations probably played a role in Werner's call to the town.[21] Werner's zealous preaching won to the Schwenkfeldian cause not only his parishioners[22] but also his landlords, the brothers Jörg and Christoph von Pannwitz, both of whom, perhaps encouraged by Eckel,[23] wrote two letters to Schwenckfeld on January 11 and January 20, 1540 inviting him to visit them should he return to Silesia.[24] Christoph even offered Schwenckfeld his castle as a domicile.[25] Schwenckfeld was negotiating at that time with Frederick II concerning his possible return to Silesia; the duke rejected this.[26]

In addition to his preaching, Werner displayed a rich literary activity, concerned primarily with edification and instruction. He first composed a *Postill*[27] in which he treated allegorically the traditional Gospel readings for Sundays and feast days. In this work he argued against any kind of mediated reality of salvation. In his discussion of John 20:22, for example, he wrote: "It is a great error to teach that the Holy Ghost comes into the hearts of men by physical means and that the grace of God is granted to the believer through the elements; since elements themselves are not capable of receiving God's grace, how can grace come through them."[28] Rather, grace can be received only through the "word of life,"[29] through the "water of life,"[30] and above all, through the spiritual reception of the "invisible life-giving bread"[31] through which man becomes deified. According to his conception, as II Peter 1:4 indicates, God became man so that "he might raise up the nature in himself and have it break forth in such glory and clarity that it might become wholly like God. Thus, through Jesus Christ, the believing human flesh may be sanctified, anointed, and made alive so that it is renewed and born again, through the Holy Ghost become a part of the divine nature."[32]

First circulated in manuscript, the *Postill,* intended for edification at home, was printed in 1558 by Georg Rab of Pforzheim.[33] Immediately after its publication, Duke Christoph of Württemberg submitted it to his theologians for a judgment. They declared that "the seductive Schwenkfeldian error was strewn throughout all of it."[34] Schottenloher has noted that because of this declaration Count Karl II of Baden-Durlach (in whose territories Pforzheim lay), the magistrates of Strassburg, and the council of Frankfurt am Main were all drawn into the affair concerning its publication.[35] Matthias Flacius Illyricus also published a sharp criticism of the *Postill*[36] because it denied the Reformation doctrine of salvation.[37] However, he had falsely believed that Schwenckfeld had written it and only published it under the pseudonym Werner.[38] The *Postill* became the most popular book among the Schwenkfelders in Glatz and especially in the Bober-Katzbach mountains.

In addition to the *Postill* Werner also wrote a Christological treatise in 1546 under the title *On the Humiliation of the Son of God.*[39] The Christology described in it is identical to that of Schwenckfeld and Crautwald, although the discussion of deification is much more extensive.[40] Like his *Catechism,* printed in the same year,[41] it is in question-and-answer form. The works were probably intended to complement each other, since in the *Catechism* Christology is not treated. His efforts for catechetical instruction must be viewed in connection with his vast pedagogical interests. He established the first school at Rengersdorf in the county of Glatz and laid one of the foundations for public education in the area, as has been mentioned in the church history of the territory.[42]

From the Schwenkfelder centers Glatz, Neurode, and Rengersdorf, Schwenkfeldianism spread through almost the whole county, particularly to Habelschwert, Grafenort, Gabersdorf, Reinerz, Volpersdorf, Wöfelsdorf, as well as to Mittelwalde and later it even extended into Moravian territory.[43] It is thus understandable that to Schwenkfelders this region must have seemed to be the Promised Land.[44]

In the county of Glatz itself, Lutheranism seemed to be powerless against the spreading Schwenkfeldianism; at least the chronicles made no mention of opposition. Opposition did, however, come from outside Glatz, since Moibanus discussed the problems of faith in Breslau, probably in 1538, with the Glatz ruler Johann von Bernstein.[45] At this meeting, he requested that Moibanus write a tract on communion for children.[46] In the tract Moibanus denied denying that the sacrament might be given to small children since they were not yet able to distinguish between sacramental and natural food. The treatise was published in 1541 along with Melanchthon's *On the Office of the Prince*[47] (which had appeared in 1539) and dedicated to Johann von Bernstein.[48] He wanted to motivate the owner of the county with this work to fight against the Schwenkfelders. Already in 1538 Melanchthon had written to Bernstein, expressly emphasizing in this tract that the political authority as divinely instituted power was compelled to move against heresy:[49] "The princes and magistrates ought to do away with the false cults and to work so that true doctrine be spread in the church and pious worship be given."[50] But Johann von Bernstein was not aroused by this to move against the Schwenkfelders.

A general decline of Schwenkfeldianism in the county of Glatz began on the death of Johann von Bernstein on September 8, 1548 when the government, with the agreement of Ferdinand I, passed from the hands of his sons and heirs, Jaroslaw, Wratislaw, and Adalbert von Bernstein, into those of Duke Ernst of Bavaria (on December 2, 1549).[51] The following year, Duke Ernst, firmly resolved to bring about the Counter Reformation in all his territories, ordered the authorities and pastors to see to it that all preaching was done according to the Catholic tradition.[52] Since as administrator of the archbishopric of Salzburg he was at first not in Glatz, the edict remained mostly without effect; only the Lutheran pastor of Habelschwerdt, Johann Tyrann, was removed from his position.[53] The situation changed, however, when the duke of Bavaria, having renounced the episcopate on July 16, 1554 took up residence in Glatz on January 28, 1556, and concentrated only on the execution of the Counter Reformation in that areas.[54]

Shortly after his arrival he announced to the assembled Lutheran and Schwenkfeldian pastors that "we shall begin the work as quickly as possible for an examination of the religious conditions."[55] Nevertheless, it was two years later, after his court preacher, Christoph Neaetius, had already debated on the Lord's Supper[56] and Christology[57] with Sebastian Eisenmann that he ordered the pastors to a hearing at his castle on July 3 and 4, 1558. Almost all of them appeared.[58] At the first meeting before the imperial commission[59] they were to answer thirty general questions.[60] The following day's questioning[61] was intended to detect who were followers of Schwenckfeld.[62] It turned out that three of the twenty-eight pastors who appeared were dedicated Schwenkfelders;[63] two others held partly to Lutheran, partly to Schwenkfeldian teachings.[64] With the exception of G. Gorlich of Volpersdorf and M. Steinberg of Gabersdorf, these were expelled. Sebastian Eisenmann, knowing the certainty of his fate, fled earlier. Nevertheless, the Schwenkfelder communities were not destroyed "since they held to each other, so that Schwenkfelders were always in the senate, and (since like things rejoice together) they always brought their interests even into the Senate."[65] According to Wedekind,[66] however, a few Schwenkfelders were converted to Catholicism in Glatz.

In an attempt fully to recatholicize the county of Glatz, Ernst of Bavaria in the fall of 1560 finally ordered that a visitation be carried out under Christoph Neaetius with the full support of the duke.[67] Neaetius began the visitation of the pastorates on on September 2, making detailed reports;[68] but this laborious work had little effect since Ernst died on December 6. Glatz then went over to Duke Albrecht V of Bavaria, the only legitimate son of his brother Wilhelm IV, from whom Ferdinand I[69] again redeemed it for himself.

After the early death of Duke Ernst of Bavaria, not only Lutheranism but also Schwenkfeldianism grew stronger again under the protection of the wealthy patrons Christoph von Pannwitz, "the Schwenkfeldian chief and headman,"[70] and David Heinrich von Tschirnhaus and Falkenkamp. Schwenkfeldianism now experienced such a new blossoming that even those "who had earlier pretended to be Catholics during the duke's life"[71] became Schwenkfelders once again. It was because of this that the bishop of Prague, Anton Brus of Müglitz, already in 1561 turned for help to Ferdinand I with the request that he defend the archpriest Christoph Neaetius as well as other Catholics in the area, and command that no one should hinder him in the pursuit of his duties.[72] At this, the emperor and his son Maximilian II, who were not in possession of Glatz, seem to have proceeded against the Schwenkfelders since, according to Elogius, Maximilian issued mandates "that none who despise word and sacrament be admitted to public office, and that those who did so be removed from their positions and expelled from the towns."[73] However, these mandates had no effect, as will be shown.

The most significant center of Schwenkfeldianism in Glatz was the small town of Mittelwalde, which was in the possession of David Heinrich von Tschirnhaus and Falkenkamp. There dwelt the learned and prosperous Schwenkfelder David Curck, the former pastor Nicolaus Detschke [Tetschke] and Adam Jäsch who is said to have known seven languages.[74] He had not only read the works of Schwenckfeld and his followers but also those of Sebastian Franck, something sharply criticized by the Schwenkfelders in the Bober-Katzbach mountains.[75] They pointed out that even Schwenckfeld had rejected Franck.[76] "I have read," wrote Antonius Oelsner, "in Caspar Schwenckfeld's *Epistolar* that he wrote and said to someone: Franck and others like him take or suck their poison from our books even as the spider does from the flowers [CS V, 523, 1] which, however, provide honey for the bee."[77]

Since the Schwenkfelders were convinced of the complete corruption of the Lutheran church and of the ineffectiveness of the word and sacrament for grace, they stayed away from its worship services, including the observance of the sacrament, and would not have their children baptized.[78] This of course piqued the opposition from the Lutherans who flourished in Glatz from 1560-1622. Their chief leaders were the ecclesiastical inspector Andreas Eising, who worked in Glatz from 1564 to 1591, and the Habelschwerdter pastor Caspar Elogius, whom Maximilian II had commissioned with the task of completely eradicating the Schwenkfelders.[79] The Lutheran pastors attempted to achieve this goal by church discipline, such as refusing proper burial rites to Schwenkfelders who had not baptized their children or observed the sacrament.[80]

Such attempts to break up the Schwenkfeldian communities and to bring the people back to Lutheranism had little effect. The Schwenkfelders were defended and protected by magistrates and landlords, especially the patron[81] David Heinrich of Tschirnhaus and Falkenkamp. Landlord of Mittelwalde, Schönfeld, and Wölfelsdorf, he even allowed the refugee Schwenkfelders from the Bober-Katzbach mountains to dwell in his territories.[82] The Lutheran pastor had no power against the Schwenkfelders as long he lived,[83] but on his death in 1563 he had a free hand and many newly-arrived Schwenkfelders returned to their homeland.[84] The Schwenkfelders did however also have strong support from the magistrates in Glatz and Habelschwerdt. This is evident in the fate of the Habelschwerdt pastor Elogius, who noted in a lengthy letter[85] to A. Brus von Müglitz that the Schwenkfelder councillors in his congregation, together with those from Glatz, under the influence of Georg Reichel in Habelschwerdt and in neighboring Landeck "had spread incendiary literature among the public, and that if the preacher of Habelschwerdt not be removed by the Feast of St. Michael, they would set the whole town afire so that there would be only a heap of ashes left.''[86] On May 1, 1577 the pastor was removed from office by the local authority Christoph von Schellendorf and Adelsdorf of Saatz and Kuna. On the following day he emigrated to Schlaupitz at Reichenbach.

At the beginning of 1623 Schwenkfeldianism began to die out in the county of Glatz since the territory, because of the law of the owner (*ius reformandi*), was recatholicized by force. Like the other secondary lands within the Bohemian Estates, Glatz, after the Bohemian Rebellion, placed itself on the side of the Bohemian Estates, and, in spite of an imperial warning on August 17, 1618, formed an alliance with them, and supported the choice of Frederick V of the Palatinate as king after Ferdinand II was deposed by the Bohemian Diet on August 19, 1619. When the Winter King (Frederick V) was defeated at the gates of Prague on November 8, 1619 by the imperial troops and the army of the Catholic League, the Bohemian Estates were defeated. Even so, the county of Glatz continued to support him, while the other Silesian princes and estates joined with Prince Elector Georg I of Saxony and reached the so-called Dresden Accord in 1621, promising to accept Ferdinand II as the legitimate overlord, to contribute regularly according to his wishes, not to join in alliance with the Palatinate, and to disband their armies. On the other hand, the county of Glatz was occupied and, after a siege of several months, the city of Glatz fell to imperial troops on October 28, 1622. The Counter Reformation was immediately inaugurated in the entire land.

By 1624 all Lutheran pastors had been gradually removed from office and replaced by Catholics.[87] In 1625 those landlords who had supported the Bohemian revolt were charged by an imperial commission with rebellion and some punished with imprisonment or fines, others with complete confiscation of their goods and belongings.[88] Finally, on July 31 an edict was issued by Ferdinand II,[89] stating that all non-Catholic subjects—who earlier had lost their rights as citizens and whose marriages had been declared invalid[90]—were ordered either to convert or to sell their goods and leave the land. While some Schwenkfelders fled to join their fellow believers in the Bober-Katzbach mountains,[91] most remained and converted to Catholicism.[92] Although they succeeded in hiding their books of edification, they apparently no longer met in conventicles. By the middle of the seventeenth century, Schwenkfeldianism had been completely eliminated from the county of Glatz.

V Schwenkfeldianism in the Regions Between Löwenberg, Goldberg, and Haynau

1. Expansion and Blossoming

As shown above, Schwenkfelders suffered persecution in the duchy of Liegnitz, especially in the town of Liegnitz itself. However, in addition to the county of Glatz, they were able to establish significant communities in the region of the Bober-Katzbach mountains from the middle of the sixteenth century.[1] They settled in the villages of Harpersdorf, Armenruh, Laubgrund, and Hockenau, all of which lay on the southwest border of the principality of Liegnitz, and particularly in the vicinities of Langneundorf, Radmannsdorf, Siebeneichen, Höfel, Lauterseiffen, and Deumannsdorf, which were located in the northern part of the principalities of Schweidnitz and Jauer, and were directly subject to the emperor. These villages could become Schwenkfeldian centers not only because many of the landlords there allowed them to settle on their estates, but also because they sympathized with them. Notable among such landlords was the wealthy Johann von Schaffgotsch,[2] provincial officer in the principality of Schweidnitz-Jauer from 1558-1559 and from 1558-1563 counselor to the royal chamber in Silesia. The chamber was responsible for the interests of the king of Bohemia as suzerain of Silesia. For many years leading up to 1573, Schaffgotsch was one of the most influential protectors of the Schwenkfelders.[3] There were also some Schwenkfelder-oriented pastors in this region, or at least pastors who tolerated the Schwenkfelders.[4] Theologically the most significant and the most influential among them in later years, mainly through his family connections,[5] was undoubtedly Michael Hiller.[6] From 1511 on he was pastor in Zobten. The parish included the villages of Siebeneichen, Höfel, Petersdorf, Radmannsdorf, Hohndorf, and Dippelsdorf. Later he joined the Reformation, but he increasingly imbibed more and more Schwenkfeldian spirituality as is evident from his writings. Schwenkfelders of the neighboring communities flocked to his services, prompting the pastor of Probsthain, Melchior Liebald,[7] to note in his parish register in 1554: "In this year they swarmed to Zobten, since a certain teacher arose there."[8] Basing his thought on the Scriptures—for example, the passage on the healing of the Phoenician woman in Mark 7:24-30,[9]—and occasionally on the Church Fathers (Ambrose and Jerome), Hiller rejected every attempt to mediate salvation through created means.[10] The external word and the sacraments could never contain or mediate grace; they could only direct the faithful to it and witness to it.[11] The faithful are given grace by God only through "the living Word of God,"[12] through the "water of life"[13] and through "an inner, heavenly, unseen, hidden food of the soul, inconceivable to all the senses but not imperceptible,"[14] that is through the deified humanity of Christ in exaltation. Through this partial partaking arises the new man in the likeness of God. On this Hiller concentrated his theological interest. In a sermon he wrote: "Christ was not born to remain in the manner of a bodily and mortal being, neither did he want that, nor was he predestined for that, but he was born to receive divine and eternal glory in his flesh, which was to be entirely renewed, transformed, deified, for the benefit of us all, but without any change or intermixture of the divine and human nature. And we shall be deified by the power of his deified flesh or humanity."[15] Though this deification progresses constantly, it finds its conclusion only after death or rather on Judgment Day.[16] Hiller emphasized that this growth must necessarily be evident already in life since "a pregnant woman does not know she will bear a child until she feels and recognizes certain obvious signs."[17] If there is no evidence of ethical renewal,[18] "we have only the delusion and misconception that God lives in us."[19]

In support of his views on the deification of man, Hiller quoted the words of the medieval Dominican mystic Johann Tauler. "Tauler says that Christ the Lord said: Christians! It is for you that I became man; now if you do not become children of God and do not let your actions show your acceptance of divine ways and proprieties, you do me an injustice."[20] Although this may well not be a genuine Tauler citation,[21] the quotation does state a basic principle of late medieval mysticism. This increased use of mystical ideas clearly distinguishes Hiller from Schwenckfeld and his first generation followers. While the notion of man's deification was by no means foreign to them, as has been pointed out, it did not have the same meaning for them as it did for Hiller. The shifting of weight from Christology to anthropology was of particular importance for the further development of Schwenkfeldianism since this shifting of weight prepared the ground for the tendency to moralize and psychologize Schwenkfeldianism at a later stage.

Because of his attack on his Lutheran colleagues—centered primarily on their doctrine of word and sacrament[22]—Hiller was suspended from his position at the urging of his Lutheran co-pastors by the magistrate of Löwenberg, who held patronage over the parish of Lobten. Accused as a heretic before the bishop of Breslau, Balthasar von Promnitz,[23] Hiller drafted a defense directed to the bishop,[24] declaring that he did by no means despise the word and the sacraments but that he would not look upon them as means of grace. The bishop, after merely exhorting him to continue administering the sacrament, reinstated Hiller.[25]

When Michael Hiller died on September 22, 1554 (1557) in Zobten,[26] the Schwenkfelders lost not only a pastor in whom they had placed great trust but also almost their last tie with the church, since the few remaining Schwenkfelder-oriented pastors in the area were soon replaced by Lutherans.[27] In subsequent years Schwenkfelders separated themselves increasingly from the established church and built their own communities. A pastor of the city of Goldberg reported that seldom did any of them attend Lutheran services; they hardly ever attended vespers, choosing instead to sit "in taverns with brandy."[28] If they felt they were attacked in the sermon they would stand up and run out of the church.[29] Sometimes they shouted at the preacher.[30] Occasionally they would send for their servants during the sermon who would then be obliged to "leave God's service and attend to the service of men."[31] Many went even further in their opposition, speaking polemically against the church.[32] Since this situation spread "in the countryside,"[33] and "quite rapidly,"[34] "some pastors were not able to distinguish pure from impure sheep any longer."[35] The situation was worsened by the activities of Martin John Sr. and Antonius Oelsner; both exponents of that third-generation Schwenkfeldianism, they brought a biblicistic, legalistic and apocalyptic strain into Schwenkfeldianism.

Martin John Sr. was born in Kauffung.[36] Believing the local pastor to be indulging in a "godless life" with "eating and drinking, [and living in] pride, avarice, gaming, dancing, and fornication,"[37] he no longer attended public worship but conducted family worship in his home.[38] For this he was banished from Kauffung by his landlord, Christoph von Redern, at the urging of the pastor Georg M.[39] He took his family and went to Harpersdorf where he purchased property with the consent of the landlord Sigismund von Mauschwitz.[40] Harpersdorf was the center of Schwenkfeldianism at the time. But here, too, his ethical rigor soon came up against the conduct of the local pastor, Georg Etzler.[41] "When I came to Harpersdorf," he wrote to Duke Frederick IV of Liegnitz, "I had to observe and listen to the same Godless conduct of the pastors as in my homeland. I did not have to go far; from my own yard I could hear how the pastor [Georg Etzler] fiddled and how the people danced and shouted and carried on even worse than in Kauffung, practising sins which God rejected in his kingdom."[42] Once again he stayed away from worship services and established Sunday conventicles in which, besides his family and servants,[43] so many Schwenkfelders from Harpersdorf and the neighboring villages took part that his house could not contain them all.[44] It is likely that he spoke against the external word of preaching and the sacraments as means of grace in these conventicles, and demanded separation from the Lutheran church.[45] This was especially necessary, he felt, because of the conduct of the Lutherans, particularly of their pastors. He was convinced that "the heathen in their idolatry were not so obedient to Satan as many Lutheran Christians are today."[46] While Schwenckfeld became radically opposed to the established church under the influence of Martin John Sr., under the influence of Antonius Oelsner it received an ecstatic-apocalyptic character. Antonius Oelsner, a shepherd from Kammerswaldau,[47] had read Schwenckfeld in his youth[48] and experienced a sudden conversion, probably in 1580.[49] After hearing voices, while seeing visions, he gave up his work at Deutmannsdorf in order to set off as a prophet like Jonah for Nineveh.[50] As a wandering preacher he roamed around in the the villages of the Bober-Katzbach mountain area[51] and soon held meetings in the forests, hoping to go unnoticed by the authorities while he spoke to the people who thronged there.[52]

The Lutheran pastors, who had been composing anti-Schwenkfeldian literature since the middle of the sixteenth century,[53] were afraid that this radical separatism would take root in their congregations. For this reason they not only preached polemically against the Schwenkfelders[54] but incited their patrons—Sigismund von Mauschwitz, landlord of Hohndorf, Langneundorf, and Armenruh, and Georg von Borwitz, landlord of Niederharpersdorf— to take action against them.[55] First to be captured was Antonius Oelsner against whom an order seems to have been issued by the Löwenberg magistrate[56] forbidding anyone to harbor him.[57] After imprisionment in Liegnitz for approximately two years by Frederick IV, Oelsner immediately resumed his preaching "day and night."[58] Some six months later, on January 13, 1587 he was once again taken into custody for questioning in Löwenberg[59] and, refusing to recant, was sent to Vienna on May 28 where he was sentenced to coercive detention, then prison, and eventually to galley service in 1595.[60] At about the same time Sigismund von Mauschwitz took action against Martin John Sr. He was ordered in 1586 either to desist from holding conventicles or to leave the estate.[61] Since the landlord was unsuccessful, John was arrested in June 1587 and placed in the stocks in Armenruh.[62] Later he was transferred to the prison in Liegnitz and from time to time transferred to the fortress in Gröditzberg.[63]

The hope of the Lutheran pastors and landlords that Schwenkfeldianism might at least be curtailed by the imprisonment of its two major leaders did not materialize. Some Schwenkfelders returned to Lutheranism[64] but the majority continued their conventicles, encouraged by the numerous circular letters and epistles of John Sr. and A. Oelsner.[65] In certain areas they continued to be protected by the gentry as well, among them Valentin von Redern Jr., landlord of Probsthain, and Johann Sigismund von Schweinichen auf Schweinhaus. Around 1590 the religious excitement of the Schwenkfelders of the Bober-Katzbach mountains increased, especially in Harpersdorf.[66]

Their gatherings, in which separatist, apocalyptic, and visionary-ecstatic emphases became increasingly stronger, were no longer led by men only but also by youths and women; this is clear from the activities of the fifteen-year-old apocalyptic Matthäus Teissner of Hartmannsdorf[67] and the ecstatic Barbara Groh of Hartliebsdorf,[68] where there is unmistakable evidence of pathological elements. An impressive portrayal of one such gathering is available in the following undated and anonymous account by a non-Schwenkfelder: "In and around Hartmannsdorf over two thousand persons, men and women, are supposed to have gathered; they performed strange gestures with their hands and bodies, they have prophets among them who said they could see the nobles and their priests sitting in hell, coupled together like dogs; furthermore, three weeks ago the judgment was to have come, but was put off, but not for more than eight days; they were forbidden to hear God's word, to go to church, or to baptize their children."[69] To deal with this movement, the bishop of Breslau, Andreas Jerin, in his capacity as the supreme provincial officer, issued an anti-Schwenkfelder mandate on October 21, 1590[70] in which all Schwenkfelder gatherings were forbidden and participation at public worship services and the reception of the sacraments was demanded. Those who did not comply were to have their goods confiscated.[71]

Since the Schwenkfelders did not obey, a persecution which lasted for decades was soon launched. On June 30, 1595 the emperor Ferdinand II, shortly after his accession to the throne, also issued an anti-Schwenkfeldian edict for his hereditary counties.[72] Supported by the landlords in the Bober-Katzbach mountains, especially those of Niederharpersdorf, Armenruh, Hartliebsdorf, and Deutmannsdorf, Frederick IV of Liegnitz and the provincial officer of the principalities of Schweidnitz and Jauer moved against them with investigations, coercive detention, imprisonment,[73] expulsion,[74] expropriations,[75] and confiscations of manuscripts and books.[76] Around 1590 twenty-eight Schwenkfelders were deported to Vienna and placed as galley slaves on the Danube during the Great Turkish War.[77] Only three survived the hardships and deprivations.[78] Paraphrasing Luther's translation of Psalm 141:7,[79] A. Oelsner wrote: "My friends lie scattered throughout Hungary in the water and on the land."[80] The three who survived were pardoned and freed by the emperor Rudolf II after the victory at Raab on March 29, 1598.[81] Yet only two, Matthäus Geissler and Melchior Weinhold, returned to their homeland,[82] soon giving up their Schwenkfeldianism.[83] Anton Oelsner remained[84] in Vienna where all traces of him are lost.[85]

Not only the leaders were affected by these anti-Schwenkfeldian measures; families and followers who could not or were not allowed to cultivate their fields experienced the greatest of economic hardships and fell into arrears in their debt payments.[86] Most of the Schwenkfelders bore the persecution with patience for years, probably not just because they were consoled by secret letters which those who were imprisoned managed to send. Thus Christoph Oelsner, who, like his brother Antonius had given up his vocation and had become a wandering preacher,[87] admonished his fellow believers in Zobten and Hohndorf on January 17, 1597 urging them to remain firm in spite of suffering.[88] His letter makes use of the medieval German mystical treatise, the *Theologia Deutsch,* which he had brought from his home to his prison in Gröditzberg:[89] "O, let us, with good will, suffer every tribulation here . . . since there is so no other way to an eternal godly life, except through the narrow way of the cross, the royal road through the narrow gate into the city of God. . . .O holy cross of my Lord Jesus! How sweet, how soft and light you are for all those who surrender themselves to God and take up the yoke of Christ."[90] In their letters they did not only try to keep alive the ethical rigor[91] and the critical attitude toward the established church among their fellow believers, but even to intensify it. "One must," wrote Antonius Oelsner in 1594 from Vienna, "shun the opponents of Christ in all spiritual and divine matters when they are known and revealed to be false and in error."[92] He advised them in this epistle neither to have their children baptized[93] as heretofore,[94] nor to have their marriages blessed in the church any longer.[95] In obedience to Isaiah 52:11, Jeremiah 50:8, II Corinthians 6:17, and Revelation 18:4, they should separate themselves entirely from the Lutheran church.[96]

After the imprisonment of Antonius Oelsner,[97] the Schwenkfelders of the county of Glatz—especially Nicolaus Detschke, Adam Jäsch, and David Curck from the small town of Mittelwalde[98]—opposed this radicalism. These men had maintained the original spiritualism, which they placed in contrast with the biblical legalism, ethical rigorism, and apocalypticism of their brethren in the Bober-Katzbach mountains. In letters[99] and personal visitations[100] they particularly charged Antonius Oelsner (whose writings they had secretly seen),[101] not entirely incorrectly, with upholding an Anabaptist position.[102] They questioned his call to preach, stated that his writings were confused, called his visions fantasies, and criticized his separatism as premature. Although they were not able to turn the Schwenkfelders in the Bober-Katzbach mountains back to the gradually waning spiritualist position, they did lead them to weaken their separatist and rigorist ethical stances. In the account of his conversion, where he defended his call to preach, Antonius Oelsner complained bitterly about these events: "If Nicolaus [Detschke] would have helped as much as he hindered, much greater things would have resulted. Nicolaus, who had wanted to help Satan to throw off the cross and to destroy it, is the greatest reason that this did not occur."[103]

During this time of persecution, the Schwenkfelders, particularly on feast days, sometimes attended services held in Langenbielau, thirty kilometres north of Glatz on the east side of the Eulen mountains.[104] This was where the Schwenkfeldian-oriented pastor Erasmus Weichenhan worked from around 1538 until his death in 1598.[105] From his pen came the sermon collection which the ''physician'' and botanist Martin John Jr., the most significant Schwenkfelder in the seventeenth century, published in 1672 on the press of Abraham Lichtenthaler[106] in Sulzbach under the pseudonym Matthias Israel,[107] ''to show those who had strayed from the truth back to the right way by the cooperating power of Christ's Spirit, to encourage those who sleep, and to strengthen the true faithful, who have the living Word of God in their hearts, by instruction in the truth.''[108] In this collection, which was the most important devotional companion next to Werner's work for the Silesian Schwenkfelders, Christology no longer stood at the center as it did in Schwenckfeld and Crautwald; an interest in the new man was now emphasized. Weichenhan was convinced that this new man arose not through the external word and sacraments[109] but rather through a continuous spiritual partaking of the deified flesh of Christ. ''For, as physical food has import for the human nature,'' he wrote, ''giving the body power, vitality, strength, ability, and life, so Christ (the food), with his transfigured flesh in God, has import for the soul of the believer, giving him consolation and life, peace and joy, and devours the lusts and desires of this same carnal man so that he no longer is what he earlier was, so that one can see from his life that he has become a new man.''[110]This shift of accent from Christology to soteriology is likely to be found in the influence of the mysticism of Tauler as well, whom Weichenhan cites frequently in his sermons.[111]

The persecution in the Bober-Katzbach mountains ended about 1600, in all likelihood because with the deaths of Martin John Sr. and Antonius Oelsner and the continuing criticism of the Glatz Schwenkfelders, further radicalization was prevented. Moreover, Caspar von Mauschwitz, the landlord of Harpersdorf and Armenruh, unlike his father before him, tolerated the Schwenkfelders,[112] and correctly pointed out that they were obedient to the political authorities.[113]

While the activity of the political authorities against the Schwenkfelders appears inconceivable to modern eyes, it was nothing compared to the imperial law of April 23, 1529 in which all those who did not baptize their children were considered Anabaptists and were to be executed. That this law was not used with rigor in Silesia is probably a result of the fact that Silesia was a secondary land of the crown of Bohemia, and thus the Silesian princes wished to demonstrate their sovereign rights over religious matters.

Even during the Thirty Years' War the Schwenkfelder communities, with the exception of those under the landlord of Langneundorf, Johann von Nimptsch,[114] were not persecuted. Both religious and political authorities were hindered in such efforts by the war. Silesia was not a primary theatre of war although imperial and Protestant union troops marched through regularly, particularly in the Bober-Katzbach mountain area.[115] Especially disastrous was the march of the 20,000-man army under Wallenstein in 1626/27[116] The protocol[117] of the peace commission in April 1654 indicate how seriously the population was decimated in the war and how seriously its economy had been affected. According to the statements of Martin John Jr., even during this period the Schwenkfelders held conventicles in the Bober-Katzbach mountains with fellow believers who fled there from the county of Glatz[118] —particularly from Mittelwalde.[119] Apparently they even received official permission to do so by Georg Rudolf of Liegnitz-Wohlau, who converted to Calvinism in 1614.[120] During this time they were twice visited[121] by the anti-clerical politico-apocalyptic publicist Ludwig Frederick Gifftheil,[122] a Swabian who had had a fleeting attachment with the last Schwenkfelders in his homeland during his youth[123] He visited Georg III of Brieg and Georg Rudolf of Liegnitz-Wohlau in order to advise them "no longer to strengthen the beast, namely, no longer to support the false prophet."[124] To the Schwenkfelders he declared that "he brought them nothing new, had never found witness to the truth purer; but they ought to live according to it, and if persecutions should come, remain steadfast."[125]

Immediately after the Treaty of Westphalia in 1648, a second period of persecution began for the Schwenkfelders; it lasted until 1657/58. Of primary impetus was the religious-political situation in Silesia after the Treaty of Westphalia.[126] The Habsburg monarchy denied certain religious freedoms of its Protestant citizens, freedoms which had been granted by the emperor to the hereditary principalities by treaty—the right to emigrate and to build a number of new churches.[127] As authorized by the six articles of the peace treaty, it now worked forcibly toward the recatholicization of the principalities of Breslau, Glogau, Schweidnitz-Jauer, Münsterberg, Oppeln-Ratibor, and Teschen,[128] which had begun earlier. Therefore, the principalities of Liegnitz, Brieg, and Wohlau saw themselves responsible to uphold their own church order and thus oppose the Hapsburg intention of making Silesia a purely Catholic, centrally-controlled land. At the same time many Schwenkfelders strengthened their opposition to infant baptism and to any ties with the Lutheran church.[129] Referring to the Scriptures and the practice of adult baptism in the early church,[130] they contended that the belief that infant baptism mediated salvation was an "abomination before God, a devastation of Christ's congregation, a rejection of the mystery of baptism,. . . the beginning of popery, . . . a basis of all error and ignorance in the congregation of Christ, and a destruction of all Godliness.''[131] Therefore, the local Lutheran pastors, especially Martin Pohl[132] of Neuford at Gröditzberg, Melchior Cupius[133] of Harpersdorf, Johann Rathmann[134] of Zobten, and Ehrhard Hubrig[135] of Deutmannsdorf and Hartliebsdorf, petitioned their landlords to punish their Schwenkfelder subjects. They also attacked them in their sermons[136] and funeral orations.[137] These landlords, especially Sigismund von Braun, owner of Zobten, Hohndorf, Langneundorf, and Petersdorf, Sigmund von Mauschwitz, landlord of Nieder-Harpersdorf, and Barbara III Bolkowskin, abbess of Trebnitz, the only Cistercian convent in Silesia to which Deutmannsdorf and Hartliebsdorf belonged,[138] did in fact move against them with imprisonment[139] and exile,[140] forbade them shelter,[141] confiscated books,[142] and levied fines against them.[143]

On the death of Georg Rudolf on January 14, 1653 an organized persecution—unlike the earlier short and localized actions—was set in motion in the principality of Liegnitz by his three nephews: Georg III, Christian, and Ludwig IV.[144] The principality of Liegnitz was initially ruled by these three nephews corporately. This persecution was obviously part of a preparation for a general church visitation,[145] which was to make possible the renewal of the Lutheran church after the Thirty Years' War.[146] In Lent of that year the Schwenkfelders were conscripted by ducal decree and a number of Schwenkfelders were seized and brought before the Lutheran consistory in Liegnitz[147] for a hearing to which Lutheran pastors had been summoned. Since the Schwenkfelders were not prepared to recant, their leaders Balthasar Jäckel and Georg Heydrich were placed in the stocks and the rest condemned to hard labor in the Liegnitz castle.[148] Nevertheless, eight weeks later they were freed with the order either to emigrate within six weeks or to return to the Lutheran church.[149] Meanwhile, they had heard that the prince of Anhalt, probably Johann Kasimir (or his son Johann Georg von Anhalt-Dessau), while on a visit to Brieg had spoken up for them, and they asked him whether it would be possible to settle in Modelsdorf, which was his property.[150] However, this plan came to naught. When the six weeks passed without their return to the Lutheran church or their voluntary emigration, they were ordered to leave the land.[151] They immediately protested and declared that the Lutheran pastors had not been able to find them in error; moreover, they insisted that the Lutheran accounts about them were false.[152] Following this, occasional hearings were held and sentences for shorter terms of imprisonment were handed down.[153] However, the order of expulsion was not executed,[154] probably because of the impending division of the three principalities among the three nephews.

A year later—in the spring of 1654—Ludwig IV, who was the only ruler of Liegnitz now, had the leading Schwenkfelders Balthasar Jäckel, Georg Heydrich, and Melchior Günther imprisoned once again and issued a general prohibition of assembly.[155] Since the order was ignored by the Schwenkfelders, five more of their members, among them Martin John Jr., were imprisoned. Hereupon the remaining Schwenkfelders ceased their gatherings, allowed their children to be baptized, their marriages to be blessed in the church, and some even converted to the Lutheran church.[156] The duke was apparently satisfied with this and gradually released the prisoners; the last to be freed was Balthasar Jäckel in June or July of 1658. He was given permission to remain in the principality.[157]

In comparison, the persecution of Schwenkfelders in the principality of Schweidnitz-Jauer was shorter and much lighter. The imprisoned Schwenkfelders were freed and allowed to continue living in the principality.[158] The reason for this was that in April 1654 the imperial commission which was passing military protection through Schweidnitz and Jauer—which was directly subject to the emperor in order to restore it to Roman Catholicism—arrived also in the area where Schwenkfelders lived.[159] It seized all the Protestant churches, confiscated church property and expelled those Lutheran pastors who had not already fled. With the opposition to the Schwenkfelders as well now driven out, they were able to live according to their religious convictions undisturbed until the arrival of the Jesuit mission in 1719. In the extant sources there is only one indication that in 1657 the abbess of the Cistercian convent of Trebnitz, Dorothea I. Bninskin, in an effort to force their conversion,[160] threatened to expel her Schwenkfelder subjects in Deutmannsdorf and Hartliebsdorf who did not attend the Lord's Supper.

For somewhat more than half a century the Schwenkfelders enjoyed peace in the principality of Liegnitz. The pastors there were far too involved with other matters to begin a controversy. Protestants from the principalities of Schweidnitz and Jauer flocked into their churches close to the border by the thousands;[161] this "great church migration" decreased only after 1707. On August 22 of that year Joseph I and Karl XII came to an agreement in the Altranstädter Convention[162] in which the emperor permitted the erection of six "grace" churches in addition to the three "peace" churches in Schweidnitz, Jauer, and Glogau, which had already been permitted: in Sagan, Freystadt, Militsch, Landeshut, Teschen, and Hirschberg. Secondly, this was a peaceful time for the Schwenkfelders because of certain landlords who were inclined toward them, as for example the widowed Hedwig von Mauschwitz, nee von Redern.[163] Finally, it is relevant that the principalities of Liegnitz, Brieg, and Wohlau—at the death of the last duke of the dynasty, Georg Wilhelm, on November 21, 1675—were returned to the crown of Bohemia as a fief and became Catholic territories. As a result, Lutheran pastors had to avoid drawing the attention of the Catholic authorities to themselves and therefore had to be satisfied merely with occasionally attacking the Schwenkfelders in sermons. Thus it was said that the Harpersdorf pastor Frederick Schröer Jr.,[164] in his funeral oration for the Schwenkfelder Susanne Dietrich (d. May 10, 1700), placed her among the foolish virgins (Matthew 25:1-13).[165]

Outward peace was combined with a severe inner crisis for the Schwenkfelders who were still tolerated or protected by local landlords.[166] An increasing number gave up their struggle for ethical perfection and radical opposition to the Lutheran church. Unhesitatingly, they participated fully in the social life of their villages,[167] allowed themselves to be married by Lutheran pastors, had their children baptized, and occasionally attended Lutheran worship services.[168] Many gave up their own confession completely and converted to Lutheranism.[169] No longer did they gather "alone in one place"[170] but were content with private reading of their devotional literature.[171] When they did meet in conventicles it was no longer in the strict manner of earlier times. Martin John Jr., for example complained bitterly about this: "When our loving forefathers met, they held Christian conversations; now, however, we chatter about useless worldly matters when we come together. . . . Earlier faithful pious Christians prayed throughout the night and worshipped, but now we can hardly endure for one hour. . . . After singing in an orderly fashion our loving fathers shared their thoughts with one another on how one thing or the other was to be understood; now our words, after the singing, are of carnal concerns. Some even talk and make plans during the singing. All of this is a sign that their hearts are not pure and that they are very little concerned with the singing."[172]

Nevertheless, there was a small circle of Schwenkfelders who held firm to the tradition under the leadership of the farmer Balthasar Jäckel of Harpersdorf, the "physician" and botanist[173] Martin John Jr.[174] of Hockenau, and the "practitioner of medicine"[175] Georg Hauptmann of Lauterseiffen.[176] In contrast to their forefathers, they did not insist on exclusiveness.[177] They were in contact both personally and by letter with Anabaptists, spiritualists, and Pietists. At times these associations were initiated by these groups themselves and sometimes by the Schwenkfelders, particularly by the intellectually active Martin John Jr.

In the fall of 1658, the year in which the second period of general Schwenkfelder persecution ended, the Schwenkfelders were visited by Christoph Baumhauer,[178] the Hutterite preacher from Sabatisch,[179] a Slovakian village close to the Moravian border.[180] With this Anabaptist emissary,[181] who was on a missionary journey to East Prussia, they held discussions and read the literature[182] he had brought with him.[183] They determined, according to a letter by Balthasar Jäckel, dated October 19, 1658 to the Hutterites in Grosschützen,[184] that "the two communities were of one mind on many important points, such as the order and practice of baptism and the Lord's Supper."[185] From this it is evident that they no longer held to Schwenckfeld's and Crautwald's spiritualism, but like the Anabaptists had adopted a literal understanding of the sacraments. They continued to correspond with the Hutterites for a long time after Baumhauer's visit but only the initial letter and the answer to it are extant.[186] Balthasar Hoffmann, one of the two Schwenkfelder delegates at the court in Vienna to petition against the Jesuit mission, traveled to Grosschützen in October 1725 when he heard of the persecution the Anabaptists had suffered there. The details of what he heard were reported to the Mennonites in Amsterdam in a letter from the Schwenkfelders on October 16, 1725.[187]

At about this time the Schwenkfelders became acquainted with some of the other famous proponents of mystical spirituality of the seventeenth century through the good offices of the Breslau embellisher Johann Georg Schüller. In 1657/58 Schüller had sent them several writings[188] along with two letters from Paul Felgenhauer, an author influenced by Schwenckfeld, Valentin Weigel, and Jacob Boehme.[189] In their answer,[190] in which they enclosed a confession of faith,[191] they praised Felgenhauer as a colleague in battle who was also striving "against the creaturists,"[192] and who taught the uncreated humanity of Christ as indicated in his *The Palm Tree of Faith and Truth.* However, they expressed their concern that he understood something different than they did, namely that Christ already possessed his celestial humanity in his preexistence and brought it with him as he took the form of a servant.[193] When they saw the difference between their Christology and his,[194] as expressed in his tripartite work *The Secret of the Lord's Temple* which Schüller had sent them, they broke off all association with him. They also could not accept his rejection of the doctrine of original sin,[195] his doctrine of purgatory,[196] and his modalistic trinitarianism.[197] On October 19, 1658 Balthasar Jäckel, then a senior member of the Schwenkfelders, wrote to Schüller, "Because the errors are so many in Felgenhauer's books and tracts, I have decided (as a layman) not to write to him any longer and commit him to God."[198]

About a decade later, likely again through Schüller, the Schwenkfelders became acquainted with Christian Hoburg's *Mystical Postils on the Evangelists* and other writings.[199] Hoburg had been converted to spiritualism[200] in Lauenburg in the mid 1630s by reading Schwenckfeld's tracts, especially *The Heavenly Balm.*[201] Convinced by Hoburg's writings that they were in theological agreement with him, they began to correspond with him. Already in his first letter to Hoburg, who was then a reformed pastor in Latum near Zutphen, Martin John Jr. wrote enthusiastically, "We, here in Silesia, have not known a teacher who has led us in the narrow way of the cross for almost ninety years now; we thought that there were no more until writings from your country came our way."[202] They also asked him if he had known of any fellow believers. In a letter of April 10, 1668[203] he named Frederick Breckling, then pastor of Zwolle, but complained that Breckling "still clung closely to his Luther."[204]

These ties of friendship with famous spiritualists were strengthened when Martin John Jr. and his bride Ursula traveled with Hans Meurer (who already had personal contacts in Amsterdam) to western Germany and Holland in the spring of 1669.[205] The journey was probably financed by honoraria gained "because of his medical care which had made him known in many places."[206] First he journeyed to Bamberg where he stayed over Easter and probably visited Georg Geelmann,[207] the "chief" of the Weigelians[208] at Bamberg. Geelmann had been expelled from Nürnberg in 1646[209] but had been received by the open-minded prince bishop Melchior Otto Voit of Salzburg in Bamberg.[210] John had originally wished to go to Nürnberg,[211] but turned instead via Frankfurt on the Main and Cologne to Latum, where Christian Hoburg was pastor. Hoburg wed John and his bride.[212] For a week and a half they remained in Amsterdam. Amsterdam was a center of religious individualists and heterogeneous groups at this time. Here John visited Johann Georg Gichtel,[213] who probably introduced him to Frederick Breckling, Johann Amos Comenius, the Dutch chiliast Petrus Serarius, and others. He traveled home via Bremen, Hamburg, Lüneburg, Magdeburg, and Leipzig.[214]

As a result of this journey, a correspondence, which is, however, only partially extant, developed between John Jr. and Hoburg,[215] Breckling,[216] Gichtel,[217] Geelmann,[218] as well as others in Amsterdam.[219] He was also acquainted with their publications, which these spiritualists occasionally added to their letters. The conservative Schwenkfelders observed this activity with great mistrust.[220] While they basically rejected the writing of Breckling, who was still too closely allied to Lutheranism and not yet in full agreement with Schwenckfeld,[221] they characteristically criticized Hoburg, on the other hand, for directing too much attention to the development of the inner man and paying no attention to moral actions.[222] They proclaimed, "The old writings, the old writings are correct."[223] Finally the greater part of the Schwenkfelders broke off with Martin John Jr. Of this, Georg Weiss,[224] later the first preacher among the Schwenkfelders who emigrated to Pennsylvania, wrote retrospectively in 1732: "When there was no contact between him [John Jr.] and us, he immersed himself in correspondence with various foreign friends so as to have Christian and kind communication; a call went out from there as if a flare went up, and the truth came clean to light as if one had never heard the truth before. Therefore he acquired the books of many of them which were then being published, such as those of Jacob Bomen [Boehme], Doctor [Johann Wilhelm] Petersen, Hiel [Immanuel, pseudonym for Heinrich Jansen von Barreveldt], [Jane] Lead, and others.''[225] Unfortunately, it is no longer possible to ascertain where he acquired the books of Boehme or those of the Philadelphian Society, which most of the Schwenkfelders rejected as philosophic speculation.[226] Perhaps they came through the Silesian Boehme circle, to which many physicians[227] belonged, or direct from Amsterdam where Gichtel and Allard de Raedt edited an eleven-volume edition of Boehme starting in 1682[228] with the support of the mayor Coenraad van Beuningen. It is striking that in the later correspondence between John Jr. and Gichtel actual theosophic problems are hardly touched upon, though Gichtel had introduced him to the writings of Boehme, the *philosophus teutonicus*.[229]

Martin John Jr. got to know some followers of Boehme personally. The most significant of these was Hilarius Prache,[230] who was pastor in Goldberg from Easter 1662. First a Weigelian, Prache later turned to Boehme and was an enthusiastic defender of the Cabbala.[231] As an ''incomparable lover of the books of fanatics''[232] he edited Jedaja Peninis' *Bakkasha* (*Desire*), Ahron ben Samuel's *Nishmat Adam* (*Breath of Adam*), and the *Bechinat Olam* (*Eternal Test*) with Latin translations and comments.[233] In March 1669 he voluntarily resigned his only very laxly run pastorate after several controversies with his fellow pastors, which he partly had initiated, and attached himself to the Schwenkfelders more closely. Shortly before he emigrated to London in 1674 together with his son-in-law Johann Georg Matern,[234] a teacher in Goldberg —in London both joined the Quakers[235]—he spent time with Martin John Jr. in Laubgrund and later with Georg Hauptmann in Lauterseiffen. It is interesting that John rejected any speculation about the millenium,[236] a subject of much interest to many theosophists at the time ''since one had no certainty and did not know if one understood the Scriptures correctly.''[237] He wished to hold to the words of Jesus rather than to the Revelation of John.[238] He searched for the kingdom of God only in himself.[239]

While most of the Schwenkfelders rejected theosophy and mystical spiritualism, they readily associated with the Pietists who had an early influence in Silesia. Obviously the Schwenkfelders were of the opinion that Pietism was like their own theological system in many ways, particularly in its demands for the vanquishing of sin through a new birth and in its emphasis on ethical renewal. Their first important contact with the Pietists came around 1690 when they sent two delegates—one of them probably G. Hauptmann—to Philipp Jacob Spener, who as the senior preacher at the court in Dresden was then the most powerful ecclesiastical authority in Protestant Germany,[240] to gain from him a recognition of their conventicles. This seemed to be possible since in the Pietist controversies in Leipzig a year before, where Spener had also been involved, there was also a question of the acceptance of conventicles. Spener did not completely condemn their criticism of the church since the Lutheran pastors had brought it on themselves by their conduct. On the contrary, however, he totally condemned their separatism as Johann Christoph Schwedler, pastor of Nieder-Wiese reported to August Hermann Francke on April 15, 1720.[241] Furthermore, Spener expressed the hope "that they might return from their false paths and separations to us as a body or one by one, if in our Protestant church more improvements occur and more preachers begin to commit themselves more earnestly to the work of the Lord in their congregations, so that the [Schwenkfelders] see powerful teaching and uplifting order in the congregations."[242]

Since 1695 the Schwenkfelders were also indirectly in touch with Francke through the theological candidate Achatius Frederick Roscius. Apparently Roscius originally wished to be a Schwenkfelder pastor, but the Schwenkfelders declined this since they believed that Christ himself must gather his scattered church before it would be allowed to call pastors, in accordance with Ezekiel 34.[243] They were also convinced that the Roman Catholic political authorities would oppose the appointment of a Schwenkfelder pastor even as they had opposed the appointment of a Lutheran pastor in the principality of Schweidnitz-Jauer.[244] They would only bring "death and persecution upon themselves without the will of God."[245] Roscius finally found a place as teacher in Halle[246] in 1695 and continued to correspond from there with the Schwenkfelders and conveyed kind regards from Francke.[247] Later Johann Christoph Schwedler,[248] a sympathizer with Francke and pastor at Nieder-Wiesa, 44 kilometres from Harpersdorf, the center of the Schwenkfelder communities, undertook a similar intermediary role.[249] The Schwenkfelders themselves never had direct contact with Francke, probably because his Pietism had a distinct ecclesiastical character.

It was through Johann Wilhelm Petersen that they came to know radical Pietism. Petersen visited them in 1707-1708 during his journey to Silesia, and associated especially with Hauptmann in Lauterseiffen and John Jr. in Laubgrund.[250] On the theological differences between them, Petersen remarked that even in him and among his followers "there are some ideas which could not stand before divine judgment. They are to be tolerated, not persecuted. On Doomsday, a different judgment will be held from what we expect."[251]

Historically by far the most significant personal contact for the Schwenkfelders, as will be demonstrated, was that with Nicolaus Ludwig von Zinzendorf, first made in the summer of 1723 during the time of the Jesuit mission. This is mentioned here only because it relates to the present topic.

As a result of these friendly contacts with Pietists, many Schwenkfelders began attending the services of the pietistically-oriented pastors Johann Christoph Schwedler in Nieder-Wiesa, Daniel Schneider in Goldberg,[252] and Johann Sturm in Adelsdorf (later in Probsthain).[253] They allowed these men to perform marriages among them and to baptize their children. In their conventicles they no longer read only the works of Schwenckfeld, Crautwald, Werner, Hiller, and Weichenhan but now also Pietistic writings, such as those of Christian Gerberg.[254] Despite the personal and literary connections to the Pietists and general theological agreement, they did not fall in with the Pietists. Spener had earlier noted[255] that the reason for this was their radical separatist stance, which had made them an independent movement.

2. *The Theological Foundations of Later Schwenkfeldianism*

The theology of later Schwenkfeldianism cannot be described here in full detail since such a project would take us beyond our primary goal. Only the basic structure can be given to indicate how far later Schwenkfeldianism continued, modified, or gave up the theological position of Schwenckfeld and Crautwald. At the center of the theology of these men was their Christology; consequently, they described themselves as "confessors of the glory of Christ." On the other hand, soteriology, from which Christology had been conceived, was of secondary importance. This emphasis changed after the middle of the sixteenth century; soteriology moved into the middle of their theology.

Schwenkfelders almost exclusively concentrated their attention on the birth and development of the new man now. "We must," wrote Hans Christoph Seibt on New Year's Day, 1703, in an epistle to his fellow believers, "concern ourselves with the source of the new man, where he receives his nourishment, strength, and growth, what his food, drink, clothing, and adornments should be; indeed, who his father and mother are and where he goes to school."[1] The new man arises, according to their belief, only through the new birth. But this does not occur through the external word or the sacrament,[2] since these can neither contain nor mediate salvation but only point to it.[3] To support this interpretation, they cited the Scriptures, especially the Johannine writings,[4] and only occasionally cited a few quotations from the Fathers. Of some importance for them was the Augustinian phrase: "Why do you prepare your teeth and stomach? Believe, and you have eaten."[5] Above all, their argument was with the practical syllogism. Thus, for example, Christoph Oelsner wrote: "The pastors are decidedly in error when they say that if a child is externally baptized he is a Christian and born anew. Grant God this were so! But, alas, this is not the case! If children, through the external waters of baptism attained to the new birth and were freed from original sin, one might rightly ask, why are youth so very sinful and lacking in virtue?''[6] The principal argument Schwenckfeld and Crautwald used against the means of grace—the philosophical principle that similar things use similar means—is markedly missing.

In all of later Schwenkfeldianism they were convinced that the new man arises in the new birth from God alone, without any outward means, through the spiritual consumption of the deified flesh of Christ.[7] In this way they went back to Schwenckfeld's Christological premises but only insofar as these were useful to describe the deification of man. Like Schwenckfeld they taught that the preexistent Christ received in his incarnation a qualitatively better human nature than that of mankind descending from Adam since God is not only the Father of the divine but also of the human nature of Christ.[8] Secondly, their argument rested on the expression of the Apostles' Creed, ''born of the virgin.'' ''Christ was begotten in a different housing,'' wrote Martin John Jr., ''not in a woman, but in a pious, pure, and mild virgin.''[9] The humanity of Christ was, according to the Schwenkfelders, progressively deified during the state of humiliation, finding its apex in the resurrection and the ascension.[10] Nevertheless, in this process of deification the human nature of Christ ''was neither exterminated nor changed into the divine nature, just as the divine nature was not given up in the incarnation, but his human nature was improved and assumed divine properties.''[11] The deified humanity of the exalted Christ now possesses the same properties as his divine nature.[12] The humanity of Christ ''was not bestowed with the heavenly power or in the sense of receiving it as a gift, or like a bridegroom makes the possessions of his father hereditary to his bride, but rather the humanity of Christ received the heavenly reign by birth, by its birth from God, since God the Father is the natural father of the human nature of Christ.''[13] The Schwenkfelders thus rejected the orthodox Lutheran teaching on the ''communication of idioms.''

This idea of deification made it possible for them to interpret the image of God as participation in the divine nature. By spiritual consumption of the deified humanity of Christ man receives, according to Martin John Jr. ''access to God, as [Christ] draws all faithful hearts to himself, like a magnet draws steel.''[14] This formulation did not originate from John Jr. himself, but is a quotation from Tauler's third sermon on the ascension of Christ.[15]

This spiritual consumption is of course bound neither to the external word nor to the sacrament, since ''the soul's food, the flesh of Christ, is not to be found in external sacramental bread.''[16] The Schwenkfelders attempted to prove this first from the Scriptures; according to their tradition, they pointed to John 6.[17] Besides that they attempted to find new proofs from Scripture, pointing out that Judas, although present at the Last Supper, was damned (John 13:27). On the other hand, the thief on the cross (Luke 23:43) was saved without having taken the sacrament.[18] Moreover, they quoted Augustine, with a quotation which is put together from two different passages in his commentary on John.[19] "Why do you prepare your tooth and stomach? Believe, and you have eaten. To believe in him is to eat the bread of life. He who believes in him has already eaten him."[20] They did not take this directly from Augustine but possibly from Gratian's *Decretum,* where this formulation is found[21] although the citation was also common in Lutheran and Calvinist literature.

To receive the new birth man must first be purified; he must be "salted throughout with the salt of the sufferings of Christ."[22] In this way the inferior powers, the concupiscent, irascible, and imaginative powers, are mortified.[23] After this, he is "to lift up his heart and look upon himself to find out whether the voice of the caller can be heard or whether the divine murmur can be perceived."[24] Secondly, he must walk the path of illumination which leads to the new birth. At this point God "bears Christ in the soul and washes it with the blood of Christ. . . pours in a new, willing spirit, directing the heart, mind, and soul so that all joy, love, and desire is turned toward God. In sum: a completely new man grows inwardly; this is the new birth."[25]

The realization of the new man, which is achieved progressively, is evident, above all, in ethical perfection. The new-born man conquers "one sin after the other" and strides from "one virtue to the other."[26] Special emphasis was placed on the rejection of all worldly life. Taverns, amusements and fairs were to be completely avoided,[27] since they were only visited "for the sake of carnal lust and amusement," "eating and drinking," and "gossip about worldly success and failure, temporal goods, money and riches."[28] Referring to Augustine, another demand was made for sexual continence between married partners. Hiller wrote in one of his sermons: "Those are not alone adulterers who sin outside their own marriage bond, but husbands and wives are adulterers as well if they love each other only for impure desires, for as Augustine says: he who loves his wife only out of impurity, is an adulterer with his own wife."[29] And B. Heydrich went so far as to write: "Saint Augustine says: A husband who loves his wife with too passionate an affection is an adulterer in the eyes of God."[30] They were convinced that this ascetic life could not be carried out without separation from society. For support they referred to the Scriptures, Jeremiah 51:45 for example, where God demands that the people of God flee from Babylon.[31] Almost all the Schwenkfelders around Harpersdorf, in contrast to those in the county of Glatz, followed this demand and very seldom took public office, such as that of a constable or a lay assessor. Almost never in their letters or writings, did they treat political, cultural, or economic matters. They praised the return to the inner life in words sometimes reminiscent of those of the late medieval mystics. Balthasar Hoffmann, for example, wrote on September 16, 1723 from the splendor of eighteenth century Vienna to his family: "My beloved, how noble is humility and how vain is pride. Blessed is the man who is able to spend his life in simplicity and knows nothing of pomposity, even if he be held in contempt. All desires, all amusements, all delights, all beauties, all adornments, all playing of stringed instruments, in short everything which in the world serves for the pleasure of the flesh, is vain."[32] Often Schwenkfelder statements concerning the ethical behavior of the new man came close to perfectionism, although they always sought to guard against this. Thus Martin John Jr. wrote in his exposition of the parable of the wheat and the tares (Matthew 13:24-30): "It is not to be denied that the faithful still have shortcomings and infirmities among themselves."[33]

The switch of theological interest from Christology to soteriology is due to the influence of late medieval mysticism, mystical spiritualism, and Pietism. The influences of Tauler[34] and of mystical spiritualism[35] are found, particularly, in the idea of participation in the divine nature. For both, salvation is a substantial participation in the Godhead. While the Schwenkfelders learned about these concepts indirectly through Hiller and Weichenhan, they were directly confronted with the complex ideas of mystical spiritualism. Besides this, especially later, came the Pietist influence with its striving to overcome sin, its esteem for the practise of piety, and its emphasis on morals. Pietism came to them not so much through the theological writings of that movement as through its biographical writings. Among other such books they read Christian Gerber's *History of the New-Born Men in Saxony*, Gottfried Arnold's *Impartial History of Church and Heresy*, and Frederick Breckling's *Catalogue of Witnesses to the Truth after Luther.*

3. *The Schwenkfelders and the Jesuit Mission*

Until the beginning of the 18th century, the Schwenkfelders were suppressed almost exclusively by Lutheran pastors and their landlords. Only after 1719, with the establishment of the Jesuit mission in Harpersdorf, for the purpose of converting them to the Catholic faith, were the Schwenkfelders persecuted by the Roman Catholic Church as well.[1] Around the turn of the eighteenth century, the Catholic Church and its authorities were made aware of the Schwenkfelder communities by several events. First, in 1698 a dissertation on Silesian radicals was published by Gottlieb Liefmann, in which he also treated the Schwenkfelders.[2] Secondly, from 1700 to 1702 a bitter controversy raged in Goldberg, centered around the Pietist pastor Daniel Schneider,[3] who had been sympathetic towards the Schwenkfelders. The controversy was also followed with interest outside Silesia. Thirdly, after 1701 the first German theological periodical, *Altes und Neues aus dem Schatz theologischer Wissenschaft* (*Old and New Things from the Treasury of Theology*), later published under the title of *Unschuldige Nachrichten von alten und neuen theologischen Sachen* (*Innocent Reports on Old and New Theological Matters*), contained numerous treatments of Schwenckfeld and his followers.[4] On October 11, 1708, the Hungarian Samuel Zelenka disputed at the University of Wittenberg with the famous Lutheran theologian Valentin Ernst Löscher presiding, on the theme *Schwenkfeldianism Reborn in Pietism*.[5] Above all, a number of Silesian Lutheran pastors, especially Johann Samuel Neander[6] from Harpersdorf, sought support from the royal authorities in Liegnitz[7] for their help in the practice of their parochial rights over the Schwenkfelders.

These were the causes leading to the establishment of the Jesuit mission. The immediate occasion was a report that Schwenkfeldianism "was making inroads among commoners and especially among the peasants."[8] Schwenckfeld's followers "went to no church and obeyed no clerical authority,[9] [because] they hold the erroneous opinion that each man is his own priest, along with countless other absurd ideas."[10] The vicar-general of Breslau turned to the Liegnitz archdeacon Christoph Mayer[11] in order to get more detailed information[12] Since "in the principality of Liegnitz there were Schwenkfelders only in this or that Lutheran parish,"[13] the matter was passed over to the archpriest of Lähn,[14] Johann Karl Alberti, "in whose district most of the Schwenkfelders"[15] lived, so that he could make further investigations "with the help of his parochial clergy."[16] After their reports had arrived, all of them emphasizing the industrious and reclusive nature of the Schwenkfelders,[17] Christoph Mayer sent these reports to the vicar-general of Breslau[18] on July 15, 1717. The vicar-general passed them on to the Royal Upper Council at Breslau on August 3.[19] The council at Breslau then ordered the Royal Council at Jauer on August 20—the Royal government at Liegnitz had already given its information on the Schwenkfelders living in Lutheran parishes there on July 7[20]—to investigate how many Schwenkfelders lived[21] in the area of Jauer.[22] The Royal Council at Jauer turned to the royal court in Löwenberg,[23] which returned the information requested on September 7.[24] The council at Jauer then reported to the upper council in Breslau.[25] On consultation with the vicar-general, the upper council reported to the emperor on February 7, 1718, recommending that the Schwenkfelder leaders be banished and the other Schwenkfelders threatened with a similar fate if they did not convert to the Roman Catholic Church.[26] Only two weeks later Karl VI gave his consent,[27] and on March 15 the Royal Council at Jauer was ordered to question the Schwenkfelders living within its jurisdiction.[28] A similar order must have reached the royal government in Liegnitz, for an investigation began there on May 19, 1718;[29] it was carried out in a friendly manner.[30] Finally, the Schwenkfelders were requested to submit their confession of faith and their most significant writings for examination. They complied a week later on May 25, 1718,[31] and submitted—together with a covering letter[32]—their devotional materials[33] and their confession of faith.[34] Johann Milan rightly noted that they now formulated their Christology more carefully.[35] On the other hand, Jauer first held its investigation in October only after repeated demands;[36] the Schwenkfelders from the villages of Zobten, Langneundorf, and Lauterseiffen were called before the Royal Council. The council then sent a report to the Royal Upper Council on October 29[37] and November 2.[38]

On December 22, 1718 the Royal Council in Breslau—informed in the meantime by the vicar-general that the the conversion of the Schwenkfelders could not be achieved by the local parish but only by a religious order[39]—reported to Karl VI on the interrogations and the projected mission of a religious order.[40] In his answer Karl agreed in principle to the establishment of a mission[41] but demanded detailed information as to which order could be trusted to carry it out and the cost per annum. The vicar-general recommended the Jesuits[42] and the Royal Upper Council consented to the proposal. This is evident from the third report to the emperor on April 16, 1719.[43] Karl once again consented[44] with the stipulation that it "be only a temporary mission, as long as it be found useful and necessary."[45] In addition to detailed instructions for the missionaries, he demanded a further report on the proposed direction of the mission.[46] Only when this had been submitted was a decree issued on September 16, 1719[47] establishing the Jesuit mission in Harpersdorf under the 57-year-old Johann Milan[48] and the 30-year-old Karl Xavier Regent.[49] On St. Thomas Day the missionaries, bearing a license from the bishop of Breslau, began their work among the 1200 to 1500 Schwenkfelders.[50] Following their instructions, they immediately invited the Schwenkfelders to voluntary disputations[51] in order to win them over to the Catholic faith. Although a general rescript had been issued by the Royal Upper Council,[52] expressly forbidding anyone, under the threat of punishment, "to put obstacles into the way [of the missionaries] or to hinder their clerical duties by any means, but rather to assist and promote them in case of necessity,"[53] the order was neglected by the Lutheran landlords, especially by the senior landlord of the principality of Liegnitz, Otto Konrad von Hohberg, owner of Zobten and other villages, Ernst Konrad von Braun, owner of Armenruh,

Harpersdorf, and Ober-Langneundorf, and also by the office of the bailiff of Siebeneichen.[54] These instead tried to fill the Schwenkfelders with fear of the Jesuits, thereby persuading many of them to receive the Lord's Supper from the hands of Johann S. Neander in order to be regarded as members of the Lutheran Church.[55] Consequently Neander[56] and all the other Lutheran pastors of the principality of Liegnitz,[57] and also the local Lutheran landlords,[58] were forbidden to admit Schwenkfelders to the Lutheran communion. The emperor belatedly confirmed this order by a rescript, dated March 14, 1720.[59]

However, when Milan and Regent found that, despite the greatest of efforts, they had only been able to achieve a few conversions after one year, the Schwenkfelders in the principalities of Schweidnitz-Jauer were informed on May 16, 1721 that even their attendance at Lutheran worship was forbidden. On the other hand, their participation at disputations with the Jesuits was made an obligation and their unexcused absence would be punishable.[60] While the priests expected greater success from this action, it was not forthcoming. By circulating an invitation list they ordered between twenty and forty Schwenkfelders to take part in religious disputations,[61] which took place in Langneundorf and Lauterseiffen on Sundays. But these orders were disobeyed by most of them,[62] since the Jesuits hesitated to levy the threatened fine. On September 7, 1721, for example, only three of the sixteen Schwenkfelders summoned from Niederlangneundorf and fifteen of the twenty-six summoned from Oberlangneundorf attended the disputation.[63]

In spring of 1721 the Schwenkfelders finally sent their own delegations to the court at Vienna to seek religious toleration,[64] after a similar plea by Ernst Conrad von Braun had failed.[65] The delegation, which included Christoph Hoffmann, his nephew Balthasar Hoffmann, and briefly also Balthasar Hoffrichter, was able during their lengthy and very expensive stay in Vienna[66] to submit seventeen petitions—unfortunately no longer extant—to the imperial court.[67] However, their pleas for toleration were unsuccessful. Their failure resulted, at least in part, from the fact that the Royal government in Liegnitz, the Royal Council at Jauer, and the Royal Upper Council in Breslau[68] as well as the Jesuit mission,[69] wrote numerous reports against any kind of toleration.

Since the Protestant pastors persisted in their attempt to attract the Schwenkfelders to the Lutheran confession, the Royal Upper Council in Breslau issued a rescript on November 5, 1772[70] forbidding them to administer baptism, marriage, and burial to the Schwenkfelders since, according to the Treaty of Westphalia, they were not one of "the tolerated religions in the empire."[71] The Lutheran pastors and landlords were only to be informed of this order orally so that "no opportunity would exist to spread it around either within or outside the country.''[72]

With this official order, which de facto removed them from the parish, the Schwenkfelders did not feel greatly disturbed insofar as baptism was concerned. They had fought against infant baptism for more than two hundred years and at the time of the Jesuit mission most of them were unbaptized. It must have been in accordance with their own wishes that the Lutheran pastors were forbidden to urge them to be baptized.[73] More problematic for the Schwenkfelders was the fact that they were refused proper church burial even in the principality of Liegnitz and they were being buried in the pastures, as was already the case in the principalities of Jauer, Langneundorf, and Lauterseiffen.[74] Through this they were placed with those who had committed suicide. The later suggestion by Regent that their bodies should not be accompanied either by Lutherans or Schwenkfelder mourners[75] was obviously not accepted. Georg Teschauer, who worked as a Catholic missionary among the Schwenkfelders from 1736 to 1756, described such a burial as follows: ''All the invited people gather with the usual grief at the home of the deceased. The body is laid on a wagon and covered with a white cloth. The closest companion of the deceased sits on the wagon in that great sorrow which is common among them; as proof that the deceased had remained obstinate in his error, the companion is dressed in black. As the body is carried away, the group follows in an orderly manner. After the interment all the people kneel and pray, and this is followed by a short address by the undertaker.''[76] The most serious punishment experienced by the Schwenkfelders was that the Protestant pastors were no longer allowed to bless their marriages in the parish church.[77] Although it was strongly forbidden, they were thus forced (if they did not wish to remain unmarried or have clandestine marriages, which was forbidden by the decree *Tametsi*),[78] to go to nearby Saxony or Brandenburg to be married by Lutheran pastors.[79] The pastor at Nieder-Wiesa, Johann Christoph Schwedler, helped them find pastors who would accommodate them. On April 15, 1723, for example, he sent a Schwenkfelder couple to the Berthelsdorf pastor Johann Andreas Rothe with the request that he bless their marriage or send them on to someone else ''not without a recommendation.''[80]

Milan and Regent not only held disputations and catechism for Schwenkfelder children but carried out an extensive literary activity as well. An anti-Schwenckdeldian tract by Milan was printed in Neisse as early as 1720.[81] In July of that year he published a short tract[82] addressing the Schwenkfelders directly, in which he declared ''that no Lutheran preacher is capable or equipped to lead you Schwenkfelders on the way to eternal salvation since none of them can show or is capable of showing that he has the true Word of God without which no salvation can be hoped for.''[83] Johann Wilhelm Jan, who had taught theology at Wittenberg since 1718, wrote a counterattack at once[84] in which he asserted that the Jesuits would use force in pursuing their mission and "would offer a human word instead of the word of God."[85] Johann Milan responded in a polemical treatise in September 1721,[86] stating, to an extent correctly, that the true persecutors of the Schwenkfelders had been the Lutherans and their landlords. Two years later Jan published yet another retort[87] in which he no longer touched upon the question of who had initiated the persecution. Between 1722 and 1724 Regent published a book in five parts, minutely examining the theology of the Schwenkfelders[88] In 1722 and 1723 he composed an introduction to the Catholic faith for Schwenkfelders;[89] the work was answered by loyal Schwenkfelders with a treatise, no longer extant, entitled *Confession of Faith of the Newly Converted Catholics*.[90] Regent replied to this in 1724[91] and in the same year wrote two further theological works. In the first[92] he attempted to show that the Schwenkfelders could convert with a clear conscience. In the second[93] he attempted to show that the Schwenkfelders had altered many hymns of the already corrupted Moravian hymnal which they used. This corruption should "convince them of their wrong path and apostasy from the very ancient Catholic church."[94] Their opponents were to be made aware that the Schwenkfelder "religious activity and way of life had only the appearance of piety."[95] Besides these, Regent wrote several other short tracts, catechetical works, and manuals of devotion.[96] The extensive literary compositions of Milan and Regent had no effect, however, since they were not concerned with the interests of the Schwenkfelders. The Schwenkfelders were concerned not with dogmatics, but with the realization of the new man.

When the two missionaries realized in 1725 that their extended attempt had been in vain, on January 8 they asked the confessor of Karl VI, Veit Georg Tönnemann, to convince the imperial court that parochial jurisdiction over the Schwenkfelders be given to them so that the conversion might be accomplished more effectively.[97] They were given such jurisdiction by the bishop's administration in Breslau on March 23, 1725.[98] Schwenkfelders were threatened with confiscation of goods and exile if they disobeyed this order.[99] However, it had scarcely been publicized—in Jauer on June 23 and in Liegnitz on July 19[100]—when both Schwenkfelders and Pastor Neander protested.[101] On August 25 and September 5 the Schwenkfelders requested that the status quo be maintained until the emperor had answered the petition of their delegation to Vienna.[102]

The hope of the Jesuits of bringing the Schwenkfelders into the Catholic fold by means of parochial jurisdiction went unfulfilled. With a few exceptions they now openly boycotted parochial jurisdiction thereafter or ignored it. To avoid baptism of their children by the Jesuits, many had them baptized elsewhere[103] or hid them in order to delay baptism as long as possible. When the missionaries discovered this, they baptized the children by force and parents were punished with fines or imprisonment.[104] To avoid obligatory marriage before a priest they arranged clandestine marriages or went secretly to Saxony, Brandenburg, or Poland to be married by Protestant pastors. As soon as these young married couples returned, their marriages were declared invalid and they had to answer to the officials for their actions.[105] If they still wished to carry on a marital relationship, they had to submit to the decree *Tametsi,* promise to raise their children as Catholics, and to be remarried by a Catholic priest in the presence of two witnesses.[106] Disobeying the order that all infant children who died be buried in the Catholic cemetery while deceased adults continued to be buried in the cattle pastures, they secretly buried their children in gardens and barns or left the bodies uninterred for days.[107]

In light of the ever-increasing suppression, the Schwenkfelders placed their entire hope on the Vienna delegation. They were thus bitterly disappointed when, in a rescript dated July 30, 1725[108] Emperor Karl VI decisively rejected their plea for toleration, refused to accept any further submissions,[109] and introduced even sharper measures against them. For example, the Schwenkfelders who stayed away from catechetical instruction without giving convincing reasons were "on a first offense to be fined according to their means and on a second offense the fine was to be doubled, and if they further disobeyed they were to be punished with imprisonment or hard labor as the occasion demanded. Schwenkfelder minors were to be looked after by Catholic guardians and sent to Catholic places to be reared in the one and only redeeming Catholic religion."[110]

When the Schwenkfelders' attempts to gain toleration had failed, they sought help from the Amsterdam Mennonites on October 16, 1725,[111] because they had heard that they had once come to the aid of the persecuted, namely in 1660 and 1661 in the case of the Bernese Anabaptists.[112] They requested that the Mennonites do the same for them and ask the assistance of the British and Dutch ambassadors to the Viennese court, asking either for toleration or for the right to emigrate—a right which they did not possess because they belonged to an illicit religion as defined by the Treaty of Westphalia. When the answer from the Dutch Mennonites was delayed and the persecution grew,[113] they saw themselves forced to leave their homeland secretly, leaving all their goods behind. Now their problem was to find a place to go. King Frederick Wilhelm I had invited them three times in 1724, according to their statements, to settle in the thinly populated area around Berlin and to establish a linen manufacturing industry there.[114] But they did not accept his invitation "for certain highly delicate reasons."[115] They apparently feared military conscription. Since Holland at the time appeared to be the Promised Land for all religiously persecuted, they decided to emigrate there. On December 3, 1725 they asked the Amsterdam Mennonites if they might come and build up a new livelihood there.[116] Once again to their "consternation and surprise" no answer came, while "the persecution increased daily and the adversaries grew more and more fierce."[117] Then they directed their sights to Oberlausitz, which was only about ten hours distance by foot, turning for help to Johann Christoph Schwedler. Schwedler immediately turned to Melchior Schäffer, pastor of Holy Trinity, Görlitz, who was likewise closely allied to Halle Pietism. Schwedler asked Schäffer to intercede for them with the magistrate of Görlitz and ask for asylum.

About the same time, on December 19, 1725, the Schwenkfelders asked Count Nicolaus Ludwig von Zinzendorf[118] if he would at least allow them to spend the winter months in Herrnhut. They had become acquainted with the count in August of 1723 when, together with Frederick von Wattenwyl and Pastor Schäffer, he had made his first journey to Silesia to visit a relative on his mother's side, Otto Conrad von Hohberg in Zobten.[119] Having seen their unfortunate situation first hand he not only drafted "several petitions for them to the imperial court,"[120] but also interceded for them personally a little later in September 1723,[121] during an audience when the imperial court stayed at Brandeis. He attempted to gain for them the right of emigration from the imperial minister Rudolph Siegmund, count of Sinzendorf and director of the Royal Upper Council of Silesia, the privy councilor Johann A. von Schaffgotsch; he was not successful. When he received this latest request from the Schwenkfelders, he immediately gave permission for them to settle in his territories.[122] As early as December 28, 1725 a delegation of them arrived in Herrnhut.[123]

On February 14, 1726 even before the Görlitz magistrate had answered Schwedler's request, the first six or seven Schwenkfelder families fled under cover of darkness from Harpersdorf to Görlitz and asked for asylum.[124] The city of Görlitz gave them a temporary permission under the condition that "they live peacefully and quietly."[125] Two days later they asked their regent, Frederick August I, elector of Saxony,[126] "how they were to deal with the present immigrants and those who were still to come."[127] On May 2 word was received through the privy councilor Gottlob Frederick von Gersdorff that the privy council had decided to tolerate the Schwenkfelders for the time being, but not to allow them to practise their beliefs publicly or to buy houses or land.[128] Some remained in the city, where they were later allowed to take lease of estates;[129] others settled in Berthelsdorf.[130] Since they all wished to reside in one place, however, they thought about moving on. On the suggestion of the Amsterdam Mennonites[131] they sent a settlement delegation to

Altona in the spring of 1726 to look for a suitable place there.[132] When this too came to naught, there arose a growing desire among many Schwenkfelders to emigrate to Pennsylvania.[133] The Amsterdam Mennonites discouraged this vigorously, both because of the political and economic situation in that British colony and the danger of the voyage; they refused any aid.[134] When all these attempts at finding a common asylum failed, they accepted the invitation of Count Zinzendorf to settle in Oberberthelsdorf, which the count had purchased in 1727 from his uncle, Gottlob Frederick von Gersdorff.[135] Here they lived in a row of houses which they built themselves and which even today are known as the Schwenkfelder houses. Generous financial assistance came from the Haarlem Collegiants[136] for the establishment of their new existence.

In Oberlausitz, as in Silesia, the Schwenkfelders maintained an industrious and quiet life in passive obedience to the political authorities.[137] They held conventicles for edification, directed mostly by Balthasar Hoffmann, but also attended the Lutheran worship services, particularly funerals. They went to Lutheran pastors for baptism, marriage, and burial.[138] However, they did not attend the Lord's Supper and stubbornly opposed all attempts to get them to accept the Lutheran confession. Consequently, some Lutheran pastors, especially Johann Adam Schön and Johann David Geissler in Görlitz, began to preach against the Schwenkfelders and to act against them with measures of church discipline.[139]

The sojourn of the Schwenkfelders in Oberlausitz was to be a short one. At the beginning of August 1731 Emperor Karl VI protested to August II of Poland through Leopold von Waldstein that Count Zinzendorf had accommodated some of his imperial subjects from Moravia. He demanded their expulsion.[140] By this he was referring not to the Schwenkfelders but only to the Moravians from Kumwald and Zauchtental. On the proposal of the privy council,[141] the king in turn ordered that Count Zinzendorf be informed that he could no longer be allowed "to attract more immigrants, through letters or messengers"[142] and in addition, he ordered Georg Ernst von Gersdorff as officer of Görlitz to submit information concerning the exiles there.[143] Since the latter said this was possible only after a detailed study on the spot,[144] Gersdorff was entrusted to undertake it himself.[145] The resulting report—the text of which is no longer available—was not unfavorable to the Schwenkfelders,[146] who had hitherto not been noticed by the political authorities of Saxony-Poland. However, the upper consistory, which was to give its opinion on the report,[147] issued a negative judgment against them.[148] It expressed the opinion that "it might have been well if Count Zinzendorf had not taken them in, since it might have been known from the beginning that it would be difficult to win them over or to bring them onto the right path."[149] As a result, the privy council through the supreme officer in Bautzen, Frederick Caspar von Gersdorff, on January 5, 1733 advised August II to command the Schwenkfelders in Oberberthelsdorf to leave the country one by one since they did not belong to any of the three religions tolerated by the Treaty of Westphalia.[150] Frederick August II, who succeeded his father Frederick August I on February 1, 1733, agreed.[151] On April 4, 1733 the supreme officer of Bautzen was instructed by a decree,[152] which was signed by Alexander von Miltitz, to order the Schwenkfelders in Oberberthelsdorf "to leave the country, but to give the command to each of them individually."[153] Since the Schwenkfelders had not been pleased with their new home because of the constant pressure to accept the Lutheran confession, they did not protest. They requested only that Zinzendorf petition that they be allowed to leave as a group.[154] It is said that they immediately attempted to gain permission to settle in Hamburg, Brandenburg, Isenburg in Wetterau, and elsewhere,[155] all to no avail.

In the meantime, the count was negotiating with the British ambassador in Copenhagen to find a place for the Schwenkfelders in Georgia.[156] The Schwenkfelders declared themselves prepared to go to Georgia if the count was successful in gaining the same promise of free passage, free land and tax abatement for them as other settlers had received.[157] Zinzendorf, likely in November 1733, submitted an anonymous request through Christoph Karl Ludwig von Pfeil, member of the Würtemberg delegates in Regensburg, to the Trustees for Establishing the Colony of Georgia in America.[158] According to Johann Philipp Fresenius[159] and Schwenkfelder tradition[160] not all the demands were met. Thus, they decided, with the count's knowledge,[161] to emigrate to Pennsylvania, since good reports had come from some Schwenkfelder families who had already gone to Pennsylvania and besides, their Dutch friends now supported their plan actively and promised them every assistance.[162]

Between April 20 and 28, 1734 forty Schwenkfelder families—180 men women and children—left Oberberthelsdorf. After a five months' journey—of which there exists an interesting contemporary account of great cultural and historical importance[163]—they arrived in Philadelphia on September 22, 1734. Here too they initially sought a single tract of land on which to settle, "to be for all others a praiseworthy example of Christian concord and union and not to be so easily contaminated by the common disease of covetousness,"[164] but when this was found to be impossible they eventually settled in small groups about a hundred miles northwest of Philadelphia near the Moravians and Mennonites, in Berks County, Northampton County, in Goshenhoppen and Skippack. These areas were climatically and geographically similar to that of their Silesian homeland. In 1782 they adopted a confession of faith in which they moved closer to the Mennonites. The Schwenkfelder church today numbers some 2,500 members.[165]

4. The Decline of Schwenkfeldianism in Silesia

Only around 200 Schwenkfelders had left Silesia during 1726, while the majority—some 300—remained in their homeland.[1] For the most part these were the ones who had married Lutherans.[2] The Jesuits continued to work with great zeal among those who remained, challenging them to discussions every Sunday by circular letters, inviting the adults to private instruction and the children to catechism classes. Only seldom did they comply with these requests, continuing vehemently to oppose the parochial jurisdiction of the Jesuits. Repeatedly several Schwenkfelders secretly brought their children to Johann Christoph Schwedler for baptism[3] and to do this at times "placed their children in pack baskets and carried them in great danger of their lives the twenty-four miles to Nieder-Wiesa in Saxony, even in the winter."[4] They also continued to have their marriages blessed by Lutheran pastors in Züllichau and Marklissa outside of Silesia.[5] On their return they were punished with imprisonment[6] and forced either to have the marriage vows repeated in the presence of a Catholic priest[7] or secretly to leave the country.[8]

On October 17, 1728 the Schwenkfelders attempted to have the parochial jurisdiction of the Jesuits removed. They requested of the authorities in Liegnitz that the Franciscans in Goldberg be allowed to solemnize their marriages and bury their dead.[9] They based their request on the fact that their work in the linen and wool trade often took them to Goldberg and thus would not force them to withdraw their labor from the community so frequently. Their request was quickly denied by the Royal Upper Council on the recommendation of the vicar-general of the Breslau diocese[10] who immediately saw through the flimsy reasoning.[11]

Although the Schwenkfelders were stubbornly opposed to the Jesuits, they gradually succeeded in causing a not insignificant number of them to convert. For example, in their report of 1732[12] the missionaries listed 324 persons who had been converted. Those who had died in the meantime were not counted; children baptized by force were indeed reckoned in the total. Moreover, there was a continually growing number of Catholic settlers—366 of them by 1732. On the order of the Royal Upper Council in Breslau, the confiscated goods of those Schwenkfelders who had fled were to be sold to Catholic farmers at a low price. The price was fixed by Catholic law courts.[13] Nevertheless, the Lutheran landlords—especially Susanne Marie Eleonore von Schweinichen, Christoph Frederick von Braun, and Karl

Nicolaus von Hohberg—did not always follow this order, and to the great displeasure of the Jesuits, sold the best farms to Lutherans.[14]

The growing number of Catholics naturally led the Jesuits to desire a church of their own in Harpersdorf. There was a problem, however, as to who would administer the parish. The vicar-general agreed to the Jesuits' request and ordered that the administration of the parish be given to the Jesuit mission until the bishop of Breslau recalled them or until the Protestant church in Harpersdorf had a Catholic priest.[15] The emperor agreed and issued a rescript to that effect on March 1, 1732.[16] A few months later—on June 4, 1732—Regent, who had become the leader of the mission upon Milan's discouraged departure on March 23, 1728,[17] laid the cornerstone for a chapel in Harpersdorf.[18] In accordance with the emperor's rescript[19] most of the cost was covered by the proceeds from the sale of confiscated Schwenkfelder goods. Thanks to the initiative of Regent the chapel was finally consecrated on September 17, 1734[20] together with a cemetery. In 1735 a Catholic school was added.[21]

By gaining the parochial administration the Jesuits had hoped to convert even more of the Schwenkfelders and to strengthen those who had already been converted. They were disappointed in both cases. Regent could report only a few new conversions in the following years.[22] Numerous Schwenkfelders requested the emperor and the imperial authorities to lift the repressive measures of the Jesuits and to consider them as Lutherans stating that after their parents' death or emigration they would adhere to the Lutheran Church.[23] The converted Schwenkfelders refused to fulfill their religious duties; above all, they refused to pay fees for clerical duties. The situation progressively worsened for the Jesuits after they had received parochial administration, because the settlement of many Roman Catholics in the area caused the Lutheran opposition to the Jesuit mission to grow. The latter at times united with the Schwenkfelders in an attempt to hinder or at least to make the work of the Jesuits more difficult. They did not even shrink from using strong-arm tactics.[24] At the end of February 1736, to the great displeasure of the Jesuits, more Schwenkfelder families from Harpersdorf and Armenruh fled to Görlitz.[25] Although the magistrate of Breslau in a letter to King August III[26] praised their industry and ability in the manufacture of flax and yarn and emphasized their religious simplicity, they were ordered to leave the country.[27]

The decline of conversions, the active or passive resistance of Schwenkfelders and Lutherans alike, and the failing support of the Roman Catholics themselves,[28] finally caused Regent to request his transfer to the Jesuit College at Liegnitz. However, Karl VI first demanded an account of property and a settlement of accounts, which took him a long time. Not until October

10, 1740 did the emperor declare that Regent's request be granted.[29]

Karl VI, in an edict issued on February 19, 1740 but no longer extant, attempted to complete the mission to the Schwenkfelders. Through the Royal Upper Council in Breslau he ordered that all remaining Schwenkfelders in the principality of Jauer either convert within a year or leave. If they chose to leave, their "possessions and inheritances were to be given to their children who converted to Catholicism or to be used for other purposes."[30] Those living in the principality of Liegnitz, on the other hand, were allowed "by a particular decree . . . out of pure clemency" to accept the Lutheran confession and remain in their homes without further "impediments like all the other adherents to the Augsburg Confession."[31] Care was to be taken, however, that they not simply attend Lutheran services *pro forma* while otherwise remaining faithful to "the Schwenkfeldian sect."[32] These orders were not executed since Karl VI, the last male offspring of the Hapsburg dynasty, died unexpectedly on October 20, 1740 at the age of only 55, whereupon Frederick II of Prussia, citing an ancient legal claim, marched a small army into Silesia on December 16. Perhaps made aware of the Schwenkfelders' situation by the Schwenkfelders themselves, the Breslau war commissioner, who was responsible for the administration of the occupied country, on May 8, 1741 issued, by the king's order, a decree for their protection.[33] According to that decree "the emigration and extirpation of the Schwenkfelders, was to be suspended now and the execution of the former decrees stopped."[34] Instead, they were "to be tolerated in the land for the time being until his majesty has finally decided the matter, with the same freedom which they enjoyed under his imperial majesty's rule several years earlier."[35] As the correspondence between the Silesian Schwenkfelders and their fellow believers in Pennsylvania clearly indicates, the edict of May 8 was intended to return them to the same status they had had before the Jesuit mission had come. They were once again placed under the parochial jurisdiction of the Lutheran church but not to be tolerated or recognized as a separate denomination. Not incorrectly did they characterize this toleration which guaranteed only an individual freedom of faith and conscience as "a restricted freedom of conscience."[36]

Apparently the Schwenkfelders found it difficult to get their former possessions returned and complained to the president of the chamber for war and domains, Ludwig Wilhelm Count von Münchow,[37] who informed Frederick II of Prussia directly.[38] On February 23, 1742, Frederick issued a cabinet order[39] instructing Münchow and the Minister of State and Justice, Samuel von Cocceji[40] "to draft the proposed edict."[41] This edict should state that the Schwenkfelders who had been driven out "by an exaggerated zeal of religion to the greatest disadvantage to commerce and to the detriment of the country in general,"[42] should not only be tolerated in Silesia but that there should be provisions for their residence,[43] since Frederick would not tolerate "such suppression or persecution in religious matters."[44] He was particularly concerned, as the cabinet order indicates, about the financial losses as a result of the persecution of Schwenkfelders.[45] His concern in this matter indicates that as a statesman and culturally concerned ruler he was not so much interested in religious freedom for the Schwenkfelders as he was in countermanding the economic losses experienced.

The edict was signed by the king at Salowitz in Moravia on March 8, 1742. It was written by von Münchow and von Cocceji along the lines of Frederick II's wishes[46] "for the aid and placation of the so-called Schwenkfelders."[47] It outlined at the beginning the reason why religious intolerance should be rejected. The edict stated that it was against reason and nature as well as against the Christian faith to violate the consciences of subjects and to persecute them "for this or that erroneous doctrine."[48] Nevertheless, the edict narrows this immediately—in this it goes beyond the suggestion of Frederick II—adding that such personal freedom of faith and conscience is guaranteed only as long as "the fundamental articles of the Christian faith"[49] are not rejected. What these fundamental articles were is not indicated, but for Frederick and the authors they surely meant only God, immortality, and virtue. The possibility existed, however, that political and religious authorities might define these articles. This restriction was most likely made and then accepted by Frederick II because he was negotiating with Maria Theresa of Austria at the time for her voluntary withdrawal of claims for Silesia.[50] The empress was personally pious and a devout churchwoman and his efforts only had prospects of success if she was assured that the articles of the Treaty of Westphalia would be upheld and the Christian religion protected.

Having established the rejection of religious intolerance while at the same time assuring the preservation of the "fundamental articles of the Christian religion,"[51] Frederick called upon the Schwenkfelders who had fled to return to Silesia. They were assured they could "live and work and move about in peace."[52] They were also given permission to settle in other Prussian territories as well. The edict further mentioned some privileges which were to be given to those who returned home. Their "farms and homes"[53] would be returned at no cost unless they had been legally purchased by their new owners. Those who settled "in other areas and villages"[54] would be "assisted financially and farms would be given to them."[55] Furthermore, they would be allowed to settle in the cities, where they would not only receive free building lots but also deferrals of the land tax for several years.[56]

This edict of Frederick II[57] was also sent to the Schwenkfelders in Pennsylvania, possibly by the chamber for war and domains directly, but certainly by the Silesian Schwenkfelders themselves. Although the Silesian Schwenkfelders urgently wished their fellow believers to return,[58] the Pennsylvania Schwenkfelders did not comply. As pacifists they feared military conscription after their return.[59] They regarded military service as belonging to "the kingdom of the devil,"[60] and they were exempted from this in Pennsylvania. Moreover, it was also important that they had no material need to take up the invitation. Eventually only a few Schwenkfelder families who had remained in Oberlausitz accepted. However, it was not easy for them even now to regain their previous possessions.[61]

The edict of Frederick II not only abolished the rights of the Jesuit mission over the Schwenkfelders, but insured that the latter were protected from all infringements on their personal faith and conscience by political and ecclesiastical authorities. The Lutheran pastors did, in fact, respect this,[62] with the occasional exception of attacks during funeral orations since the Schwenkfelders still did not attend public worship.[63] However, baptism, marriage in the parish church, and burial remained obligatory for Schwenkfelders.[64] The pastors were delegates of the political authorities and had kept parish registers which were also registers of births and burials. The political authorities recognized as lawful only those marriages which had been blessed in the parish church. Nevertheless, the toleration they enjoyed was broad enough that a new period of growth could have started among the Schwenkfelders. But renewal did not come; the Schwenkfelders instead declined in number and their theological ideas became unimportant. During the last epoch of their history, from 1741 to 1826, the Silesian Schwenkfelders did not compose a single book. Only on the request of their brethren in Pennsylvania did they accept the task of editing and publishing *The Vindications for Caspar Schwenckfeld,* which was prepared in Pennsylvania by Christoph Schultz; Caspar and Christoph Kriebel, Balthasar Hoffmann and others assisted in the preparation of this work, which was begun in December 1768 and completed in February 1769.[65] Published in Jauer in 1771 and dedicated to Frederick II of Prussia,[66] the book, containing a description of the history of the Schwenkfelders and excerpts of Schwenckfeld's writings, fomented dissonance among them, because the volume was filled with editorial additions, abbreviations,[67] and numerous misprints which had not been corrected.[68] This dissonance was intensified a year later when in gratitude to their fellow believers for earlier help,[69] the Silesian Schwenkfelders printed their confession.[70] The confession's title indicates that it is the same confession which was submitted to the royal government in Liegnitz on May 25, 1718. The only signer of this confession, who was still living in 1772, Balthasar Hoffmann, however, declared that the new confession differed from the earlier one;[71] C. E. Heintze had admitted that from the beginning.[72]

The reason that Schwenkfeldianism in Silesia was not able to renew itself lay primarily in the social structure of its adherents, whose numbers constantly dwindled.[73] As indicated in the extant correspondence, these were, for the most part, old, single, or widowed persons;[74] the number of families with children was very small.[75] Young Schwenkfelders had to marry Lutherans,[76] or remain single[77] since there were no eligible Schwenkfelders. If they married Lutherans, they almost always became Lutherans and broke their ties with the Schwenkfelders.[78] Vocations were changing as well during this period. Whereas the first generation had usually been nobles, theologians, or physicians and the second often farmers, landowners, craftsmen, and independent employers, they were now mostly day-laborers or tenant farmers earning their living mostly by spinning. A cultural decline also went along with this social decline. Whereas earlier some Schwenkfelders knew Latin, Greek, and Hebrew, these people could hardly read or write their native language.

There are also theological reasons for the absence of renewal among the Schwenkfelders. In the many letters which the Silesian Schwenkfelders wrote to Pennsylvania, one looks in vain for that distinctive mark of later Schwenkfeldianism: the realization of the new man. Even the original, ethically-motivated exclusiveness had also been given up, especially by the youth, a fact which troubled the few remaining conservatives[79] but which was greeted with unmistakable satisfaction by the Lutheran pastors. Johann Adam Hensel, Lutheran pastor of Neudorf at Gröditzberg and Silesian church historian wrote: "Their former zeal has disappeared almost completely; they go to amusements which young people like. They are no longer distinguishing themselves by that old-fashioned clothing which had been their mark in former times, but are now dressing themselves like other farmers in the area and living with other Protestants on friendly terms."[80] Moreover, they no longer met in conventicles after the emigration of their brethren. "I hope," Heintze wrote to Balthasar Hoffmann in May 1765, "that you will not misuse your freedom of conscience as is unfortunately happening among us; each person goes his own way and there are no longer any gatherings nor true community."[81] Although in the answer of June 16, 1767 the Pennsylvania Schwenkfelders exhorted the Silesian Schwenkfelders to gather "at least occasionally . . . [with] prayers, readings, singing, exhortation, and admonition as in times past our forefathers did who loved Jesus Christ."[82] This, as well as later admonitions, remained without success.[83]

Even in this final stage of Silesian Schwenkfeldianism a few held fast to the tradition. Their leading figure was, undoubtedly, the unmarried Karl Ehrenfried Heintze, who was born about 1720 in Probsthain as the son of a Lutheran magistrate and by trade a print cutter and a cloth printer.[84] Following a long religious search in Calvinism, Catholicism, and especially in

Lutheranism and extensive reading of Luther,[85] he was directed to Schwenkfeldianism by a dream in 1756.[86] He immediately studied Schwenckfeld's writings which were loaned to him by Balthasar Kurtz, the only Schwenkfelder he knew.[87] He experienced a religious conversion[88] and together with his relatives, joined the Schwenkfelders.[89] The Schwenkfelders in Pennsylvania set their hopes on him to bring new life to the waning movement in Silesia.[90]

However, Heintze read not only the works of Schwenckfeld, but also Paracelsus, Boehme, Jane Lead, Johann Georg Gichtel, and above all, Gottfried Arnold.[91] He was convinced that these writings were in full agreement with those of the Silesian nobleman.[92] This was denied emphatically by his fellow believers in Pennsylvania, who declared that Boehme and the English mystic Jane Lead,[93] ''did not agree with the doctrine and teaching of Schwenckfeld.''[94]

Central to Heintze's theology was his teaching on the new man. He wrote passionately against forensic justification. For example, he wrote to the Schwenkfelders in Pennsylvania on February 15, 1768: ''Our country has a multitude of preachers and teachers, but they preach Christ right out of the land. Everyone according to his own sectarian ideas speaks of a Christ external to us, for us, but not within us. Their whole construction remains a Babylon, which is so clearly prefigured and described by the prophet Zechariah in Chapter 5.''[95] For Heintze the sign of the new man was moral perfection, but he saw in his time only signs of a general moral decline evidenced by many natural calamities and heavenly portents.[96]

Although Heintze basically retained the earlier Schwenkfelder teaching on the image of God, he did not succeed in renewing the movement in Silesia. A significant reason was that in his last years he experienced another fundamental theological change. Under the influence of the writings of the Enlightenment rationalist Johann Christian Edelmann, which Heintze had borrowed in Liegnitz,[97] his spiritualism changed to pantheistic rationalism. Unfortunately, this change from spiritualism, theosophy, and radical Pietism to rationalism cannot be described in detail, since few documents are available. It is not even known which writings he read, although he likely was familiar with the publication *Unschuldige Nachrichten* (*Impartial Information*), which appeared between 1735 and 1742.[98] In any case, he was convinced that Edelmann would lead in knowledge ''even beyond Schwenckfeld''[99] and, for this reason, he endeavored unsuccessfully[100] to get the Silesian Schwenkfelders to accept Edelmann's writings.[101] Meanwhile, Pennsylvania Schwenkfelders urgently warned Heintze[102] and their friends in Silesia against Edelmann,[103] especially against Edelmann's doctrine of the Logos as presented in the eighth dialogue of the *Unschuldige Nachrichten* (*Impartial*

Information).[104]

After the death of Heintze on December 31, 1775 Schwenkfeldianism in Silesia quickly lost its significance. Correspondence from Silesia to Pennsylvania became rarer and rarer. Unlike the replies from America, letters from Silesia contained no theological discussions and scarcely any political information. For the most part they are concerned with family matters or with the fate of the Schwenkfelder devotional literature in Silesia.[105] Those writings which had not been confiscated by the mission and sent to the Jesuit college in Liegnitz were to be purchased at the request of the Pennsylvania Schwenkfelders and were to be sent over to them.[106]

In October 1857, having received no mail for many years, the Schwenkfelders in Pennsylvania wrote to Probsthain asking if Schwenkfelder congregations still existed in Silesia. They were immediately answered by the Lutheran pastor there, Oswald Kadelbach, who informed them that the last Schwenkfelder, the farmer Melchior Dorn, had died in Harpersdorf in 1826.[107] Thus, exactly one hundred years after the flight of the Schwenkfelders out of Silesia, Schwenkfeldianism there finally expired.

VI Conclusion

This study has made it evident that Schwenckfeld and his followers at first understood themselves as followers of the Wittenberg movement and endeavored to establish the Reformation in Silesia. In accordance with their humanist and mystical-spiritualist tradition, they believed that the reformation of Christianity was also Luther's real concern. They maintained this position even when they thought that in the territories touched by the Reformation there was no renewal of all areas of life as they had awaited. They explained this initially by suggesting that the proclamation of the Gospel first made wickedness perceptible.

However, when no renewal was forthcoming, they explained it by Luther's rejection of his previous spiritualism. They began cautiously to criticize the Lutheran doctrine of forensic justification which they regarded as misleading or even false. In contrast to the Lutherans, they developed a concept of justification effected directly by the Spirit, the basis of which was a "disposition to grace" and the criterion of which was good works. In this it is evident that they did not understand Luther's concept of the justice of God by which the sinner is set without any condition in a correct relationship with God through the Word.

Schwenkfeldianism first became conscious of its own unique identity during its lengthy controversy on the sacrament with Lutherans and later with South Germans and the Swiss. On the basis of its spiritualism, Schwenkfeldianism rejected all realistic and—after some vacillation—all significatory explanations of the Lord's Supper. Basing their argument on the Gospel of John's statement on the bread of life and a philological-grammatical exegesis of the words of institution, they taught instead a spiritual consumption which they did not identify with faith. In the development of this sacramental mysticism they were not only influenced by the Patristic tradition but also by Karlstadt and Zwingli. The person who developed this concept of the sacrament and later inaugurated and formed the characteristic elements of Schwenkfeldian theology was the learned, trilingual canon, Crautwald. Schwenckfeld, on the other hand, on the basis of his social position and uncommon ability to communicate, was more or less only the influential propagator of this doctrine. Schwenckfeld was less independent in his theology than has been previously thought.

Spiritualism, which according to the Schwenkfelders was alone capable of opening the way to the inner man and of making a renewal of Christianity possible, gradually became the key to its theology. In permanent argument with the Lutheran doctrine of the "means of salvation" and with Anabaptist biblicism, they developed their concept of the internal word, referring to

Scripture, the Fathers, and to the philosophical axiom of "similar similarities." This inner word is never *a priori* in man, but must always first be given by the Spirit from outside. This emphasis on the "extra nos" (outside of man) distinguishes the Schwenkfeldian movement from the late medieval tradition and ties it to the Reformation. The final consequence of their spiritualism was developed in their Christology. It was once again Crautwald who made the major contribution. After various earlier stages of development they came to the conclusion after 1538 that the human nature of Christ, which had been different from the human nature of ordinary men from the beginning, gradually became deified. Their soteriology is found in its final form together with their Christology, which in the final analysis allows of no incarnation and for this reason was sharply attacked by South Germans, Swiss, and Lutherans alike. The "confessors of the glory of Christ," as they called themselves now, believed they had made it clear why man would be deified by the spiritual consumption of the deified body of Christ according to II Peter 1:4. However, they strongly rejected any kind of apotheosis.

Within the course of the controversy on justification, the Lord's Supper, and the external word, Schwenkfeldianism succeeded in spreading throughout not only the territories of Duke Frederick II of Liegnitz but into other areas of Silesia despite the opposition of the Lutherans. This was possible because many nobles and theologians united or sympathized with the movement. This changed when its most influential protector, Frederick II, for political reasons (Schwenckfeld had to leave Silesia in 1529 under the pressure of the Hapsburgs) and probably also from personal conviction, eventually sought closer ties with the Schmalcald League. After initially moving with edicts of exile only against radical Schwenkfelder theologians who refused to associate with the Lutherans, Frederick II in his later years eventually suppressed Schwenkfeldianism without exception. Many Schwenkfelders then emigrated to the county of Glatz and into the area of the Bober-Katzbach mountains.

After a short period of blossoming, Schwenkfeldianism in Glatz was completely extinguished by the Counter Reformation. Yet many, in some cases large, conventicles remained for almost three centuries in the villages between Löwenberg, Goldberg, and Haynau. Under the influence of Anabaptist ideas and an increasing receptivity to mystical ideas, spiritualism—which presupposes a certain amount of abstract thinking—was gradually lost because the social structure of Schwenkfelders became increasingly peasant. Schwenkfeldianism became concerned chiefly with the rise and development of the new man. This soteriological interest, which was ever more reduced to moralism, led them into a sharp conflict with Lutheran orthodoxy—which attacked the Schwenkfelders in sermons and writings and not infrequently incited political authorities to move against them. In the seventeenth and eighteenth centuries, the Schwenkfelders gave up their anxiously-guarded exclusiveness and sought contact with other theological and intellectual movements. Their intellectual contacts with many leading mystical spiritualists, with whom they felt themselves connected because of their radical criticism of the church and their ethical rigorism, was particularly intense, though they rejected their ideas of natural philosophy, theosophy, and millenarianism. Not insignificant was their contact with separatistic Pietists, whose literary production they eagerly read in their conventicles. Characteristically, they remained distant from Lutheran Pietism, an indication that mystical spiritualism has an internal relationship to radical Pietism but not necessarily to Lutheran Pietism.

When in 1726 those Schwenkfelders who were more firmly rooted in the tradition had fled under the pressure of recatholicization, the movement, now made up largely of the lower social classes, became less and less significant theologically and historically. With few exceptions—a move toward rationalism—the Schwenkfelders let themselves be satisfied with a formal critique of Lutheranism or embraced the Lutheran church. In 1826 Schwenkfeldianism, a movement in which the manifold nature of Protestantism was especially impressive, finally expired in Silesia.

NOTES

I The Beginnings of Schwenkfeldianism

1. Origins and Early Growth.

[1] Extensive but incomplete bibliographies on Schwenckfeld are found in Schl II, 19575-19720; V, 49233-49272; VII, 58077-58140; *Bibliographie de la reforme* 1450-1648. Ouvrages parus de 1940 à 1955. (Fascicule I-IV; Leiden 1958-1963), I, 96, 355, 656, 1583, 1732; II, 1600, 1852; IV, 764. See also Franz Michael Weber, *Kaspar Schwenckfeld;* Martha Kriebel, *Schwenckfeld and the Sacraments;* E.J. Furcha, "Key concepts in Caspar von Schwenckfeld's Thought"; and Norman Dollin, *The Schwenkfelders in eighteenth century America.*
[2] Here and following see Selina Gerhard Schultz, *Caspar Schwenckfeld von Ossig,* 1-3.
[3] See Gustav Bauch, "Zur älteren Liegnitzer Schulgeschichte," 96-135.
[4] CS XIV, 876, 21. His name is not found in the registers of the University of Cologne.
[5] Ernst Friedlaender, *Aeltere Universitäts-Matrikeln,* I, 19, 26-27.
[6] CS VI, 489, 22-23; XIV, 876, 21-22.
[7] CS XIV, 47, 28-32. Cf. IV, 781, 17; VI, 489, 23-24. On the beginning of his service see Schultz, 5, n. 29.
[8] Cf. CS IV, 781, 17; VI, 489, 23-24; XIV, 47, 28-32. O. Hampe, *Zur Biographie Kaspars v. Schwenckfeld,* 8 holds that he went to Brieg in 1515 for the marriage of Georg I.
[9] Joachim Curaeus, *Gentis Silesiae annales,* 243.
[10] CS XIV, 876, 30-31.
[11] See Johann Hess to Willibald Pirckheimer, December 21, 1517 in Johannes Heumann, *Documenta literaria,* 116-118.
[12] See CS XVI, 795, 20; Cf. IV, 248, 17-22. The assertion (cf. Albrecht Wachler, "Leben und Wirken Caspar Schwenckfeld's," 97, 126 and Heinrich Wilhelm Erbkam, *Geschichte der protestantischen Sekten,* 364) that Schwenckfeld underwent a religious awakening in the pre-Reformation period is clearly false.
[13] Cf. here and following David Erdmann, *Luther und seine Beziehungen zu Schlesien,* 2-8.
[14] See Josef Benzing, *Lutherbibliographie,* 108, 350, 355, 362, 414.
[15] CS XIII, 212, 5-9.
[16] Emanuel Hirsch, *Schwenckfeld und Luther,* 35-67, especially 36-37.
[17] CS IV, 832, 23-24.
[18] CS IX, 33-34,6; End 15, 275-277. No. 3343. Cf. WAT 5, 300, 15-302, 9, No. 5659.
[19] CS IX, 660, 36-661, 1.
[20] Schultz, *Schwenckfeld,* 3, n. 19.
[21] CS VI, 489, 24-490, 1.
[22] On this and the following see above all Ferdinand Bahlow, *Die Reformation in Liegnitz,* 32-33, and Wolfgang Knörrlich, *Kaspar v. Schwenckfeld,* 49-50.
[23] CS I, 36, 9-10.
[24] On Sebastian Schubart see Ferdinand Bahlow, "Sebastian Schubart 1498-1580," 28-54.
[25] His name is not found in the town register at the Kulmbach Stadtarchiv.
[26] This is indicated in the preface to his *Vorrede Wieder die Lehre der Schwenckfelder* (hereafter: Schubart, "Vorrede"). The work itself is no longer extant. The preface is printed in Bahlow, *Reformation,* 149-154.
[27] Valentin Crautwald to Ursula Thumb von Stetten November 11, 1540, Wolfenbüttel HAB, Cod. Guelf. 45.9 Aug. fol. 420r: "My parents and forefathers were simple farmers." Cf. Gerhard Eberlein, "Der kirchliche Volksunterricht," 6.
[28] See Hans Bahlow, *Schlesisches Namenbuch,* 30, 88.
[29] See Gustav Bauch, "Schlesien und die Universität Krakau," 155.
[30] Ibid.

[31] Ibid.
[32] Ibid. Cf. August Kastner, *Archiv für die Geschichte des Bisthums Breslau,* IV, 31.
[33] Valentin Crautwald to Ursula Thumb von Stetten November 11, 1540, Wolfenbüttel HAB, Cof. Guelf. 45.9 Aug. fol. 420r.
[34] See Gustav Bauch, "Beiträge zur Literaturgeschichte des schlesischen Humanismus," 240-241.
[35] See Johann Heyne, *Dokumentirte Geschichte des Bisthums und Hochstifts Breslau,* III, 599; Richard Völkel, *Die persönliche Zusammensetzung des Neisser Kollegiatkapitels,* 143; Fritz Luschek, *Notariatsurkunde und Notariat in Schlesien,* V, 236.
[36] Völkel, 143.
[37] Ibid.
[38] See Adam Reisner, *Vita Valentini Crautuualdi,* München SB, CLM 718, fol. 549r: "Valentin Crautwald, canon priest, trained in languages, the arts and good writing from his youth, rose to the highest pinnacle of humanist erudition. He was, because of his learning, [gained] over many years in private and public study, admitted to the circle of Johann Turzo, bishop of Breslau."
[39] Johannes Hess to Willibald Pirckheimer, December 21, 1517, printed in Heumann, *Documenta literaria,* 116-118.
[40] Ibid.
[41] After the death of Crautwald in 1545 his library went to the church library of Sts. Peter and Paul. (Cf. Ferdinand Bahlow, "Die Kirchenbibliothek von St. Peter und Paul in Liegnitz," 140-175; and his "Aus der Peter-Paul-Kirchenbibliothek," 302-303.) In 1945 it was placed in the university library in Wroclaw.
[42] See Karol Glombiowski, "Über die Verbreitung der Schriften des Erasmus von Rotterdam in Schlesien," 135-136.
[43] Cf. Philipp Melanchthon to Johann Hess, April 17, 1520, CR 1, 155-161, No. 69; and to Michael Wittiger, April, 1520, ibid., 161-162, No. 71.
[44] See Ambrosius Moibanus to Johann Hess, December 8, 1521, printed in CKGS 9 (1904), 48-49 and Georg Kretschmar, *Die Reformation in Breslau,* 56. It is not known from the sources whether or not Crautwald visited Wittenberg at that time.
[45] Reisner, *Vita,* CLM 718, fol. 549r.
[46] Above all see Gerhard Eberlein, "Zur Würdigung des Valentin Krautwald," 269-270; Bahlow, *Reformation,* 46-47 and Knörrlich, 51.
[47] Legnica StA M 375: "On July 11, 1524 the venerable man, Valentin Crautwald, Canon of Neisse, was invested to the vacant canonate and prebend in the church of Liegnitz because of the resignation of Johannis Punitz, earlier possessor of the same canonate and prebend. This took place in the presence of the illustrious prince and lord Frederick." (Cited from Gustav Bauch, *Valentin Trozendorf,* 67.)
[48] Valentin Crautwald to Margarete Engelmann, 1537, in Gottfried Arnold, *Supplementa,* 139: "I am a stranger here; I was ordered to come by our princes to teach at the seminary what is in the divine Scriptures."
[49] Valentin Crautwald to Ursula Thumb von Stetten, November 11, 1540, Wolfenbüttel HAB, Cod. Guelf. 45.9 Aug. fol. 420v: "I must not, however, forget the goodness of God, the Lord, who has visited and kept me here now for seventeeen years in freedom, without taking monastic rule or wearing the habit or tonsure. May the Lord let these things increase his glory through Jesus Christ."
[50] CS II, 76, 16-17.
[51] See G. Bauch, *Aus dem Hausbuche des Goldberger Lehrers Zacharias Bart,* 19.
[52] See Schubart, "Vorrede," 149. F. Bahlow, *Die Reformation in Liegnitz, 47; Kn*örrlich, *Kaspar von Schwenckfeld,* 51-52.
[53] See Schubart, "Vorrede," 150. On Wenzel Küchler see above all Bahlow, *Reformation,* 177-178.
[54] See Schubart, "Vorrede," 150. On Valerius Rosenhayn see above all Franz Xaver Görlich,

Versuch einer Geschichte der Pfarrkirche zu Schweidnitz, 11; Bahlow, *Reformation,* 49-50; and Knörrlich, 49-50.

[55] On Ambrosius Kreusig see Hermann Söhnel, "Zur Kirchengeschichte des Fürstentums Wohlau," 52-53 and Gottfried Kliesch, *Der Einfluss der Universität Frankfurt (Oder) auf die schlesische Bildungsgeschichte,* 149.

[56] Friedlaender, I, 21, 26-27.

[57] On Bernhard Egetius see Söhnel, 52-55.

[58] CS VII, 116, 24-25.

[59] CS, VI, 490, 5-8.

[60] Ibid.

[61] Johann Scaurus was pastor at Ossig from 1522 to 1534 and pastor and senior minister in Steinau until 1553.

[62] After the death of his brother Georg I of Brieg in 1521, Frederick II inherited the principality of Brieg. In 1523 he purchased the territories of Wohlau, Steinau and Raudten from Baron Hans Turzo, and in 1525 the baronial towns of Herrnstadt, Rützen and Winzig from the brothers Hans and Heinrich Kurzbach. Through these purchases he established the Dukedom of Wohlau. To these were later added as securities whole principalities such as Glogau between 1540 and 1544, and Münsterberg and Frankenstein after 1542.

[63] On November 26, 1515 Frederick II married Elisabeth, the daughter of King Kasimirs of Poland and the youngest sister of Sigismund I of Poland and Ludwig II of Hungary. After her death on February 16, 1517, he married a niece of his first wife, Sophie, daughter of Margrave Frederick V of Brandenburg-Ansbach on November 14, 1518.

[64] Heinrich Wuttke, "Zwei Wallfahrten von Schlesiern nach dem gelobten Lande," 502-515., Heinrich Meisner and Reinhold Röhricht, "Die Pilgerfahrt des Herzogs Friedrich II von Liegnitz und Brieg nach dem heiligen Lande," 101-131, 177-215, and Gerhard Eberlein, "Die Wallfahrt Herzog Friedrichs II von Liegnitz nach Jerusalem," 31-33.

[65] CS XVIII, 14, 16-17.

[66] Ibid., 14, 19-20.

[67] See Ibid., 36, 10-11.

2. The Attempts of the Schwenkfelders to Bring About the Reformation in Silesia

[1] On Johann V. Turzo see Schl I, 8326; III, 29965-29969; VII, 61133a, 61135. On the Turzo family see Kurt Bathelt, "Die Familie Thurzo in Kunst und Kultur Ostmitteleuropas," 115-124, and Götz von Pölnitz, *Jakob Fugger,* I, 53-54; II, 23, 264.

[2] Allen III, 343-345, No. 850; IV, 134-135, No. 1047, 331-332, No. 1137. The correspondence was transmitted through Caspar Ursinus Velius (Cf. Ibid., III, 346, 37-44, No. 851).

[3] Cf. WAB 2, 152-153, 30-32, No. 318; CR I, 209-210, No. 84.

[4] WAB 2, 153, No. 318; CR I, 209-210, No. 84.

[5] WAB 2, 214, 31-32, No. 352.

[6] On Jacob von Salza see Schl II, 19670; III, 29961-29964; V, 51224; VII, 61133a.

[7] On this and the following see Karl Otto, "Über die Wahl Jacobs von Salza zum Bischof von Breslau," 303-327.

[8] See August Kastner, *Archiv für die Geschichte des Bisthums Breslau,* I, 9-10. Cf. Kurt Engelbert, "Die Anfänge der lutherischen Bewegung in Breslau und Schlesien," 161-162.

[9] This was treated at the cathedral chapter on September 23, 1523. See Acta Capituli Wratislaviensis, Wroclaw DA, III, b. 1b, 146. Cf. Kastner, I, 19. The Latin letter of Hadrian VI to the municipal council of Breslau on July 23, 1523 is found in Wroclaw SA, Sammlung-Klose, 42, fol. 41r-42v (Copied from the original) and G. Buckisch, "Schlesische Religionsakten,"

I Teil, 1517-1607, Wroclaw DA, I, 13a. 112-116. Printed in Jakob Schickfuss, *Neue vermehrete schlesische Chronica,* III, 55-58 (in Latin, with German trans.), and Michael Joseph Fibiger, *Das in Schlesien gewaltthätig eingerissene Lutherthum,* I, 76-81 (in Latin, with German trans.).

[10] Wroclaw SA, Sammlung-Klose, 42, fol. 42r.

[11] See Acta Capituli Wratislaviensis, Wroclaw DA, III, b. 1b, 94-95.

[12] An undated copy of this letter is found in München SB, CLM 965, fol. 334v-335r, a German trans. of which is given in Hermann Hoffmann and Kurt Engelbert, "Aufzeichnungen des Breslauer Domherrn Stanislaus Sauer," 158-159. See fol. 335r: "With greatest concern we ask your majesty in all your dominions to press down and extirpate by severe edicts and diligent care this plague of religion (arising out of license and insolence and now perpetrated with impunity) and the zeal for novelties among the unlearned populace such that great perturbation and certain grave divine castigation is to be feared."

[13] The mandate of Ludwig II on December 24, 1521 is found in Wroclaw SA, Sammlung-Klose, 42, fol. 13r-14r.

[14] See Acta Capituli Wratislaviensis, Wroclaw DA, III, b, 1b, 102-103. Cf. Kastner, I, 11.

[15] The mandate of Ludwig II on April 16, 1523 is printed in Wroclaw SA, Sammlung-Klose, 42, fol. 30v-31v.

[16] Cf. Bahlow, *Reformation,* 35.

[17] Sigismund I's letter to the municipal council at Breslau on September 13, 1523 is found in Wroclaw SA, Sammlung-Klose, 42, fol. 46v-47r, printed in Fibiger, I, 83, and Sigismund Justus Ehrhardt *Presbyterologie,* I, 75. Note also his letter to the Breslau council of October 10, 1523 in Wroclaw SA, Sammlung-Klose, 42, fol. 50v-51r.

[18] Breslau municipal council to Sigismund I, September 22, 1523, Wroclaw SA., Sammlung-Klose, 42, fol. 47r-50v.

[19] CS XVIII, 3, 21-22.

[20] The neighboring regions of Troppau, Teschen and Jägerndorf were under the spiritual jurisdiction of the Bishop of Olmütz. The county of Glatz and part of the principalities of Glogau and Krakau (Pless/Beuthen) belonged to the archbishopric of Prague.

[21] On Hans Magnus von Axleben see CS I, 358-362.

[22] Ibid., (211) 242-283.

[23] Ibid., 244, 5.

[24] Ibid., 246, 23-24.

[25] Ibid., 254, 22ff.

[26] Ibid., 250, 3-8; 252, 19-25.

[27] Ibid., 272, 25-32.

[28] Ibid., 250, 9-15.

[29] Ibid., 264, 4-10.

[30] Ibid., 272, 30-32.

[31] Ibid., 276, 25-28.

[32] Ibid., 274, 8-10.

[33] Ibid., 274, 31-276, 16.

[34] Ibid., 274, 14-18.

[35] CS II, 94, 11-96, 9.

[36] On the diet in Grottkau on January 17, 1524 see Paul Konrad, "Die Einführung der Reformation in Breslau und Schlesien," 45-46, Engelbert, 198-200, and Kretschmar, 100-101.

[37] On the April 4, 1524 diet in Breslau see Kastner, I, 27-29.

[38] On the diet in Breslau on April 11, 1524 see Acta Capituli Wratislaviensis, Wroclaw DA, III, b. 1b, 190-194. Cf. Kastner, I, 29-30.

[39] Acta Capituli Wratislaviensis, Wroclaw DA, III, b. 1b, 190. Cf. Kastner, I, 29.

[40] Note especially Kretschmar, 104-115.

[41] CS II (1) 28-103.

[42] Ibid., 28-41, 7.

[43] This was suggested by Knörrlich, 79 among others.

[44] Veit Ludwig von Seckendorf, *Commentarius,* II, III. Ad Indicem I. Historicum. Scholia sive Supplementa No. 28 (unpaginated). Seckendorf bases his statement on a 1617 letter of the Superintendent Simon Grunäus to Abraham Scultetus.
[45] CS XIV, 290, 20-23.
[46] Knörrlich, 33.
[47] CS I, 36, 1-2; XIII, 26, 22-28.
[48] Ibid., XIV, 290, 20-23.
[49] Prince Albert visited Liegnitz in October, 1524 for example. See Paul Tschackert, *Urkundenbuch,* II, 261.
[50] See Konrad Klose, "Schwenckfeld und die Schwenckfelder in Lüben," 195, and his *Beiträge zur Geschichte der Stadt Lüben,* 76-77.
[51] CS I, 118, 7-121, 7.
[52] Ibid., 270, 23-24.
[53] Ibid., 36, 3-5.
[54] Ibid., IX, 82, 2-4.
[55] Ibid., II, 262, 10-11.
[56] Paul Scholz, "Vertreibung der Bernhardiner aus Liegnitz," 359-378.
[57] Valentin Crautwald to Margarete Engelmann, 1537, printed in Arnold, *Supplementa,* 139.
[58] On this and the following see Schubart, *Vorrede,* 149-150. Cf. Bahlow, *Reformation,* 48.
[59] Certainly it may have happened that the sacrament was given in both species earlier. This was suggested by Johann, baron of Rechenberg auf Windisch-Borau and Freystadt, a friend and admirer of Melanchthon's at the Breslau diet of April 11, 1524. See Acta Capituli Wratislaviensis, Wroclaw DA, III, b. 1b, 191: "To this, lord Johann Rechenberg knight in Freystadt etc. in a clear voice stated that he had received the Supper under both species and did not wish to participate in the sacrament in any other way as long as he lived." Cf. Kastner, I, 30.
[60] CS II, 660, 17-24.
[61] Ibid., XVIII, 8, 3-11.
[62] Ibid., 8, 11-12.
[63] Printed in Theodor Wotschke, "Zur Reformation in Liegnitz," 155-158, and in CS XVIII (6) 8-10.
[64] On this and the following cf. Knörrlich, 108-110.
[65] München SB, CLM 718, fol. 37r-55v, printed in Ferdinand Cohrs, *Die Evangelischen Katechismusversuche vor Luthers Enchiridion,* IV, 204-218. In 1536 Schwenckfeld translated this catechism of Crautwald's into German and in an expanded version printed it under the title *Catechismus Christi.* See CS V, (559) 568-603. A revised edition was also published two more times (see ibid., 562-565).
[66] München SB, CLM 718, fol. 26r-36r, printed in Eberlein, "Volksunterricht," 34-40 (faulty edition), and in Cohrs, IV, 196-203.
[67] München SB, CLM 718, fol. 56r-63r, printed in Cohrs, IV, 219-225.
[68] CS IX, (448) 453-493. Cf. ibid., II, 376.
[69] Ibid., IV, (208) 216-238. Partially printed in Johann Michael Reu, II, Abt. II, 757, 22-762, 18.
[70] SC IX, (731) 737-756. Partially printed in Reu, 762, 19-773, 13.
[71] On dating see CS V, 235, 30-31.
[72] Cf. Joachim Heubach, "Die Aufgabe der christlichen Unterweisung bei den Böhmischen Brüdern," 327-349.
[73] Cohrs, IV, 196-197, 15.
[74] Ibid., 197, 16-20.
[75] Ibid., 198, 33-200, 32.
[76] Ibid., 200, 33-202, 28.
[77] Ibid., 202, 30-203, 11.
[78] Ibid., 203, 12-25.
[79] CS V, (221) 222-246.
[80] Valentin Crautwald to Michael Wittiger, May 20 and 27, 1526, München SB, CLM 718, fol. 310v-311r, 319r-320v.

[81] CR I, 643-644. No. 261.
[82] Valentin Crautwald to Dominicus Schleupner, 1526, München SB, CLM 718, fol. 292r-v.
[83] Valentin Crautwald to Johann Hess, ibid., fol. 272r.
[84] Extant only in München SB. On this and the following see WA 10, 2, 347-348, and Paul Althaus Sr., *Forschungen zur Evangelischen Gebetsliteratur,* 26-29.
[85] WA 10, 2, 347.
[86] Althaus, 29.
[87] See WA 10, 2, 347-348, and Althaus, 30-32.

3. *The Liegnitz Brotherhood and Other Reformation Centers*

[1] The poem is found in a supplement to Ambrosius Moibanus, *Catechismi capita decem,* Wittenberg 1538, fol. H 8r, and is printed in Kretschmar, 112, 114.
[2] On this and the following see Gerhard Eberlein, "Die erste evangelische Predigt in Schlesien," 65-77.
[3] See Konrad, "Einführung," 21-23.
[4] See ibid., 23.
[5] See Gottfried Seebass, *Bibliographia Osiandrica,* 3, 1-4.
[6] Cf. Gustav Kawerau, "Liturgische Studien zu Luther's Taufbüchlein von 1523," especially 472-473, 526-547.
[7] See Johann Grünewald, "Das älteste schlesische Gesangbuch," 61-66, and Günter Birkner, "Die beiden ältesten evangelischen Gesangbuch-Drucke Schlesiens 1525 und 1525/26," 141-152.
[8] Nikolaus Pol, *Jahrbücher,* III, 38.
[9] See for example Ambrosius Moibanus to Johannes Hess, December 8, 1521 printed in *CKGS* 9 (1904) 48-49, and Kretschmar, 56.
[10] Probably the April 1520 anti-papal dialogue *Vadiscus.*
[11] CS I, 11, 15-17.
[12] Philipp Melanchthon to Johannes Hess, March 25, 1522 printed in CR 1, 566-576, No. 206.
[13] CS 1, 10-12, especially 10, 9-11, 14.
[14] Ibid., 35, 8-9.
[15] Ibid., 37, 1.
[16] Ibid., 37, 2.
[17] Printed in Gustav Koffmane, "Zu Luthers Briefen und Tischreden," 133-136; Gustav Bauch, "Analekten zur Biographie des Johann Hess," 45-48; Nikolaus Müller, *Die Wittenberger Bewegung 1521 und 1522,* 15-19; and Kretschmar, 46, 48, 50, 52, 54.
[18] Note the error in Bahlow, 26 in this regard: "So great was the first impression which Luther made on Schwenckfeld that the Silesian hurried personally to Wittenberg at the end of 1518 or the beginning of 1519 to allow himself to be directed more deeply into the truth at Luther's feet."
[19] Printed in Bauch, "Analekten," 48-49. See Kretschmar, 56.
[20] Note, for example, Franz Hoffmann, *Caspar Schwenckfelds Leben und Lehren,* 19.
[21] CS IX, 82, 2-4.
[22] CR 1, 155-161, No. 69.
[23] WAB 2, 118-119, No. 296; CR 1, 161-162, No. 71; 201-202, No. 78; 613-614, No. 242; 643-644, No. 261.
[24] Tschackert, *Urkundenbuch,* II, 55. See also Walther Hubatsch, *Albrecht von Brandenburg-Ansbach,* 103.
[25] Tschackert, *Urkundenbuch,* II, 55 and 261.
[26] The correspondence between Schwenckfeld and Albert of Prussia began between October 1524 and May 1525 (cf. CS II, 109-112), but is lost until 1528.
[27] CS XIV, 281, 38-282, 1.

[28] See Albert Clos, ''Beziehungen zwischen der preussischen und der Liegnitzer Reformation,'' 25-26.
[29] Heinrich Laag, ''Die Einführung der Reformation im Ordensland Preussen,'' 860-861.
[30] Friedlaender, I, 4, 27-28.
[31] Hubatsch, 115.
[32] CS II, (113) 120-125.

4. *The Liegnitz Brotherhood and the Left Wing of the Reformation*

[1] Konrad, ''Einführung,'' 80.
[2] Friedlaender, I, 34, 10-11.
[3] Weimar LHA, Reg. N. No. 623, fol. 46r-46v, printed in End 6, 271-273, No. 1331; WAB 4, 571-573, No. 1328, Beilage. Cf. Hermann Barge, *Andreas Bodenstein,* II, 386-388, 391-392.
[4] WAB 4, 571, 3-5, No. 1328, Beilage.
[5] On the back of this letter of Karlstadt's, Luther wrote ''D. Karlstadts Manuscript and seal.''
[6] WAB 4, 568-571, No. 1328.
[7] CS II, 243, 15-16; 253, 1-2.
[8] Crautwald, *De sensu verborum coenae dominicae,* n.d. (ca.1525), München SB, CLM 718, fol. 96r.
[9] Ernst Freys and Hermann Barge, ''Verzeichnis der gedruckten Schriften des Andreas Bodenstein,'' 18.
[10] WAB, 3, 544, 545, No. 903.
[11] Johann Bugenhagen, *Eyn Sendbrieff / widder den newen yrrthumb / bey dem Sacarament des / leybs vnd blutts vn=/sers HERRN / Jhesu Chri=/sti.* / Wittenberg 1525.

5. *Schwenckfeld's Criticism of the Reformation Doctrine of Justification*

[1] CS I, 36, 20-21.
[2] Ibid., (211) 242-283.
[3] Ibid., 268, 17-20.
[4] Ibid., 268, 20-22.
[5] Ibid., 268, 29-35.
[6] Ibid., 270, 6.
[7] Ibid., 270, 1-6.
[8] Ibid., II, 70, 14.
[9] Ibid., 70, 2-24.
[10] Ibid., 121, 7-8.
[11] Ibid., 121, 6-122, 11.
[12] Ibid., 280, 14-281, 6.
[13] On this and the following see my ''Sebastian Franck und die lutherische Reformation,'' 13-20.
[14] Cf. Sebastian Franck, *Trunkenhayt,* fol. B 4r: ''If a preacher notices that someone is not extending the gospel but that it is being misapplied for self-righteousness and hypocrisy, he will not remain there if he is of God. For he likes the pearl enough that he would rather strew it before swine and give the gospels to the dogs. Therefore he remains completely silent or he flees. For we have just as much a commandment to be silent and leave as we do to preach and come to give aid.''
[15] Cf. Here and following see Georg Baring, ''Hans Denck und Thomas Müntzer,'' 145-181.
[16] Hirsch, 145-170.
[17] Ibid., 147.
[18] Ibid.

[19] CS I, 270, 15-17.
[20] Ibid., 270, 17.
[21] Ibid., 270, 18-20.
[22] Ibid., 270, 25-26.
[23] Ibid., 270, 24.
[24] Ibid., 270, 28-31.
[25] Ibid., II, 40, 15-20.
[26] Ibid., 44, 9. Cf. 44, 25-46, 7.
[27] Ibid., 46, 21-22.
[28] Ibid., 46, 24-25: ". . .through the cross and suffering, suppression of carnal desire, rejection of the world and a similar mortification of their flesh." Cf. 46, 8-33.
[29] Ibid., 56, 22-68, 22.
[30] Ibid., XIII, 997, 31-35.
[31] Ibid., 997, 34-35.
[32] Ibid., 998, 2.
[33] Ibid., 997, 36-998, 2.
[34] Ibid., 60, 14-16.
[35] Ibid., 62, 6.
[36] In any case, Schwenckfeld used Melanchthon in his later writings. Cf. ibid., XIII, 991, 1-998, 37.
[37] In the *De hominis viribus adeoque de libero arbitrio* he writes: "There is no liberty in either external or internal works, but all things result according to divine will." Philipp Melanchthon, *Werke in Auswahl,* II, 1, 17, 3-6.
[38] CS II, 281, 8.
[39] Ibid., III, (24) 25-33.
[40] Ibid., 28, 23-31.
[41] Ibid., 558-569.
[42] Ibid., 560, 18-19.
[43] Ibid., II, 72, 29-78, 26.
[44] Ibid., 74, 9-11.
[45] Ibid., 74, 28-29.
[46] Ibid., 74, 29-31.
[47] Ibid., 74, 35-76, 5.

6. Schwenckfeld's Early Doctrine of Justification

[1] CS I, 239-243.
[2] Crautwald, *Ein nutzbar Edell / Buchleinn von be=/reytunge zum sterben / mit vnder=/richt wie sich in den anfechtungen / doselbst zu haldenn sey / auss / dem latein / mit eyll vnd / eynfeldig gedeutscht./* Breslau 1524. Hereafter: *Von bereytunge zum sterben.* (In a future study I intend to discuss this *Ars moriendi*).
[3] Ibid., fol. A IV (Vorwort).
[4] On Georg Jeschko see Luschek, 171, 401. He is noted in Acta Capituli Wratislaviensis, Wroclaw DA, III, b. 1a, fol. 315r, 479r, 547v. I am thankful to A. Sabisch for indicating this to me.
[5] On Erasmus Heyland see Gerhard Pfeiffer, *Das Breslauer Patriziat im Mittelalter,* 302.
[6] Crautwald, *Von bereytunge zum sterben,* fol. A IV (Preface).
[7] CS II, 44, 26-27.
[8] Ibid., 44, 28-29.
[9] Ibid., XI, 509, 5-9; 510, 8.
[10] Ibid., 583, 14-16.
[11] WA 26, 508, 32-36 (English tranlation: LW, 37, 371).
[12] CS II, 44, 8-46, 7.

[13] Ibid., 46, 6-7.
[14] Ibid., I, 256, 14-15.
[15] Ibid., 256, 15-16.
[16] Ibid., 262, 15-16.
[17] Ibid., II, 80, 31-33.
[18] Ibid., 80, 34-35.
[19] Ibid., 34, 17-20.
[20] Ibid., 48, 28-31.
[21] The *Devotio Moderna,* in which the ideal of bearing the cross is central, clearly did not influence the young Schwenckfeld. The Brethren of the Common Life played no role in Silesia. Cf. Bernhard Windeck, *Die Anfänge der Brüder vom gemeinsamen Leben in Deutschland.*
[22] CS II, 86, 4-7.
[23] See ibid., 50, 26-30. "Only through faith in Christ alone do we receive the Spirit, and the same Spirit assures our spirit that we are the children of God (Romans 8). And again St. Paul says, we have not received the Spirit from this world. The Spirit comes only from God that we may know what is given us by God."
[24] On this see Reinhold Pietz, *Der Mensch ohne Christus.*
[25] CS II, 72, 11-13.
[26] Ibid., 48, 29-31.
[27] Ibid., 52, 30-31; 60, 26-29; 64, 30-33.
[28] Ibid., XIII, 857, 6-10.
[29] Ibid., I, 276, 17-24.
[30] Ibid., II, 80, 19-26. "We must all become one through the suffering of Christ; we must bear all that the eternal God sends with patience and meekness. In our flesh we must fulfill the suffering of Christ, for everyone who wishes to be resurrected with Christ in joy must first die with him in suffering."
[31] Ibid., VIII, 50, 18-20; 52, 23-25.
[32] Ibid., 70, 1-3. Cf. 68, 36-72, 3.

7. The Theological and Spiritual Roots of Schwenckfeld's Early Doctrine of Justification

[1] Karl Ecke, *Schwenckfeld,* 33.
[2] Hirsch, 36.
[3] Pietz, especially 155-158.
[4] Knörrlich, 40; Cf. ibid., 41: "Thus Schwenckfeld stands almost fully in the bond of Luther, makes Luther's thoughts his, and propagates his teaching. His first extant writings indicate Schwenckfeld's firm Lutheran position." Ibid., 44: "Until 1525 he fought on Luther's side against the Roman system which he saw as "antichrist" opposed to the clear words of Scripture and the law of God and leading to evil practices and errors."
[5] Ibid., 64.
[6] Ibid., 88.
[7] Erbkam, 359.
[8] Ibid., 358.
[9] Ibid., 473.
[10] Gottfried Maron, *Individualismus und Gemeinschaft bei Caspar von Schwenckfeld,* 160.
[11] Erich Seeberg, "Der Gegensatz zwischen Zwingli, Schwenckfeld und Luther," 60.
[12] Richard H. Grützmacher, "Schwenckfeld," in RE XVIII, 72-81. According to Grützmacher, "in the development of his thought, Schwenckfeld built on the thought of Augustine, German mysticism, and above all on Tauler" (ibid., 76, 57-58), and in his "mystical concept. . . of faith the middle ages" was reborn (80, 59-60). Cf. also his *Wort und Geist,* 158-173.
[13] Joachim Wach, *Types of religious experience,* 139.

[14] CS I, 11, 15-17.
[15] Ibid., XII, 554, 2-3.
[16] Ecke, 45.
[17] CS I, 252, 26-28. In the 1521 Basel edition of Tauler, the phrase reads ". . . that God himself does not begin a work of which he is not the beginning and the end" (fol. 83v, b).
[18] Ecke, 45.
[19] Hirsch, 41-42.
[20] CS II, 68, 12-14.
[21] Cf. Engratis Kihm, "Die Drei-Wege-Lehre bei Tauler," 268-300.
[22] CS II, 83, 12-14.
[23] Hirsch, 36-41.
[24] These writings are: *In epistolam Pauli ad Galatas M. Lutheri commentarius*, 1519 (WA 2, [436] 443-618;English trans.: LW, 27, 153-4 10); *Resolutiones Lutherianae super propositionibus suis Lipsiae disputatis*, 1519 (WA 2, [388] 391-435); *Von der Freiheit eines Christenmenschen*, 1520 (WA 7, [12] 20-38;English trans.: LW, 31, 333-377); *Von dem Papsttum zu Rom wider den hochberühmten Romanisten zu Leipzig*, 1520 (WA 6, [277] 285-324;English trans.: LW, 39, 55-104); *Von den guten Werken*, 1520 (WA 6, [196] 204-276;English trans.: LW, 44, 21 -114); *Das Magnificat verdeutscht und ausgelegt*, 1521 (WA 7, [538] 544-604;English trans.: LW, 21, 297-358); *Eine treue Vermahnung M. Luthers zu allen Christen, sich zu hüten vor Aufruhr und Empörung*, 1522 (WA 8, [670] 676-687; English trans .: LW, 45, 57-74); *Acht Sermone D.M. Luthers von ihm gepredigt zu Wittenberg in der Fasten* (WA 10, 3, 1-64;English trans.: LW, 51, 70-100); *Vorrede auf die Epistel S. Pauli an die Röhmer*, 1522 (WAB 7, 28-79;English trans.: LW, 25, 4-524); *Kirchenpostille*, 1522 (WA 10, 1, 1, 1-739 and 10, 1, 2, 1-208); *Von Menschenlehre zu meiden und Antwort auf Sprüche, so man führet, Menschenlehre zu stärken*, 1522 (WA 10, 2, [61] 72-92;English trans.: LW, 35, 131-153); *Wider den falsch genannten geistlichen Stand des Papsts und der Bischöfe*, 1522 (WA, 10, 2, [93] 105-158;English trans.: LW, 39, 247-299); *Dass eine christliche Versammlung oder Gemeine Recht und Macht habe, alle Lehre zu urteilen und Lehrer zu berufen, ein- und abzusetzen, Grund und Ursach aus der Schrift*, 1523 (WA 11, [401] 408-416;English trans.: LW, 39, 305-314).

II Controversies Over the Lord's Supper

1. Schwenckfeld's Doctrine of the Supper before 1525

[1] CS I, 250, 21-31.
[2] Ibid., XIV, 802, 17.
[3] Ibid., II, 249, 21-25.
[4] Ibid., (325) 329-333.
[5] Ibid., 330, 8-9.
[6] Ibid., 330, 10-13.
[7] In his treatise *Vom Anbeten des Sakraments des heiligen Leichnams Christi (WA 11, 431-456;English trans.: LW, 36, 275-305)* Luther separated himself from Honius who since the spring of 1521 had begun to treat the words of institution as signifying the body of Christ.
[8] In his work *Wider die himmlischen Propheten, von den Bildern und Sakrament*, Luther defended the Supper as a means of grace against Karlstadt (for example WA 18, 136, 9-19; 136, 24-144, 2; 182, 21-33;English trans.: LW, 40, 79-143), who in his spiritualism had rejected the external word.
[9] CS II, 122, 14-125, 1.
[10] Ibid., 242, 24-243, 1.

[11] Ibid., 249, 21-25. Cf. 253, 21-25; 255, 29-256, 1; 256, 6-10; 258, 9-13; 258, 17-21, 23-24.
[12] WA 17, 1; 175, 17.
[13] For example, ibid., 12, 480, 2-4.
[14] CS XIV, 802, 19-24. Cf. 803, 15-19.
[15] Ibid., 820, 24-34. Cf. 803, 5-8.
[16] Ibid., 802, 35-37. Cf. 803, 11-14.
[17] Ibid., 803, 5-7: "I will not become troubled over the words: *This is my body* (Matthew 26:26). I stand firm in my stated position based on John 6." Ibid., 803, 18-23: "The [turmoil] concerning *This is my body* may be as it will. As I see it God the Lord will call [us] to the correct meaning. Certainly, however, as I understand it, the Lord Christ is not speaking of bread and wine as one can see when one says *Hoc est sanguis meus.*"
[18] Ibid., 802, 39-803, 4.
[19] Ibid., 802, 17-23. It must be noted that this statement is from 1556 so that his comments on the value of this conception of the sacrament and his review of the specific elements are not reliable in detail.
[20] Ibid., 803, 24-27. Cf. ibid., II, 127-140.
[21] The treatise was probably reworked in 1529 *(Ein Christlich bedencken. Ob Judas vnd die ungleubigen falschen Christen / den Leib vnnd das blut Jhesu Christi / jm Sacrament des Nachtmals etwan empfangen / oder auch noch heüt empfahen vnd niessen mögen,* ibid., III, [(492)] 498-507) since it treats the same question as his treatise to Markus Zimmermann of 1556 in 12 points (ibid., esp. 506, 1-6). If this is true then it is highly likely that in his early sacramental teaching Schwenckfeld used *credere* (to believe) and *edere* (to eat) synonymously. In his treatise he described spiritual eating as a metaphysical description of an inner communion in faith. "Just as the lord Christ wishes to live alone spiritually in the faithful heart, in the Holy Spirit, so he also wishes to nourish true Christians with his flesh and blood spiritually in the word . . . through true faith. He directs the faithful heart from all which is opposed and against him from earthly being and life above itself and into itself into a nobler being into the spiritual heavenly being in which he refreshes, feeds, fills, and satisfies it with his divine grace and with the bread of eternal life (ibid., 506, 8-15).
[22] Ibid., XIV, 803, 27. Cf. II, 147-164.
[23] Ibid., XIV, 803, 27-28. Cf. II, 141-146.
[24] Cf. ibid., II, 145-146.
[25] Ibid., 194, 10-11.
[26] Ibid., XIV, 803, 28.
[27] Ibid., 802, 16-20; 803, 24-27.
[28] Ibid., II, 242, 24-243, 1.
[29] Ibid., 122, 14-123, 2. Although Schwenckfeld does not make it clear which book of Zwingli's he read, it is likely to have been the *Ad Matthaeum Alberum de coena dominica epistola* (CR 90, [322] 335-354) and the *De vera et falsa religione commentarius* (ibid., [590] 628-912).
[30] Ibid., 242, 24-243, 1; 251, 7-11.
[31] CR 90, 340, 8-12.
[32] See Wessel Gansfort, *De sacramento Eucharistiae et audienda missa,* Chapters VII-IX, in Wessel Gansfort, *Opera,* 670-677.
[33] CR 91, (505) 512-519.
[34] Ibid., 514, 2-4.
[35] Walter Köhler, *Zwingli und Luther,* I, 272.
[36] CS II, 242, 24-243, 1.
[37] Ibid., 272, 20-21.
[38] Ibid., 272, 21-22.
[39] Cf. ibid., 272, n. 5.
[40] Erhard Peschke, *Die Theologie der Böhmischen Brüder in ihrer Frühzeit,* I, 1, 279-304.
[41] Ibid., 280.
[42] Valentin Ernst Löscher, *Ausführliche Historia motuum zwischen den Evangelish-Lutherischen und Reformirten,* I, 147-148 and Ehrhardt, IV, 39.

[43] CS II, 253, 1-4.
[44] Ibid., 281, 8-9.

2. *Crautwald's Doctrine of the Lord's Supper*

[1] CS II, 194, 8-10; XIV, 803, 28-32.
[2] Ibid., XIV, 803, 28-32.
[3] Ibid., 803, 33-34.
[4] Ibid., 803, 34-804, 3. Cf. II, 194, 10-14.
[5] Ibid., II, 194, 14-196, 6. Cf. XIV, 804, 2-3.
[6] Ibid., II, (173) 194-209.
[7] Ibid., XIV, 804, 4-5.
[8] Ibid., 804, 5-6.
[9] Ibid., II, (173) 194-209.
[10] Ibid., 196, 6-9.
[11] Ibid., 196, 10-11.
[12] Ibid., 196, 11-12.
[13] Ibid., 196, 12-17.
[14] Ibid., 196, 17-19.
[15] Ibid., 196, 23-198, 2. Unfortunately Crautwald does not indicate which letter of Cyprian he read. It was possibly the sixty-third (CSEL 3, 1, 701-717).
[16] Ibid., 198, 2.
[17] Ibid., 198, 12-21.
[18] Ibid., 198, 30-200, 2.
[19] Ibid., 200, 2-8.
[20] Ibid., 200, 8-17.
[21] Ibid., 200, 17-21.
[22] Ibid., 200, 30-31.
[23] Ibid., 200, 31-202, 2.
[24] Crautwald also read Gratian's *Decretum* (ibid., 202, 2). He must have been particularly concerned with the third part since in *Decretum* 2, de consecratione, there are many citations from the Fathers, particularly Cyprian and Augustine (cf. c. 2, 3, 13, 26, 44, 45, 46, 47 D. 2 de cons.). Certainly he found support for his new doctrine of the Supper in c.47 D.2 de cons.
[25] Ibid., 202, 2.
[26] Ibid., 202, 3-5.
[27] Ibid., 202, 6-7.
[28] Ibid., 202, 7-9.
[29] Ibid., 202, 10-12. This is notably missing in the German trans.. This may be because of the later differences between Schwenckfeld and Egetius.
[30] Cf. ibid., 244, 11-12.
[31] Ibid., 202, 12-13. The letter is no longer extant.
[32] Ibid., 202, 13-15.
[33] Ibid., 204, 1-209, 28.
[34] Schubart, "Vorrede," 150: ". . . and through him [Crautwald] as the most learned and public lector, the other pastors and preachers were also drawn into error, even Wentzeslaum Küchler, preacher in St. Peters."
[35] CS II, 204, 8-10.
[36] Ibid., 307, 13-14. Cf. Valentin Crautwald to Bernhard Egetius, December 1525. München SB, CLM 718, fol. 214v: "The use of the bread in the meal is not that in or with or through which Christ gave his body to the disciples."
[37] CS II, 307, 15-16.
[38] Ibid., 204, 8-10.

[39] Valentin Crautwald to Bernhard Egetius, December 10, 1525. München SB, CLM 718, fol. 212r.
[40] CS II, 198, 25-26.
[41] Note, for example, ibid., 204, 11-12: "The words of the Lord's Supper ought to be expanded and explained with these words of Christ in John 6: *My body is truly food.*"
[42] Ibid., 198, 24-25.
[43] Ibid., 307, 26-29.
[44] Ibid., 302, 4-10.
[45] Valentin Crautwald to unknown addressee (before April 13, 1526), München, SB, CLM 718, fol. 243v: "In no other way than inwardly is Christ or food capable of being eaten, that is with the teeth of faith."
[46] Note, for example, CS II, 313, 33-314, 10.
[47] Ibid., 304, 22-27. Cf. Valentin Crautwald to Bernhard Egetius, December 10, 1525, München SB, CLM 718, fol. 214v: "In the Supper Christ represents and shows in the bread of the meal, the nature of his body, exhibiting in true bread, true bread in true eating, true eating in true nourishment and vivification, true nourishment and vitality: he joins and sets forth true things with true things." "They teach that the nature of the body of Christ, that is the celestial bread [is] from the bread which is eaten."
[48] CS II, 303, 25-26.
[49] Crautwald, *Institutiuncula de signis seu symbolis sacris sacramentis,* (presumably 1525), München SB, CLM 718, fol. 60r-v.
[50] CS II, 306, 31-34.
[51] Ibid., 312, 12-21.
[52] Ibid., 313, 7-14.
[53] This is grammatically correct. See Bl-Debr 171, 273.
[54] CS II, 204, 16-17: "This is my body which is given for you. Construe it as follows: My Body which is given for you is this, namely bread."
[55] Ibid., 206, 2. Cf. *Das Neue Testament ins Hebräische,* translated by F. Delitzsch (Luke 22:19).
[56] CS II, 206, 1-8. Cf. W. Gesenius, *Hebräische Grammatik.* Fully revised by E. Kautzsch, 472, 141, 1.
[57] Note, for example, Valentin Crautwald to Adam Adamus, June 17, 1526, München SB, CLM 718, fol. 224r-225r. Especially fol. 225r: "It is enough to say that it is not possible to turn *this* grammatically into the masculine or to indicate the masculine, since it has no sex and is neuter." A similar argument can be found in Karlstadt. Cf. Gottfried Krodel, *Die Abendmahlslehre des Erasmus von Rotterdam,* 202.
[58] CS II, 424, 22-24.
[59] Ibid., 208, 4-6.
[60] Ibid., (297) 301-323.
[61] Ibid., 303, 31-32.
[62] CS II, 208, 17-19: "Thus Tertullian states against Marcion: Christ represents his body as bread saying: Behold, he begins with the body, not with the bread. These are Tertullians's words. Jerome on Matthew says the same." Cf. CSEL, 47, 308, 22. On the concept of *repraesentare* in Tertullian see Karl Ludwig Leimbach, *Beiträge zur Abendmahlslehre Tertullians,* 6-32.
[63] Valentin Crautwald to unknown addressee, (before April 13, 1526). München SB, CLM 718, fol. 257r. Cf. CSEL 47, 560, 1-2. On the use of *figura* in Tertullian see Leimbach, 62-90.
[64] CS II, 208, 1-11. Cf. CSEL, 3, 3, 2, 754, 6.
[65] Ibid., 208, 12-21.
[66] Ibid., 208, 20.
[67] Ibid., 208, 20.
[68] Ibid., 208, 20-21.
[69] Note, for example, CS II, 307, 13-16: "Look not to the earth, nor to the earthly, nor to the bread, nor above, nor below, nor read in a book, or in the statement or outer word of the

celebrant for they neither have nor give the heavenly bread of eternal life or daily sustenance for the children of God."

70 Note, for example, ibid., 198, 11-200, 21.

71 Ibid., 306, 1.

72 On Sebastian Eisenmann see CS XV, 205-207.

73 Schubart, "Vorrede," 151: "As soon as this hallucinatory revelation came and was preached in Liegnitz things happened as they might be expected to happen. Lo there came a spirit out of Germany with the name Sebastian N. After this he was for a long time Crautwald's famulus until Crautwald died; he shot poison with Schwenckfeld from the pipe which Crautwald made, flying to Liegntz, bringing a head full of revelations."

74 See Valentin Crautwald to Margarete Engelmann, 1537, printed in Arnold, *Supplementa*, 139: ". . . This man is everything in one: a cook, a waiter, a housekeeper, a shepherd and servant, a cleaner and ostler, and has served me now for nine or ten years. He has in this time improved himself in art, speech, and reading." Sebastian Eisenmann, *Von der Schul des heiligen Geists*, 1557, SchLP, Ms. Sb. XXV, fol. 28v: ". . . until God the Father of all comfort, embraced me and revealed to me his son Jesus Christ in the school of the Holy Spirit Anno 1527." Cited from CS XV, 205-206. Reisner, *Vita*, München SB, CLM 718, fol. 549r: "He had for his colleague or assistant Sebastian Eisenmann who was his butler, steward and cook, and with whom he lived for more than twenty years."

75 Johann Christian Hermann Weissenborn, *Acten der Erfurter Universität*, II, 306, 4: "Sebastianus Isenman de Frickenhusen."

76 Eisenmann, *Schul*, fol. 27r: "In all I heard Bugenhagen, Fuker, Jonas, and Mennius preach, and Melanchthon read and I knew other writings in many colleges and towns in Germany but they could not satisfy or bring peace to my soul and conscience." Cited from CS XV, 205.

77 See Valentin Crautwald to Margarete Engelmann, 1537, printed in Arnold, *Supplementa*, 139: ". . . Beside me is my helper. Earlier he was a very young man, a pastor and preacher."

78 Schubart, "Vorrede," 151: "Many came and counsel was given, that private prayer be begun in the school of the Church your blessed mother. Those who wished to have revelations of the Spirit, fasted and prayed and, advised in this stupidity, they imagined that what came to them in their fasts and prayers was a spiritual revelation. The cantor [G. Tag] wrote these down."

79 Ibid., 152.

80 Ibid., 151-152.

81 WAB 4, 138, 1-139, 3, No. 1055.

82 CS XVII, 1014, 16-19.

83 In his important study *Thomas Müntzer in Zwickau und die "Zwickauer Propheten."* Paul Wappler indicates the significant role of revelations of the Spirit in the thought of Nikolaus Storch (ibid., 46-47), Markus Thomae (ibid., 58-60), and Thomas Drechsel (ibid., 78-81).

84 CS II, 196, 10-12; 204, 8-10; 208, 25-26.

85 Ibid., 208, 25-26.

86 See Joachim Ernst Scheibel, *Geschichte der Stadtbuchdruckerey*, 12.

87 Crautwald's library contained the following works by Zwingli: *Usslegen vnd gründ der schlussreden oder Artickle* (1523) (CR 89, 1-457); *Von götlicher un menschlicher grechtigheit* (1523) (ibid., 458-525); *Der Hirt* (1524) (ibid., 90, 1-68); *Antwurt eins Schwytzerpurens* (1524) (ibid., 86-91); *Ain Epistel Huldrych Zwinglis . . . an den Ersamen landsradt von gantzen gemeind . . . der Graffschafft Doggenburg* (1524) (ibid., 95, 206-212, No. 342); *De vera et falsa religione* (1525) (ibid., 90, 590-912). Of Oecolampadius' works he owned *In epistolam Joannis apostoli catholicam primam Joannis Oecolampadii demegorise, hoc est: homiliae unna et XX* (1524).

88 In addition to the *Lucubratiunculae* (published by Matthias Schürer in Strassburg, 1515), Crautwald's library contained the following works by Erasmus: *De bello Turcis inserendo Consultatio* (1517) (Le Clerc 5, 345-368): *Paraphrasis in Epistolam Pauli ad Romanos* (1518) (ibid., 7, 773-848); *Apologia ad Jac. Fabrum Stapulensem* (1518) (ibid., 9, 67-80);

Paraphrasis in duos Epistolas Pauli ad Corinthios (1519) (ibid., 7, 859-942); *Antibarbarorum* (1520) (ibid., 10, 1691-1744). Cf. Glombiowski, 125-152, especially 136.

89 CS II, 323, 17-22. Cf. Le Clerc 7, 565 D.

90 Cf. G. Krodel, *Die Abendmahlslehre des Erasmus v. Rotterdam.*

91 CS II, 208, 1-24.

92 Valentin Crautwald to Bernhard Egetius, December 10, 1525, München SB, CLM 718, fol. 219r.

3. The Attempts of the Schwenkfelders to win the Lutherans

1 CS II, 241, 3-4; XIV, 803, 26-27

2 Ibid., XIV, 804, 7-8.

3 Ibid., II, 240, 21-241, 2; 241, 11-14.

4 Cf. ibid., 240, n. 3.

5 Ibid., 243, 2.

6 Ibid., (173) 194-209.

7 Ibid., (383) 391-408.

8 This is likely the second part of his 1526 *Collatio et consensus verborum coenae dominicae* (ibid., (383) 389-408); the selection is from 403-408.

9 Ibid., 275, 20-21.

10 Ibid., 244, 11.

11 It is likely that Schwenckfeld had other writings along. Cf. esp. ibid., 244, 10 and CS XIV, 804, 7.

12 CS II, (235) 240-282.

13 Ibid., 240, 16-20.

14 WAT 3, 125, 8-15, No. 2971b; cf. 24-30, No. 2971b; 5, 300, 2-6, No. 5659.

15 CS II, 241, 19-245, 24.

16 Ibid., 245, 17-18.

17 Ibid., 244, 9-12.

18 Ibid., 274, 3.

19 Ibid., 273, 11-274, 2.

20 Ibid., 276, 5-16.

21 Ibid., 245, 25-247, 3; 248, 14-264, 8; 264, 24-273, 5.

22 Ibid., 263, 18-20.

23 Ibid., 244, 13-16.

24 Ibid., 267, 22-23.

25 Köhler, *Zwingili,* I, 199-200.

26 CS III, 264, 11-25.

27 Otto Vogt, publisher, *Dr. Johannes Bugenhagens Briefwechsel,* 58-59, No. 17.

28 CS II, 264, 27-272, 22.

29 Ibid., 273, 7.

30 Ibid., 273, 8-9.

31 Ibid., 274, 14-15.

32 On December 2, Schwenckfeld took part in a Vesper service at which Bugenhagen preached on John 3 (ibid., 248, 6-13). On December 3, he went with Bugenhagen to distribute money from a common collection (ibid., 253, 17-19) and on the same day he was at the baptism of Justus Jonas' second son, Justus (ibid., 263, 20-21). On December 4 there was a marriage service which Schwenckfeld likely attended (ibid., 275, 23-24.).

33 Ibid., 280, 15.

34 Ibid., 280, 21-23.

35 Ibid., 280, 23-26.

36 Ibid., 281, 1.

[37] Ibid., 281, 3-4.
[38] Ibid., 281, 4-6.
[39] Heinrich Hermelink, ''Zu Luthers Gedanken über Idealgemeinden,'' 267-322, demonstrated that Luther maintained this position in all his writings. Cf. Walter Köhler, ''Kirchengeschichte vom Beginn der Reformation,'' 508-509.
[40] Maron, 110-116.
[41] WA 19, 75, 5 (English trans.: LW 53, 63). Cf. Hermelink, ''Zu Luthers Gedanken,'' 314. Note as well Theodor Kolde, ''Luther's Gedanke von der ecclesiola in ecclesia,'' 552-555.
[42] WA 19, 75, 20.
[43] See ibid., especially 485, 25-483, 19.
[44] CS II, 279, 23-24.
[45] Ibid., 272, 4.
[46] Cf. ibid., 289-294.
[47] See ibid., 292.
[48] Ibid., 391, 14-15.
[49] Ibid., 393, 4-11.
[50] Crautwald, *De imagine et veritate sive umbra et corpore de duplici pane et potu in coena dominica,* (1526), München SB, CLM 718, fol. 127r: ''For truly this body Christ represents true bread. After the consumption of the broken bread he says: ''This is my body which is given for you.'' And the image of bread is not [the image] of truth.''
[51] Ibid., fol. 127v: ''And the broken bread is able to represent the Body of Christ given for us and the likeness of the bread broken on the cross and distributed as food for the nourishment of souls is not able to truly be the body of Christ.''
[52] Ibid., fol. 131r.
[53] Ibid., fol. 143r: ''The early Fathers did not doubt that Christ both bestowed favors and was present to the congregation or church gathered to break bread in his memory, but that faithful minds ate his body and blood in spirit and spiritually by spiritual means.''
[54] CS II, 279, 15-19.
[55] WAB, 3, 653, 5-9, No. 653.
[56] WA 19, 123, 1-5.
[57] WAB 4, 33, 10-11, No. 982.
[58] Ibid., 42, 39-43, No. 989.
[59] CS XIV, 804, 17.
[60] Ibid., 804, 17-20.
[61] Vogt, 61-62, No. 19.
[62] Ibid., 62, No. 19.
[63] WAB 4, 52-53, No. 995.
[64] Ibid., 53, No. 996.
[65] Ibid., 52, 5-10, No. 995; 53, 6-12, No. 996.
[66] Ibid., 52, 10-11, No. 995; 53, 12 and 16, No. 996.
[67] Ibid., 52, 12-13, No. 995.
[68] Ibid., 53, 18-19, No. 996.
[69] Cf. ibid., 53, 12-16, No. 996: ''I ask you now, if there is any place for my wish, that you abstain from that opinion which is so great a danger for souls lest you also be a criminal and increase the danger in the church. If, moreover, you are given to your opinion that you do injury (you do do injury) how much does Christ suffer.''
[70] CR I, 809-810, No. 396. This letter and that in Suppl. Mel. 6, 1, 332, No. 493 (beginning of September) may be dated too late. Moibanus' marriage took place before April 30, 1526.
[71] Gustav Kawerau, *Briefwechsel,* I, 100, No. 98.
[72] On Schwenckfeld's correspondence with Hess see CS II, 295-296. From Crautwald to Hess two letters are extant, April 8, 1526 (probable date) and 1526, München SB, CLM 718, fol. 271r to 280v and fol. 281r-288r.
[73] Schwenckfeld's correspondence with Moibanus is lost. Cf. CS II, 361-362. Only one letter

of Crautwald's to Moibanus, on June 24, 1526 remains. It is located in München SB, CLM 718, fol. 380r-390r.

74 Crautwald to Adam Adamus, June 17, 1526 and August 15, München SB, CLM 718, fol. 222r-225v and fol. 234r-241v (printed in CS II, 430-438).

75 Crautwald to Matthias Funck, (April/June 1526), München SB, CLM 718, fol. 226r-233v (printed in CS II, 422-429).

76 The correspondence of Schwenckfeld with Wittiger is lost. See CS II, 295, 334-335. Letters from Crautwald to Wittiger do remain for April 8, May 20, May 27, June 3, June 10, 1526, München SB, CLM 718, fol. 299r-307r, 308r-313v, 314r-318v, 318v-320v, 321r-349v.

77 On Süssenbach see Kliesch, 188.

78 See Ewald Wernicke, *Chronik der Stadt Bunzlau,* 172.

79 WAB 4, 60-61, No. 1001.

80 CR 1, 809-810, No. 396.

81 CS II, (165) 169-171; (363) 367-374. Cf. Tschackert, II, 517.

82 CS II, 273, 15-16.

83 Ibid., 330, 7-13.

84 Ibid., 330, 15-16.

85 Ibid., 330, 17-22.

86 Ibid., 330, 22-25.

87 Ibid., 331, 1-3.

88 Ibid., 331, 4-10.

89 Ibid., 331, 10-13.

90 Hirsch, 51.

91 CS II, 329, 9-11.

92 See Johann Soffner, ''Schlesische Fürstenbriefe aus der Reformationszeit,'' 401.

93 Printed in ibid., 401-402.

94 Ibid., 402.

95 CS II, 329, 5.

96 Ibid., (325) 329-333.

97 Paul Speratus, Johann Briesmann and Johann Poliander to Albert of Prussia, (Nov. 13, 1526) printed in P. Tschachert, *Urkundenbuch,* II, 522a.

98 Breslau preachers to Valentin Crautwald and others, November 29, 1526, printed in August Friedrich Heinrich Schneider, *Verlauf der Reformation in Liegnitz,* 34-35, Beilage II.

99 See CR I, 809-810, No. 396.

100 See Valentin Crautwald to Adam Adamus, June 17, 1526, München SB, CLM 718, fol. 222r.

101 CS II, 644, 17-21.

102 Ibid.

103 Paul Speratus, Johann Briesmann and Johann Poliander to Albert of Prussia, [November 13, 1526], printed in Tschackert, II, 522a. See also Karl Johann Cosack, *Paulus Speratus Leben und Lieder*, 83-87.

104 Paul Speratus to Caspar Schwenckfeld and Valentin Crautwald, November 13, 1526, printed in Tschackert, II, 522a. See also Cosack, 87.

105 The address. See note 104.

106 Printed in Schneider, *Verlauf,* 34-35, Beilage II.

107 Ibid., 35, Beilage II.

108 CR I, 812, No. 400.

4. The Approach of the Schwenkfelders to the South Germans and Swiss

1 On this and the following see especially Köhler, *Zwingli,* I, 273-274 and Knörrlich, 137-140.

2 See Franz Bernhard von Bucholtz, *Geschichte der Regierung Ferdinand des Ersten,* II, 407-425.

[3] On the decisions of the diet see Schickfuss, III, 171, and Georg Thebesius, *Liegnitzische Jahr-Bücher,* III, 28.
[4] Ibid.
[5] See Bucholtz, II, 407-425.
[6] Name according to CR 96, 100, 12, No. 607, but note CR 95, 567, 3, No. 470 where it is written Winkler. In the latter, a copy was being used.
[7] CR 95, 559, No. 466.
[8] Ibid., 559, 10-14, No. 466.
[9] Ibid., 567, 3-5, No. 470.
[10] Ibid., 568, 17-20, No. 470.
[11] Ibid., 568, 19-20, No. 470.
[12] Ibid., 568, 1-3, No. 470.
[13] Ibid., 567-570, No. 470.
[14] Ibid., 568, 21-569, 1, No. 470.
[15] Ibid., 569, 1-7, No. 470.
[16] Ibid., 569, 7-9, No. 470.
[17] Ibid., 91, (880) 893-941, No. 77.
[18] Ibid., 95, 569, 9-11, No. 470.
[19] Ibid., 558, 9-11, No. 465.
[20] Ibid., 569, 9-30, No. 470.
[21] CS II, 447, 23-30.
[22] On this and the following see Gustav Koffmane, "Eine schlesische Universität in der Reformationszeit," 34-38; Eberlein, "Die erste evangelische Universität," 281-282, 289-290, 297-298; Hans Reitzig, "Erste evang. Universität Deutschlands einst in Liegnitz," 6; and Karlheinz Goldmann, *Verzeichnis der Hochschulen,* 230.
[23] Seckendorf, III. Ad Indicem I. Historicum. Scholia sive Supplementa. No. 28 (unpaginated). His information is based on a letter which the Superintendent Simon Grunäus sent to Abraham Scultetus in 1617.
[24] See CR I, 811, No. 398; 812-813, No. 400; 814, No. 402.
[25] See Josef Benzing, *Lutherbibliographie,* 65.
[26] CR I, 811, No. 398.
[27] Ibid., 812-813, No. 400.
[28] On the beginning of the lectures see Eberlein, "Die erste evangelische Universität," 281-282, 289-290.
[29] On Ziegler's stay in Liegnitz see especially Hermann Jordan, *Reformation und gelehrte Bildung in der Markgrafschaft Ansbach-Bayreuth,* 137-139.
[30] Johann Clajus, *Variorum carminum libri quinque,* fol. 1r: "Ziegler, famed for his knowledge of Hebrew, came."
[31] Reisner, *Vita,* fol. 549v: "He interpreted wisely the books of the New Testament and the Psalms in public lectures." Crautwald's lectures are known partly through imprints and partly through student notes. They are: commentaries on the first three chapters of Genesis (Berlin SB, Ms. theol. lat. quart. 880) which a student of Crautwald's, Johann Schweintzer, had printed in 1530 (CS III, 582-611); part of a commentary on Matthew (München SB, CLM 718, fol. 170r-187r); one on John (München SB, CLM 718, fol. 459r-477r); one on Romans (Wolfenbüttel HAB, Cod. Guelf. 37.27 Aug. fol. 229-259); part of a commentary on I and II Corinthians (München SB, CLM 718, fol. 370r-379r, Wolfenbüttel HAB, Cod. Guelf. 37.27 Aug. fol. 421-445, 447-456); lectures on Galatians (Wolfenbüttel HAB, Col. Guelf. 37.27 Aug. fol. 447-456); lectures on Colossians (Wolfenbüttel HAB, Cod. Guelf. 37.27 Aug. fol. 521-542). I am planning an edition of Crautwald's lectures.
[32] Reisner, *Vita,* fol. 549v.
[33] On Trotzendorf's stay in Liegnitz see Bauch, *Trotzendorf,* 66-71.
[34] WAB 4, 138-140, No. 1055.
[35] Ibid., 163, No. 1076.

[36] On Rurer's stay in Liegnitz see Karl Schornbaum, *Die Stellung des Markgrafen Kasimir von Brandenburg zur reformatorischen Bewegung,* 109, n. 315.
[37] CR 96, 100, 2-4, No. 607.
[38] Ibid., 100, 6-7, No. 607.
[39] Ibid., 102, 1-26, No. 607. Cf. Fritz Heusler, "Petrus Gynoraeus", 120-122.
[40] Ibid., 100, 7-11, No. 607; 102, 25-26, No. 607.
[41] Emil Egli, *Actensammlung zur Geschichte der Zürcher Refomation,* 886, No. 2002, S 11.
[42] CR 96, 170, 4, No. 633; 224, 28-29, No. 656.
[43] Ibid., 170, 4-5, No. 633; 224, 19-23, No. 656.
[44] On Buchmann's work at the Liegnitz Academy see Emil Egli, *Analecta Reformatoria,* II, 9-13.
[45] Cr 95, 567-570, No. 470.
[46] On the editions of the *Syngramma* see Walther Köhler, *Bibliographia Brentiana,* 13, 14, 305, 390, 573, 600. The Syngramma are cited from Christoph Matthäus Pfaff, *Acta et Scripta Ecclesiae publica Wirtembergicae,* Tübingen 1719, 153-198.
[47] On this and the following see Köhler, *Zwingli,* I, 126-127; Friedrich Wilhelm Kantzenbach, "Johannes Brenz und der Kampf um das Abendmahl," 561-580; Martin Honecker, "Die Abendmahlslehre des Syngramma Suevicum," 39-68; and Martin Brecht, "Die frühe Theologie des Johannes Brenz," 73-87.
[48] This composition by Oecolampadius was translated by Ludwig Hätzer into German and appeared in 1525 on the press of Christopher Froschauer. Cf. Gerhardt Goeters, *Ludwig Hätzer Spiritualist und Antitrinitarier,* 67-86.
[49] Krodel, 237.
[50] Pfaff, 63.
[51] Ibid., 156.
[52] Ibid., 43-44. Oecolampadius used in particular the first chapter of *Distinktion X De haeresi illorum qui dicunt, corpus Christi non esse in altari nisi in signo.* See Petrus Lombardus, *Libri IV Sententiarum.* Published by P.P. Collegii S. Bonaventurae, Ad Claras Aquas 1916, 796-800.
[53] Ibid., 159.
[54] Ibid., 82.
[55] Ibid., 162.
[56] Valentin Crautwald to Adam Adamus, June 17, 1526, München SB, CLM 718, fol. 238v, printed in CS II, 435, 13-18.
[57] On further controversies over the *Syngramma* see Kantzenbach, 570-580.
[58] WA 19, (474) 482-523 (English trans.: LW 36, 335ff.)
[59] Ibid., 482, 17-18.
[60] Ibid., 483, 14.
[61] Ibid., 482, 19-20.
[62] Ibid., 483, 15-18.
[63] Ibid., 498, 16-30; 503, 25-504, 15.
[64] Ibid., 484, 21-25.
[65] Ibid., 498, 26-28.
[66] CS II, (439) 445-580.
[67] Ibid., 446, 24-30.
[68] See for example ibid., 461, 25-30: "As in all cases this is the sum, ground and basic point of the error, that they place the body of Christ in the bread or in the substance of bread, hold the bread to be the body of Christ, and mix and unite the indifferent creature with God the Creator. From this are born virtually all other errors of the Christian church."
[69] Note, for example , ibid., 470, 20-23: "This is also the body and flesh of our Lord Jesus Christ in the Word; through this food only can the power of the almighty Word be received and eaten in the Last Supper by all believers." Cf. ibid., 483, 8-10; 491, 9-492, 10; 529, 3-10; 551, 27-34.
[70] Köhler, "Zwingli," I, 458.
[71] Schultz, 153-154.

72 Albert of Prussia to Caspar Schwenckfeld, May 9, 1527, printed in Tschackert, *Urkundenbuch,* II, 548.

73 CS II, 607, 7-8.

74 WA 23, (38) 64-283 (English trans.: LW 37, 13-150).

75 Ibid., 107, 8-10, 24-27.

76 Ibid., 193, 31-33.

77 Albert of Prussia to Caspar Schwenckfeld, May 9, 1527, printed in Tschackert, *Urkundenbuch,* II, 548.

78 Cf. A. Clos, 42-43.

79 See CS II, 622-623.

80 Ibid., 628, 17-18.

81 Ibid., 629, 2-4.

82 Ibid., 629, 13-18.

83 See Tschackert, *Urkundenbuch,* II, 555. The marginalia were not printed in CS II, 628-629.

84 Albert of Prussia to Caspar Schwenckfeld, August 7, 1527, in Tschackert, *Urkundenbuch,* II, 558.

85 CS III, 42, 9-11. Cf. II, 630.

86 Ibid., III, 42, 8-11.

87 WA 23, 377, 28-31: "They wrote a lengthy answer to my book. I am surprised that it has still not come to Wittenberg. I will, if God allows, answer them once more and then let them go."

88 Printed in Bucholtz, II, 523-526, Beilage IV. Partially printed in Schickfuss, III, 171-172. On this and the following see Colmar Grünhagen, "Schlesien unter der Herrschaft König Ferdinands," 66-69; Grünhagen, *Geschichte Schlesiens,* II, 37-39; Gerhard Eberlein, "Die Verhandlungen besonders der Breslauer in den Jahren 1526 u. 1527," 33-42.

89 Printed in Bucholtz, II, 526-528, Beilage V. Partially printed in Schickfuss, III, 172-173.

90 Pol, III, 47. Cf. Fibiger, I, 14. See also Ferdinand I to the Magistrate of the City of Breslau, March 10, 1527, Wroclaw SA, Sammlung-Klose, 42, fol. 91r-v.

91 CS XVIII, 13, 5-9.

92 Ibid., (II) 13-23. On the imprint see Hans Volz, "Die Breslauer Luther- und Reformationsdrucker Adam Dyon und Kaspar Libisch," III, No. 29.

93 The influence of Schwenckfeld can already be seen in the changed vocabulary.

94 On this and the following see Grünhagen, "Schlesien unter Ferdinand," 69-76; Grünhagen, *Geschichte Schlesiens,* II, 39-45, and Eberlein, "Die Verhandlungen," 44-54.

95 On Johannes Fabri see Adalbert Horawitz, "Johann Heigerlin (Fabri) bis zum Regensburger Convent," 83-220; Karl Czerwenka, *Dr. Johann Fabri als Generalvikar von Konstanz;* Karl Schottenloher, "Johann Fabri in Rom;" Ignaz Staub, *Dr. Johann Fabri, Generalvikar von Konstanz (1518-1523);* and Leo Helbling, "Dr. Johann Fabri."

96 See Acta Capituli Wratislaviensis, Wroclaw DA, III, b. 1b. 493-494. Cf. August Kastner, *Archiv für die Geschichte des Bisthums Breslau,* I, 55.

97 Ibid., 500-501. (56).

98 Ibid., 500. (56).

99 Printed in Fibiger, *Das in Schlesien gewaltth*ätig eingerissene Lutherthum, II, 23-24; Abraham Gottlob Rosenberg, *Schlesische Reformationsgeschichte,* 49-51. CS XVIII, (24) 26. On dating the work see Eberlein, "Die Verhandlungen," 49, n. 4.

100 Printed in Fibiger, II, 20-23 and Pol, III, 51.

101 See Fibiger, II, 20-23 and Pol, III, 52. Cf. Grünhagen, "Schlesien unter Ferdinand," 72; Grünhagen, *Geschichte Schlesiens,* II, 41, and Eberlein, "Die Verhandlungen," 51.

102 Michael Steinberg, *Chronik von Schweidnitz,* 137. Cf. Gustav Croon, "Zur Frage: Hinrichtung auf der Schweidnitzer Judenwiese oder auf der Juden Weise," 407-408.

103 This is the general consensus of historians of Silesian territorial history and Schwenkfelder church history.

104 CS II, 664, 24-29.

[105] Pol, III, 54. See also Grünhagen, "Schlesien unter Ferdinand," 75 and Grünhagen, *Geschichte Schlesiens,* II, 43-44.
[106] Eberlein, "Die Verhandlungen," 54, correctly suggests that Pol shifted the proceedings of 1527 and 1528.
[107] Johann Soffner, *Geschichte der Reformation in Schlesien,* 105.
[108] CS II, (631) 637-670.
[109] Ibid., 642, 14-17.
[110] Ibid., 647, 25-648, 8.
[111] Ibid., 655, 23-28.
[112] Ibid., 655, 28-34.
[113] Ibid., XVIII, 30, 27-38.
[114] Ibid., 31-32, 35.
[115] Ibid., 31, 34-32, 2.
[116] Ibid., 31, 31-34.
[117] Ibid., 29-30.
[118] Ibid., 32, 36-33, 15.
[119] Ibid., (27) 29-33. On the imprint see Volz, III, No. 30.
[120] On this and the following see Acta Capituli Wratislaviensis, Wroclaw, DA III, b. 1b., 534-535. Cf. Kastner, I, 57-58.

5. *The Final Position of the Liegnitz Brotherhood on the Sacrament*

[1] CS III, (1) 5-23.
[2] Ibid., II, (439) 445-580.
[3] Ibid., III, 7, 16-18.
[4] For a list of the reasons see ibid., 5, 16-22.
[5] Ibid., 5, 23-7, 14.
[6] Ibid., 5, 25-27.
[7] Ibid., 7, 15-23, 12.
[8] Ibid., 11, 2-7.
[9] Ibid., 9, 37-38.
[10] Ibid., 8, 25-26 (WA 15, 584, 21 [English trans.: LW 43, 135]).
[11] Ibid., 10, 29 (WA 23, [38] 64-283 [English trans.: LW 37, 13-150]).
[12] Ibid., 8, 7-9 (WA 5, 175, 23-24); 14, 30-33 (WA 5, 379, 1-14).
[13] Ibid., 7, 12 (WA 10, 1, 58, 4-95, 8); 7, 13 (WA 10, 1, 142-180, 3); 8, 24 (WA 10, 1, 224, 1-7); 9, 32-36 (WA 10, 1, 224, 2-7); 13, 31-33 (WA 10, 1, 186, 15-16.).
[14] Ibid., 7, 13-14 (WA 10, 1 [61] 72-92).
[15] Ibid., 7, 10-12 (WA Bib 8, 10-32.).
[16] Cf. Maron, 101-105.
[17] CS III, 23, 13-20.
[18] Ibid., 23, 14-17.
[19] Ibid., 407, 8-9.
[20] Ibid., 35, 13-20.
[21] Cf. ibid., 36, n. 1.
[22] WA 26, 433, 1-437, 29. Luther also turned against Schwenckfeld's treatise *Cause and Reason,* to which he alluded in WA (26) 434, 20 (English trans.: LW 37, 262).
[23] Ibid., 434, 20-38; 434, 39-436, 11; 436, 12-25; 436, 26-31; 436, 32-437, 8; 437, 9-18.
[24] Ibid., 437, 15-16.
[25] Ibid., 437, 22-24.
[26] Valentin Crautwald to Martin Bucer, April 28, 1528, printed in TA Elsass 1, 157, 18-21, No. 131.

[27] This is suggested by Staedtke (CR 93, 2, 250) on the basis of CS III, 407, 14-26. Certainly Schwenckfeld stated "that he was never entreated by the Strassburgers for it" (CR 93, 2, 250, n. 2), but he does not say that the Strassburgers did not ask him about it. The passage "Thus I was caused to send [my opinions] regarding this to certain Strassburg scholars known to me" from CS III, 407, 14-15 may be interpreted in both ways.

[28] This is suggested without proof in Köhler, *Zwingli,* 1, 573.

[29] Wolfgang Capito to Johann Oecolampadius, April 9, 1528, printed in Ernst Staehelin, *Briefe und Akten zum Leben Oekolampads,* II, 171-172, No. 566; Wolfgang Capito to Zwingli, April 15, 1528, CR 96, 425, 1-19, No. 712; Martin Bucer to Zwingli, April 15, 1528, ibid., 426, 1-427, 2, No. 713.

[30] CS III, 407, 19-23.

[31] Ibid., 407, 3; CR 93, 2, 256-257.

[32] Ibid., 407, 14.

[33] Ibid., 407, 15-19.

[34] Ibid., 407, 19-23.

[35] Valentin Crautwald to Martin Bucer, April 28, 1528, printed in TA Elsass, 157, 18-21, No. 131.

[36] Ibid. Cf. this with CS III, 407, 23-26. Staedtke is mistaken in his contention that further discussion was also rejected by the Strassburgers.

[37] CR 96, 505-506, No. 737.

[38] Ibid., 505, 5-6, No. 737.

[39] Ibid., 93, 2, 194, 4-7.

[40] Ibid., 210, 13-14.

[41] Ibid., 210, 14-15.

[42] Ibid., 210, 15-18.

[43] Ibid., 210, 18-20.

[44] For example, Staedtke claims this (ibid., 251).

[45] CS III, 4, 3-11 (CR 93, 2, 249, 11-19.).

[46] Ibid., 16-18 (CR 93, 2, 249, 25-250, 3.).

[47] Ibid., 19 (CR 93, 2, 250, 3.).

[48] Ibid., 19 (CR 93, 2, 250, 3-4).

[49] Hirsch's contention (44, n. 5) that "the cause for a break just arose in the spring of 1530 (CS III, 620)" is false, as Köhler, [*Zwingli,* I, 574, n. 1] correctly indicated.

[50] CS III, (34) 35-60.

[51] Ibid., 36, 6-21; 41, 34-37.

[52] Ibid., 44, 5-19.

[53] Ibid., 44, 19-22.

[54] Ibid., 44, 37-38.

[55] Cf. Köhler, *Zwingli,* I, 76-77, 321-322, 483-484.

[56] CR 93, 2, 210, 5 marginalia.

[57] CS III, 42, 25-45, 13.

[58] Ibid., 45, 34-46, 33.

[59] Ibid., 47, 12-60, 19.

[60] Ibid., II, (581) 590-599.

[61] Valentin Crautwald to Johann Oecolampadius, April 28, 1528, printed in Ernst Staehelin, *Briefe und Akten zum Leben Oekolampads,* II, 177, No. 573.

[62] CR 96, 100, 4-7, 13-14, No. 607.

[63] CS II, 686, 13-14.

[64] Ernst Staehelin, *Oekolampad-Bibliographie,* 142.

[65] CS II, 590, 4-5.

[66] Ibid., 590, 9.

[67] Ibid., 590, 10.

[68] Ibid., 590, 11-13.

69 Valentin Crautwald to Johann Oecolampadius, April 28, 1528, printed in Staehelin, *Briefe und Akten,* II, 177, No. 573.

70 Ibid.

71 Caspar Schwenckfeld to Johann Oecolampadius, May 3, 1528, printed in ibid., 181, No. 574 and CS III, 62, 7-9.

72 Ibid., and CS III, 62, 15.

73 G. Buckisch, "Schlesische Religionsakten," I. Teil. 1517-1607, Wroclaw DA, I, 13a, 178-187. Printed in Abraham Gottlob Rosenberg, *Schlesische Reformations-Geschichte,* 416-428. Partially printed in Fibiger, II, 39-42 and in Johann Adam Hensel, *Protestantische Kirchen-Geschichte der Gemeinden in Schlesien,* 169-170.

74 Ibid, 179-181, (420).

75 Ibid., 181, (420).

76 Ibid., 181: "Whoever preaches or teaches scornfully against this shall pay as the greatest slanderer of God with his life," (420).

77 CS III, (99) 100-118.

78 Ibid., 102, 37-103, 13; 105, 9-11, 27-28; 106, 18-20.

79 Note for example, ibid., 103, 36-38; 107, 13-14.

80 Note for example, ibid., 107, 8-9.

81 Note for example, ibid., 103, 21-25: "He [Luther] broke off from the good works and laws of God far too often and built up a dead un-understandable faith on the basis of the letters alone as did many in the time of James. Because James' epistle lifts up works and strives against pretended faith, Luther does not wish to allow it in his Bible."

82 Ibid., 106, 21-24.

83 Ibid., 106, 23.

84 Ibid., 110, 5-6.

85 Printed in Rosenberg, 416-428, and partially in Fibiger, II, 39-42.

86 Printed in Rosenberg, 85-88; Fibiger, II, 45-47; CS XVIII, (34) 36-38.

87 CS XVIII, 36, 5-6.

88 Ibid., 37, 28-34.

89 Ibid., 38, 2-5.

90 Ibid., 37, 5-21.

91 Printed in Rosenberg, 432-439.

92 Ibid., 434.

93 Ibid., 435.

94 Ibid., 436.

95 See especially Horawitz, 138ff; Czerwenka, 58ff; and Staub.

96 Johann Fabri, *Christenliche ableynung,* fol. h 4v.

97 Ibid., fol. a 4r-v.

98 Thebesius, III, 45.

99 CS II, 645, 18-646, 29.

100 Ibid., 645, 21-22.

101 On the reasons for the closing of the University of Liegnitz see Koffmane, "Eine schlesische Universität," 34-38.

102 Valentin Trotzendorf, *Precationes,* fol. C IV-C 3V (Vorrede). Cf. also Lorenz Hartranfft, *Ware, Christliche, und glimpffliche Widerlegung des Irrthumbs der Schwenckfelder.*

103 Clajus, fol. 0 IV.

104 How long Ziegler remained in Liegnitz cannot be said. It is only known that there were negotiations regarding his return to Ansbach after July 1529. Duke Georg of Brandenburg was in Liegnitz from March 7-14, 1529 (see Louis Neustadt, "Aufenthaltsorte des Markgrafen Georg von Brandenburg," 243) and there met Ziegler. On the reasons for the final closing of the University of Liegnitz see Koffmane, "Eine schlesische Universität." 34-38.

105 CS XVIII, (39) 41-43.

106 Ibid., 41, 4-5.

107 Ibid., 42, 29-30.

108 Ibid., 42, 19-23.
109 Ibid., 42, 23-25.
110 Ibid., 43, 5-6.
111 Ibid., 43, 6-8.
112 Ibid., III, (432) 435-439.
113 Wolfgang Capito to Zwingli, May 18, 1529, CR 97, 124, 2, No. 842.
114 The long period of time between his departure from the principality of Liegnitz (before February 15, 1529; cf. CS XVIII, 42, 29-30), and his arrival in Strassburg (before May 18, 1529; cf. CR 97, 124, 2, No. 842) is striking. It is likely that after a stay in Brieg (CS XIV, 282, 34-283, 17) and perhaps elsewhere in Silesia (according to Martin John Sr., Schwenckfeld first left Silesia on April 19, 1529; cf. Schultz, 162, n. 14) he went to Nürnberg for a short time. See my "Sebastian Franck und Caspar Schwenckfeld," 3, n. 4.
115 See Schultz, 3.
116 M. Bucer, "Vergleichung D. Luthers und seins Gegentheyls," in Martin Bucer, *Opera omnia.* Series I. Deutsche Schriften, II, 371, 30-34.
117 Valentin Crautwald to Wolfgang Capito, Martin Bucer and others, April 13, 1529, printed in TA Elsass I, 237, No. 182a.
118 CR 97, 124, 2-3, No. 842.
119 Ibid., 126, 13-14, No. 842.
120 CS III, (391) 402-431.
121 Ibid., 394-397.

III The Golden Age of Moderate Schwenkfeldianism

1. The Controversy of the Liegnitz Brotherhood with the Anabaptists

1 CS III, (269) 271-343.
2 Ibid., 272, 3.
3 Ibid., 271, 7-8, 13-15.
4 Ibid.
5 Ibid., 271, 18-19.
6 Ibid., (83) 87-98.
7 Cf. ibid., 83-84.
8 Ibid., 301, 14-18; 331, 22-28.
9 Ibid., 305, 13.
10 Ibid., 305, 14.
11 Ibid., 305, 15.
12 Ibid., 306, 3; 331, 39-332, 2.
13 Ibid., 306, 3.
14 Ibid., 305, 40-306, 1.
15 Ibid., 308, 22-24.
16 Ibid., 305, 14-15.
17 Ibid., 305, 16.
18 Ibid., 305, 24-25.
19 Note for example, ibid., 331, 5-10: "Everything which is done is born either of flesh or of Spirit and every birth brings forth its own kind. Flesh brings forth flesh and Spirit spirit. The external water is not spirit but flesh. Therefore it brings forth nothing but flesh and cannot give or bear spiritual [things]. In a like manner each and every external thing cannot receive spiritual [things]."
20 Note for example, ibid., 301, 23-25 (John 3:5); 305, 30-306, 3 (Acts 8:16); 331, 38-332, 3 (Titus 3:4-6).

[21] Ibid., 308, 37-39.

[22] On this and the following see the materials gathered by Klose (Wroclaw SA, Sammlung-Klose, 4, 100-109). Cf. also Gustav Koffmane, "Die Wiedertäufer in Schlesien." Against these the partially hypothetical, partially false work of Wilhelm Wiswedel, *Bilder und Führergestalten aus dem Täufertum,* III, 222-227, is almost useless.

[23] Friedrich Wilhelm von Sommersberg, *Silesiacarum rerum scriptores,* I, 220: "At Stoltz near Franckenstein half the farmers were Anabaptist because many were placed in the pillory in Franckenstein, and were exiled after having their ears cut off. Duke Karl would not tolerate them in the land."

[24] WAB 4, 371-372, No. 1215; cf. ibid., 311, 6-8, No. 1190.

[25] Christian Meyer, "Zur Geschichte der Wiedertäufer in Oberschwaben." 230: "He [Hans Hut] knew them [Anabaptist leaders] but he could not name them. According to him there were two in Breslau, an Oswald and a Hess, ten in Moravia and many more in other places. He was with them much and had spoken with them." On the problem as to whether Hut himself was in Silesia see Gottfried Seebass, *Müntzers Erbe. Werk, Leben und Theologie des Hans Hut. (d. 1527).*

[26] Such orders were issued on April 2, 1528, January 30, 1530, and June 6, 1535; see Wroclaw SA, Sammlung-Klose, 42, fol. 190r, 191r-v.

[27] See Wroclaw SA, Sammlung-Klose, 4, 105-106. Cf. Wiedertäufferischen Gesindleins in Mähren und Schlesien seltsame Beschaffenheit. Ao 1535, Brno SA, Becksche Sammlung, G 10/49, No. 68, fol. 22v.

[28] CS IV, 242, 36-243, 5. Cf. Schwenckfeld to Martin Bucer, July 3 and 7, 1528, ibid., III, (74) 76-82. On this and the following see Hans Urner, "Die Taufe bei Caspar Schwenckfeld," 329-342.

[29] On this and the following see Wilhelm Heberle, "W. Capito's Verhältniss zum Anabaptismus"; Johann Wilhelm Baum, *Capito und Butzer, Strassburgs Reformatoren;* Johann Martin Usteri, "Die Stellung der Strassburger Reformatoren Bucer und Capito zur Tauffrage"; Johann Adam, *Evangelische Kirchengeschichte der Stadt Strassburg,* 109-122.

[30] See Wolfgang Capito to Zwingli, December 26, 1526, CR 95, 820, 9, No. 564.

[31] Ibid., 96, 87, 14, No. 605.

[32] See Manfred Krebs, "Einleitung zu M. Bucers Getrewe Warnung gegen Jacob Kautz," in Bucer, *Opera omnia,* Series I, Deutsche Schriften, II, 227-233.

[33] Printed in TA Elsass I, 116, 17-121, 9, No. 90.

[34] For a summary of the judgment which Capito wrote on the Anabaptists in his commentary on Hosea see ibid., 152, 4-153, 10, No. 126.

[35] A short selection from Bucer's long discussion of baptism and the Anabaptists in his commentary on Matthew is found in ibid., 79, 2-21, 78.

[36] Bucer, *Opera omnia,* Series I, Deutsche Schriften, II, (225) 234-258.

[37] The selection from the commentary on John in which Bucer defended infant baptism is printed in TA Elsass I, 149, 16-151, 5, No. 124.

[38] CR 96, 426-429, No. 713.

[39] Crautwald to Martin Bucer, April 28, 1528, prinited in TA Elsass I, 155, 20-160, 31, No. 131. Schwenckfeld's answer to Bucer is lost (cf. CS III, 60).

[40] Crautwald to Wolfgang Capito, June 29, 1528, printed in TA Elsass I, 165, 3-173, 8, No. 141; Schwenckfeld to Martin Bucer, July 3 and 7, 1528, CS III, (74) 76-82; Crautwald to Martin Bucer, July 5, 1528, printed in TA Elsass I, 174, 10-178, 12, No. 144.

[41] TA Elsass, I, 167, 22-25, No. 141.

[42] Ibid., 167, 25-31, No. 141.

[43] Ibid., 160, 3-12.

[44] Ibid., 160, 12-13.

[45] Ibid., 168, 13-15.

[46] Ibid., 168, 25-31.

[47] Ibid., 168, 31-36.

[48] CS III, 79, 20-21.

[49] TA Elsass I, 158, 35-159, 7; 170, 3-8.
[50] Ibid., 158, 33-34; 159, 8.
[51] Ibid., 177, 6-7.
[52] CS III, 81, 36-37.
[53] Ibid., 79, 21-22.
[54] Ibid., 79, 27-29.
[55] Ibid., 79, 26-27.
[56] CR 96, 487-488, No. 729; cf. also Martin Bucer to Zwingli, June 24, 1528, ibid., 492-493, No. 732.
[57] On this and the following see Torsten Bergsten, *Balthasar Hubmaier,* 398-422.
[58] Johann Kessler, *Sabbata mit kleineren Schriften und Briefen,* published by E. Egli and R. Schoch, 164, 37-39.
[59] Seckendorf, *Commentarius,* III, 116.
[60] Rudolf Rican, *Die Böhmischen Brüder,* 92.
[61] On the Nikolsburg Colloquy see Bergsten, 452-475.
[62] On Glaidt see Johann Loserth, "Oswald Glayt," 70-73; Wilhelm Wiswedel, "Oswald Glait von Jamnitz," 550-564; Gerhard F. Hasel, "Sabbatarian anabaptists of the sixteenth century," 107-121.
[63] Balthasar Hubmaier, *Schriften,* edited by G. Westin and T. Bergsten, (398) 400-431.
[64] On Froschauer see Paul Leemann van Elck, *Die Offizin Froschauer,* 13-15.
[65] On Froschauer's work as a printer of Hubmaier's works see Hubmaier, 37.
[66] CR 96, 554, 2-555, 1, No. 760.
[67] On Froschauer's work as a printer in Liegnitz see Koffmane, "Wiedertäufer," 36-37; Hans Bahlow, *Die Anfänge des Buchdrucks zu Liegnitz,* 7-14; Leemann van Elck, 15.
[68] On Fischer see Petr Ratkos, "Die Anfänge des Wiedertäufertums in der Slowakei," 41-59; and Hasel, 111-121.
[69] Ratkos, 46-51.
[70] Ibid., 52.
[71] Crautwald, *Bericht vnd anzeigen,* Berlin SB, Ms. germ. 527, fol. 53v.
[72] Ibid., fol. 54r.
[73] Note, for example, CS IV, 457, 24-32.
[74] Note, for example, ibid., 479, 22-23.
[75] Ibid., 513, 28-29.
[76] Crautwald, *Bericht vnd anzeigen,* Berlin SB, Ms. germ. 527, fol. 37v.
[77] Willy Rordorf, *Der Sonntag,* 140-151.
[78] CSEL 20, 196, 21-23 (De oratione, 23); 292, 25-293, 11 (De ieiunio adversus psychicos, 14); 47, 454, 5-27 (Adversus Marcionem, 4, 12).
[79] CS IV, 454, 24-25.
[80] Ibid., 453.
[81] Its contents may be reconstructed from the following: Wolfgang Capito to the Preacher Leonhard von Lichtenstein, before December 21, 1531, printed in TA Elsass I, 363, 16-385, 31, No. 290 a; Capito's critical comments on Glaidt's *Vom Sabbat* printed in ibid., 386, 5-393, 26, No. 290 b; Schwenckfeld to Leonhard von Lichtenstein auf Nikolsburg, January 1, 1532, CS IV, 444-518; Crautwald, *Bericht vnd anzeigen,* Berlin SB, Ms. germ. 527, fol. 36r-55r.
[82] Crautwald, *Bericht vnd anzeigen,* Berlin SB, Ms. germ. 527, fol. 36r.
[83] Ibid., fol. 36r-v.
[84] Ibid., fol. 53v.
[85] Ibid., fol. 36r-v.
[86] Ibid., fol. 36v.
[87] Ibid., fol. 37r.
[88] Ibid., fol. 36r.
[89] Ibid., fol. 45r-v.
[90] Ibid., fol. 45v.
[91] Ibid.

92 Ibid.
93 Ibid.
94 Ibid., fol. 37v.
95 CS IV, 489, 18-25.
96 Ibid., 489, 22.
97 Crautwald, *Bericht vnd anzeigen,* Berlin SB, Ms. germ. 527, fol. 36v.
98 Ibid., fol. 46r-48v.
99 Ibid., fol. 46v.
100 Ibid.
101 Ibid., fol. 46r.
102 Ibid., fol. 46v.
103 Ibid., fol. 46r.
104 Ibid., fol. 52v-53r.
105 Ibid., *Zur Interpretation von IgnMagn,* 9 (MSG 5, 766-770). See Rordorf, 138-140.
106 CS III, (835) 836-844.
107 Ibid., XIV, 597, 4-8.
108 Schwenckfeld to Jacob Kautz, July 19, 1529, printed in TA Elsass I, 242, 12-246, 14, No. 193.
109 Strassburg city council proceedings of October 9, 1529, printed in ibid., 249, 4-10, No. 195.
110 Strassburg city council proceedings of November 29, 1529, printed in ibid., 250, 3-13, No. 196.
111 CS IX, 802, 34.
112 On this colloquy and the later relationship between Schwenckfeld and Marpeck see ibid., XVIII, 47 and Torsten Bergsten, ''Pilgram Marbeck und seine Auseinandersetzung mit Caspar Schwenckfeld.''
113 Willem Izaak Leendertz, *Melchior Hofmann,* 41, asserts that Schwenckfeld had already met Hofmann in December of 1525 in Wittenberg. This is not possible, however, since Hofmann had left Wittenberg for Dorpat in the fall of 1525 at the latest. See Kawerau, 3.
114 CS III, 836, 3-837, 8; 838, 23-840, 16.
115 Ibid., 838, 18-19.
116 Ibid., 838, 6 (MSL 10, 5, C).
117 Ibid., 838, 14-15 (MSG 20, 652-653).
118 Ibid., 838, 16-18 (MSL 2, 190 A).
119 On the problem of infant baptism in the patristic period see J. Jeremias, *Die Kindertaufe in den ersten vier Jahrhunderten* [English trans. by David Cairns, *Infant Baptism in the First Four Centuries* (London: SCM, 1960)]. K. Aland, *Die Säuglingstaufe im Neuen Testament und in der alten Kirche;* J. Jeremias, *Nochmals: Die Anfänge der Kindertaufe;* K. Aland, *Die Stellung der Kinder in den frühen christlichen Gemeinden und ihre Taufe.* [English trans. by G. R. Beasley-Murray, *Did the Early Church Baptise Infants?* (Philadelphia: Westminster, 1963)]. Crautwald often overinterpreted the Fathers and thus explained them falsely. To give only one example, he thought he could prove on the basis of Eusebius' *Ecclesiastical History* that faith always preceded baptism in the ancient church (CS III, 838, 15; MSG 20, 652-653). If one examines the context of the Eusebius catechism, it is clear that it is from a fragment of a letter by Dionysius of Rome in which the former is explaining his opposition to the Novatians. He had hesitated to allow the lapsed to receive penance and the Eucharist, ''because our most merciful Lord Jesus Christ was attacked as implacable; he thus obliterated the holy baptismal washing.'' For Dionysius of Alexandria the reception of the Novatians has set aside both the mercy of Christ and baptism because as an act of God baptism still had validity even if the baptized person was untrue to his faith and baptismal confession. For Dionysius baptism stands above faith and confession. The passage cited by Crautwald from Eusebius says nothing about the relationship of faith and baptism.
120 Thebesius, III, 27-28 and Ehrhardt, IV, 33.
121 CS VI, 20, 7-9.
122 Note especially his baptismal tract *Von der Wiedergeburt und Herkummen eines Christen Menschen,* ibid., (5) 12-36.

[123] Ibid., 25, 30-31.
[124] Ibid., 13, 3-4; cf. 14, 7-15.
[125] Ibid., 22, 4-9 (MSL 6, 431 B; 433 A; 753 C).
[126] Ibid., 21, 35-36.
[127] Ibid., III, 836, 21-22; 836, 27-837, 1.
[128] Ibid., 837, 9-13.
[129] Ibid., 840, 28-30.
[130] Ibid., 840, 9-11.
[131] Ibid., 840, 13.
[132] Ibid., 840, 17-21.
[133] Printed in : Cohrs, IV, 219-225.
[134] Ibid., 220, 16-20.
[135] CS III, 837, 21-22.
[136] Ibid., (835) 836-844.
[137] Ibid., (260) 261-262.
[138] Ibid., XIV, 597, 6-8.
[139] Ibid., 597, 4-5.
[140] On Schwenckfeld's concept of baptism see Seeberg, 57-63, and Urner.
[141] Urner, 334-337.
[142] Peter Chelcicky, "Von den Sakramenten," printed in German trans. in Peschke, *Theologie,* I, 2, 77, 1-26.
[143] Ibid., 93, 6-8.
[144] Ibid., 93, 18-35.
[145] Ibid., 93, 13-18.
[146] On this and the following see Erhard Peschke, "Der Kirchenbegriff des Bruder Lukas von Prag," 284.
[147] Cf. CS II, 272, n. 5.
[148] See Peschke, *Böhmischen Brüder*, 109-110.
[149] See the foreword to the hymnal *Von Christo Jesu, unserem säligmacher, seiner Menschwerdung, Geburt, Beschneidung. . . ,etlich christliche vnd tröstliche Lobgesäng, auss einem vast herrlichen G'sangbuch gezogen.* Psalm 98:81, 146. Strassburg 1534 and 1535. Cf. August Friedrich Heinrich Schneider, *Zur Literatur der Schwenckfeldischen Liederdichter bis Daniel Sudermann,* 21; and Eduard Emil Koch, *Geschichte des Kirchenlieds,* I, 2, 120-121.
[150] Zdenek Vaclav Tobolka, *Michael Weisses's Ein new Gesangbüchlein aus d. J. 1531 und sein Drucker Georg Styrsa.*
[151] "Wiedertäufferischen Gesindleins in Mähren und Schlesien seltsame Beschaffenheit," Ao. 1535, Brno SA, Becksche Sammlung G 10/49, No. 68, fol. 22r.
[152] Partially printed in Bucholtz, IV, 476-477.
[153] Crautwald, *Bericht vnd anzeigen,* Berlin SB, Ms. germ. 527, fol. 49v.
[154] Ibid.
[155] Ibid.
[156] In his library Crautwald had two Hebrew grammars (Elia Levita, *Grammatica hebraica absolutissima,* Basel 1525; and his *Tabula omnium coniugationum,* Basel 1525), part of Sebastian Münster's edition of the Hebrew Bible (Ecclesiastes, Basel 1525; Canticum canticorum, Basel 1525) and Johann Reuchlin's *De arte cabbalistica* (Hagenau 1517). He also knew the controversial *Evangelium secundum Matthaeum* (Basel, 1537) by Münster. See Crautwald to Johann Althansen, November 1537, Wolfenbüttel HAB, Cod. Guelf. 37.27 Aug. fol. 5r. Münster believed he had found the original of Matthew's Gospel. He was dealing with a forgery, however.
[157] Ratkos, 53.
[158] The writings of von Lichtenstein and his preacher are no longer extant.
[159] Wolfgang Capito to the preachers of Leonhard von Lichtenstein, before December 21, 1531, printed in TA Elsass I, 363, 16-385, 31, No. 290a. See also ibid., 386, 5-393, 26, No. 290b.
[160] CS IV, (444) 453-518.

[161] Wiswedel, "Glait," 562. See also WA 50, 309-310. Cf. also Wilhelm Maurer, "Die Zeit der Reformation," in *Kirche und Synagoge*, I, 404-407, Johannes Mathesius, *Ausgewählte Werke*, III, 90 and 341, and WA 50, (309) 312-337 (English trans.: LW 47, 65-98).

2. The Suppression of Radical Schwenkfeldianism

[1] See Paul Sartori, "Lätare," in *Handwörterbuch des deutschen Aberglaubens*, V, 921.
[2] Pol, *Jahrbuücher*, III, 60.
[3] Bauch, *Valentin Trozendorf*, 50-51.
[4] Ibid.
[5] I am in agreement with Bauch, *Trozendorf*, 51 that the story of Eckel in Goldberg is not a "fabrication" of Schubart's as Gerhard Eberlein (*Aus Kirchen-Rechnungen des Reformations-Jahrhunderts*, 107) states.
[6] On Heydeck see Paul Tschackert, "Friedrich von Heideck, Herr auf Johannisburg und Lötzen"; Theophil Besch, *Friedrich von Heydeck;* Martin Lackner, *Geistfrömmigkeit und Enderwartung*, 13-29.
[7] In the spring of 1525 Heydeck stayed with Albert of Prussia and married the former nun Hedwig von Falkenhain. See Besch, 25.
[8] Albert of Prussia to Frederick von Heydeck, March 12, 1529, printed in Tschackert, *Urkundenbuch*, II, 618.
[9] Cf. Albert of Prussia to Frederick von Heydeck, May 20, 1529, ibid.
[10] Frederick von Heydeck to Johann Hess, February 8, 1530, printed in A.F.H. Schneider, *Verlauf der Reformation in Liegnitz*, 38, Beilage V.
[11] Ibid.
[12] Frederick II to Johann Hess, February 7, 1530, printed in ibid., 38, Beilage IV.
[13] Frederick von Heydeck to Johann Hess, February 8, 1530, printed in ibid., 38-39, Beilage V.
[14] Melanchthon to Ambrosius Moibanus, August 14, 1526, CR I, 812-813, No. 400.
[15] Later Heydeck also held the position at Lötzen by which he became the most influential person in Masuren.
[16] See Clos, 31-33.
[17] Ibid., 33-35.
[18] The marriage settlement is printed in Alfred Nicolovius, *Die Bischöfliche Würde in Preussens evangelischer Kirche*, 36-38.
[19] Adolf Meckelburg, "Chronik des Johannes Freiberg," 486.
[20] Ibid.
[21] Ibid.
[22] Cf. P. Speratus, *Gantzer handel der unterredung vom abendmahl des herrn, 1531 Dezember 29 u. 30*, Göttingen Staatliches Archivlager (Königsberg SA, HBA), Schrank 4, Fach 22, No. 63 (I), fol. 43v.
[23] Ibid., 43v. In this protocol written by Speratus there is a citation from Eckel's rejoinder.
[24] Wolfenbüttel HAB, Cod. Guelf. 37, 27 Aug. fol. 421r-432r.
[25] See CS IV, 581, 8-11; 593, 33-34; 594, 11-12.
[26] Printed (with errors) in Nicolovius, 116. Cf. Tschackert, *Urkundenbuch*, II, 787.
[27] Printed in Cosack, 374-382. Cf. Tschackert, *Urkundenbuch*, II, 794.
[28] See above all, ibid., I, 192-194; and Lackner, 18-20.
[29] Speratus, *Gantzer handel der unterredung vom abendmahl des herrn.*
[30] Ibid., fol. 47v.
[31] P. Speratus, *Gantzer handel der unterredung vom abendmahl des herrn*, printed in *Erleutertes Preussen*, I, 269-280, 448-463; *Unschuldige Nachrichten, 1732*, 183-195; Cosack, *Paulus Speratus Leben und Lieder*, 383-404. The following notes refer to the manuscript.
[32] Ibid., fol. 49v.
[33] Ibid., fol. 49r-v.
[34] Ibid., fol. 50v.

[35] Ibid., fol. 139v.
[36] Ibid., fol. 28v.
[37] Ibid., fol. 28v-30r.
[38] Ibid., fol. 30v.
[39] Ibid.
[40] Ibid., fol. 53r.
[41] Ibid., fol. 38r.
[42] Ibid., fol. 41v.
[43] Ibid., fol. 55v.
[44] The most significant treatise by Schwenckfeld on the problem of the external work is *De cursu verbi Dei* (CS II, [581] 591-599). The most important tract by Crautwald on the same theme is *Von der gnaden Gottes* (ibid., III, [837] 87-98). In these works they attempt by means of the Scriptures, the philosophic axiom of *similia similibus,* the practical syllogism, and the Fathers to demonstrate that God does not deal with man through the external preached word but directly through the spirit.
[45] P. Speratus, *Gantzer handel der unterredung vom abendmahl des herrn.*
[46] Ibid., fol. 56v.
[47] Ibid., fol. 65r.
[48] Ibid., fol. 60r.
[49] Ibid., fol. 62r.
[50] Ibid., fol. 44r.
[51] Ibid., fol. 41v.
[52] Ibid., fol. 42v.
[53] See Georg von Polentz, Paul Speratus, Johann Briesmann, Johann Poliander, and Michael Meurer to Albert of Prussia, before August 26, 1532, ibid., fol. 47v.
[54] Partially printed in Tschackert, *Urkundenbuch,* II, 831.
[55] See Fabian Eckel to Johann Hess, March 18, 1532 printed in ibid., 840.
[56] Göttingen Staatliches Archivlager (Königsberg SA, HBA), Schrank 4, Fach 22, No. 63 (I), fol. 27r-36v.
[57] Ibid., fol. 27r-33r.
[58] Ibid., fol. 28v.
[59] Ibid., fol. 33r-36v.
[60] Ibid., fol. 36r.
[61] Besch, 43.
[62] Göttingen Staatliches Archivlager (Königsberg SA, HBA), Schrank 4, Fach 22, No. 63 (I), fol. 38r-44r.
[63] CS IV, (564) 567-606.
[64] This date can be established by a letter of Eckel's to Johann Hess, March 18, 1532. Cf. n. 55.
[65] It is certain that this work is by Eckel (CS IV, 599, 33ff).
[66] Ibid., 567-577.
[67] Ibid., 577-581.
[68] Ibid., 581-593.
[69] Ibid., 576, 9-26.
[70] Paul Speratus to Martin Luther, Philipp Melanchthon and Justus Jonas, August 31, 1534 printed in ZKG II (1890), 302-304; cf. Tschackert, *Urkundenbuch,* II, 934. See also CS IV, 609, 7-13.
[71] Cf. CS IV, 600, 2-3.
[72] Its contents are noted by Crautwald; cf. n. 73.
[73] CS IV, (607) 609-631.
[74] Göttingen Staatliches Archivlager (Königsberg, SA, HBA), W 19, 2, fol. 53 to 92.
[75] Wolfenbüttel HAB, Cod. Guelf. 37. 27 Aug. fol. 2r.
[76] See Tschackert, *Urkundenbuch,* II, 873, 886.
[77] See ibid., 930, 932, 938, 946.
[78] Meckelburg, 485-486.

[79] Paul Speratus to Albert of Prussia, after December 11, 1542, partially printed in Tschackert, *Urkundenbuch,* III, 1490.
[80] See WA 30, 3, 547, 4-16.
[81] Ibid., 547-553.
[82] Ibid., 547, 11-13.
[83] Ibid., 552, 4-5.
[84] Ibid., 552, 12-15.
[85] Ibid., 552, 24-26.
[86] See Wolfgang Höhne, *Luthers Anschauungen über die Kontinuität der Kirche,* 20-29.
[87] Tschackert, *Urkundenbuch,* I, 197.
[88] WA 30, 3; 552, 32-553, 10.
[89] Friedrich Samuel Bock, *Grundriss von dem Merkwürdigen Leben des Durchlauchtigen Fürsten und Herrn, Herrn Albrecht des ältern,* 223-224; Cosack, 141, and Tschackert, *Urkundenbuch,* II, 867.
[90] WAB 6, 474-475, No. 2025.
[91] Ibid., 474, 18-21, No. 2025.
[92] Ibid., 474, 21-23, No. 2025.
[93] Ibid., 475, 27-28, No. 2025.
[94] Ibid., 475, 28-30, No. 2025.
[95] Ibid., 475, 31-32, No. 2025.
[96] Ibid., 475, 33-35, No. 2025.
[97] Printed in *Erleutertes Preussen,* I, 270-277. Cf. Tschackert, *Urkundenbuch,* II, 868.
[98] See n. 31.
[99] On this and the following see above all Cosack, 141-158; Tschackert, *Urkundenbuch,* I, 199-203; and Lackner, 24-29.
[100] Tschackert, *Urkundenbuch,* II, 959.
[101] Partially printed in ibid., 975.
[102] Ehrhardt, IV, 267.
[103] Matth. Alber, *Methodus,* fol. o 3v. Enders, (V, 1012, n. 1), from which this is cited, ascribes the account falsely to Crautwald.
[104] Eberlein, "Aus Kirchen-Rechnungen des Reformations-Jahrhunderts," 267.
[105] See Bahlow, *Reformation,* 186, n. 216.
[106] Thebesius, III, 33.
[107] On October 4, 1532, Speratus wrote to Eckel in Liegnitz (Tschackert, *Urkundenbuch,* II, 873). Eckel answered on March 3, 1533 from Neurode in Glatz (ibid., 886) without commenting on the change of address.
[108] Schubart, "Vorrede," 151.
[109] Ibid.
[110] Gustav Bossert, "Kleine Mittheilungen. I. Zu Hans Bünderlin's späterer Geschichte," 54.
[111] Thebesius, *Liegnitzische Jahrbücher,* III, 32.
[112] CR 4, 734-735, No. 2422. Bretschneider's dating of the letter in 1541 is false.
[113] Bahlow, *Reformation,* 121.
[114] Ibid., 187, n. 218.
[115] Magistrate of the City of Breslau to Frederick II, October 13, 1533, Wroclaw SA, Sammlung-Klose, 42, fol. 115r-v. Cf. Koffmane, "Die Wiedertäufer in Schlesien," 43. The bracketed pagination in the following quotations is based on Koffmane.
[116] Ibid., fol. 115r: ". . . likewise certain Anabaptists, particularly one named Clemens, who reside in the lands of the Lord of Bernstain are at times active, preach to the people and draw a great many people to them" (43).
[117] Frederick II to the Magistrate of the City of Breslau, October 16, 1533, Wroclaw SA, Sammlung-Klose, 42, fol. 113r-114r (43-44).
[118] Ibid., fol. 113v (44).
[119] Ibid.

3. Moderate Schwenkfeldianism

[1] See Crautwald to Johannes Schnabel and Johann Hoffmann, March 4, 1534, printed in CKGS 3, (1887), 30-31.
[2] See Crautwald to Margarete Engelmann, 1537, partially printed in Arnold, *Supplementa,* 139.
[3] Crautwald, *Bericht vnd anzeigen,* Berlin SB, Ms. germ. 527, fol. 53v.
[4] See Crautwald to Margarete Engelmann, 1537, partially printed in Arnold, *Supplementa,* 139.
[5] Ibid.
[6] Crautwald to Ursula Thumb von Stetten, November 11, 1540. Wolfenbüttel HAB, Cod. Guelf. 45. 9 Aug.fol. 420v: "Now I see how the poor live, in pain and need, poverty and suffering with many visitations of God to children and cattle. Visit their homes, crawl into their hovels; see how some work hard in the sight of God, how others living in abundance and in the of midst of wealth die. Hear of their needs, difficulty and situations."
[7] Crautwald to Margarete Engelmann, 1537, partially printed in Arnold, *Supplementa,* 140.
[8] Ibid.
[9] Ibid., 139-140.
[10] CS V, (221) 222-246.
[11] Ibid., 223, 10-16.
[12] Ibid., 223, 19-29.
[13] Ibid., IX, (731) 739-756.
[14] That is, the *Bekantnuss vom H. Sacrament des leibs unnd bluts Christi* (ibid., III, [712] 719-752) and *Catechismus von ettlichen Hauptartickeln des Christlichen glaubens* (ibid., IV, [208] 216-238).
[15] Ibid., V, 235, 24-33.
[16] Ibid., IX, 739, 1-745, 19.
[17] Ibid., 745, 20-749, 4.
[18] Ibid., 749, 5-756, 10.
[19] Ibid., 748, 23-28.
[20] Ibid., 748, 2-7.
[21] Ibid., 737-738.
[22] On the printing and editions of Werner's catechisms see ibid., 731-733. Cf. also ibid., V, 235, 30-32.
[23] Val. Trotzendorf, *Catechesis scholae Goltpergensis,* fol. B 5r; printed in Reu, I, 2, Abteilung, II, 775, 25-27: "It is now sixteen years since certain fanatics (sophoi) on a questionable pretext wished to deprive me of my catechetical office and cast me from the school."
[24] Ibid., fol. B 5r; in Reu, 775, 29-30: "I responded: If my catechetical position is taken, I have an open mission, for catechesis is something substantial for a scholar."
[25] CS VI, (193) 203-229. See also my *Sebastian Franck,* 76, No. 12.
[26] CS IV, in Apparat, 225 (to line 30), 227-229.
[27] On Franck's concluding remarks see my *Sebastian Franck,* 12.
[28] On Wolfhart see Karl Wolfhart, *Beiträge zur Augsburger Reformationsgeschichte, II, Zur Biographie des M. Bonifacius Wolfhart,* 167-180; the same, *Beiträge zur Augsburger Reformationsgeschichte, III, Caspar Schwenckfeld und Bonifacius Wolfhart,* 97-114, 145-161.
[29] CS VI, 203, 17-20; 211, 11-13; 223, 2-5; 32-34.
[30] Ibid., (5) 11-36.
[31] Ibid., 24, 8-9, 12-13; cf. 13, 23-25; 14, 7-9, 31-33; 20, 5-9; 27, 24-26; 31, 33-34; 34, 10-17.
[32] Ibid., 14, 33-36; 21, 10-13; 25, 29-30; 29, 17-18; 30, 24-29; 34, 18-23.
[33] Ferdinand I's June 6, 1535 order that Moravian Anabaptists were not to be tolerated in Silesia was forwarded to Bishop Jacob von Salza, Duke Karl I of Münsterberg-Oels, Duke Frederick II of Liegnitz, Brieg and Wohlau and the council of Breslau by Ladislaus Popel of Lobkowitz and Heinrich Treuschen. See F.B. Bucholtz, *Geschichte der Regierung Ferdinand des Ersten,* IV, 477-478.
[34] See Fr. Hruby, *Die Wiedertäufer in Mähren,* 9-12.
[35] Ferdinand I to Jacob von Salza (after June 6, 1535) partially printed in Franz Bernhard von

Bucholtz, "Geschichte der Regierung Ferdinand des Ersten," IV, 478.
[36] Ferdinand I to Frederick II, October 28, 1536, mentioned in ibid., 477.
[37] On this and the following see Koffmane, "Wiedertäufer," 47-48.
[38] CS XI, 812, 30.
[39] Ibid., 812, 31: "The Lord Christ has helped you through my poor service."
[40] Klose, "Schwenckfeld," 4 and *Beiträge,* 76-82.
[41] On Hirsenberger see Konrad Klose, "Wer war die erste evangelische Pfarrer in Lüben?" 167, and *Beiträge,* 77-80, 487.
[42] CS XI, 812, 32; cf. 812, 27-28.
[43] Ibid., 816, 26.
[44] See ibid., VI, 165, 18-22. Cf. ibid., V, (15) 23-96.
[45] Ibid., VI, (154) 157-175.
[46] Ibid., IX, 411, 32-33.
[47] Ibid., 706, 5-19.
[48] Ibid., XI, 919, 14-19.
[49] Cited from Paul Pfotenhauer, "Die Pförtner von Neumarkt und ihre Aufzeichnungen," 267.
[50] Crautwald to Johannes Schnabel and Johann Hoffmann, March 4, 1534, printed in CD KG g GS S 3 (1887), 30-31.
[51] The letters of Crautwald to Michael Wittiger in 1526 are in München SB, CLM 718, fol. 299r-307r (April 8, 1526); 308r-313r (May 27, 1526); 314r-318v (1526); 318v-320v (June 3, 1526); 321r-349v (June 17, 1526).

IV The Decline of Schwenkfeldianism

1. Frederick II's Approaches to the Lutherans

[1] Melancthon to Frederick II, June 25, 1533, CR IV, 1019-1020, No. 1118b; Melanchthon to Jerome Wittich, , ibid., 1020-1021, No. 1121b. The (July) 1533 date of the editor is certain.
[2] Ibid., 1019-1020, No. 1118b.
[3] Ibid., 1020, No. 1121b: "I am not horrified by any moderation concerning the Lord's Supper which is reflected in your composition."
[4] Ibid.
[5] Ibid.
[6] Ibid.
[7] Ibid., 1021, No. 1121b: "It is correct that I do not attack that moderation which is in your composition."
[8] Ibid., 1020, No. 1121b.
[9] On this and the following see above all Gerhard Eberlein, "Die evangelischen Kirchenordnungen Schlesiens im 16. Jahrhundert," 215-234; Sehling III, 418-420.
[10] On this and the following see Acta Capituli Wratislaviensis, Wroclaw DA, III, b.1b, 682-684. Cf. Kastner, I, 71.
[11] Cf. Eberlein, "Kirchenordnungen," 217.
[12] Hellmut Eberlein, "Die sogenannte Synode zu Strehlen."
[13] See Acta Capituli Wratislaviensis, Wroclaw DA, III, b. 1b, 695-696. Cf. Kastner, I, 71.
[14] For this title see note 15.
[15] This order is printed without the baptismal service in Fibiger, II, 106 ff; Rosenberg, 449-455; Aemilius Ludwig Richter, *Die evangelischen Kirchenordnungen des sechszehnten Jahrhunderts,* I, 239-241. It is fully printed in Sehling, III, 436-439 and Bahlow, *Reformation,* 158-163. Sehling is cited below.
[16] Ibid., 436-437.
[17] Ibid., 437.
[18] Ibid., 438-439.

[19] Ibid., 436.
[20] Ibid.
[21] Ibid., 438.
[22] Ibid., 439.
[23] Gereon Sailer to Wolfgang Capito, October 3, 1533, printed in TA Elsass II, 132, 28-29, No. 423.
[24] CS IV, 219, 23-24.
[25] Ibid., 219, 24-25.
[26] Ibid., 219, 23-225, 30.
[27] Ibid., 219, 25-27; 219, 35-221, 2.
[28] Ibid., 221, 18-19.
[29] Ibid., 219, 26-27; 219, 35-221, 2.
[30] Ibid., 223, 2-5.
[31] Ibid., 219, 27-29.
[32] See above all Köhler, ''Zwingli,'' II, 432-455; Ernst Bizer, *Studien zur Geschichte des Abendmahlsstreits im 16. Jahrhundert,* 25-130.
[33] Köhler, ''Zwingli,'' II, 448-449, 453-455 but note the opposite view in Bizer, 125-127.
[34] CS V, (507) 510-516.
[35] Crautwald to Schwenckfeld, December 1, 1536, München SB, CLM 718, fol. 512r-525v. Reisner entitled the work *De Concordia Et Vnione Sacramentali Quae facta est Anno Salutis M.D. XXXVI. Epistola Item Explicatio Loco I Corinth. XI. De Dignitate & Proba Manducantium. D. Valent: Craut: Silesij Theologi.*
[36] Ibid., fol. 513r.
[37] Ibid.
[38] Bizer, 118.
[39] Crautwald to Schwenckfeld, December 1, 1536, München SB, CLM 718, fol. 514r.
[40] Ibid., fol. 514v.
[41] Ibid., fol. 518v: ''Whoever eats, eats worthily or unworthily in the Lord, for Paul made two such orders. The impious therefore are those who eat unworthily in the Lord.''
[42] CS V, 514, 31-32; 515, 2-3.

2. The Christological Controversies

[1] On Schwenckfeld's Christology see above all Ferdinand Christian Baur, *Die christliche Lehre von der Versöhnung in ihrer geschichtlichen Entwicklung,* 459-463; *Die christliche Lehre von der Dreieinigkeit und Menschwerdung Gottes in ihrer geschichtlichen Entwicklung,* III, 219-256; ''Zur Geschichte der protestantischen Mystik,'' 502-528; Georg Ludwig Hahn, *Schwenckfeldii sententia de Christi persona et opere exposita;* Erbkam, *Geschichte der protestantischen Sekten,* 357-475; Isaak August Dorner, *Entwicklungsgeschichte der Lehre von der Person Christi,* II, 575-581, 624-636; Dorner, *Geschichte der protestantischen Theologie, besonders in Deutschland,* 178-182; Frederick William Loetscher, ''Schwenckfeld's Participation in the Eucharistic Controversy of the Sixteenth Century,'' 352-386, 454-500; Ecke, 124-128, 201-203; Theodor Sippell, ''Caspar Schwenckfeld,'' 865-871, 897-900, 925-927, 955-957, 963-966; Hirsch, 60-66; Hans Joachim Schoeps, *Vom himmlischen Fleisch Christi,* 25-36; Paul L. Maier, *Caspar Schwenckfeld on the Person and Work of Christ* and ''Caspar Schwenckfeld: A quadricentennial evaluation,'' 89-97; and Maron, 35-66.
[2] Note for example CS II, 574, 23-25: ''The bodily food is changed into our nature but the spiritual food changes into itself, that is into the divine nature in which we participate, II Peter 1.''
[3] Note for example ibid., III, 10, 11-14.
[4] Ibid., 202, 3-4.
[5] Pietz, 53, notes correctly that their spiritualism was contained by their biblicism.
[6] CS II, 481, 31-32; cf. 520, 1-3: ''This then is honor to God that man (with the exception of

Christ the man and natural son of God) cannot place such divine eternal being in any creature here or elsewhere.''

[7] Ibid., 555, 2-3.

[8] Ibid., 555, 3-556, 36.

[9] Wolfenbüttel HAB, Cof. Guelf. 37. 27 Aug. fol. 455v-456r.

[10] CS II, 574, 21-22.

[11] Ibid., 574, 30-575, 2.

[12] Ibid., 555, 13.

[13] Ibid., 555, 1-14.

[14] Maier, 37, n. 1.

[15] Hirsch, 61, n. 1.

[16] They emphasized this themselves. Note for example CS III, 629, 30-630, 36; ibid., V, 262-265; ibid., VI, 132, 4-133, 4; 496-497; 572, 11-573, 5; ibid., VII, 525, 25-33; 575, 17-31; ibid., VIII, 600, 3-8.

[17] Note particularly Crautwald's writings of 1529, CS III, (269) 271-343: *De cognitione Christi seu diiudicatione corporis et sanguinis Domini,* München SB, CLM 718, fol. 422r-458r; *Vorlesung über Joh 6,* ibid., fol. 459r-477r. Reisner gave it the title: *Ex Praelectione D. Valentini Cautw: In Euangelii Diui Johannis. VI. Caput. Annotata.*

[18] CS III, 317, 39-40.

[19] Note for example ibid., 218, 27-219, 7; Crautwald, *De cognitione Christi,* München SB, CLM 718, fol. 427v: ''The word of God in the body moreover was not contained by the body.''

[20] CS III, 325, 8. Cf. Crautwald, *De cognitione Christi,* München SB, CLM 718, 426v: ''True man according to the likeness of our humanity but of a different origin and property of flesh, in the whole course of his life without sin and guile.''

[21] Note for example, CS III, 296, 13-32; 325, 4-23.

[22] Note for example, ibid., 296, 13-15; Crautwald to Johannes Haner, (1536), München SB, CLM 718, fol. 536v.

[23] Note for example, Crautwald, *De cognitione Christi,* München SB, CLM 718, fol. 426v: ''True man according to similitude.''

[24] Note for example, CS III, 219, 1; 258, 30, 39; 559, 5; 635, 2.

[25] Note for example, ibid., 202, 28-34; 247, 30-36.

[26] Wolfenbüttel HAB, Cod. Guelf. 37.27 Aug. fol. 23r.

[27] Crautwald, *De cognitione Christi,* München SB, CLM, 718, fol. 434r.

[28] Note for example, CS III, 202, 37-38.

[29] Note for example, ibid., 559, 3-8: ''It is in no way fitting to call Christ a man, a creature, whom the Father ordained as the first born and the Lord of all creatures. Whatever was creaturely in him was taken away through his death and resurrection and ascension. [He is] in every way like the Father in the indivisible being of the Holy Trinity.''

[30] Ibid., 253, 26-28.

[31] For example ibid., 261, 25-30: ''Christ remains in his place (that is a manner of speaking since one cannot speak concerning this matter outside of time and space of how something happened beyond time and space). Christ remains as the Bible says at the right hand of the Father in heaven and rules over all through the right hand and the fingers of the right hand of God where he sits. That is through the Word in the Holy Spirit.''

[32] Note for example, Crautwald, *Vorlesung über Joh 6,* München SB, CLM 718, fol. 472r: ''Who eats the flesh of Christ is a partaker of the divine nature.''

[33] Ibid., fol. 472r-v: ''As physical bread is not eaten before it is baked and made ready for eating, so the flesh of Christ is not able to be the bread of souls unless it is first made spiritual and taken up into God. Therefore he says: My flesh is truly food, that is eternal food.''

[34] CS III, (269) 271-343.

[35] Ibid., 296, 4-11. Unfortunately Crautwald does not say which passages from the two works he had in mind.

[36] MSL 10, 357. On the Christology of Hilary see especially Anton Beck, *Die Trinitätslehre des heiligen Hilarius von Poitiers,* 208ff.; Pierre Smulders, *La doctrine trinitaire de S. Hilaire*

de Poitiers, 37ff; Paul Löffler, "Die Trinitätslehre des Bischofs Hilarius von Poitiers zwischen Ost und West," 26-36.

37 In addition to Hilary, Schwenckfeld cites above all Apollinaris of Laodicea, Cyril, Ambrose and Irenäus, A study of Schwenckfeld's use of patristic citations is necessary.

38 This is made particularly clear in his letter to Johann Bader (CS IV, [1] 3-49) which Schwenckfeld composed in December, 1530, a year and a half after he left Silesia.

39 That Schwenckfeld's Christology was not attacked by Luther or his followers is explained by the fact that it is not fully distinct from Luther's in the writings on the Lord's Supper, as has been indicated above. Nevertheless it is false to minimize the differences betweeen the two Christologies (note for example, Dorner, *Entwicklungsgeschichte der Lehre von der Person Christi,* 575-577: "Among the many reformers, none, we doubt, had more similarity to Luther's Christological premises than Andreas Osiander and among those who held themselves aside from the church, C. Schwenckfeld") or to negate it altogether (note Hirsch, 60: "Schwenckfeld's Christology, as we know it, is however only an imitation of the Lutheran [position]")

40 CS V, 340, 28-30.

41 Ibid., 340, 31-37.

42 Ibid., 340, 38-341, 13.

43 Indicated here above all was Luther's *Vom Abendmahl Christi, Bekenntnis* (WA 26, [242] 261-509).

44 CS V, 341, 16-17.

45 On this and the following see Crautwald to Margarete Engelmann, (before September 30, 1538), Wolfenbüttel HAB, Cod. Guelf. 45. 9 Aug., fol. 74r-81r.

46 Ibid., fol. 77r.

47 Ibid., fol. 77r-v.

48 Ibid., fol. 78v. marginalia (Commentary to I Cor. 2:8: MSL 17, 205 B) and fol. 80r (Commentary to Phil. 2:10-12: MSL 17, 434 A-B).

49 Ibid., fol. 79r (Commentary to Zach. 6:9-15: MSL 25, 1458 A).

50 Ibid., 79v.

51 See Schultz, 242-252.

52 See Heinold Fast, *Heinrich Bullinger und die Täufer,* 43-47.

53 See Werner Näf, *Vadian und seine Stadt St. Gallen,* II, 450-462.

54 See Karl Kern, "Sebastianus Coccius, Rektor der Schwäbisch Haller Lateinschule," 78-108.

55 CS VI, 136, 27-137, 3. See also Maier, 36.

56 Wolfenbüttel HAB, Cod. Guelf. 37. 27 Aug., fol. 33-45.

57 Ibid., fol. 42-43.

58 Ibid., fol. 49-52.

59 Ibid., fol. 51.

60 Cf. Maier, 52-66.

61 Crautwald to Katharina Streicher (after September 29, 1539), Wolfenbüttel HAB, Cod. Guelf. 45. 9 Aug., fol. 182r.

62 Ibid., fol. 182v.

63 See below section 4.

3. The Suppression of Schwenkfeldianism

1 Seckendorf, *Commentarius,* III, 160.

2 Ibid.

3 Ibid.

4 Hans Volz, publisher, *Urkunden und Aktenstücke zur Geschichte von Martin Luthers Schmalkaldischen Artikeln,* 109, n. 7. Volz's spelling of Wunschelt and Egetius here, on page 120, note 1, and in the register of persons is wrong.

5 Ibid., 120, n. 1.

[6] No Silesian prince took part in the Augsburg diet of 1530. Georg, the eighteen-year-old son of Duke Karl I of Münsterberg-Oels, was in the company of Count Georg of Brandenburg-Ansbach.

[7] Seckendorf, *Commentarius,* III, 160.

[8] Ibid., 160-161.

[9] Ibid., 160.

[10] Ibid., 160-161.

[11] CR 3, 128-131, No. 1458.

[12] Seckendorf, *Commentarius,* III, 161. The assertion in Protestant territorial church histories that Silesia was at this time more or less a completely Protestant land is false.

[13] Ibid.

[14] On this see Paul Fuchtel, "Der Frankfurter Anstand vom Jahre 1539," 168 and 174.

[15] Frederick II's promise to support Ferdinand I with troops was forced from him. The troops were never supplied.

[16] The full title is given in WA 50, 118. On this work by Moibanus, which is printed in W[1] 9, (2546) 2576-2747 and which is cited below, see Erdmann, 49-51; Soffner, *Geschichte der Reformation in Schlesien,* 117-118; Paul Konrad, *Dr Ambrosius Moibanus,* 68-70; "Die Einführung," 123 and Bahlow, *Reformation,* 130-132.

[17] W[1] 9, 2730.

[18] Ibid., 2677.

[19] WA 50, (117) 119-120.

[20] Ibid., 120, 9-15.

[21] Pol. III, 96.

[22] See CS V, 778-779.

[23] See Johann Scaurus to Schwenckfeld, May 23, 1540, Wolfenbüttel HAB, Cod. Guelf. 37. 27 Aug., fol. 69-72 and Cod. Guelf. 45. 9 Aug., fol. 102r-106v; Scholastica von Kitlitz to the same, June 2, 1540, ibid., Cod. Guelf. 37. 27 Aug., fol. 57-61 and Cod. Guelf. 45. 9 Aug., fol. 151r-156r.

[24] Schwenckfeld to Johann Scaurus, August 1, 1540, CS VII, (105) 107-117; Crautwald to Caspar von Wohlau, (before August 10, 1540), ibid., (118) 120-130; Schwenckfeld to Scholastica von Kitlitz, August 10, 1540, ibid., (149) 151-160; the same to Johann Scaurus, March 126, 1542, ibid., VIII, (106) 107-110; the same to Scholastica von Kitlitz, October 5, 1542, ibid., (300) 301-305 and May 13/14, 1543, ibid. (605) 607-611.

[25] On Schwenkfeldianism in the principality of Wohlau see above all Johann Christian Köllner, *Wolaviographia,* 287-288; Johann Heyne, *Urkundliche Geschichte der Stadt und des Fürstenthums Wohlau,* 312-313; and Söhnel, 51-63.

[26] Thebesius, III, 32-33.

[27] Berlin SB, Ms. germ. 153, fol. 1r-59r.

[28] Jerome Wittich, *Kurtze vnnd gründtliche widderlegung der vier Schlusreden die Johan Sigmund / Werner / etwa Pfarherr zu Lignitz aus Schwenckfelds Büchern gezogen,* Magdeburg 1555. After Wittich's death (1553) the piece was published by Sebastian von Zedlitz in Neukirch and dedicated to Georg II of Brieg-Wohlau.

[29] Frederick II to Schwenckfeld, April 4, 1540, Wolfenbüttel HAB, Cod. Guelf. 45. 9 Aug., fol. 139r-v. The judgments which were brought in have not been found and must be considered to be lost.

[30] Ibid., fol. 139v. Frederick II declared that he was prepared to make possible Werner's and Eckel's trip out of Silesia if Schwenckfeld would help to find them positions in the Empire. If they were "with the learned" there would be nothing to prevent their return to Liegnitz. He would "eagerly take them in as preachers and see that they would be supported with the previous and with a better livelihood (than they had had)."

[31] Ibid., fol. 139r-v.

[32] Ibid., fol. 139v.

[33] Georg Bock von Polach to Schwenckfeld, November 18, 1539, Wolfenbüttel HAB, Cod. Guelf. 45. 9 Aug., fol. 456r-v.

[34] CS VII, (14) 18-34; (131) 132-148.
[35] Seckendorf, *Commentarius,* III, 244.
[36] Ibid.
[37] WAB 8, (597) 598-599, No. 3406.
[38] Luther's answer is not extant. See Seckendorf, *Commentarius,* III, 244.
[39] Johann Frederick to Frederick II, November 10, 1539, WAB 8, 597-598 (extracts printed).
[40] Seckendorf, *Commentarius,* III, 244.
[41] On Faber see Heinrich Schnell, *Heinrich V, der Friedfertige,* 14, 24, 34-37.
[42] Crautwald to Katharina Streicher, after September 29, 1539, Wolfenbüttel HAB, Cod. Guelf. 37. 27 Aug., fol. 44: "... with thanks that God the Lord has still granted us a place here, since for a long time my chair was at the door and I might have spent my old age wandering if it had happened that my Lord and God had not protected me and had allowed me again to sit in my corner."
[43] See Crautwald to Margarete Engelmann, 1537, extracts printed in G. Arnold, *Supplementa,* 139-140.
[44] See Crautwald to Johann Schnabel and Johann Hoffmann, April 14, 1534 printed in CKGS 3 (1887), 30-32.
[45] In 1538 for example he was sick for a month. See Crautwald to Jacob Held von Tieffenau, Sepetember 30, 1538, Wolfenbüttel HAB, Cod. Guelf. 45. 9 Aug., fol. 62r-73v.
[46] WA 39, (92) 93-95, 4.
[47] Wolfenbüttel HAB, Cod. Guelf. 45. 9 Aug., fol. 428v.
[48] CS IX, 437, 11.
[49] On Neff see Gustav Bossert, *Quellen zur Geschichte der Wiedertäufer,* I, 114; Weber, 23.
[50] Wolfenbüttel HAB, Cod. Guelf. 37. 27 Aug., fol. 543r.
[51] Printed in Sehling, III, 439-441. See also ibid., 420-421. The church order is not dependent on that of Wittenberg in 1533 as Gottlieb Biermann, *Geschichte des Protestantismus in Österreichisch-Schlesien,* 45, asserted , nor on any others. It is original and grew out of the needs of the principalities of Liegnitz and Brieg.
[52] Ibid., 440.
[53] Ibid.
[54] Ibid.
[55] Ibid.
[56] Ibid.
[57] Ibid., 440-441.
[58] Ibid.
[59] Ibid., 441.
[60] Ibid.
[61] Partially printed in ibid., 441-442. Cf. ibid., 421-422.
[62] Eberlein, "Kirchenordnungen," 225, suggested this earlier.
[63] Sehling, III, 421.
[64] Ibid., 440.
[65] Partially printed in Rosenberg, 135-136.
[66] Ibid., 136.
[67] On February 24, 1547 the patron allowed these new positions to be established. The document is printed in Schneider, *Verlauf,* 39, Beilage VI.
[68] G.Thebesius, *Liegnitzische Jahr-Bücher,* III, 71.
[69] Ibid.
[70] The pastors of Liegnitz, Goldberg, Haynau and Lüben to Georg II, 1554, October 9, 1554, Wroclaw SA, Rep. 28. Fürstentum Liegnitz, X, 5, g (original): "... and especially because of the ruinous rising of Schwenckfeldian radicalism, which as time went on cut into the localities even more, and all pastors and ministers together with the entire principality came under great mistrust and suspicion, as if we were all part of the heresy and the whole of your principality infected with this poison." Cf. their letter to Georg II, November 8, 1554, ibid. (original)

71 Sebastian von Zedlitz to Georg II, March 13, 1555, ibid., (original): ''Although your worship, in the present difficult and dangerous times, has graciously ordained for the principality of Liegnitz two learned, pious, God-pleasing men, who are free from doubt, as superintendents, the visitation is most necessary in that place; there Schwenckfeld has sowed his seed among spiritual and secular, learned and laity, to such a degree that he hopes and intends that it stand firmly and be solidly rooted.''

72 Sebastian von Zedlitz to Georg II, May 27, 1555, ibid., (original).

73 Heinrich Dietrich and Georg Seiler to Georg II, April 22, 1555, ibid., (original).

74 The same to Georg II, (on the reverse appears the date 1556), ibid., (original).

75 Ibid.

76 Cf. for example, ibid.: ''For them [i.e.Schwenkfelders who remain firm] we have ordered anew an examination to be held before the council. Because they remained steadfast we wish to surrender them to the council according to your command.''

77 Frederick IV to Georg II, April 9, 1585, ibid., (original).

78 Ibid.

79 Ibid.

80 On this and the following see Klose, ''Schwenckfeld,'' 190-208 and *Beiträge,* 80-98.

81 Cf. Franziskus Rosentritt to Georg II, November 27, 1561, Wroclaw SA, Rep. 28. Fürstentum Liegnitz, X, 5, g (original): ''After Caspar Schwenckfeld had brought his false teaching among the people for years, he had in every way here and in Lyben a rather significant following. Concerning this both of my predecessors, preachers here, complained not a little.''

82 Ibid.

83 Ibid.

84 Ibid.

85 On Rosentritt see n. 80 and Konrad Klose, ''M. Franziskus Rosentritt.''

86 Franziskus Rosentritt to Georg II, November 27, 1561, Wroclaw SA, Rep. 28. Fürstentum Liegnitz, X, 5, g (original).

87 Ibid.

88 Ibid.

89 Ibid.

90 Ibid.

91 Franziskus Rosentritt to Georg II, November 27, 1561, Wroclaw SA, Rep. 28. Fürstentum Liegnitz, X, 5, g: ''. . . and because Paul Neugebauer, an important man among the artisans, was in the guild, the guild in which the mayor was a member, took up his case and called its elders members and agreed together that [Paul Neugebauer's wife, a Schwenckfelder] should be buried. On this matter they went to the local government official.''

4. Schwenkfeldianism in Glatz

1 On the relationship between owners see Joseph Kögler, ''Kurzgefasste Regenten-Geschichte der Grafschaft Glatz,'' 13-14.

2 On the beginning of the Reformation in the county of Glatz see Georg Aelurius, *Glaciographie,* 295-296; Rosenberg, 200-202; Aloys Bach, *Urkundliche Kirchengeschichte der Grafschaft Glatz,* 97; Soffner, 415-417; Alfred Zobel, ''Die Reformation in der Grafschaft Glatz,'' 107-108; 113-114; and Josef Fogger, ''Beiträge zur Geschichte der evangelischen Kirche in der Grafschaft Glatz,'' 106-109.

3 Note for example, Bohuslav Balbinus, *Miscellanea historica regni Bohemiae,* III, 44.

4 See Kögler, ''Regenten-Geschichte,'' 15.

5 Ibid.

6 Soffner, 416, n. 2.

7 See Bach, 100.

8 Aelurius, 299.

9 On Eckel's stay in Glatz see Aelurius, 296-297; Gottlieb Liefmann, *Dissertatio historica de fanaticis Silesiorum,* fol. B 3r; Johann Heinrich Cunrad, *Silesia togata,* 62; Daniel Gomolcke, *Der heutigen Schlesischen Kirchen-Historie,* III, 75-77; Johann Gottlieb Kahlo, *Denkwür-*

digkeiten der preussischen Grafschaft Glatz, 139-140; Caspar Keseler, "Catalogus pastorum Ecclesiarum Lignicensium Petro-Paulinae et Marianae," 772; Rosenberg, 313; Bach 99-101; Eduard Ludwig Wedekind, *Geschichte der Grafschaft Glatz,* 238; Soffner, 110-114; Franz Volkmer, "Denkwürdige Männer aus und in der Grafschaft Glatz. Erster Nachtrag," 225; Paul Heinzelmann, "Beiträge zur Predigersgeschichte der Grafschaft Glatz," 10-11; and Fogger, 110.

10 Bach, 100.

11 On the Anabaptists in Habelschwerdt see Kögler, 23; Franz Volkmer, *Geschichte der Stadt Habelschwerdt,* 12.

12 CS IV, (240) 241-244.

13 Franz Volkmer, "Auszüge aus einer Reihe Glatzer Chroniken. I. Aus der Chronik des lutherischen Schneiders Pankraz Scholz zu Glatz und seines Sohnes Nickel," 317: "Since he could not be satisfied with abusing and insulting God's word and scorning the holy and precious sacrament, God himself had to stop his mouth. He called the sacrament only poor bread and an illusion of bread. Often he said that men ran after a bit of bread like dogs did after a piece of meat and it was not even bread but an illusion of bread and [he said] similar devilish things about divine matters."

14 On Eisenmann's stay in Glatz see Aelurius, 297-298; Liefmann, fol. B 4r; Kahlo, 140; Wedekind, 238-239; Heinzelmann, 11; and Fogger, "Beiträge," 111.

15 On Rosenhayn's stay in Neurode see Keseler, 773-774; Ehrhardt, IV, 265; Bach 102; W. Klambt, *Urkundliche Chronik der Stadt und Herrschaft Neurode,* 37; Wedekind, 242; Fogger, "Beiträge," 111.

16 Schubart, "Vorrede," 153: "The master Valerius who was at the same time the pastor at Ronnerssdorff in the county of Glatz was struck so that he could no longer preach. He wandered about for a time, and finally became like a child and died in the house he had bought."

17 See CKGS 4 (1888), 106.

18 On Werner's stay in Rengersdorf see Aelurius, 296; Liefmann, fol. B 3v; Ehrhardt, IV, 158-160; Bach, 101; Soffner, 417; Volkmer, "Denkwürdige Männer." 236; Fogger, "Beiträge," 110-111.

19 On Rengersdorf see Joseph Kögler, "Historische und topographische Beschreibung der im Glatzer District gelegenen und zur Rengersdorfer Pfarrei gehörigen 5 Dörfer," 89-123, 213-232.

20 Ibid., 90.

21 Cf. Bach, 101.

22 Cf. ibid., 102.

23 Cf. CS VII, 48.

24 Ibid., 48-50.

25 Ibid., 50.

26 Ibid., 12, 7-9.

27 Ibid., XV, (395) 407-1031.

28 Ibid., 630, 33-37.

29 Ibid., 508, 11-12.

30 Ibid., 661, 21.

31 Ibid., 462, 5.

32 Ibid., 670, 16-21.

33 See Karl Schottenloher, "Der Pforzheimer Buchdrucker Georg Rab und die beschlagnahmte Postille des Schwenckfeldjüngers Johann Werner," 400-411.

34 Christoph von Würtemberg to Karl II of Baden-Durlach, October 30, 1558, printed in ibid., 400.

35 Ibid., 400-401.

36 See Wilhelm Preger, *Matthias Flacius Illyricus und seine Zeit,* I, 309-310.

37 Matthias Flacius, *Funnffzig grobe Irthumen,* fol. F 3r-G iv.

38 Ibid., fol. F 3r.

39 CS X, (129) 131-154.

[40] Ibid., 146-154.
[41] Ibid., IX, (731) 735-756.
[42] See Volkmer, "Denkwürdige Männer," 236.
[43] See Christoph Neaetius, "Liber Proventuum," printed in *Geschichtsquellen der Grafschaft Glatz,* III, 25-28.
[44] Bach, 101.
[45] Ambrosius Moibanus, *Ad magnificum ac generosum. . .An commio infantium. . .probetur Ecclesiae* fol. B 2v-3v.
[46] Ibid., fol. A 2r-B 8r.
[47] Ibid., fol. G 8r-L 8r. Cf. CR 3, 240-258, Melanchthon, I, (387) 388-410.
[48] The dedication is in Moibanus, *Ad magnificum ac generosum,* fol. A 2r-B 8r.
[49] CR 3, 485-486, No. 1649.
[50] Ibid., 240, No. 1520; A. Moibanus, fol. G 8v.
[51] Neaetius, 15.
[52] Ibid.
[53] See Joseph Thamm, *Geschichte der Stadt Habelschwerdt,* 19; Kögler, 24; and Volkmer, *Geschichte der Stadt Habelschwerdt,* 12.
[54] On the Counter-Reformation activities in the county of Glatz by Duke Ernst of Bavaria see Aelurius, 298; Kahlo, 31-32; Bach, 109-110; Wedekind, 252-257; Alfred Zobel, "Die Reformation in der Grafschaft Glatz," 107-108, 113-114; Joseph Schmidt, "Herzog Ernst von Bayern und die erste Glatzer Gegenreformation," 22-50; Fogger, 114-116.
[55] Neaetius, 15.
[56] CS XV, (195) 197-204.
[57] Ibid., (205) 208-213.
[58] A list of the pastors who did not appear is found in Schmidt, 38-39.
[59] Among others the following belonged to the commission: the secretary, Georg Mehl of Strolitz, the representative of the Grandmaster of the Knights of Malta, Wenzel von Haugwitz auf Pischkowitz, the Count of Prague, Petrus Pechin, and the Provost of Holy Cross in Breslau, Sebastian Schleupner.
[60] Steinberg, 171-172.
[61] Ibid., 173-174.
[62] Ibid.
[63] The following pastors were involved: Georg Raufeisen from Wölfelsdorf, Thomas Schweiker from Rengersdorf, and Michael Steinberg from Gabersdorf.
[64] These were the two preachers: Caspar Stender from Habelschwerdt and Georg Görloch from Volpersdorf.
[65] Caspar Elogius to Anton Brus von Müglitz, May 2, 1577, Prag SB, C 113/3 Karton 2050. Cf. Maximilian II to Christoph von Schellendorff, January 18, 1572, printed in Aelurius, 305 , and Gomolcke, III, 80-81.
[66] Wedekind, 255.
[67] The visitation warrant is in Neaetius, 16.
[68] See Neaetius, 33-62.
[69] See Kögler, 16.
[70] Valentin Jeckel to Anton Brus von Müglitz, February 8, 1561, Prag SB C 66.
[71] Anton Brus von Müglitz to Ferdinand I, [n.d., before September 5, 1561] Prag SB, C 67.
[72] Ibid.
[73] Caspar Elogius to Anton Brus von Müglitz, May 2, 1577, Prag SB, C 113. von Kitlitz to the same, June 2, 1540, ibid., Cod. Guelf. 37. 27 Aug., fol. 57-61 and Cod. Guelf. 45. 9 Aug., fol. 151r-156r.
[74] Martin John Jr. to Achatius Frederick Roscius, SchLP, VC 5-1, 818-820; "Nicolaus Tetschke preached in Mittelwald and at first defended infant baptism. Thereafter he had questions [about the practice] and gave up his post." Martin John, *Bericht von den Schwenckfeldern,* SchLP, VC 5-3, n.d., 1224: "There were still two men in Mittelwald who stood by Detschke. One

was Adam Jesch, the other David Curke. Both were learned men. Adam Jesch knew seven languages."

75 See Antonius Oelsner to Christoph Oelsner, SchLP, VC 5-3, n.d., 544.

76 Cf. my *Sebastian Franck,* 3-19.

77 Antonius Oelsner to Christoph Oelsner, SchLP, VC 5-3, n.d., 544.

78 See Caspar Elogius to Anton Brus von Müglitz, May 2, 1577, Prag SB, C 113. Cf. M. John, *Bericht von den Schwenckfeldern,* SchLP, VC 5-3, 1222: "And when the sacraments and teachings were changed, the people whose consciences were against it took no part in it. Most of the them favored infant baptism. On this Schwenckfeld did not write much; his teaching of the Spirit and fire baptism pointed out that man himself must search for it and must enter into the new birth out of Spirit and water from above. For some this manner of infant baptism was hard to accept."

79 Caspar Elogius to Anton Brus von Müglitz, May 2, 1577, Prag SB, C 113.

80 Ibid.

81 See Valentin Jeckel to Anton Brus von Müglitz, February 8, 1561, Prag SB, C 66.

82 M. John Jr., *Bericht von den Schwenckfeldern,* SchLP, VC 5-3, 1227: "A man at Deutmansdorff who did not have confidence in the pastors whom he could not consider to be faithful but who wished to marry, went into the county of Glatz in Mittelwald. The lord of the area had the same ideas and took these people in willingly."

83 Ibid.: "And the Lutheran pastor had to leave these people be as long as the old lord lived. To them my grandmother, Mrs. Martin John went with her children."

84 Ibid.: "When the old lord died [1563], his wife under pressure from the pastor began to persecute. Then the Silesians one after the other returned to Silesia where persecution had decreased somewhat. The young lord did not wish to let my father do so, however, since he did not have any equally clever man in the whole area."

85 Caspar Elogius to Anton Brus von Müglitz, May 2, 1577, Prag SB, C 113.

86 Ibid.

87 See Fogger, 125. Cf. Martin John Jr. to Achatius Frederick Roscius, SchLP, VC 5-1, 820: "Hereafter the Counter-Reformation began and the priest and authority [in Mittelwald] had to leave."

88 See Fogger, 125-126.

89 Printed in Balbinus, VIII, 135-138; cf. Bach, 288-290; Wedekind, 379-380.

90 See Fogger, 127.

91 M. John Jr., *Bericht von den Schwenckfeldern,* SchLP, VC 5-3, 1227: "My father remained until the Counter-Reformation began and he had the house full of soldiers who threatened him with the worst threats one can think of. Because of these he fled one night with his wife and child and one sister. The other sister, however, a stubborn daughter, stayed."

92 On this and the following see M. John Jr., *Bericht von den Schwenckfeldern,* SchLP , VC 5-3, 1227: ". . .he allowed his children to be baptized. I knew all of them as adults. They were all Catholic; they knew of the former creed but could not let themselves be noticed. They had a piccard hymnal but kept it hidden since they did not wish to be persecuted. The same thing happened to others. In some there was spiritual knowledge or the flame of love; among the youth however one noticed nothing. I noted it died out completely with the adults. God forbid that in other places where one pays so little attention to the truth, the same thing occur."

V Schwenkfeldianism in Löwenberg, Goldberg, and Haynau

1. Expansion and Blossoming

1 On the problem of dating the beginning of Schwenkfeldianism in the Bober-Katzbach mountains see Hensel, 201; Benjamin Gottlieb Sutorius, *Die Geschichte von Löwenberg,* II, 140; Soffner, 246-247, 249; Koffmane, "Wiedertäufer, " 55.

[2] On Johann von Schaffgotsch see Elizabeth Zimmermann, "Über den Ursprung der Schwenckelder im Iser-und Riesengebirge," 149-162; and Emil Voigt, "Die Burg Kynast und ihre Besitzer," II, 221-225.

[3] Ibid.

[4] See Soffner, 246-247.

[5] Hiller was married to Elizabeth von Lest, nee von Redern.

[6] None of Hiller's works appeared in print. The originals must be considered lost, but copies of the following works are found in SchLP:

1. *Postilla und Auslegung der Evangelia durchs gantze Jahr; Geprediget durch den Gott gelehrten Mann Michael Hiller—Pfarrherr zum Zobten—(Ein Dorff in Schlesien im Fürstenthum Jauer). Der in Gott verschieden ist den 22. Octobris, an einem Montage zu nachts, Im Jahre 1557. (Es wird sein Abscheid auch geschrieben funden 1554). Abgeschrieben und zusammen getragen von Nicolaus Detschken. (Es wird auch geschrieben funden von Nicolaus Detschken, dass ers zusammen getragen 1564. Doch ist das letztere vil volkommener; und ist auch dieses dem letzteren nach abgeschrieben worden.) Abgeschrieben im Jahre Christi MDCCLIV.* (VB 5-5). In its four parts the manuscript contains sermons about the church year and on various themes of Christian faith as well as Hiller's Confession. Two copies from 1571 (SchLP VA 5-3 and 5-6) contain only the first two parts. For this reason the later manuscript (1754) is cited below as *Postille.*

2. *Von der Christlichen Busse.* The oldest extant copy (VA 2-12) is dated 1717. The manuscript contains six prayers and six hymns on repentance.

3. *Ein Schöner Christlicher Tractatt Des von Gott Hochbegnadetten und Gelertten Michael Hillers Lehrers zum Zobten in Schlesien. Darinnen enthalten sind sein Treu u. Tauff und Communion Ceremonien Sampt den Gebetten wie er es üblich gehalten hatt Wie auch Die Besuchung der Krancken Sampt Den Leich Sermonen und Predigten. Welcher Michael Hiller gelebett und gelehrtt hatt Nach Christi geburtt im Sechzehenden Seculi und verschiden 1557 anitzo abgeschriben von Maria Weissen MDIII (error for MDCCC).* (VA 4-11). This manuscript contains orders of service for baptism, marriage, the Lord's Supper, and funerals, as well as funeral and burial hymns.

4. *Auserlesene Hertz-anmuthige Trost-volle Sterbens-Seuffzer und Gebette, frommer liebhabenden in Gott sich tröstenden Seelen. Aufgesetzt von Hn. Michael Hillern, seel. weyland Pfarrherrn zum Zobten in Schlesien, Psal. 90. Ach Herr! lehr unss bedencken dass wir sterben müssen, auf dass wir klug werden. Geschrieben im Jahr 1753.* (VB 1-19).

[7] On Liebald see Oswald Kadelbach, *Geschichte des Dorfes Probsthayn,* 19.

[8] Ibid., 145.

[9] *Postille,* I, 250.

[10] Ibid., II, 65 and 138.

[11] Ibid., I, 118: "The sacraments are not aids for or capable of making man holy; they are the practice and confession of faith and an internalization and reconsideration of the death and blood offering of Christ." Ibid., 132-133: "The verbal Gospel or preached word today gives no faith or holiness. It is only a word of service, witness, exhortation and serves those who are already faithful. . . He who properly understands the matter will see clearly that the preached word gives us witness, teaches and points to Christ who gives, increases and strengthens faith rather than that out of it we should or can become faithful or Christians." Ibid., 277: "The sermon, where it is correct and true, can give witness to faith but cannot give faith." Ibid., 301: "Thus one calls our sacrament the body of Christ, and baptism, the baptism of Christ, since it internalizes, points, and directs to a reconsideration of the true baptism."

[12] Ibid., 197.

[13] Ibid., 55.

[14] Ibid., II, 224.

[15] Ibid., I, 57. The last sentence may be read: ". . . his deified, even transformed-into-God flesh." Cf. ibid., 68, 96-97; II, 22.

[16] Ibid., I, 99-100: "And as Christ's humanity was reduced by his ephemerality and each day became more one with God, so the faithful man each day sets aside the essential nature of

the old man and moves to divinization in all purity and piety, and the body of the Christian man becomes daily purged and polished through good practices and especially through much suffering and sorrow . . . and thus deification becomes daily stronger in the whole man . . . and on the last day, when the Christians arise, their deification will be complete.'' Cf. ibid., 57; II, 5, 24 and 52.

[17] Ibid., I, 57.

[18] Note for example, ibid.: ''However, these are the marks: firstly, knowledge of our nothingness; secondly, justification through Jesus Christ by which the conscience is certain and happy; thirdly, eternal abhorrence of sinners; fourthly, desire and eagerness for God's words and Christian activity; fifthly, desire for truth; sixthly, improvement of life; seventhly, tendency to the love of God and neighbor; eighthly, striving against sin especially of one's own flesh, so that he no longer lives after his own desires.''

[19] Ibid.

[20] Ibid., 100.

[21] It could not be ascertained which Tauler imprint was used by Hiller. The citation is not found in the Basel 1521 Tauler edition which contains pseudo-Tauler sermons.

[22] Michael Hiller, *Michael Hillers Bekäntnis, welches er gethan hat vor Se. Fürstl. Gnaden den Bischoffe zur Neisse, Balthasar Promnitzen,* in *Postille,* IV, 324-325.

[23] Ibid., 324.

[24] Ibid., 324-327.

[25] See Sutorius, II, 367.

[26] On Hiller's death date see ibid., 368.

[27] See Soffner, 246-247.

[28] The pastors of Goldberg to Georg II, n.d. [ca. 1560], Wroclaw SA, Rep. 28. Fürstentum Liegnitz X, 5, i.

[29] Ibid.: ''However they seldom came to the preaching service; but if [they] heard something which affected them, they stood up [or shouted out?] and left.''

[30] Ibid.: ''At times someone would shout at the preacher in the pulpit.''

[31] Ibid.

[32] Ibid.: ''Thus there were still many people in certain churches who held to the false radical teachings and who also sometimes spoke abusively about the church.''

[33] Heinrich Diettrich and Georg Seiler to Georg II, n.d. [1556 on the reverse side], Wroclaw SA, Rep. 28, Fürstentum Liegnitz, X, 5, g (original). In this letter the villages of Probsthain, Armenruh, and Hartmannsdorf [Gross-Hartmannsdorf or Harpersdorf], are mentioned in particular.

[34] Ibid.

[35] Ibid.

[36] M. John Sr. to the Schwenkfelders in Harpersdorf, n.d. SchLP, VC 5-3, 386. M. John Sr. to Frederick IV, n.d., ibid., 393. Cf. M. John Jr., *Bericht von den Schwenckfeldern,* n.d., ibid., 1225.

[37] M. John Sr. to Frederick IV, n.d., ibid., 393. Cf. M. John Jr. to the Schwenkfelders in Harpersdorf, ibid., 386: '' . . . and there [at Kauffung] I saw the Godless life of the priests, how they were busy with eating and drinking, with card playing and the playing of nine pins sitting in beer houses and taverns, how they caused disturbances and practiced vice; I cannot tell you enough about their sins.'' M. John Sr. to Emperor Rudolf II, n.d., ibid., 408: ''And the priest at Kauffung made a place to play nine-pins on the church property and invited other priests in and they played together.''

[38] M. John Sr. to the Schwenkfelders in Harpersdorf, ibid., 386-387: ''And because of this I was forced to stay in my home and read to my wife and children and admonish them to penance insofar as God gave me grace.'' M. John Sr. to Frederick IV, n.d., ibid., 393.

[39] M. John Sr. to the Schwenkfelders in Harpersdorf, n.d., ibid., 387; M. John Sr. to Frederick IV, n.d., ibid., 393. M. John Jr., *Bericht von den Schwenckfeldern,* n.d., ibid., 1225.

[40] M. John Sr. to the Schwenkfelders in Harpersdorf, n.d., ibid., 387; M. John Sr. to Frederick IV, n.d., ibid., 393-394; Ursula John Sr. to Frederick IV, n.d., ibid., 397. Cf. M. John Jr.,

Bericht von den Schwenckfeldern, n.d., ibid., 1225.

41 On Etzler see Eberhard Goldmann, "Zur Geschichte der Kirchengemeinde Harpersdorf," I, 29; H. Grünewald, *Predigergeschichte von Goldberg,* 19.

42 M. John Sr. to Frederick IV, n.d., SchLP, VC 5-3, 394. Cf. M. John Sr. to the Schwenkfelders in Harpersdorf, n.d., ibid., 387.

43 M. John Sr. to the Schwenkfelders in Harpersdorf, n.d., ibid., 387. M. John Sr. to Frederick IV, ibid., 394; Ursula John Sr. to Frederick IV, n.d., ibid., 397. Cf. M. John Jr., *Bericht von den Schwenckfeldern,* n.d., ibid., 1225.

44 M. John Sr. to Frederick IV, n.d., ibid., 394; Ursula John Sr. to Frederick IV, n.d., ibid., 397. Cf. M. John Jr., *Bericht von den Schwenckfeldern,* n.d., ibid., 1225.

45 M. John Sr. to N.N., n.d., ibid., 362: "And the person who is not baptized and does not receive or wish to receive the holy Sacrament, is now no Christian. And he who does not believe that a child in its baptism is washed of all sins is a great sinner. And he who does not believe that the bread and wine give the body and blood of the Son of God, is held to be a despiser of God. And he who does not seek the kingdom of God with them cannot find it, they say." M. John Sr. to Andreas Jerin, ibid., 378: "The false teachers wish that we be based on a foundation other than God. And it is their foundation on which they want us to build, namely the holy baptism, the holy Sacrament, and their oral, preached word. In this they wish to bind holiness for us and to tie it down which we are not able and will not consent to do without going against our consciences." John Sr. to N.N., n.d., ibid., 1316: "Thus no Christian will accept that he should take the doctrine of their Godless teachers or hold to their baptism or Sacrament; God the Lord will not accept a half man, but he wants to have us completely and totally or dispense with us. And thus we must accept the whole Christ in faith and not half a Christ, since he is not divided in God but totally and alone one. Therefore God does not wish that his faithful ones participate with the community of the devil. The man who goes to Satan's teachers goes to Satan."

46 M. John Sr. to Ursula John Sr., 1592, ibid., 415.

47 M. John Jr., *Bericht von den Schwenckfeldern,* n.d., ibid., 1225.

48 Antonius Oelsner to Peter Heinrich, n.d., ibid., 447-448. Antonius Oelsner to Christoph Oelsner and the Schwenkfeldrer, 1597, ibid., 545.

49 A. Oelsner, *Ein Gründtlicher bericht von Antonie Ölssnern seiner Bekehrungh, Offenbarungh undt erkenthnis,* n.d. [after 1594], (hereafter cited: *Bekehrungsbericht*), SchLP, VC 4-1, 3-4: "When I became an honorable and reasonable man and feared God and his judgment like a servant and when I was able to read the Scriptures, I began with zeal to search in them and I studied what was the correct faith and the foundation of the community of God. And then one night God caused a deep sleep to fall over me, and when I awoke I found myself different than before, namely fear and anxiety had gripped me and I had come into fire and water, for it was as if my shirt had been pulled out of hot water. My feelings and thoughts were tied to this so that I could no longer think of earthly things, as earlier, and I began to shake and quiver for dread and pain and did not know what to do. Then I heard inwardly a thought and command: I was to pray. As I began with weak reverence to pray the Lord's Prayer, I was immediately heard and God worked quickly in me and immediately and he filled me from above to below and purified me in a moment."

50 Antonius Oelsner to Peter Heinrich, n.d., SchLP, VC 5-3, 451. Cf. A. Oelsner, *Bekehrungsbericht,* n.d., SchLP, VC 4-1, 5.

51 Antonius Oelsner to Peter Heinrich, n.d., SchLP, VC 5-3, 451.

52 Ibid., 451-452: "Then I made use of great bravery and freedom and I went into the field to admonish and make it known to others. And I did this for the following reason: the houses were too small for the large company of people, and I thought that in the village the light-minded and the enemies would come too often, cause an uproar, make fun of the word so that the houses who took us in and protected us would be taken by the authorities. Therefore I went into the fields to admonish people since I noted that the enemies who hated the word and believed the doctrine was false would not come so far, but those who had a desire and love for the word of God and the Spirit of the Lord and who wished to be counseled and in-

structed through me according to his doctrine. These would come to the field without hesitation and indeed did so."

53 The most significant anti-Schwenkfeldian writings were: Caspar Radecker, *Gegründetes Auschreiben von den Aufheben der Bücher Caspar von Schwenckfelds* (Wittenberg, 1556); Caspar Radecker, *Bericht ob weltlich Gewalt die Schrifften und Bücher der Schwermer frey zu zulassen, oder aber weg zu nemen, schüldig sey. Wider jtzige unchristliche Rotten und Secten gestellet.* (Wittenberg,1556); Caspar Radecker, *Eine ernste Ermanunge an die Kirche zu Lewenberg, das man die Prediger hören soll, so das liebe selige wort Gottes, und die heiligen Sacramenta, rein und gesund führen* (Wittenberg, 1563); Caspar Radecker, *Erklärung dreier Fragen zum nothdürftigen Unterrichte der Kirchen zu Löwenberg,* (Görlitz 1567); L. Krentzheim, *Leicht-Predigt über Jungfrau Sabina—Tochter des Bartel zu Logau von Olbersdorf Fürstl. Liegnitz Rath und Hofmeister. Darinnen zugleich kürzlich mit eingebracht eine gründliche Verlegung des Schwenckfeldischen Irrthumbs vom Wort Gottes. Gepredigt zu Liegnitz den 17. Mai 1570* (Görlitz, 1571); L. Hartranft, *Ware, christliche und glimpfliche Widerlegung des Irrthumbs der Schwenckfelder* (Görlitz, 1578); A. Herfart, *Drei gute Predigten vom heiligen Abendmahl aus den Worten Sankt Pauli I. Cor. II* (Frankfurt a.O., 1578).

54 M. John Sr. to N.N., n.d., SchLP, VC 5-3, 400: "You have yourself heard how he [the preacher] went into the pulpit and with a fierce heart ridiculed us and shamed us to his greatest ability and knowledge."

55 M. John Sr. to N.N., n.d., ibid., 359 and 363; M. John Sr. to Frederick IV, n.d., ibid., 394; M. John Sr. to N.N., n.d., ibid., 400; M. John Sr. to N.N., n.d., ibid., 404; M. John Sr. to Emperor Rudolf II, n.d., ibid., 408; M. John Sr. to Sigismund von Mauschwitz, n.d., ibid., 411.

56 Sutorius, II, 383.

57 A. Oelsner, *Bekehrungsbericht,* n.d., SchLP, VC 4-1, 20. On this and the following see Sutorius, II, 383-384.

58 Ibid., 23.

59 Ibid., 24.

60 Ibid., 28-29; Antonius Oelsner to Markus Domitz, 1595, SchLP, VC 5-3, 532-540, partially printed in Christoph Schultz, *Erläuterung,* 25-27; Christoph Schultz to Peter Heinrich, n.d., ibid., 437; M. John Sr. to Emperor Rudolf II, n.d., ibid., 409-410.

61 M. John Sr. to the Schwenkfelders in Harpersdorf, n.d., ibid., 388-389; Ursula John Sr. to Frederick IV, n.d., ibid., 397.

62 M. John Sr. to N.N., n.d., ibid., 361; M. John Sr. to the Schwenkfelders in Harpersdorf, n.d., ibid., 389; Ursula John Sr. to Frederick IV, n.d., ibid., 397.

63 M. John Sr. to the Schwenkfelders, n.d., ibid., 390-392.

64 M. John Sr. to the Schwenkfelders, n.d., ibid., 367-368.

65 Note for example, Antonius Oelsner to the Schwenkfelders in Harpersdorf, n.d., ibid., 512; Antonius Oelsner to Georg Geissler, n.d., ibid., 515; Christoph Oelsner to the Schwenkfelders in Harpersdorf, 1594, ibid., 617; Christoph Oelsner to Melchior Schulderte, 1595, ibid., 642.

66 M. John Sr. to the Schwenkfelders in Harpersdorf, n.d., ibid., 390-391: "When the two years were up, a great stir began among the people. It was said to me that they would imprison more people. . . .Then the people came and there was a great stir among the people, and children and old people complained and wept over the false pastors, over the sins of the people and the arrogance they showed, and many were so moved—and many men are still affected today—and this lasted about fourteen days." Christoph Oelsner to Antonius Oelsner, September 18, 1594, ibid., 633-634: "And in the year 1590, the almighty Lord and God drew some men graciously to us, enlightened and visited them particularly in Hartsdorff [Gross-Hartmannsdorf near Gröditzberg in the principality of Jauer?] at Christoph Teissner's where for several days many people gathered. There a number of men, servants, maids, women, boys, girls, young and old fell down with shaking and murmuring. They wept, cried and shouted for mercy for their sins and the sins of others and over the Godless life and customs, especially over the false pastors and over all idolatry and the great pomp, the harmful and

evil pride of men. They admonished men earnestly and faithfully to repentance and a better way of life.''

67 M. John Sr. to the Schwenkfelders in Harpersdorf, n.d., ibid., 390: ''They also told me that Christoph Theissner's son was afflicted and that he went around for a whole week so that they did not know what would happen to him. The boy's name was Matteus, and he was fifteen. He became sick and for three days would not eat or drink nor did he speak much. Later he did speak, eat and drink again. They asked him what had happened and he said he could tell them much if God wanted him to, but that he did not yet so wish. Then he began to call [men] to penance and said God would do great wonders. People came to him, and he said he had seen the angels of God with trumpets and that they should have already blown. Then an angel of God came, stepped before God, and begged him to spare them.''

68 Christoph Oelsner to Antonius Oelsner, June 2, 1594, ibid., 634: ''Then Martin Grohn's widow of Hartliebsdorff, Barbara, who now was married to Balthasar Adolf also began shaking and fell down to the floor in the room, crawled on the floor among the people and when she arose she asked and called for me. But I was out in the garden. She said I should come in. Then she came quickly to me and begging, weeping and in joy embraced me and said: Oh brother Christoph and sister Ursula! And she took Ursula's right hand and my right hand and placed them together and said we belonged together (God help us in Christ) as she and Balthasar Adolf did. I was somewhat astounded by this and said: 'May that occur according to God's will in Christ. Amen.'''

69 This account is printed in Nikolaus Henel van Hennenfeld, *Silesiographia,* 291-292; Gerhard Eberlein, ''Die Bauernprediger,'' 81-82; Elizabeth Zimmermann, *Schwenckfelder und Pietisten in Greiffenberg und Umgegend,* 4 (with slight variations in her ''Ursprung,'' 158; according to which is cited below). A similar account is in G. Buckisch, *Schlesische Religionsakten, I. Teil. 1517-1607,* Wroclaw DA, I, 13a, 528-529: ''Again they say there is a tree in hell which lowers itself every day and on which hangs all kinds of pomp, great collars, silk caps, cloaks and other such things, and were there still a small branch not yet adorned, if it were adorned, the tree would sink and on the Last Day will come and this will happen before the harvest. Again they say there is a mountain in a small land from which two people went out; they are said to have converted around 5,000 people to their belief, that one should not call elders fathers, since there is only one Father in Heaven. They destroyed all jewelry and such like, confessed their sins to each other, fell on their knees and faces and beat their heads on the ground, ate, drank and slept little. Some wished not to eat at all.'' Cf. the accounts of the disturbances in Schickfuss, II, 237-238; and Koffmane, ''Wiedertäufer,'' 48-55.

70 Printed in summary in Anton Balthasar Walther, *Silesia diplomatica,* I, 94, 146.

71 Cf. M. John Sr. to N.N., n.d., SchLP, VC 5-3, 406: ''And our lords let it be known they wanted to take our property and send us to the galleys.''

72 Sutorius, II, 384.

73 M. John Sr. to the Schwenkfelders in Harpersdorf, n.d., SchLP VC 5-3, 390; M. John Sr. to Frederick IV, n.d., ibid., 394-395; M. John Sr. to Emperor Rudolf II, n.d., ibid., 408-410; M. John Jr., *Bericht von den Schwenckfeldern,* n.d., ibid., 1223: ''A persecution arose and these people were sent to prison in Löwenberg [Lemberg] and in the Grötzberg [on which was a large castle]. Men and women, young women and young men . . . sat there for eight, ten or more years.'' On this and the following see also Schultz, *Erläuterung,* 27-34.

74 M. John Sr. to Emperor Rudolf II, n.d., ibid., 410.

75 M. John Sr. to the Schwenkfelders in Harpersdorf, n.d., ibid., 391; M. John Sr. to Frederick IV, n.d., ibid., 395.

76 M. John Sr. to the Schwenkfelders in Harpersdorf, n.d., ibid., 391. Cf. Sutorius, II, 384.

77 Antonius Oelsner to Markus Domitz, 1595, ibid., 532-540; M. John Jr., *Bericht von den Schwenckfeldern,* n.d., ibid., 1223. Cf. Schultz, *Erläuterung,* 22-27.

78 Antonius Oelsner to Markus Domitz, 1595, ibid., 538; A. Oelsner, *Bekehrungsbericht,* n.d., SchLP, VC 4-1, 18.

79 WA Bibel 10, I, 566 (verse 7).

80 Antonius Oelsner to Markus Domitz, 1595, SchLP, VC 5-3, 540. Cf. Schultz, *Erläuterung*, 27.

81 M. John Jr., *Bericht von den Schwenckfeldern*, n.d., ibid., 1223.

82 Ibid.

83 Ibid., 1226-1227.

84 Ibid., 1223.

85 Ibid., 1223-1224.

86 M. John Sr. to Frederick IV, n.d., ibid., 395; Ursula John Sr. to Frederick IV, n.d., ibid., 398.

87 Christoph Oelsner to Antonius Oelsner, September 18, 1594, ibid., 630-631.

88 Christoph Oelsner to the Schwenkfelders in Zobten and Hohndorf, January 17, 1596, ibid., 653-657.

89 Christoph Oelsner to Barbara Wörner, June 19, 1595, ibid., 653.

90 Christoph Oelsner to the Schwenkfelders in Zobten and Hohndorf, January 17, 1596, ibid., 655-656.

91 Note for example Christoph Oelsner to Caspar Anders, March 6, 1593, ibid., 614: "May God grant that we renounce the world along with its joys and desires completely and willingly take the cross upon us and follow Christ in the small way through the narrow gate to the city of God"; Christoph Oelsner to the Schwenkfelders in Harpersdorf, n.d., ibid., 617;: "The young people among you who fear the Lord, whether girls or boys, dear brothers and sisters, do not follow the flesh as earlier when they were disbelievers and lived in the lusts of the flesh. Now flee the lust of youth, all useless, unchaste language and evil companionship; be chaste, moral, virtuous, wise, and fear God and be obedient to your elders"; Christoph Oelsner to the Schwenkfelders in Zobten and Hohndorf, January 17, 1596, ibid., 654: "O the wretched, rotten flesh, that from youth is ever inclined to evil. Truly, we must learn to strive against our evil flesh and harm it, and take pains that it does not live in sin and withstand the Holy Spirit"; Christoph Oelsner, *Vom Spruche Matth. 24:40*, n.d., ibid., 700: "Since he who wishes to learn to know Christ in faith and trust, must go into the field away from the world, that is, he must separate himself with his heart, life, activity, faith and trust, he must lift forth his heart and note in himself if he might learn in any way the voice of the caller and receive the divine inspiration."

92 Antonius Oelsner to the Schwenkfelders, 1594, ibid., 494.

93 M. John Jr., *Bericht von den Schwenckfeldern*, n.d, ibid., 1222.

94 Antonius Oelsner to the Schwenkfelders, 1594, ibid., 477-493. Note for example 478: "And I have acknowledged that the common practice of infant baptism is an abomination, the foundation and beginning of all errors, and [leads] to the greatest and most remarkable evil and breakdown of Christendom . . . in short, infant baptism is an abomination and yet mere child's play, and brings horror and sorrow of heart to Christian parents, children and Godparents. . . . In infant baptism a friendship is established which is the enemy of God . . . and makes the one the other. The lust of the eye and the lust of the flesh is the virtue of youth among worldly men; that is, immodesty, unchastity and impurity, the lust of the flesh; from this comes the lust of the eye, that is envy, sorrow and eagerness for wealth; from this a life of pride, that is the pride, pomp and pageantry of the world. All this results from infant baptism. After children are born into the world (oh what a wretched birth) the parents, father and mother, immediately choose and ask for Godparents for the child, who are pleasing to them and rich and who give much."

95 Ibid., 493: "But as to the institution of marriage, the young people who wish to marry should marry believers who are themselves the obedient children of believing parents. The parents, especially the father, should go to his closest friend or faithful brother and neighbor or some other worthy, reasonable man and ask him to go to the girl's father and mother as an intermediary and ask them if they will give their daughter to his son to marry, be she virgin or widow. This, neither before or after the young man speaks with the girl as to whether they wish to marry and love one another. Such a marriage is to begin in the fear of God and in Christ without elaborate language or long wooing."

96 Ibid., 496.

97 A. Oelsner, *Bekehrungsbericht,* n.d., SchLP, VA 4-1, 30; M. John Jr., *Bericht von den Schwenckfeldern,* n.d., SchLP, VC 5-3, 1224.

98 Here see especially A. Oelsner, *Bekehrungsbericht,* n.d., SchLP, VC 4-1, 1-62; A. Oelsner to Christoph Oelsner, 1597, SchLP, VC 5-3, 540-589; M. John Jr., *Bericht von den Schwenckfeldern,* n.d., ibid., 1224.

99 Note for example Antonius Oelsner to Christoph Oelsner, n.d., ibid., 544, 545, 549; A. Oelsner, *Bekehrungsbericht,* n.d., SchLP, VA 4-1.

100 Note for example Antonius Oelsner to Christoph Oelsner, 1597, SchLP, VC 5-3, 559-560.

101 M. John Jr., *Bericht von den Schwenckfeldern,* n.d., ibid., 1224.

102 Antonius Oelsner to Christoph Oelsner, 1597, ibid., 552; Antonius Oelsner to the Schwenkfelders, 1594, ibid., 485-486.

103 A. Oelsner, *Bekehrungsbericht,* n.d., SchLP, VA 4-1, 40. Cf. ibid., 40: "Nicolaus did not wish to allow anything to result, but he armed himself with his full power to strive against the will of God, scorned me and my faithful admonition in the Lord, spoke against me and held me for untimely. Should such a man who has so great a reputation not be able to hinder very, very much?"

104 M. John Jr., *Bericht von den Schwenckfeldern,* n.d., SchLP, VC 5-3, 1225. Cf. Schultz, *Erläuterung,* 35.

105 On Weichenhan see Liefmann, fol. B 4v; Otto Schultze, *Predigergeschichte des Kirchenkreises Schweidnitz-Reichenbach,* 7; Johannes Grünewald, *Predigergeschichte des Kirchenkreises Schönau,* 12.

106 Hans Wiedemann, "Das Sulzbacher Geistesleben unter Herzog Christian August," 30.

107 The full title reads: *Postilla, Das ist: Geistliche Hertzstärckung und Labsal / Wie auch Auslegung über die Evangelien / So man pfleget zu lesen an den Sonntagen und heiligen Festen. Christlich und einfältig geprediget und beschrieben / Durch ERASMUM Weichenhan / Pfarrern zu Langen-Bielau.* (Sultzbach, 1672.)

108 Ibid. Vorwort, fol. B 1r-v.

109 Ibid. Especially I, 269-270, 278-280; II, 126-129, 185-196.

110 Ibid., I, 129. Cf. especially I, 70-76; II, 82-90, 464-472.

111 Note for example ibid., I, 124; II, 187, 212, 221.

112 Sutorius, II, 384-385.

113 Ibid., 385.

114 M. John Jr., *Bericht von den Schwenckfeldern,* n.d., SchLP, VC 5-3, 1230. Cf. Schultz, *Erläuterung,* 36-37.

115 On this and the following see Richard Roepell, "Das Verhalten Schlesiens zur Zeit der böhmischen Unruhen;" H. Palm, "Die Conjunction der Herzöge von Liegnitz, Brieg und Oels, sowie der Stadt und des Fürstentums Breslau mit der Krone Schweden in den Jahren 1633-35"; H. Palm, "Schlesiens Antheil am dreissigjährigen Kriege vom Juli bis December 1620"; J. Athanasius Kopietz, "Wallensteins Armee in Schlesien im Jahre 1626 und im Frühjahr 1627"; H. Palm, "Der Dresdner Accord 1621"; Julius Krebs, "Zur Geschichte der inneren Verhältnisse Schlesiens von der Schlacht am Weissen Berge bis zum Einmarsche Waldsteins"; Krebs, "Schlesien in den Jahren 1626 und 1627."

116 See Krebs, "Schlesien."

117 Printed in Christian Friedrich Fischer, *Geschichte und Beschreibung der schlesischen Fürstenthums-Hauptstadt Jauer,* II, 144-145; A. Teichmann, *Chronik der Stadt Bolkenhain,* 87-94.

118 M. John Jr., *Bericht von den Schwenckfeldern,* n.d., SchLP, VC 5-3, 1227.

119 Ibid., 1229 and 1235.

120 Schultz, *Erläuterung,* 36-37.

121 On Gifftheil see Gottfried Arnold, *Fortsetzung der Unparteiischen Kirchen- und Ketzerhistorie,* I, 98-102, 761; Christoph Kolb, "Abraham und Ludwig Friedrich Gifftheil"; Ernst Eylenstein, "Ludwig Friedrich Gifftheil. Zum mystischen Separatismus des 17. Jahrhunderts in Deutschland"; Arnold Schleiff, *Selbstkritik der lutherischen Kirchen im 17. Jahrhundert;* Friedrich Fritz, "Friedrich Gifftheil"; Friedrich Fritz, "Konventikel in Würt-

temberg von der Reformationszeit bis zum Edikt von 1743,'' 135-143; Heinrich Hermelink, *Geschichte der evangelischen Kirche in Württemberg,* 165.

122 On Gifftheil's stay with the Silesian Schwenkfelders see M. John Jr., *Bericht von den Schwenckfeldern,* n.d., SchLP, VC 5-3, 1229-1232. Cf. Schultz, *Erläuterung,* 37.

123 On the Schwenkfelders in Württemberg see Fritz, ''Konventikel,'' 103-115; Weber, *Kasper Schwenckfeld und seine Anhänger.*

124 M. John Jr., *Bericht von den Schwenckfeldern,* n.d., SchLP, VC 5-3, 1229.

125 Ibid., 1231. Cf. ibid., 1230: ''And as they spoke with one another and rejoiced together, they went with him to Feldhaüser [a hamlet near Harpersdorf] since understanding men were there. He rejoiced greatly over this, and said he had traveled far and had met no one other than a young nursemaid who had had the Holy Spirit. And as they spoke with him about one thing and another and asked him many questions, just as he asked them many; he said that he was bringing the world unknown things but to them was bringing nothing new. They already had the correct [teaching] and this was what he sought. They should adhere to it. He encouraged them to stand firm, and said they should not, if persecution should come, be like a pile of leaves; if the storm winds came, God would protect them.''

126 On this see Fritz Dickmann, *Der Westfälische Frieden,* 462-463.

127 Johann G. v. Meiern, *Acta pacis Westphalicae publica,* V, 507.

128 See J. Berg, *Die Geschichte der gewaltsamen Wegnahme der evangelischen Kirchen u. Kirchengüter in den Fürstenthümern Schweidnitz und Jauer.*

129 Individual Schwenkfelders still brought their children to baptism, as for example the conventicle leader Hans Liebwitz who was charged with this by Georg Heydrich. See Georg Heydrich to Hans Liebwitz, 1650, SchLP, VC 5-3, 796-797.

130 On their understanding of baptism see especially G. Heydrich, *Fragen vom Sacrament der Tauffe,* June 19, 1649, ibid., 747-760; B. Jäckel, *Christliches Glaubens Bekäntnis,* n.d., ibid., 743-744.

131 Heydrich, 759.

132 On Pohl see Gottlob Kluge, *Schlesischer Jubelpriester,* 137-138; Grünewald, ''Predigergeschichte von Goldberg,'' 5.

133 On Cupius see Goldmann, I, 30; Grünewald, ''Predigergeschichte von Goldberg,'' 20. Cf. Georg Heydrich and Balthasar Jäckel to Georg Rudolf, January 28, 1651, SchLP VC 5-3, 761; Valentin, Melchior and Balthasar Jäckel to the ducal government in Liegnitz, April 7, 1654, ibid., 764; Balthasar Jäckel and Georg Heydrich to the prince of Anhalt [Johann Kasimir or Johann Georg von Anhalt-Dessau?], May 16, 1653, ibid., 780.

134 On Rathmann see Grünewald, ''Predigergeschichte Löwenberg,'' 40. Cf. N.N. to Johannes Rathmann, October 20, 1651, SchLP, VC 5-3, 811.

135 On Hubrig see Gruünewald, ''Predigergeschichte Löwenberg,'' 10. Cf. Georg Kriebel to Barbara III. Bolkowskin, June 10, 1651, SchLP, VC 5-3, 807.

136 N.N. to Johannes Rathmann, October 20, 1651, ibid., 310: ''We were not able to refrain from writing to you when we heard that on the 18th Sunday after Trinity [Sept. 28], among other things, you preached about us few believers who are called Schwenkfelders, who alone hope in Christ; that we, like the Sadducees, did not believe in the resurrection of the flesh—as you will well remember. This is not the first time that you have charged us with errors of which we take no part.''

137 Balthasar Heydrich and Valentin Jäckel to Martin Pohl, February 8, 1652, partially printed in Hensel, 330-331.

138 Margarete Stumpf, *Beiträge zur Geschichte des Klosters Trebnitz,* 41.

139 Georg Kriebel to Barbara III. Bolkowskin, June 10, 1651, SchLP, VC 5-3, 807; Balthasar Heydrich and Valentin Jäckel to Martin Pohl, February 8, 1652, partially printed in Hensel, 331.

140 Georg Heydrich and Balthasar Jäckel to Georg Rudolf, January 28, 1651, SchLP, VC 5-3, 730; Valentin, Melchior and Balthasar Jäckel to the ducal government in Liegnitz, April 7, 1654, ibid., 764.

141 Georg Hanig to Sigismund von Braun, June 16, 1651, ibid., 809.

[142] Georg Kriebel to Barbara III. Bolkowskin, June 10, 1651, ibid., 808.

[143] Ibid., 807.

[144] This date is from M. John Jr. to Achatius Friedrich Roscius, April 29, 1695, SchLP VC 5-1, 778.

[145] See Gerhard Eberlein, *Die General-Kirchenvisitation im Fürstentume Liegnitz von 1654-1655.*

[146] Cf. Hensel, 407.

[147] Valentin, Melchior and Balthasar Jäckel to the ducal government in Liegnitz, April 7, 1654, SchLP, VC 5-3, 764-765; M. John Jr., "Bericht," n.d., ibid., 1223. In the following two notes the first number refers to the letter, the second to the *Bericht.*

[148] Ibid., 765; 1223.

[149] Ibid., 765; 1223.

[150] Balthasar Jäckel and Georg Heydrich to the Duke of Anhalt [Johann Kasimir or Johann Georg von Anhalt-Dessau?], May 16, 1653, ibid., 779-782. Because of the plague in 1633 Modelsdorf was "nearly emptied of men" (J.G. Bergemann, *Beschreibung und Geschichte der alten Burgveste Gröditzberg,* 158).

[151] Valentin, Melchior and Balthasar Jäckel to the ducal government in Liegnitz, April 7, 1654, ibid., 765; M. John Jr., *Bericht,* n.d., ibid., 1223.

[152] Valentin, Melchior and Balthasar Jäckel to the ducal government in Liegnitz, April 7, 1654, ibid., 765-766.

[153] M. John Jr., *Bericht,* n.d., ibid., 1223.

[154] Valentin, Melchior and Balthasar Jäckel to the ducal government in Liegnitz, April 7, 1654, ibid., 766; M. John Jr., *Bericht,* n.d., ibid., 1223.

[155] On this and the following see M. John Jr., *Bericht,* n.d., ibid., 1233-1234.

[156] Balthasar Jäckel to Martin John Jr., n.d., ibid., 784.

[157] On the date and the terms of the release see B. Jäckel to Ludwig IV, July 4, 1658, ibid., 789-790; B. Jäckel to Johann Georg Schüller, n.d. [after June 3, 1658], ibid., 792. Cf. against them, M. John Jr., *Bericht,* n.d., ibid., 1233.

[158] M. John Jr., n.d., ibid., 1233; Balthasar Jäckel to Ludwig IV, n.d. [1657], ibid., 784.

[159] On this and the following see Berg, 209-210, 219-220.

[160] Schwenkfelders in Deutmannsdorf and Hartliebsdorf to the administrators of Abbess Dorothea I. Bninskin von Trebnitz, May 8, 1657, SchLP, VC 5-3, 801-806.

[161] On the pilgrimage to the border churches in the southeast of the duchy of Liegnitz see especially Kadelbach, *Geschichte des Dorfes Probsthayn,* 89-108; Gerhard Eberlein, *Die schlesischen Grenzkirchen im XVII. Jahrhundert,* especially 36, 39; Goldmann II, 63-73; S. Knörrlich, *Die Zufluchtskirche zu Harpersdorf,* especially 21-26.

[162] Printed in *Kayser-und Königl. das Erb-Hertzogthum Schlesien concernirende Privilegia,* III, 919-928.

[163] Cf. Dorothee von Velsen, *Die Gegenreformation in den Fürstentümern Liegnitz-Brieg-Wohlau,* 21.

[164] On Schröer Jr. see E. Goldmann, I, 33 and Grünewald, *Predigergeschichte von Goldberg,* 20.

[165] Heinrich Seipt to Georg and Elizabeth Wörner, SchLP, VA 3-12, 586.

[166] Cf. Church Visitation Record of 1674 (for Harpersdorf), Legnica StA, A 1059, 573.

[167] M. John Jr. to Georg Kriebel, February 6, 1668, SchLP, VC 5-3, 1001: "One final matter I must consider: If the adults realize they are not able to change the evil ways of their children, why then do they make marriage feasts for them that in many places are practiced in a more Luciferian manner than those of the worldly people? I myself have seen them laughing behind their backs, saying: Look at them; are they any better than we?" M. John Jr. to Heinrich Schultz, Nov. 1, 1668, ibid., 1008: "Ah, dear God, how great a shame it is that those who wish to be and should be faithful send their children with pomp to church or help them with suitable means so that even the pastors themselves derisively say that these people don't want to come to the church themselves, but send their children in utter display of splendor. Is their derisiveness not well founded? Thus the worldly people and Epicureans can very correctly say that those who call themselves Schwenkfelders, their children are the worst of all, as I myself have heard and have had to blush with shame. When these Schwenkfelders joined with

those who were banging away with guns, shouting and playing games at wedding ceremonies, the worldly then said: See these, see; where are they better than we? It doesn't show. Ah, how scornful a statement must often be heard when these people's children behave in such Luciferian ways, when those people speak who believe they have a right to it. Indeed, don't they act just like we do? I thought that these people didn't behave in such ways."

168 M. John Jr. to Hans Mäuer, June 17, 1665, ibid., 943; M. John Jr. to N.N. ibid., 982. Especially significant here are the remarks which are found in the records concerning the Schwenkfelders which were furnished by the archdeacon Johann Maximilian Strauss concerning the visitation of the Liegnitz archdeaconates in 1677 and 1678. See Joseph Jungnitz, *Visitationsberichte der Diözese Breslau,* IV, 1, 127-128, 317-319.

169 Thus for example Johann Rüdel, pastor at Seebnitz, declared in the general church visitation of 1655 that the many Schwenkfelders in the parish of Gross Kotzenau "were often found in church, but that he no longer knew any by name." Cited from Eberlein, *Die General-Kirchenvisitation im Fürstentum Liegnitz von 1654/55,* 108.

170 Church Visitation Record of 1674 (for Harpersdorf), Legnica, StA, A 1059, 573.

171 Ibid.

172 M. John Jr., *Ein Bedencken und Auslegung über Matth. 13.24. Vom Unkraut und der Leute Schlaff,* SchLP, VC 5-3, 919.

173 Liefmann, fol. B 4v: "He was good in medicine and particularly in botany."

174 On M. John Jr. see ibid., fol. B 4v.

175 Ibid., fol. C 1r.

176 On Hauptmann see ibid., fol. B 4v-C 1r; Hensel, 408-409.

177 See for example Church Visitation Record of 1674 (for Harpersdorf), Legnica, StA, A 1059, 573.

178 On Baumhauer see Christian Hege, Article: "Baumhauer, Christoph," in ML I, 141; R. Friedmann, *Die Schritten der Huterischen Täufergemeinschaften,* 112-113; Hege, Article: "Baumhauer, Christoph," in ME, I, 251.

179 Sobotiste.

180 Balthasar Jäckel to the elders of the Hutterites in Grossschützen, October 19, 1658, SchLP, VC 5-3, 792.

181 The mission of the Hutterites has not yet been studied enough.

182 Balthasar Jäckel to the elders of the Hutterites in Grossschützen, October 19, 1658, SchLP, VC 5-3, 792-793. It is not known which writings were used.

183 Ibid.

184 Velké Levary.

185 Balthasar Jäckel to the elders of the Hutterites in Grossschützen, October 19, 1658, SchLP, VC 5-3, 792.

186 Ibid., 792-794; Andreas Ehrenpreis to Balthasar Jäckel, March 17, 1660, ibid., 794-796. See also Friedmann, 112-113.

187 Schwenkfelders to the Mennonites in Amsterdam, October 16, 1725, Amsterdam BD, No. 2908.

188 It is certain that Schüller sent the following writings of P. Felgenhauer to the Schwenkfelders: *Das Geheimnis vom Tempel des Herrn in seinem Vorhof, Heiligen und Allerheiligsten in drei verschiedenen Teilen* (Amsterdam 1631); *Deipnologia* (Amsterdam 1650); *Postillion oder Neuer Kalender und prognosticon astrologicum propheticum* (Amsterdam 1655); *Palma fidei et veritatis in cruce Christi ad salutem* (Amsterdam 1656); *Confession und Glaubensbekenntnis in dreyen Puncten als von Gott, Christo dem Sohne Gottes und von der neuen Geburt aus Gott* (n., 1658).

189 Balthasar Jäckel to Johann Georg Schüller, December 5, 1657, SchLP, VC 5-3, 769; Balthasar Jäckel to Paul Felgenhauer, March 9, 1658, ibid., 770.

190 Balthasar Jäckel to Paul Felgenhauer, March 9, 1658, ibid., 770-771.

191 Balthasar Jäckel, *Christliches Glaubens Bekäntnis,* n.d., ibid., 739-747.

192 Balthasar Jäckel to Paul Felgenhauer, March 9, 1658, ibid., 770.

193 Ibid.

[194] Balthasar Jäckel to Johann Georg Schüller, June 3, 1658, ibid., 772-774.
[195] Ibid., 774-776.
[196] Ibid., 776-778.
[197] Balthasar Jäckel to Johann Georg Schüller, October 19, 1658, ibid., 791.
[198] Ibid., 791.
[199] M. John Jr. to Christian Hoburg, n.d. [before 1667], ibid., 990-992.
[200] CS IX, (512), 524-624.
[201] On the influence of Schwenckfeld's writings on Hoburg see Martin Kruse, *Speners Kritik am landesherrlichen Kirchenregiment und ihre Vorgeschichte,* 142-143.
[202] M. John Jr. to Christian Hoburg, n.d. [before 1667], SchLP, VC 5-3, 991.
[203] Christian Hoburg to the Schwenkfelders, April 10, 1668, ibid., 892-895.
[204] Ibid., 893.
[205] On John's journey see M. John Jr. to Hans Brochmann, November 2, 1669, ibid., 1235-1237.
[206] Anonymous, *Des zu den Quackern übergetretenen Hilarii Prachii und J.C. Matern seines Eydams Brieffe,* 445.
[207] On Geelmann see Jöcher-Adelung, II, 1377; J.H. Jäck, *Pantheon der Literaten und Künstler Bambergs,* 302; Hermann Clauss, "Weigelianer in Nürnberg," 267-271.
[208] Bamberg, *Sterberegister der Oberpfarre Unser Lieben Frau,* 75, No. 337.
[209] Clauss, 267-271.
[210] Jäck, 302.
[211] M. John Jr. to Hans Brochmann, November 2, 1669, SchLP, VC 5-3, 1235.
[212] Ibid., 1235-1236.
[213] Johann Georg Gichtel to M. John Jr., September 15/25, 1669, printed in Johann G. Gichtel, *Theosophia Practica,* I, 12-16.
[214] M. John Jr. to Hans Brochmann, November 2, 1669, SchLP, VC 5-3, 1236.
[215] In the Schwenkfelder Library, besides a letter of M. John Jr. to Christian Hoburg, n.d. [before October 25, 1667], ibid., 990-992 are the following letters of Christian Hoburg to M. John Jr., October 25, 1667, ibid., 891-892; April 10, 1668, 892-895; January 2, 1669, 899-901; January 12, 1670, 901-903; August 12, 1670, 903-905; January 20, 1674, 905-906; January 7, 1675, 910-912; 1675, 912-914. Christian Hoburg also wrote an epistle to the Schwenkfelders on January 20, 1674, ibid., 906-909.
[216] Neither John's correspondence nor that of the Schwenkfelders with Breckling has been found. Breckling must have esteemed the Schwenkfelders since he listed their most important leaders, namely Balthasar Jäckel, M. John Jr., and Georg Hauptmann in his *Catalogus testium veritatis post Lutherum* (printed in Arnold, *Fortsetzung der Unparteiischen Kirchen- und Ketzerhistorie,* II, 776). In addition, John Jr. read the writings of Breckling eagerly. Cf. M. John Jr. to Georg Kriebel, February 6, 1668, SchLP, VC 5-3, 993: "I have yet found no treatises which described Babel more clearly than does Breckling's."
[217] Gichtel's letters to M. John Jr. and Hauptmann are in Gichtel, I (see Register).
[218] Besides a single letter of Georg Geelmanns to M. John Jr., May 1, 1671, the rest of the correspondence was not available and must be considered lost.
[219] See Achatius Friedrich Roscius in M. John Jr., February 18, 1695, SchLP, VC 5-1, 774.
[220] M. John Jr. to Georg Kriebel, February 6, 1668, SchLP, VC 5-3, 992-1002.
[221] Ibid., 993, 996-997.
[222] Ibid., 996-997: "It was no great surprise to me that they attacked Breckling with such vigor. But if Christian Hoburg's *Postille* often overemphasizes the death of the old Adam and agrees in the essential points with Caspar Schwenckfeld's doctrine, why then is it so despised? . . . So many say it treats only the inner man. Indeed? What more does Schwenckfeld aim for ? Look only in his *Passional,* in his *Unterricht wie man betten soll* (Instruction on how to pray), [CS VI, (651) 659-748 and XVII, (844) 848-986], and you will see whether or not he has made an external thing of the worship. Paul says that one is not a Jew who is outwardly a Jew. Jacob Boehme says that one is not a Schwenkfelder who is externally a Schwenkfelder." Cf. M. John Jr. to the wife of Hans Dehnst, n.d., ibid., 1068, 1070.
[223] M. John Jr. to Georg Kriebel, February 6, 1668, ibid., 994.

[224] On Weiss see L.E. Kriebel and S.G. Schultz, *Georg Weiss.*

[225] Georg Weiss to A.W. [Abraham Wagner?], July 9, 1732, SchLP, VA 3-12, 520-521.

[226] Ibid., 519-522.

[227] See Koffmane, 17-24.

[228] Cf. W. Buddecke, *Die Jacob Böhme-Ausgaben,* I, 1-11.

[229] Johann Georg Gichtel to Martin John Jr., August 20, 1678, printed in Gichtel, I, 97-102.

[230] On Prache see Friedrich Lichtstern, *Schlesische Fürsten-Krone,* 182; Liefmann, fol. D 4r-E 1r; *Nova Literaria Germaniae,* 290-292; Hensel, 408-409; Ehrhardt, II, 343-348; Karl W. Peschel, *Die Geschichte der Stadt Goldberg,* 378; Ludwig Sturm, *Geschichte der Stadt Goldberg in Schlesien,* 684, 701-702; Grünewald, "Predigergeschichte Goldberg," 12; Braithwaite, *The Second Period of Quakerism,* 526, 705.

[231] Hilarius Prache to M. John Jr., October 9, 1676, printed in *Unschuldige Nachrichten von Alten und Neuen Theologischen Sachen,* 1706, 432-441.

[232] Liefmann, fol. D 4r.

[233] See *Nova Literaria Germaniae,* 290; Julius Fürst, *Bibliotheca Judaica,* I, 26; III, 74, 118.

[234] On Johann Georg Matern see Hensel, 408-409; Braithwaite, 526, 705.

[235] Prache worked for a Quaker press in London (see Hilarius Prache to M. John Jr., October 9, 1676, printed in *Unschuldige Nachrichten von Alten und Neuen Theologischen Sachen,* 1706, 432-441). His son-in-law Matern worked as a teacher in Waltham Abbey, the boys' school founded in 1668 by George Fox (see Johann Georg Matern to M. John Jr., September 30, 1676, printed in ibid., 432-441). There he took part in a revival (Braithwaite, 526-527).

[236] See M. John Jr., *Ein Dialogus oder Gespräche vom tausendjährigen Reiche,* n.d.,SchLP, VC 5-3, 1048-1053; M. John Jr. to Georg [Kriebel], February 28, 1689, ibid., 1045-1046; M. John Jr. to N.N., n.d., ibid., 1055.

[237] M. John Jr., *Ein Dialogus,* n.d., ibid., 1052.

[238] Ibid., 1049; M. John Jr. to N.N., n.d., ibid., 1055.

[239] Ibid., 1053, 1056.

[240] On this and the following see Philipp Jakob Spener to N.N., 1690, printed in Philipp Jakob Spener, *Theologische Bedencken,* I, 314-315; P.J. Spener to N.N., July 10, 1690, printed in P.J. Spener, *Letzte Theologische Bedencken,* III, 687-692; Johann Christoph Schwedler to August Hermann Francke, April 15, 1720, Berlin SB, Francke-Nachlass.

[241] Ibid.

[242] P.J. Spener to N.N., 1690, printed in Spener, *Theologische Bedencken,* I, 315.

[243] M. John Jr. to Achatius Friedrich Roscius, n.d., SchLP, VC 5-1, 782.

[244] Ibid.

[245] Ibid.

[246] In the list of the regular lecturers (Jerome Freyer, *Programmata latino-germanica cum additamento miscellaneorum vario,* 693-715) his name is not found but it is listed in the Halle University matriculation register (F. Zimmermann, 324, left column: "Roscius, Acthat. Frid. Luben. Lusat. 30. 1. 1694").

[247] Note for example Achatius Friedrich Roscius to M. John Jr. n.d. [after April 29, 1595], SchLP, VC 5-1, 803-804.

[248] On Schwedler see above all E. Zimmermann, *Schwenckfelder,* passim.

[249] Note for example: J.C. Schwedler to August Hermann Francke, April 15, 1720, Berlin SB, Francke-Nachlass.

[250] Johann Wilhelm Petersen, *Lebens-Beschreibung,* 321-322.

[251] Ibid.

[252] On Schneider see above all Anonymous, *Kurtzer Bericht von Hn. Dan. Schneider / Pfarrers in Goldberg / gefährlichen Unternehmen;* Anonymous, *Daniel Schneiders Prüfung des Caspar Schwenckfelds;* Valentin E. Löscher [Zelenka Collection], *Dissertatio de Schvengfeldismo in Pietismo renato,* Section 21-23; Hensel, 513-514, 553-554; Ehrhardt, IV, 431-434; Peschel, 394-401; Koffmane, 50-51; Sturm, 685, 703-708; Zimmermann, *Schwenckfelder,* 61-63; Grünewald, *Predigergeschichte Goldberg,* 13.

[253] On Sturm see Ehrhardt, IV, 495-497; Zimmermann, *Schwenckfelder,* 49, 69, 112-114; Grünewald, *Predigergeschichte Goldberg,* 34.
[254] Christian Gerber, *Historia derer Wiedergebohrnen in Sachsen,* IV, 267-268.
[255] Philipp Jakob Spener to N.N., 1690 printed in Spener, I, 315.

2. *The Theological Foundations of Later Schwenkfeldianism*

[1] Hans Christoph Seibt to the Schwenkfelders, January 1, 1703, SchLP, VA 3-12, 236.
[2] Note for example M. John Jr., *Bekantnis meines Glaubens,* n.d., SchLP, VC 5-3, 1266, 1272, 1280-1281.
[3] Note for example ibid., 1266-1267: ''I am not lying when I say that we dare not call the Holy Scriptures God's Word, since they give witness to the true living Word of God and also contain the words which God spoke to and with the prophets and which the Son of God himself spoke. But I wish that people would note the difference (as the Scripture notes it) between the living Word of God and the words of Scripture.'' Ibid., 1272: ''Physical water does not in itself contain the Holy Spirit. Much less is the Spirit able to be given through it.'' Ibid., 1280: ''We believe also that one cannot be holy through external bread and wine, which itself has no life.''
[4] John 5:39 (e.g. B. Jäckel, *Christliches Glaubens Bekäntnis,* n.d., ibid., 746); John 6:35 (e.g. Christoph Oelsner to N.N., n.d., ibid., 595); John 6:55: (e.g. John Sr. to N.N., n.d., ibid., 363; John Sr. to the prince-bishop of Breslau, n.d., ibid., 379); I John 2:27 (e.g. Antonius Oelsner to Sigismund von Mauschwitz, September 26, 1590, n.d., ibid., 439.
[5] Christoph Oelsner to N.N., 1592, ibid., 595; M. John Jr. to Georg Kriebel, ibid., 1074.
[6] Christophr Oelsner to N.N., 1592, ibid., 594.
[7] On the point that salvation cannot be mediated see M. John Jr.'s two short tracts on natural philosophy, *Ein Bedencken von den Bienen,* ibid., 934-937, and *Ein Bedencken, was die Natur der Bienen bedeutet* ibid., 937-940.
[8] Note for example M. John Jr., *Ein Bedencken und Auslegung über Matth. 13.24. Vom Unkraut und der Leute Schlaff,* n.d., ibid., 923. ''He [Christ] took for himself a true human body and soul from Mary. His origin was not from her, however, but the origin of Christ the man is from God the Father through the work of the Holy Spirit, so that God the Father in both natures is the natural Father of the whole natural Son, Christ.'' M. John Jr., Ein Bedencken von den Bienen, ibid., 935: ''The queen bee is begotten in a dwelling other than that of the other bees. Christ likewise was begotten in another vessel, namely not in a woman, but in a pious, pure and gentle virgin.'' M. John Jr., *Bekantnis meines Glaubens,* n.d., ibid., 1256: ''. . . that God the Father is thus the natural Father of the whole Christ according to his two natures.''
[9] M. John Jr., *Ein Bedencken von den Bienen,* n.d., ibid., 856.
[10] Note for example, M. John Jr., *Bekantnis meines Glaubens,* n.d., ibid., 1257-1258: ''And after the full dispensation of the resurrection, he ascended to heaven and sat at the right hand of God and received all divine power to himself. Rev. 1:18. From this it is clear that Christ in his humanity as well, had received all divine power to himself.'' M. John Jr. to N.N., n.d., ibid., 1039: ''In temporality the flesh of Christ was a mortal flesh and was subject to all temptations (but without sin) for us; this flesh has now a different form: for it is now inseparably joined with the word in the same divine joy.'' Ibid., 1040: ''But now I believe the divine took humanity into itself in an eternal uniformity, so that now in eternity he remains man and God at the right hand of God.''
[11] M. John Jr., *Bekantnis meines Glaubens,* n.d., ibid., 1258.
[12] Note for example M. John Jr., *Ein Bedencken und Auslegung über Matth. 13.24. Vom Unkraut und der Leute Schlaff,* n.d., ibid., 923: ''And Christ both according to his humanity and his divinity is exalted above all the heavens and has inherited all power in heaven and on earth, so that, according to his humanity, he also sent out the Holy Spirit. This humanity of Christ has no less power, strength, glory and splendor than does the divinity.''
[13] Ibid.

[14] J. John Jr., *Bekantnis meines Glaubens,* n.d., ibid., 1259.
[15] Johannes Tauler, *Predigten,* ed. by G. Hofmann, 139.
[16] Christoph Oelsner to the commandant of Gröditzberge, 1592, SchLP, VC 5-3, 593.
[17] Note for example B. Heydrich, *Ist ein Christlicher Unterricht,* ibid., 834.
[18] Balthasar Heydrich and Valentin Jäckel to Martin Pohl, February 8, 1652, printed in Hensel, 331.
[19] Note for example M. John Jr. to Georg Kriebel, n.d., SchLP, VC 5-3, 1074.
[20] Chapter 25:12 (MSL 35, 1602) and 26:1 (MSL 35, 1607).
[21] *Decretum Gratiani,* Part III. *De consecratione,* Dist. II, can. 47.
[22] Christoph Oelsner, *Erklärung des Spruchs Matth. 24.40,* n.d., SchLP, VC 5-3, 697.
[23] Ibid., 697: "That will be very bitter for the young pupils and servants whom Christ has taken into his training school, when, through the grace of God in penance, the wantonness of the flesh, the lust, wit, desire, extravagant thoughts and the wanderings of the emotions are not taken under the discipline of the cross."
[24] Ibid., 700.
[25] M. John Jr., *Fragen von dem bethlehemitischen Kinder-Mord,* 1698, ibid., 929.
[26] M. John Jr. to Georg Schoeps, January 3, 1671, ibid., 1021.
[27] Note for example Caspar Breuer to Dorothea N., n.d., ibid., 813-815.
[28] Ibid., 813.
[29] Michael Hiller, *Postille,* IV, 273. According to David Lenfant (*Concordantiae Augustinianae,* Vol. 2, Paris 1656-1665) this is not a direct citation, but is in keeping with Augustine's views on marriage. Note for example Sermon IX, chapter XI (MSL 38,88): "When you wish to use a wife more than is necessary for bearing children, it is sin." On Augustine's view of marriage see Johann Peters, *Die Ehe nach der Lehre des hl. Augustinus.*
[30] B. Heydrich, *Ist ein Christlicher Unterricht,* n.d., SchLP, VC 5-3, 847.
[31] See for example, M. John Jr., *Ein Bedencken und Auslegung über Matth. 13.24. Vom Unkraut und der Leute Schlaff,* n.d., ibid., 921.
[32] Balthasar Hoffmann to his family and Ursula Hoffmann, September 16, 1723, SchLP, VOC-H[37] (original).
[33] M. John Jr., *Ein Bedencken und Auslegung über Matth. 13.24. Vom Unkraut und der Leute Schlaff,* n.d., SchLP, VC 5-3, 926. Cf. M. John Jr., *Fragen von dem bethlehemitischen Kinder-Mord,* 1698, ibid., 933: "Question: Does the believer then escape the temptation to sin? Answer: He certainly feels tempted to sin but does not yield, and rather fights against the temptation and chases it out the door by which it entered."
[34] Kihm, 268-300.
[35] M. Schmidt, "Teilnahme an der göttlichen Natur. 2. Petrus 1,4 in der theologischen Exegese des mystischen Spiritualismus, des Peitismus und der lutherischen Orthodoxie." in *Dank an Paul Althaus, ed. by W. Künneth and W. Joest, 171-201, and also expanded in Schmidt, Wiedergeburt und Neuer Mensch,* 238-298.

3. *The Schwenkfelders and the Jesuit Mission*

[1] On the Jesuit mission see the studies of A.F.H. Schneider, whose manuscript notes are in SchLP and Berlin SB. Unfortunately Schneider never completed evaluating his work other than in a summary of his studies in an 1862 publication of the Elisabeth School in Berlin.
[2] Liefmann, fol. B 2v ff.
[3] On Schneider see 232, n. 252; and on Zimmermann, *Schwenckfelder,* 179, n. 5
[4] Citations in Maron, 17.
[5] Ibid., 18-20.
[6] On Neander see E. Goldmann, I, 34-36; Grünewald, *Predigergeschichte Goldberg,* 20; S. Knörrlich, 12.
[7] Christoph Schultz to Anton N., April 6, 1768, SchLP, VC 3-7, 6; K.X. Regent, *Irrthümer,* III, 66. Cf. Schultz, *Erläuterung,* 47-48.

[8] Attachment to the writings of the Breslau Vicariate-general. Christoph Mayer, May 21, 1717, Wroclaw SA, Rep. 28. Fürstentum Liegnitz, X, 5, b.

[9] Ibid.

[10] Ibid.

[11] The archdeaconate's authority reached into the principality of Jauer.

[12] The Breslau Vicariate-general to Christoph Mayer, May 21, 1717, Wroclaw SA, Rep. 28, Fürstentum Liegnitz, X, 5, b., and in summary in Wroclaw DA, Harpersdorf 5, 2 and JAH, *Diarium,* SchLP, VN 73-5, 673. Cf. also K.X. Regent, *Irrthümer,* I, 21-22 and V, 27-28; Schneider, *Jesuit-Mission,* 5.

[13] Christoph Mayer to the Breslau Vicariate-general, July 5, 1717, Wroclaw SA, Rep. 28, Fürstentum Liegnitz, X, 5, b.

[14] Ibid.

[15] Ibid.

[16] Ibid.

[17] The account is found in the supplement to Christoph Mayer's letter to the Breslau Vicariate-general, July 5, 1717.

[18] Ibid.

[19] The Breslau Vicariate-general to the Breslau Royal Upper Council, August 3, 1717, printed in Regent, *Irrthümer,* I, 21-22 and V, 28-29, and in summary in Wroclaw DA, Harpersdorf, 5, 2 and JAH, *Diarium,* SchLP, VN 73-75, 673-674.

[20] The Royal government in Liegnitz to the Breslau Vicariate-general July 7, 1717, Wroclaw, DA, Harpersdorf, 5, 2 and JAH, *Diarium,* SchLP, VN 73-5, 675 (in summary).

[21] The archdeacon Christoph Mayer clearly indicated that the Schwenkfelders lived for the most part in the principality of Jauer.

[22] Available as a summary of the letter in Wroclaw DA, Harpersdorf, 5, 2 and JAH, *Diarium,* SchLP, VN 73-5, 673-674.

[23] Royal Council Jauer to the court judge of Löwenberg, August 21, 1717, Wroclaw DA, Harpersdorf, 5, 2 and JAH, *Diarium,* SchLP, VN 73-5, 674 (in summary).

[24] Available as a summary of the letter in Wroclaw DA, Harpersdorf 5, 2 and JAH, *Diarium,* SchLP, VN 73-5, 674.

[25] Royal Council Jauer to the Breslau Royal Upper Council, September 24, 1717, Wroclaw DA, Harpersdorf, 5, 2 and JAH, *Diarium,* SchLP, VN 73-5, 674 (in summary).

[26] Available as a summary of the letter in Wroclaw DA, Harpersdorf, 5, 3-4, and JAH, *Diarium,* SchLP, VN 73-5, 677-678.

[27] Karl VI to the Breslau Royal Upper Council, February 22, 1718, Wroclaw DA, Harpersdorf 5, 3 and JAH, *Diarium,* SchLP, VN 73-5, 676 (in summary). Cf. Regent, *Irrthümer,* I, 14.

[28] Available as a summary of the letter in Wroclaw DA, Harpersdorf, 5, 4 and JAH, *Diarium,* SchLP, 73-5, 678.

[29] John Milan, *Examinator methodi jesuiticae convertendi Schwenckfeldianos,* 108-109.

[30] Georg Jäckel and eight other Schwenkfelders to the Royal Government in Liegnitz, May 25, 1718, printed in J.W. Jan, *Verum Dei verbum,* I, 4-6, Beilage I; Gerber, IV, 269-273; Adam Koepke, *Historische Nachricht von dem vor zweyhundert Jahren berühmten und verruffenen Schlesischen Edelmann, Herrn Caspar Schwenckfeld von Ossig, samt beygef*ügter Anzahl seiner Schrifften, 48; Oswald Kadelbach, *Ausführliche Geschichte,* 34-36.

[31] Available as a summary of the letter in Wroclaw DA, Harpersdorf, 5, 5, and JAH, *Diarium,* SchLP, VN 73-5, 680-681.

[32] See note 30.

[33] Unfortunately it is not known which of their books of edification were submitted.

[34] Printed in Jan, *Verum Dei verbum,* I, 7-17, Beilage I; Milan, *Examinator,* 110-117; partially printed in Hensel, 679-680.

[35] See Milan, *Examinator,* 110.

[36] The Breslau Royal Upper Council to the Royal Council of Jauer, October 24, 1718, Wroclaw DA, Harpersdorf, 5, 4 and JAH, *Diarium,* SchLP, VN 73-5, 678-679 (in summary).

[37] As a summary of the letter in Wroclaw DA, Harpersdorf, 5, 4 and JAH, *Diarium,* SchLP, VN 73-5, 679.

[38] As a summary of the letter, ibid.

[39] The Breslau Vicariate-general to the Breslau Royal Upper Council, April 2, 1718, Wroclaw DA, Harpersdorf, 5, 4 and JAH, *Diarium,* SchLP, VN 73-5, 678 (in summary).

[40] As a summary of the letter in Wroclaw DA, Harpersdorf, 5, 4-5 and JAH, *Diarium,* SchLP, VN 73-5, 680.

[41] Karl VI to the Breslau Royal Upper Council, January 26, 1719, Wroclaw DA, Harpersdorf, 5, 5 and JAH, *Diarium,* SchLP, VN 73-5, 681 (in summary).

[42] The Breslau Vicariate-general to the Breslau Royal Upper Council, April 16, 1719, Wroclaw DA, Harpersdorf, 5, 5 and JAH, *Diarium,* SchLP, VN 73-5, 682 (in summary).

[43] As a summary of the letter in Wroclaw DA, Harpersdorf 5, 5 and JAH, *Diarium,* SchLP, VN 73-5, 681-682.

[44] Karl VI to the Breslau Royal Upper Council, May 12, 1719, *Diarium,* SchLP, VN 73-5, 100-103. Cf. the summary of the letter in Wroclaw DA, Harpersdorf, 5, 5.

[45] Ibid., 101.

[46] Ibid., 102.

[47] Karl VI to the Royal Government in Liegnitz, September 16, 1719, JAH, *Instrumenta,* SchLP, VN 73-6, 539-542. Cf. the summary in Wroclaw DA, Harpersdorf, 5, 6. Printed in J. W. Jan, *Verum Dei verbum,* I, 42, Beilage III; *Unschuldige Nachrichten,* Leipzig, 1720, 499-501.

[48] On Johann Milan see Jöcher, IV, 1725-1726. For a list of his writings see Sommervogel, V, 1089-1091.

[49] On Karl Xaver Regent see Jöcher, VI, 1547; ADB, 27, 552; B. Duhr, *Geschichte der Jesuiten in den Ländern deutscher Zunge,* IV, I, 446-449. For an incomplete and faulty list of his writings see Sommervogel, VI, 1584-1586.

[50] Episcopal document, November 14, 1719, JAH, *Diarium Instructionis,* SchLP, VN 73-11, 15-16, printed in Schneider, *Jesuiten-Mission,* 43-44, Beilage II.

[51] Instruction, November 14, 1719, ibid., 116-118, printed in ibid., 44, Beilage II.

[52] The Breslau Royal Upper Council to the Royal Councils, October 9, 1719, printed in Hensel, 677-678. Cf. Wroclaw DA, Harpersdorf, 5, 6 and JAH, *Diarium,* SchLP, VN 73-5, 684 (in summary).

[53] Ibid., 678.

[54] The Breslau Royal Upper Council to the Royal Council of Jauer, March 12, 1720, JAH, *Instrumenta,* SchLP, VN 73-6, 90-91.

[55] JAH, *Summarissimus Extractus Operationum,* SchLP, VN 73-7, 59-60: "At the beginning of the mission the brothers Baron von Braun [sc. Christoph Friedrich and Ernst Konrad], their administrators and their Lutheran pastors drove the Schwenkfelders to Lutheranism by coaxing and punishment. Thereafter, some received the eucharist here in Harpersdorf in the mission station."

[56] The Royal Government in Liegnitz to Johann Samuel Neander, March 2, 1720, JAH, *Instrumenta,* SchLP, VN 73-6, 104-106.

[57] Royal Consistory in Liegnitz to the pastors of the principality of Liegnitz, March 2, 1720, ibid., 95-99, printed in J.W. Jan, *Verum Dei verbum,* I, 47-48, Beilage VII.

[58] The Royal Government in Liegnitz to Ernst Konrad von Braun, March 2, 1720, ibid., 107-108.

[59] Karl VI to the Breslau Royal Upper Council, March 14, 1720, ibid., 80-83. As a summary of the decree in Wroclaw DA, Harpersdorf, 5, 7 and JAH, *Diarium,* SchLP, VN 73-5. 685.

[60] Summary of the record from the Royal Council of Jauer, May 16, 1721, ibid., 47-53.

[61] The Breslau Royal Upper Council to the Liegnitz Royal Government, January 7, 1723, ibid., 54-58.

[62] The Breslau Royal Upper Council to the Jauer Royal Council, March 22, 1725, ibid., 59-60.

[63] *Verzeichnis derer unter dem Conrad Freyherr von Hohberg von Zobten in Niederlangneundorf der Jaurischen Fürstenthumb befindlichen Schwenckfelder,* SchLP, VN 73-4, 166-168. Only two of the 27 summoned from Lower and Middle Langneundorf and 26 from Upper Schwenkfelders of the 27 summoned from Lower and Middle Langneundorf and only two of the 26 from Upper Langneundorf appeared on January 1, 1724 (ibid., 403-405).

[64] For this and the following see Christoph Schultz to Anthon N., April 6, 1768, SchLP, VC

3-7, 8-9; Christoph Hoffmann, *Kurze Lebens-Beschreibung Balthasar Hoffmanns,* 1777, SchLP, VR 22-9; Wroclaw DA, Harpersdorf 3, *Gravamina,* 10, and JAH, *Gravamina,* SchLP, VN 73-7, 569-570. Cf. Chr. Schultz, *Erläuterung,* 59; Schneider, *Jesuiten-Mission,* 11-12.

65 Wroclaw DA, Harpersdorf 3, *Gravamina,* 9 and JAH, *Gravamina,* SchLP, VN 73-7, 569: "In 1720 Baron von Braun [Ernst Konrad] of Armenruhe was paid 300 Kroener by the Schwenkfelders to go to Vienna to negotiate toleration for the sect."

66 Ibid., 10 and 569-571: "Subsequently three Schwenkfelders, Christoph and Balthasar Hoffmann and Balthasar Hofrichter were in Vienna, remaining there most of the time from around 1721 to 1725 inclusive; and through the offices of a bankrupt clothmaker of Goldberg, Hertel, they spent 19,000 Thaler in the effort to gain toleration, as the chief spokesperson Melchior Scholtz freely testifies. There are handwritten notes extant, that one time 1,000 Kroener had been sent, namely from Hirschberg. At the same time because of other events and opposing campaigns, many levies took place during these years, for such amounts as 200 Thaler, 22 Ducates, 300 Reichsthaler, etc." Cf. H.W. Kriebel, *The Schwenkfelders in Pennsylvania,* 23.

67 Christoph Hoffmann, *Kurtze Lebens-Beschreibung Balthasar Hoffmanns,* 1777, SchLP, VR 22-9 (these petitions are no longer extant).

68 The Liegnitz Royal Government to the Breslau Royal Upper Council, May 19, 1721; Jauer Royal Council to the Breslau Royal Upper Council, June 10, 1721; Breslau Royal Upper Council to Karl VI, July 12, 1721, Wroclaw DA, Harpersdorf 5, 9-10 and JAH, *Diarium,* SchLP, VN 73-5, 691-692, 695 (in summary).

69 K.X. Regent to the Jauer Royal Council, June 6, 1721; Regent to Karl VI, November 13, 1721, Wroclaw DA, Harpersdorf 5, 9, 11 JAH, *Diarium,* SchLP, VN 73-5, 692-693, 696-697 (in summary).

70 Breslau Royal Upper Council to the Royal Government in Liegnitz, November 5, 1722, JAH, *Diarium Instructionis,* SchLP, VN 73-11, 52-56.

71 Ibid., 54.

72 Ibid., 55.

73 Ibid., 54.

74 Ibid.

75 The Jauer Royal Council to the Breslau Royal Upper Council, April 16, 1723, ibid., 61-62.

76 Cited from Schneider, *Jesuiten-Mission,* 32, note 40.

77 Breslau Royal Upper Council to the Liegnitz Royal Government, November 5, 1722, JAH, *Diarium Instructionis,* SchLP, VN 73-11, 55.

78 Denzinger, 990-992.

79 Johann Christoph Schwedler to August Hermann Francke, April 14, 1720, Berlin SB, Francke-Nachlass.

80 Johann Christoph Schwedler to Johann Andreas Rothe, April 15, 1723, Herrnhut ABU, R 20 C, No. 15.74.

81 Milan: "Fünff kurtze und gründliche auss allgemeinen von jedem so nur den Christlichen Nahmen führen will zugestandenen Lehr-Sätzen gezogene Beweissthümer: Dass niemand obey gutem Gewissen der Schwenckfeldischen Sect beypflichten Oder Mit gesunder Vernunft in selbiger verbleiben könne," Neisse, 1720. Cf. Sommervogel, V, 1089.

82 Printed in *Unschuldige Nachrichten,* 1720, 503-504; Jan, *Verum Dei verbum,* I, 17; Schneider, *Jesuiten-Mission,* 10.

83 Cited in Jan, *Verum Dei verbum,* I, 17.

84 Jan, *Methodus Jesuitica convertendi Schwencfeldianos,* Wittenberg 1721. Cf. Sommervogel, V, 1098.

85 Cited in Jan, *Verum Dei verbum,* I, 32.

86 Milan, *EXAMINATOR METHODI JESUITICAE Convertendi Schwenckfeldianos* Prague 1721. Cf. Sommervogel, V, 1089-1090.

87 J.W. Jan, *Repetita demontratio quod non hodiernae romanae sed evangelicae ecclesiae ministri habeant verbum dei.* Wittenberg 1723. Cf. Sommervogel, V, 1090. After J.W. Jan's death, this, as well as his first polemical treatise which appeared in 1721, reappeared under

the title: *Verum Dei verbum ecclesiae evangelicae assertum,* Wittenberg 1726. Cf. Sommervogel, V, 1090. To this Milan countered with: *Verum Dei verbum soli Romanae Ecclesiae,* Breslau 1724. Cf. Sommervogel, V, 1090. A second edition followed in 1737. Cf. Sommervogel, V, 1090. Ten years later, Milan replied again with his own polemic publication *Lang geborgt, ist nicht geschenckt. Teil I-III,* Augsburg 1736-1737. Cf. Sommervogel, V, 1090. In this publication Milan tried to show that the understanding of the scripture of the Lutherans was obscure and that of the Catholics lucid; the work of the Jesuits among the Schwenkfelders was not even mentioned.

88 K.X. Regent, *Zusatz derer übrigen Irrthümer welche die im Hertzogthum Schlesien befindliche Schwenckfelder in denen (so genannten) Glaubens-Bekandtnüssen arglistig verschwiegen. Teil I-V.,* Neisse, 1722-1724. Cf. Sommervogel, VI, 1584.

89 K.X. Regent, *Der Neu-bekehrte Catholische Christ,* Neisse 1723. Cf. Sommervogel, VI, 1584.

90 K.X. Regent, *Christliche Ablehnung Derer Haupt-Unwahrheiten / Welche Die Schwenckfelder in einer Schrifft / so genannte Glaubens-Bekandtnuss der Neu-bekehrten Catholischen / Höchst-sträfflich und vermessentlich auffgesetzet haben,* Neisse, 1724, 4-5.

91 Title in note 90 above. Cf. Sommervogel, VI, 1584.

92 K.X. Regent, *Gewissens-Scrupel / Warumb es wider das Gewissen der Schwenckfelder seyn soll; ihre Lehr zu verlassen / hingegen den Catholischen Glauben anzunehmen / Gewissenhafft auffgelöset,* Neisse 1724. Cf. Sommervogel, VI, 1585.

93 K.X. Regent, *Der Auss eigenem Gesang-Buch / Und Sonsten gebrauchlichen Büchern / Dess Irrthums / Uberzeugte Schwenckfelder,* Neisse 1724. Cf. Sommervogel, VI, 1584-1585.

94 Ibid., 4.

95 Ibid.

96 Note for example K.X. Regent, *Exempel der Schlesier / Oder Vorstellung der fürnehmsten Christlichen Tugenden / welche die vormahlen Durchleuchtigste Hertzogin in Schlesien anjetzo Glorwürdigste Himmels-Fürstin / Gnädigste Schutz-Frau und Landes-Mutter S. HEDWIG zur Lebens-Zeit heylsam geübet / und nach dem Tod zur Nachübung hinterlassen,* Neisse 1723. Cf. Sommervogel, VI, 1585.

97 Wroclaw DA, Harpersdorf 3, *Fructus Jurisdictio,* 2-3 and JAH, *Fructus Jurisdictio,* SchLP, VN 73-3, 252-253.

98 *Decretum Officii Administrationis in Spiritualibus,* March 23, 1725, JAH, *Instructiones,* SchLP, VN 73-11, 119. The instruction is found in ibid., 120-125. It is printed in Schneider, *Jesuiten-Mission,* 45-46, Beilage IV.

99 *Instructio,* Section 4.

100 Wroclaw DA, Harpersdorf 5, 15 and JAH, *Diarium,* SchLP, VN 73-5, 706-707; JAH, *Instrumenta ad Modum Operandi,* SchLP VN 73-6, 33; Wroclaw DA, Harpersdorf 3, *Fructus Jurisdictio,* 22-23 and JAH, *Fructus Jurisdictio,* SchLP, VN 73-7, 280 (in summary).

101 Johann Samuel Neander to the Royal Government in Liegnitz, September 7, 1725, Wroclaw DA, Harpersdorf 5, 16 and JAH, *Diarium,* SchLP, VN 73-5, 710 (in summary).

102 Schwenkfelders from the principalities of Liegnitz and Jauer to the Breslau Royal Upper Council, August 25 and September 5, 1725, Wroclaw DA, Harpersdorf 5, 16 and JAH, *Diarium,* SchLP, VN 73-5, 708 (in summary).

103 Wroclaw DA, Harpersdorf 3, *Fructus Jurisdictio,* 14-15 and JAH, *Fructus Jurisdictio,* SchLP, VN 73-7, 268.

104 Wroclaw DA, Harpersdorf 3, *Fructus Jurisdictio,* 12-15 and JAH, *Fructus Jurisdictio,* SchLP, VN 73-7, 264-268.

105 Note for example, the Jauer Royal Council to Karl Nikolaus von Hohberg, March 28, 1725, JAH, *Instructiones,* SchLP, VN 73-11, 86-88.

106 A "Paradigma Stipulationis ante Matrimonium" of July 23 appears in ibid., 91-98.

107 Wroclaw DA, Harpersdorf 3, *Fructus Jurisdictio,* 18-19 and JAH, *Fructus Jurisdictio,* SchLP, VN 73-7, 270-274.

108 Karl VI to the Breslau Royal Upper Council, July 30, 1725, JAH, *Instrumenta ad Modum Operandi,* SchLP, VN 73-6, 19-24.

[109] Ibid., 22-23.
[110] Ibid., 22.
[111] Schwenkfelders to the Doopsgezinden in Amsterdam, October 16, 1725, Amsterdam BD, No. 2908.
[112] K. Guggisberg, *Bernische Kirchengeschichte,* 365.
[113] Adam Wiegner to [Daniel Hoovens], December 3, 1725, Amsterdam BD, No. 2909.
[114] Ibid.
[115] Ibid.
[116] Ibid.
[117] Adam Wiegner to [Daniel Hoovens], January 14, 1726, ibid., No. 2911.
[118] Schwenkfelders to Nikolaus Ludwig von Zinzendorf, December 19, 1725, printed in part in A.G. Spangenberg, *Zinzendorf,* II, 326-327. Cf. N.L. von Zinzendorf, *Kurze Relation von Herrnhut,* 56. See also A.G. Spangenberg, *Zinzendorf,* II, 324; E. Beyreuther, *Zinzendorf und die sich allhier beisammen finden,* 152.
[119] See N.L. von Zinzendorf, *Die Geschichte der verbundenen vier Brüder,* 99. Cf. A.G. Spangenberg, *Zinzendorf,* II, 262.
[120] Ibid.
[121] On this and the following see N.L. von Zinzendorf, *Kurze Relation von Herrnhut,* 46. Cf. A.G. Spangenberg, *Zinzendorf,* II, 266-267; E. Beyreuther, *Zinzendorf und die sich allhier beisammen finden,* 1.
[122] Nikolaus Ludwig von Zinzendorf to the Schwenkfelders, December 25, 1725, excerpted in A.G. Spangenberg, *Zinzendorf,* II, 327. Cf. N.L. v. Zinzendorf, *Kurze Relation von Herrnhut,* 56; E. Beyreuther, *Zinzendorf und die sich allhier beisammen finden,* 152.
[123] See N.L. v. Zinzendorf, *Kurze Relation von Herrnhut,* 56.
[124] The magistrate of Görlitz to August II, February 23, 1726, Dresden LA, loc 5861, Vol. I, fol. 11r (original). Excerpts are printed in Chr. G. Jähne, *Dankbare Erinnerung,* 27-28. Cf. Adam Wiegner to [Daniel Hoovens], March 16, 1726, Amsterdam BD, No. 2914; Adam Wiegner, Melchior Kriebel, Balthasar Jäckel and Georg Wiegner to the Doopsgezinden in Amsterdam, April 3, 1726, ibid., No. 2915.
[125] The magistrate of Görlitz to August II, February 23, 1726, Dresden LA, loc 5861, Vol. I, fol. 12v (original).
[126] Ibid., fol. 11r-13r.
[127] Ibid., fol. 12v.
[128] Gottlob Friedrich von Gersdorff to the magistrate of Görlitz, May 2, 1726, ibid., fol. 15r (in summary).
[129] Gottlob Friedrich von Gersdorff to the magistrate of Görlitz, July 9, 1727, ibid., fol. 29v.
[130] Frederick Caspar von Gersdorff to August II, September 13, 1732, Dresden LA, loc. 5854, fol. 57v-58r (original).
[131] Adam Wiegner, Melchior Kriebel, Balthasar Jäckel and Georg Wiegner to the Doopsgezinden in Amsterdam, April 3, 1726, Amsterdam BD, No. 2915.
[132] [Christian Hänisch] to the Doopsgezinden [in Haarlem], June 17, 1726, ibid., No. 2920 (incomplete).
[133] Adam Wiegner to Ameldonk Leew, Jan Schalle and Cornelius van Putten, September 12, 1726, ibid., No. 2921 (original); Adam Wiegner to the Doopsgezinden [in Amsterdam], January 6, 1727, ibid., No. 2923 (original).
[134] Ameldonk Leew, Jan Schalle and Cornelius van Putten to the Schwenkfelders, April 1, 1727, excerpted in O. Kadelbach, *Ausführliche Geschichte Kaspar v. Schwenckfelds und der Schwenckfelder in Schlesien,* 59-62.
[135] Cf. Frederick Caspar von Gersdorff to August II, September 13, 1732, Dresden LA, loc 5854, fol. 58r (original).
[136] Isaak Crajesteijn to Christian Hänisch, May 10, 1726, partially printed in O. Kadelbach, *Ausführliche Geschichte,* 58-59.
[137] Nikolaus Ludwig von Zinzendorf to Frederick Caspar von Gersdorff, n.d. [about August 1732], Herrnhut ABU, R 5 AN 20, 40; Frederick Caspar von Gersdorff to August II,

September 13, 1732, Dresden LA, loc 5854, fol. 58v (original); Frederick Caspar von Gersdorff to August II, December 19, ibid., fol. 74v (original).

138 On this and the following see Frederick Caspar von Gersdorff to August II, September 13, 1732, Dresden LA, loc 5854, fol. 58v-59r (original).

139 O. Kadelbach, *Ausführliche Geschichte*, 63.

140 Karl VI to Leopold von Waldstein, n.d. [before August 15, 1731], Dresden, LA, loc 5854, fol. 3r-v; excerpted in F. Körner, *Die kursächsische Staatsregierung*, 16. Cf. Leopold von Waldstein to Karl VI, August 17, 1731, JAH, *Instrumenta ad Modum* SchLP, VN 73-6, 528-531.

141 Privy Council to August II, August 16, 1731, Dresden LA, loc 5854, fol. 5v-6r.

142 August II to the Privy Council, August 20, 1731, ibid., fol. 8r.

143 August II to Georg Ernst von Gersdorff, August 20, 1731, ibid., fol. 7r.

144 Georg Ernst von Gersdorff to August II, September 15, 1731, ibid., fol. 12r-v.

145 Privy Council to Georg Ernst von Gersdorff, November 8, 1731, ibid., fol. 17r-v; Georg Ernst von Gersdorff to August II, March 15, 1732, ibid., fol. 41r-v (original).

146 Georg Ernst von Gersdorff to August II, March 15, 1732, ibid., fol. 41r-50v (original). On the investigations see F. Körner, *Die Kursächsische Staatsregierung*, 15-25; F.S. Hark, *Der Konflikt der kursächsischen Regierung mit Herrnhut*, 5-10.

147 Privy Council to the Upper Consistory, n.d., Dresden LA, loc 5854, fol. 54r-55r.

148 Upper Consistory to August II, November 1732, ibid., fol. 61r-65v (original). A copy of it is found in loc 1892, fol. 13r-15r.

149 Ibid., fol. 65r and 14v, respectively.

150 Privy Council to Frederick August II, January 5, 1733, Dresden LA, loc 6854, fol 78r.

151 Friedrich August II to the Privy Council, March 31, 1733, ibid., fol. 83r.

152 Friedrich August II to Frederick Caspar von Gersdorff, April 4, 1733, ibid., fol. 82r-v, printed in N.L. v. Zinzendorf, *B*üdingische Sammlung, III, 12-13.

153 Ibid., fol. 82v and p. 13, respectively.

154 Nikolaus Ludwig von Zinzendorf to N.N., n.d., [about 1733 (autumn)], Herrnhut ABU, R 5 A 2a, 57; partially printed in English in E.S. Gerhard and S.G. Schultz, *The Schwenkfelders and the Moravians in Saxony*, 12.

155 H.W. Kriebel, *The Schwenkfelders in Pennsylvania*, 29-30.

156 A.G. Spangenberg, *Zinzendorf*, IV, 803-804; G. Reichel, *August Gottlieb Spangenberg, Bischof der Brüderkirche*, 97-98.

157 [Schwenkfelders] to Nikolaus Ludwig von Zinzendorf, n.d. [after October 23, 1733], Herrnhut ABU, R 14 AN 2,2a (R 6 A 5,20); Melchior Kriebel, Georg Weiss, Balthasar Hoffmann, Balthasar Jäckel and others to Nikolaus Ludwig von Zinzendorf, n.d. [after October 23, 1733], ibid., R 14 A 2,2c (R 14 N 2,2e; R 5 A 5,21), printed in English in Gerhard and Schultz, 11-12.

158 [Nikolaus Ludwig von Zinzendorf] to N.N., n.d. [before November, 1733], Herrnhut ABU, R 5 10. Cf. A.G. Spangenberg, *Zinzendorf*, IV, 803.

159 Johann Ph. Fresenius, *Bewährte Nachrichten von Herrnhutischen Sachen*, III, 754.

160 H.W. Kriebel, *The Schwenkfelders in Pennsylvania*, 31.

161 Nikolaus Ludwig von Zinzendorf to N.N., n.d. [ca. autumn, 1733], Herrnhut ABU, R 5 A 2a, 57, partially printed in Gerhard and Schultz, 12. Cf. in contrast J.M. Levering, *A History of Bethlehem*, 32.

162 Schultz, *Erläuterung*, 64. Cf. Christoph Schultz to Anton N., April 6, 1768, SchLP, VC 3-7, 4.

163 Christoph Schultz, *Reise-Beschreibung von Altona bis Pensylvanien*, printed in Schultz, *Erläuterung.*, 450-461.

164 Fresenius, III, 112.

165 On the history of Schwenkfelders in Pennsylvania see above all H.W. Kriebel. For an extensive list of literature see E. Meynen, *Bibliographie des Deutschtums der kolonialzeitlichen Einwanderung in Nordamerika insbesondere der Pennyslvanien-Deutschen und ihrer Nachkommen*, 147-148; Kriebel and H.G. Hein, "Schwenckfelder," in ML, IV, 139-140; G. Maron, "Schwenckfelder," in RGG, V, 1622-1623.

4. The Decline of Schwenkfeldianism in Silesia

1 Cf. Adam Wiegner, Melchior Kriebel, Balthasar Jäckel and Georg Wiegner to the Doopsgezinden in Amsterdam, April 3, 1726, Amsterdam BD, No. 2915.

2 Kadelbach, *Ausführliche Geschichte*, 46.

3 Wroclaw DA, Harpersdorf 3, *Fructus Jurisdictio*, 14-15 and JAH, *Fructus Jurisdictio*, SchLP, VN 73-7, 268.

4 Ibid., 14-15 and 268-269.

5 Ibid., 16-17 and 270.

6 Ibid., 16-17 and 270-271.

7 Ibid.

8 Ibid., 16-17 and 271.

9 On this and the following see ibid., 4-7 and 255-259.

10 Breslau Vicariate-general to the Breslau Royal Upper Council, February 8, 1792, JAH, *Instrumenta ad Modum Operandi*, SchLP, VN 73-6, 500-503.

11 Breslau Royal Upper Council to the Liegnitz Royal Government in Liegnitz, February 25, 1729, ibid., 498-499.

12 Statistics based on K.X. Regent's statement for the year 1732 are found in Schneider, *Jesuiten-Mission*, 20.

13 Breslau Royal Upper Council to the Liegnitz Royal Government, January 16, 1726, JAH, *Instrumenta ad Modum Operandi*, SchLP, VN 73-6, 368-372.

14 Wroclaw DA, Harpersdorf 3, *Gravamina*, 7-9 and JAH, *Gravamina*, SchLP, VN 73-7, 566-569.

15 Breslau Vicariate-general to the Breslau Upper Royal Council, October 8, 1728, Wroclaw DA, Harpersdorf 3, *Extractus ex instructione episcopali*, 25-27 and JAH, *Gravamina*, SchLP, VN 73-7, 317-321.

16 Karl VI to the Breslau Royal Upper Council, March 1, 1732, Wroclaw DA, Harpersdorf 3, *Extractus ex instructione episcopali*, 33-36 and JAH, *Gravamina*, SchLP, VN 73-7, 327-331 as well as Wroclaw SA, Rep. 28. *Fürstentum Liegnitz*, X, 7, and I, fol. 1r-2r.

17 The successor to Johann Milan was Franz Weigelsfeldt, S.J.

18 JAH, *Berechnungen wegen der Sustentation der Kapelle in Harpersdorf*, SchLP, VN 73-10, 90.

19 See note 16.

20 JAH, *Berechnungen wegen der Sustentation der Kapelle in Harpersdorf*, SchLP, VN 73-10, 92.

21 JAH, *Inventaria*, SchLP, VN 73-9, 18.

22 He could only register 19 conversions from 1732 to 1736.

23 Numerous transcripts of petitions are found in Wroclaw SA, Rep. 28, *Fürstentum Liegnitz*, X, 7 and II, fol. 1r-53v.

24 See for example the investigation report of the two counselors of the Liegnitz Royal Government, Franz Joseph von Kernis and Franz Wilhelm von Larisch, May 3, 1736, ibid., X, 5, b.

25 Cf. Kadelbach, *Ausführliche Geschichte*, 65-66.

26 Mayor and magistrate of Görlitz to August III, May 28, 1736, Dresden LA, loc 5854, fol. 100r-105r (original).

27 Privy Council to Frederick Caspar von Gersdorff, May 30, 1736, ibid., fol. 106r-v.

28 K.X. Regent to Franziskus Retz, May 11, 1737, JAH, *Diarium*, SchLP, 73-5, 760-761: They are dead who loved me and protected me.

29 Karl VI to the Breslau Royal Upper Council, October 10, 1740, JAH, *Reskripte*, SchLP, VN 73-8, II, 238-240.

30 Breslau Royal Upper Council to the Jauer Royal Council, March 14, 1740, ibid., 563.

31 Breslau Royal Upper Council to the Liegnitz Royal Government, March 14, 1740, Wroclaw SA, Rep. 28. *Fürstentum Liegnitz*, X, 5, b (original).

32 Breslau Royal Upper Council to the Liegnitz Royal Government, March 5, 1740, ibid. (original).

33 The decree is printed in J.A. Hensel, *Protestantische Kirchengeschichte der Gemeinen in Schlesien*, 738; Kadelbach, *Ausführliche Geschichte*, 49. For this and the following see

Weigelt, *Frederick II von Preussen und die Schwenckfelder in Schlesien.*

[34] J.A. Hensel, *Protestantische Kirchengeschichte,* 738.

[35] Ibid.

[36] Karl Ehrenfried Heintze to Christoph Kriebel, February 11, 1722, SchLP, VC 3-7, XXXIX.

[37] Cf. Frederick II to Ludwig Wilhelm von Münschow, February 23, 1742, Merseburg DZA, Hist. Abt. II, Rep. 96, Geheimer Zivilkabinett, B. Minuten, Vol. 25, 1742, fol. 48r.

[38] This report is no longer available.

[39] Frederick II to Ludwig Wilhelm von Münchow, February 23, 1742, ibid.

[40] Frederick II to Samuel von Cocceji, February 23, 1742, ibid., fol. 48r-v.

[41] Frederick II to Ludwig Wilhelm von Münchow, February 23, 1742, ibid., fol. 48r.

[42] Frederick II to Samuel von Cocceji, February 23, 1742, ibid., fol. 48r-v.

[43] Ibid., fol. 48v.

[44] Ibid.

[45] Ibid., fol. 48r-v.

[46] An original edition of this *Edikt wegen Unterbringung und Placierung der sogenannten Schwenckfelder in Sr. Königl. Schlesischen und übrigen Landen* is found in Merseburg DZA, Hist. Abt. II, Rep. 46 B, No. 131, Fasz. 2. Printed in *Gesamlete Nachrichten und Documente den gegenwärtigen Zustand des Hertzogthums Schlesiens betreffend,* III, 2-4; *Sammlung aller in dem souverainen Herzogthum Schlesien und dessen incorporirten Grafschafft Glatz in Finanz=Criminal=Geistlichen=Consistorial=Kirchen=Sachen etc. publicirten und ergangenen Ordnungen,* II, 41-42; *Acta Historico-Ecclesiastica,* VI, 380-381; A. Köpke, *Historische Nachricht von Caspar Schwenckfeld,* 2-3; *Helden=, Staats= und Lebens=Geschichte Friedrichs des Andern,* II 581-582; Chr. G. Jähne, *Dankbare Erinnerung,* 34-36; partially printed in C. Grünhagen, *Schlesien unter Friedrich dem Grossen,* I, 483-484.

[47] Merseburg DZA, Hist. Abt. II, Rep. 46 B, No. 131, Fasz. 2.

[48] Ibid.

[49] Ibid.

[50] See C. Grünhagen, *Geschichte des Ersten schlesischen Krieges,* II, 269-337.

[51] Merseburg DZA, Hist. Abt. II, Rep. 46 B, No. 131, Fasz. 2.

[52] Ibid.

[53] Ibid.

[54] Ibid.

[55] Ibid.

[56] Ibid.

[57] According to the excerpts in Schneider, Berlin SB, Handschriften-Abteilung (Collectaneum 25b, fol. 132), the edict was publicized verbally in Silesia; its announcement in the rest of the Prussian lands was, however, left to the discretion of the chief justice minister Samuel von Cocceji by the directorate of finances, war and the dominion. Regrettably Schneider gives no reference so that it remains unclear as to whether he used the proceedings from Rep. 46 B, Schlesien seit 1740, or those of the registrar of the Silesian provincial ministry (1740-1806), which earlier were housed in the Geheimen Staatsarchiv at Berlin but after 1881 were given over to the then Prussian archives at Breslau. The records (Rep. 99) were totally destroyed in Breslau at the end of the war.

[58] Note for example Rosina Scharffenberger to Hans Christoph Hübner, April 28, 1742, SchLP, VOC-H[6] (original); Barbara Wiegner to Maria Drescher, April 20, 1742, SchLP, VC 2-5, 5.

[59] Note for example Hans Christoph Hübner to Rosina Scharffenberger, December 20, 1744, SchLP, VOC-H[6].

[60] Ibid.

[61] Cf. Barbara Wiegner to Maria Drescher, April 20, 1742, SchLP, VC 2-5, 4-5.

[62] Note for example Christoph Groh to Christoph Schultz, March 17, 1776, SchLP, VC 3-7, 230: "We [that is, the Schwenkfelders in Silesia] are not now treated with as much scorn as we were during the time of the Mission. I have equal standing with anyone, before the baron, the pastor and the magistrate; the pastor sent me food from a baptismal meal, having said that even though I was not attending church, I was nevertheless a good old *wit* [*wit* = wood;

likely a metaphorical expression having reference to being made of good, solid wood or having good roots, being a good old chum].''

63 Cf. for example, Karl Ehrenfried Heintze to the Schwenkfelders in Pennsylvania, August 22, 1771, SchLP, VOC-H[10].

64 Cf. for example, Karl Ehrenfried Heintze to Christoph Kriebel, February 11, 1772, SchLP, VC 3-7, XXXIX (original): ''1. The dead are being buried, without exception, at the command of the king, in the church cemeteries. . . . The teaching is taking place under Lutheran preachers. . . . 2. As to marriage, it is the same as it was before the Mission, for you must not assume that our freedom of conscience is at all comparable to yours. 3. The baptism of small children remains as of old an anti-Christian practice''; Georg Fliegner, Christoph Groh and Karl Ehrenfried Heintze to the Schwenkfelders in Pennsylvania, February 15, 1768, ibid., 28; Georg Fliegner to Caspar Seibt, February 15, 1768, SchLP, VOC-F[2].

65 On this and the following see S.G. Schultz, *History of the ''Erläuterung,''* 21-24.

66 To this they were prodded by the reading of the anonymously-published nine-volume histories of *Helden-, Staats- und Lebens- Geschichte Friedrichs des Anderen,* which in volume two (576-582) contains the edict of toleration and a short excerpt of the history of the Schwenkfelders.

67 See note 65.

68 According to the subsequently attached erratum, there were no less than 463 printing errors, not counting minor errors such as the transposition of letters.

69 Cf. Karl Ehrenfried Heintze, Georg Fliegner and Christoph Groh to the Schwenkfelders in Pennsylvania, June 1, 1772, SchLP, VOC-H[10].

70 *Der Schwenckfelder Glaubens-Bekäntniss welches sie auf kayserlichen Befehl an die damalige Regierung in Liegnitz eingehen müssen im Jahre 1718. den 25. Mai. Denen Pensylvanischen Brudern zu Lieb und Ehren ans Licht gegeben von etlichen Mitbekennern in Schlesien im Jahr Christi 1772.* Jauer 1772.

71 Christoph Schultz, Balthasar Hoffmann (and others) to Balthasar Kurtz, Christoph Groh and Karl Ehrenfried Heintze, May 15, 1773, SchLP, VC 3-7, 154. Cf. E.S. Gerhard, ''Balthasar Hoffmann (1687-1775). Scholar, Minister, Writer, Diplomat,'' 36, n. 2.

72 Karl Ehrenfried Heintze, Georg Fliegner and Christoph Groh to the Schwenkfelders in Pennsylvania, June 1, 1772, SchLP, VOC-H[10]; Karl Ehrenfried Heintze to the Schwenkfelders in Pennsylvania, August 17, 1773, ibid. (original).

73 The number of Schwenkfelders in Silesia was only 44 in 1768 (see Georg Fliegner, Christoph Groh and Karl Ehrenfried Heintze to the Schwenkfelders in Pennyslvania, February 15, 1768, SchLP, VC 3-7, 62-63) and finally, in 1776, only 23 (see Helena Heydrich to Melchior Jäckel, 1776, SchLP, VOC-H 13; original).

74 According to the list of persons which accompanied the letter of Georg Fliegner, Christoph Groh and Karl Ehrenfried Heintze to the Schwenkfelders in Pennsylvania (February 15, 1768, SchLP, VC 3-7, 37), 17 of the total of 44 Schwenckfeld adherents in 1760 were single.

75 The total of Schwenkfelder families which included children was seven; see ibid.

76 Cf. for example Georg Fliegner to Christoph Hoffmann, February 15, 1772, SchLP, VC 2-6, 43: ''My two sons are still with me and remain unmarried, having little opportunity to do so since no woman of our people is left.''

77 Cf. for example, Christoph Beer to Christoph Hoffmann, May 24, 1789, ibid., 86.

78 Cf. Karl Ehrenfried Heintze to Balthasar Hoffmann, May, 1765, SchLP, VC 3-7, 11; Georg Fliegner, Christoph Groh and Karl Ehrenfried Heintze to the Schwenkfelders in Pennsylvania, February 15, 1768, ibid., 22; Helena Heydrich to Christoph Hoffmann, February 1770, SchLP, VC 2-6, 28; Melchior Heydrich to Christoph Hoffmann, n.d., ibid., 19.

79 Cf. for example Georg Fliegner, Christoph Groh and Karl Ehrenfried Heintze to the Schwenkfelders in Pennsylvania, February 15, 1768, SchLP, VC 3-7, 21.

80 Hensel, *Protestantische Kirchengeschichte,* 739.

81 Karl Ehrenfried Heintze to Balthasar Hoffmann, May 1765, SchLP, VC 3-7, 11.

82 The Schwenkfelders in Pennsylvania to the Schwenkfelders in Silesia, June 16, 1767, ibid., 21.

83 Cf. for example Christoph Kriebel to the Schwenkfelders in Silesia, February 28, 1769, ibid., 42.

84 Karl Ehrenfried Heintze to the Schwenkfelders in Pennsylvania, May 1765, ibid., 10.

85 Ibid., 10-11.

86 Ibid., 11.

87 Ibid.

88 Ibid.

89 Ibid.

90 Cf. for example Christoph Kriebel to the Schwenkfelders in Silesia, February 28, 1769, ibid., 49: "We cannot help but add in regard to the dear brother C.E.H. [Heintze] for your own sake. We observe from the writings that we have received that he is a man full of love and that he has been imbued with a wonderful knowledge of Christian teachings and a particular gift for speaking and writing. And we also observe that you who have been raised from childhood on Schwenckfeld's teachings, are fast losing ground to the extent that it appears your very existence is threatened. Think about and pay attention to the following: What might God's will be for H. [Heintze]? Might he not be your gift from God, to lift your sunken spirits and to encourage you again to retrieve Schwenckfeld's teachings from the dust, truly to seek Christ's honor and to model his love according to his admonition among yourselves."

91 See especially Christoph Schultz to Christoph Groh, July 1, 1799, ibid., LXI. There appears here a compilation of the authors which C.E. Heintze had read. But there is no indication either here or elsewhere which writings are referred to. On the high regard in which C.E. Heintze and other Silesian Schwenkfelders held G. Arnold see Karl Ehrenfried Heintze to Christoph Schultz, n.d., SchLP, VOC-H[10] (original); Georg Fliegner, Christoph Groh and Karl Ehrenfried Heintze to the Schwenkfelders in Pennsylvania, February 15, 1768, ibid., 27.

92 Karl Ehrenfried Heintze to the Schwenkfelders in Pennsylvania, May 1765, SchLP, VC 3-7, 11.

93 Christoph Kriebel to Karl Ehrenfried Heintze, February 16, 1771, ibid., XXXI.

94 Ibid.

95 Georg Fliegner, Christoph Groh and Karl Ehrenfried Heintze to the Schwenkfelders in Pennsylvania, February 15, 1768, ibid., 24.

96 Karl Ehrenfried Heintze to the Schwenkfelders in Pennsylvania, February 20, 1768, ibid., 34-35; Georg Fliegner, Christoph Groh and Karl Ehrenfried Heintze to the Schwenkfelders in Pennsylvania, February 16, 1770, ibid., 63.

97 Helena Heydrich to Christoph Kriebel, March 11, 1776, ibid., LV.

98 Cf. Christoph Kriebel to the Schwenkfelders in Pennsylvania, December 1774, ibid., 183. This part of the letter was, however, not sent.

99 Cf. Helena Heydrich to Christoph Kriebel, March 11, 1776, ibid., LV.

100 See Jeremias Heydrich to Christoph Schultz and Christoph Kriebel, March 6, 1776, SchLP, VOC-H[14] (original); Helena Heydrich to Christoph Kriebel, March 11, 1776, SchLP, VC 3-7, LV; Christoph Groh to Christoph Schultz and Christoph Kriebel, March 17, 1776, ibid., LX; Christoph Groh to Christoph Schultz, March 17, 1776, ibid., 229.

101 Ibid.

102 Christoph Kriebel to Karl Ehrenfried Heintze, December 22, 1774, SchLP, VC 3-7, LIII.

103 Cf. for example Christoph Kriebel to Helena Heydrich, December 1774, ibid., LIV.

104 Christoph Kriebel to the Schwenkfelders in Silesia, 1774, ibid., 181.

105 Cf. for example Helena Heydrich to Melchior Jäckel, March 1786, SchLP, VOC-H[13] (original).

106 Georg Fliegner, Christoph Groh and Karl Ehrenfried Heintze to the Schwenkfelders in Pennsylvania, February 15, 1768, SchLP, VC 3-7, 28.

107 Oswald Kadelbach to the Schwenkfelders in Pennsylvania, December 2, 1857, SchLP, VOC-K[2].

Bibliography

Bibliography

1. Primary Sources

Not all of the primary documents cited or referred to below can be described here in detail. However, the location and identifying signature are accurately recorded.

Amsterdam, Bibliotheek der Verenigde Doopsgezinde Gemeente (Universiteitsbibliotheek):

Signature:No. 2908-2909, 2911, 2914-2915, 2920-2921, 2923. (Verhouding tot niet-Doopsgezinde Gemeenten en tot Maatschappijen. Schwenckfelders.)

Berlin, Staatsbibliothek Preussischer Kulturbesitz:

Signature: Ms. germ. 153. (Joh. Sig. Werner: Bekanntnus unnd Rechenschafft der furnemesten articul vonn der Justification oder gerechtmachung Christy unnd vom diennste des Evangelij.)

Signature: Ms. germ. 527, fol. 36r-55v. (Val. Krautwald: Bericht und Anzeigen, wie gar one Kunst und guotten verstandt, Andreas Fischer vom Sabbat geschrieben.)

Signature: Ms. theol. quart. 88a. (Val. Krautwald: In tria priora capita Geneseos Commentaria.)

Francke-Nachlass, Kapsel 25.

A.F.H. Schneider-Collectaneum, 25 b.

Brno, Staatsarchiv:

Signature: G 10/49, Nr. 68. (Becksche Sammlung, Wiedertaufferischen Gesindleins in Mähren und Schlesien seltsame Beschaffenheit. Ao 1535.)

Dresden, Staatsarchiv:

Signature: loc 1892. (Acten des Oberconsistoriums: Verschiedene aus den kaiserlichen Landen emigrirte, auf denen Zinzendorfschen Gütern Bertheldsdorf und Herrnhut sich niedergelassene Leut betr. 1732-1738.)

Signature: loc 5854. (Acten der geh. Canzlei: Den Grafen von Zinzendorf und die auf seinem Gütern Berthelsdorf und Herrnhut befindlichen mährischen Exulanten betr. 1731 ssq.)

Signature: loc 5861, Vol. I.

Signature: loc 6854.

Göttingen, Staatliches Archivlager:

Signature: Schrank 4, Fach 22, Nr. 63 (I). (Staatsarchiv Königsberg—Nachlass Speratus. Gantzer handel der unterredung vom abendmahl des herrn leibs und bluts.)

Signature: W 19,2. (Staatsarchiv Königsberg. Fab. Eckel: Auf Einn Poliander schrifft.)

Herrnhut, Archiv der Brüder-Unität:

Signature: R 5 10; R 5 A 2a,57; R 5 A 5,21; R 5 AN 20,40; R 6 A 5,20; R 14 A 2,2c; R 14 AN 2,2a; R 14 N 2,2e; R 20 C 15,74. (Letters from and to N.L. v. Zinzendorf. Photostat in the Schwenckfelder Library, Pennsburg, Pa.)

Legnica Stadtarchiv:

Signature: A 1059. (Visitation protocol of 1654)

Merseburg, Deutsches Zentralarchiv, Historische Abteilung II:

Signature: Rep. 46 B Nr. 131, Fasz. 2. (Edict wegen Unterbringung und Placierung der sogenannten Schwenckenfelder.)

Signature: Rep. 96, Geheimes Zivilkabinett, B. Minuten, Bd. 25, 1742, fol. 48r-v. (Kabinettorder und Reskript Friedrichs II.)

München, Bayerische Staatsbibliothek:

Signature: CLM 718. (Val. Krautwald: Cratoaldi Silesii Cophinus fragmentorum sive reliquiarum de mensa domini.)

Signature: 965. (St. Sauer: Stanislai Saweri doctoris et canonici Wratislauiensis chronica [Silesiae] a tempore regis Matthiae, Wladislai et Ludouici.)

Pennsburg, Schwenkfelder Library:

Signature: Ms. Sb. XXV; VA 2-12, 3-12, 4-11, 5-3; VB 1-19; VC 2-5, 2-6, 3-7, 4-1, 5-1, 5-3; VR 22-9; VOC F^2, H^{10}, H^{13}, H^{14}, H^{37}, K^2, . (Schwenckfeldiana of the 16th to 19th centuries.)

Signature: VN 73-3, 73-4, 73-5, 73-6, 73-7, 73-8, 73-9, 73-10, 73-11. (Complete copy of the archives of the Jesuit Archives, Harpersdorf.)

Prag, Staatliches Zentralarchiv:

Signature: C 66-67. (Korrespondenz des Anton Brus v. Müglitz, Eb. v. Prag.)

Signature: C 113. (Erzbischöfliches Archiv.)

Weimar, Landeshauptarchiv (Staatsarchiv):

Signature: Reg. N.Nr. 623. (Ernestinisches Gesamtarchiv, Religionswesen.)

Wolfenbüttel, Herzog August Bibliothek:

Signature: Cod. Guelf. 37. 27 Aug. (Sendschreiben und Briefe, die Valentin Crautwaldt und Caspar von Schwenckfeldt mit einander, solche, die letzterer mit verschiedenen Personen, Männern und Frauen, gewechselt hat, theologische Abhandlungen beider und biblische Auslegungen Schwenckfeldts.)

Signature: Cod. Guelf. 45, 9 Aug. (Etliche Sändbriefe von mancherlei Stucklen vnd vnderredung beim christlichen glauben 1543 [von Kaspar von Schwenckfeld und Valentin Crautwald].)

Wroclaw, Diözesan-Archiv:

Signature: DA, I, 13a. (G. Buckisch: Schlesische Religionsakten. I. Teil. 1517-1607.)

Signature: DA, III, b. 1a u. 1b. (Acta Capituli Wratislaviensis.)

Signature: DA, Harpersdorf, 3 u. 5. (Archivalien des Jesuiten-Archivs Harpersdorf.)

Wroclaw, Staatsarchiv:

Signature: Sammlung-Klose, 4 u. 42.

Signature: Rep. 28. Fürstentum Liegnitz, X, 5, b; 5, g; 5, i; 7.

2. Secondary Sources

In the following secondary source bibliography are listed only those works referred to or directly cited from in the monograph. Titles mentioned in the text are not listed here again.

Adam, Johann: *Evangelische Kirchengeschichte der Stadt Strassburg bis zur französischen Revolution* (Strassburg 1922).

Aelurius, Georg: *Glaciographia, oder Clätzische Chronica, das ist: Gründliche historische Beschreibung der berümbten vnd vornemen Stadt, ja gantzen Graffschafft Glatz, nach allen vornemsten Stücken* (Leipzig 1625).

Aland, Kurt: *Die Säuglingstaufe im Neuen Testament und in der alten Kirche. Eine Antwort an Joachim Jeremias* (München 1961).

———: *Die Stellung der Kinder in den frühen christlichen Gemeinden und ihre Taufe* (München 1967).

Althaus, Paul Sr.: *Forschungen zur Evangelischen Gebetsliteratur* (Gütersloh 1927).

Anonymous: *Kurtzer Bericht von Hn. Dan. Schneider, Pfaffers in Goldberg, gefährlichen Unternehmen. Unschuldige Nachrichten von Alten und Neuen Theologischen Sachen... auff das Jahr 1703* (2nd edition, Leipzig 1706), pp. 598-605.

Anonymous: *Des zu den Quackern übergetretenen Hilarii Prachii und J. C. Matern seines Eydams Brieffe. Unschuldige Nachrichten von Alten und Neuen Theologischen Sachen... auf das Jahr 1706* (2nd edition, Leipzig 1709), pp. 432-441.

Anonymous: *Von der Wiederaufnahme der Schwenkfelder in Schlesien. Acta historico-ecclesiastica, oder gesammlete Nachrichten von den neuesten Kirchen-Geschichten. Bd. VI* (Weimar 1742), pp. 373-381.

Arnold, Gottfried: *Fortsetzung und Erläuterung oder dritter und viertder Theil der unpartheyischen Kirchen- und Ketzer-Historie, bestehend in Beschreibung der noch übrigen Streitigkeiten im XVIIden Jahrhundert* (Frankfurt am Main 1700).

———: *Supplementa, illustrationes und emendationes zur Verbesserung der Kirchen-Historie* (Frankfurt am Main 1703).

Bach, Aloys: *Urkundliche Kirchen-Geschichte der Grafschaft Glaz. Von der Urzeit bis auf unsere Tage. Nebst einem Anhange: Geschichtlich statistische Darstellung aller Gläzer Pfarreien und Kirchen mit deren geistlichen Vorsteheren, so wie der Schulen im Jahre 1841* (Breslau 1841).

Bahlow, Ferdinand: "Die Kirchenbibliothek von St. Peter und Paul in Liegnitz." *Mitteilungen des Geschichts- und Altertumsvereins für die Stadt und das Fürstentum Liegnitz 2* (1908), pp. 140-175.

———: "Aus der Peter-Paul-Kirchenbibliothek." *Mitteilungen des Geschichts-und Altertumsvereins für die Stadt und das Fürstentum Liegnitz 3* (1910), pp. 301-304.

———: *Die Reformation in Liegnitz* (Liegnitz 1918).

———: "Sebastian Schubart 1498-1580," *JSchlKG* 29 (1939), 28-54.

Bahlow, Hans: *Die Anfänge des Buchdrucks zu Liegnitz. Ein Beitrag zur Literatur- und Kulturgeschichte des deutschen Ostens* (Liegnitz 1928).

———: *Schlesisches Namenbuch. Mit einer Kartenskizze* (Kitzingen am Main 1953).

Balbinus, Bohuslav: *Miscellanea historica regni Bohemiae, quibus natura bohemicae telluris. . . explicantur* (Prag 1681-1688).

Barge, Hermann: *Andreas Bodenstein von Karlstadt* (Leipzig 1905).

Baring, Georg: "Hans Denck und Thomas Müntzer in Nürnberg 1524," *ARG* 50 (1959), 145-181.

Bathelt, Kurt: "Die Familie Thurzo in Kunst und Kultur Ostmitteleuropas (1450 bis 1650)." *Deutsche Monatshefte. Zeitschrift für Geschichte und Gegenwart des Ostdeutschtums N.F.* 7 (1940), 115-124.

Bauch, Gustav: "Analekten zur Biographie des Johann Hess," *Correspondenz-Blatt* 8 (1902), 161-185; 9 (1904), 34-64.

———: "Beiträge zur Literaturgeschichte des schlesischen Humanismus," *ZVG Schles.* 26 (1892), 213-248.

———: "Faber, Franciscus," in *ADB* 48, 472-473.

———: *Aus dem Hausbuche des Goldberger Lehrers Zacharias Bart. 1529-1612* (Breslau 1907).

———: "Schlesien und die Universität Krakau im XV. und XVI. Jahrhundert," *ZVG Schles.* 41 (1907), 99-180.

———: "Zur älteren Liegnitzer Schulgeschichte," *Mitteilungen der Gesellschaft für deutsche Erziehungs- und Schulgeschichte* 18 (1908), 96-135.

———: *Valentin Trozendorf und die Goldberger Schule* (Berlin 1921).

Baum, Johann Wilhelm: *Capito und Butzer, Strassburger Reformatoren. Nach ihrem handschriftlichen Briefschatz, ihren gedruckten Schriften und anderen gleichzeitigen Quellen dargestellt* (Elberfeld 1860).

Baur, Ferdinand Christian: "Zur Geschichte der protestantischen Mystik; die neueste Literatur derselben," *ThJB* 7 (1848), 453-528.

———: *Die christliche Lehre von der Dreieinigkeit und Menschwerdung Gottes in ihrer geschichtlichen Entwicklung. Teil III. Die neuere Geschichte des Dogmas, von der Reformation bis in die neueste Zeit* (Tübingen 1843).

———: *Die christliche Lehre von der Versöhnung in ihrer geschichtlichen Entwicklung von der ältesten Zeit bis auf die neueste* (Tübingen 1838).

Beck, Anton: *Die Trinitätslehre des heiligen Hilarius von Poitiers* (Mainz 1903).

Benzing, Josef: *Lutherbibliographie. Verzeichis der gedruckten Schriften Martin Luthers bis zu dessen Tod*. Bearbeitet in Verbindung mit der Weimarer Ausgabe unter Mitarbeit von Helmut Claus (Baden-Baden 1966).

Berg, J.: *Die Geschichte der gewaltsamen Wegnahme der evangelischen Kirchen und Kirchengüter in den Furstenthümern Schweidnitz und Jauer während des siebzehnten Jahrhunderts. Mit zum grossen Theile noch ungedruckten Urkunden und Belägen. Eine Säcularschrift, als Beitrag zur schlesischen Kirchengeschichte und zur Begründung einer angemessenen Auseinandersetzung der äusseren Verhältnisse der evangelischen Kirche mit dem State und der römisch-katholischen Kirche* (Breslau 1854).

Bergemann, J.G.: *Beschreibung und Geschichte der alten Burgveste Gröditzberg* (Löwenberg 1827).

Bergsten, Torsten: *Balthasar Hubmaier. Seine Stellung zu Reformation und Täufertum 1521-1528* (Kassel 1961).

———: "Pilgram Marbeck und seine Auseinandersetzung mit Caspar Schwenckfeld," *Kyrkohistorisk Arsskrift* 57 (1957/58), 39-100.

Besch, Theophil: *Friedrich von Heydeck, ein Beitrag zur Geschichte der Reformation und Säkularisation Preussens* (Königsberg in Pr. 1897).

Beyreuther, Erich: *Zinzendorf und die sich allhier beisammen finden* (Marburg/Lahn 1959).

Bibliographie de la réforme 1450-1648. Ouvrages parus de 1940 à 1955 (Fascicule I, Leiden 1959. Fascicule II, Leiden 1960. Fascicule IV, Leiden 1963).

Biermann, Gottlieb: *Geschichte des Protestantismus in Österreichisch-Schlesien* (Prag 1897).

Birkner, Günter: "Die beiden ältesten evangelischen Gesangbuch-Drucke Schlesiens 1525 und 1525/26," *ArSKG* 26 (1968), 141-152.

Bizer, Ernst: *Studien zur Geschichte des Abendmahlsstreits im 16. Jahrhundert* (Darmstadt 1962).

Bock, Friedrich Samuel: *Grundriss von dem merkwürdigen Leben des Durchlauchtigen Fürsten und Herrn, Herrn Albrecht des ältern, Marggrafen zu Brandenburg* (Königsberg 1745).

Bossert, Gustav: "Kleine Mittheilungen. 1. Zu Hans Bünderlins späterer Geschichte," *JGPrÖ* 13 (1892), 54.

———: *Quellen zur Geschichte der Wiedertäufer. Bd. I. Herzogtum Württemberg* (Leipzig 1930).

Braithwaite, William Charles: *The Second Period of Quakerism.* (2nd. ed.; Cambridge 1961).

Brecht, Martin: *Die frühe Theologie des Johannes Brenz* (Tübingen 1966).

Bucer, Martin: *Vergleichung D. Luthers und seins Gegentheyls*, in *Opera omnia. Series I. Deutsche Schriften* (Gütersloh 1962).

Bucholtz, Franz Bernhard v.: *Geschichte der Regierung Ferdinand des Ersten. Aus gedruckten und ungedruckten Quellen* (Wien 1831 and 1833).

Buddecke, Werner: *Die Jakob Böhme-Ausgaben. Ein beschreibendes Verzeichnis* (Göttingen 1937).

Clajus, Johannes: *Variorum carminum libri quinque* (Görlitz 1568).

Clauss, Hermann: "Weigelianer in Nürnberg," *BBKG* 21 (1915), 267-271.

Clos, Albert: "Persönliche und literarische Beziehungen zwischen der preussischen und der Liegnitzer Reformation. Eine Untersuchung Zum Eindringen der Schwenckfeldschen Lehre in Preussen," *Jahrbuch für Ostpreussische Kirchengeschichte* 6 (1940), 23-63.

Cohrs, Ferdinand: *Die Evangelischen Katechismusversuche vor Luthers Enchiridion* (Berlin 1902).

Cosack, Carl Johann: *Paulus Speratus Leben und Lieder. Ein Beitrag zur Reformationsgeschichte, besonders zur Presussischen, wie zur Hymnologie* (Braunschweig 1861).

Croon, Gustav: "Zur Schlesischen Ortsnamenkunde. III. Zur Frage: Hinrichtung auf der Schweidnitzer 'Judenwiese' oder auf der 'Juden Weise,'" *ZVG Schles.* 41 (1907), 407-408.

Cunrad, Johann Heinrich: *Silesia togata, sive Silesiorum doctrina et virtutibus clarissimorum elogia, singulis distichis comprehensa...edidit Caspar Theophil. Schindlerus* (Liegnitz 1706).

Curaeus, Joachim: *Gentis Silesiae annales complectentes historiam de origine, propagatione et migrationibus gentis, et recitationem praecipuorum eventuum, qui in Ecclesia et Republica usque ad necem Ludovici Hungariae et Bohemiae regis acciderunt* (Wittenberg 1571).

Czerwenka, Karl: *Dr. Johann Fabri als Generalvikar in Konstanz (mit besonderer Berücksichtigung seiner Stellung zur Reformation)* (Diss. phil. Wien 1903).

Decretum Gratiani: *Corpus Iuris Canonici* (Graz 1955).

Dickmann, Fritz: *Der Westfälische Frieden* (Münster 1959).

Dollin, Norman: The Schwenckfelders in Eighteenth Century America

(Ph.D., Columbia University 1971).

Dorner, Isaak August: *Entwicklungsgeschichte der Lehre von der Person Christi von den ältesten Zeiten bis auf die neueste dargestellt* (Berlin 1853).

———: *Geschichte der protestantischen Theologie, besonders in Deutschland, nach ihrer principiellen Bewegung und im Zusammenhang mit dem religiösen, sittlichen und intellectuellen Leben betrachtet* (München 1867).

Duhr, Bernhard: *Geschichte der Jesuiten in den Ländern deutscher Zunge* (München and Regensburg 1928).

Eberlein, Gerhard: "Die Bauernprediger vom Jahre 1587 flgd.," *Correspondenz-Blatt* 4 (1894), 81-82.

———: *Die General-Kirchenvisitation im Füstentume Liegnitz von 1654-1655. Protokolle und Beilagen* (Liegnitz 1917).

———: *Die schlesischen Grenzkirchen im XVII. Jahrhundert* (Halle 1901).

———: "Die evangelischen Kirchenordnungen Schlesiens im 16. Jahrhundert," in *Silesiaca. Festschrift des Vereins für Geschichte und Alterthum Schlesiens zum siebzigsten Geburtstage seines Präses Colmar Grünhagen* (Breslau 1898), pp. 215-234.

———: "Aus Kirchen-Rechnungen des Reformations-Jahrhunderts," *Correspondenz-Blatt* 4 (1895), 102-110.

———: "Die erste evangelische Predigt in Schlesien," *Correspondenz-Blatt* 5 (1894), 65-77.

———: "Die erste evangelische Universität," *Evangelisches Kirchenblatt für Schlesien* 4 (1901), 281-282, 289-290, 297-298.

———: "Die Verhandlungen besonders der Breslauer in den Jahren 1526 und 1527," *ZVG Schles.* 36 (1902), 29-58.

———: "Der kirchliche Volksunterricht nach den Anschauungen der Schwenckfeldischen Kreise in Schlesien im ersten Drittel des 16. Jahrhunderts. Zugleich ein Beitrag zur Würdigung des Valentin Krautwald," *Correspondenz-Blatt* 7 (1900), 1-49.

———: "Die Wallfahrt Herzog Friedrichs II. von Liegnitz nach Jerusalem," *Evangelisches Kirchenblatt für Schlesien* 2 (1899), 31-33.

———: "Zur Würdigung des Valentin Krautwald," *Correspondenz-Blatt* 8 (1903), 268-286.

Eberlein, Hellmut: "Die sogenannte Synode zu Strehlen. (Am 15. September 1534.)," *JSchlKG* 25 (1935), 12-19.

Ecke, Karl: *Schwenckfeld, Luther und der Gedanke einer apostolischen Reformation* (Berlin 1911).

Egli, Emil: *Actensammlung zur Geschichte der Zürcher Reformation in den Jahren 1519-1533. Mit Unterstützung der Behörden von Canton und Stadt Zürich* (Zürich 1879).

———: *Analecta Reformatoria* (Zürich 1901).

Ehrhardt, Siegismund Justus: *Presbyterologie des Evangelischen Schlesiens* (Liegnitz 1782 and 1789).

Engelbert, Kurt: "Die Anfänge der lutherischen Bewegung in Breslau und Schlesien. I. Teil," *ArSKG* 18 (1960), 121-207.

Erbkam, Heinrich Wilhelm: *Geschichte der protestantischen Sekten im Zeitalter der Reformation* (Hamburg and Gotha 1848).

Erdmann, David: *Luther und seine Beziehungen zu Schlesien, insbesondere zu Breslau* (Halle 1887).

Eylenstein, Ernst: "Ludwig Friedrich Gifftheil. Zum mystischen Separatismus des 17. Jahrhunderts in Deutschland," *ZKG* 41 (1922), 1-62.

Fabri, Johannes: *Christenliche ableynung des erschröckenlichen yrrsal, so Caspar schwenckfelder in der Schlesy, wyder de warheyt des hoch wirdigenn Sacraments leibs vnd bluts Christi, auffzurichten vnderstandenn hat* (Mainz 1529).

Fast, Heinold: *Heinrich Bullinger und die Täufer. Ein Beitrag zur Historiographie und Theologie im 16. Jahrhundert* (Weierhof [Pfalz] 1959).

Fibiger, Michael Joseph: *Das in Schlesien gewaltthätig eingerissene Lutherthum, und die dadurch erfolgte schwere Verfolgung der Römischen Kirchen und Geistligkeit, denen Lutherischen Beschwer-Führungen... entgegengeleget* (Breslau 1723 and 1724).

Fischer, Christian Friedrich: *Geschichte und Beschreibung der schlesischen Fürstenthumshauptstadt Jauer* (Jauer 1804).

Flacius, Matthias: *Funnffzig grobe Irthumen der Stenckfeldischen Schwermerey, aus seinen eigenen Büchern trewlich zusamen gelesen vnd verzeichnet, damit sich die einfeltigen Christen desto fleissiger für seinem Gifft schewen vnd hüten. Vrteil von der Stenckfeldischen schwermerey der getrewen Diener in der Kirche zu Braunschweig vnd Hannouer. Der hochgelerten Theologen, zu Schmalkald Anno 1540. versamlet Vrteil von der Schwenckfeldischen Schwermery. Von den grewlichen jrthumen der newen Schwenckfeldischen Postill, vnter dem name des Johans Wörners, newlich ausgangen* (Jena 1559).

Fogger, Josef: "Beiträge zur Geschichte der evangelischen Kirche in der Grafschaft Glatz," in *Die Grafschaft Glatz. Deutschlands Erker, Gesundbrunnen und Herrgottswinkel. Bd. V. "Der Herrgottswinkel Deutschlands." Kirche und kirchliches Leben in der Grafschaft Glatz in einem Jahrtausend* Herausgegeben von Alois Bartsch und Leo Christoph (Lüdenscheid 1968), pp. 104-131.

Francke, Sebastian: *Von dem greüwlichen laster der trunckenhayt* (Augsburg 1528).

Freher, Paul: *Theatrum virorum eruditione clarorum* (Nürnberg 1688).

Fresenius, Johann Philipp: *Bewährte Nachrichten von Herrnhutischen Sachen. Bd. III* (Frankfurt and Leipzig 1748).

Freyer, Hieronymus: *Programmata latino-germanica cum additamento miscellaneorum vario* (Halle 1737).

Freys, Ernst and Barge, Hermann: *Verzeichnis der gedruckten Schriften des Andreas Bodenstein von Karlstadt* (Nieuwkoop 1965).

Friedlaender, Ernst: *Aeltere Universitäts-Matrikeln. I. Universität Frankfurt a. O. Aus der Originalhandschrift unter Mitwirkung von Georg Liebe und Emil Theuner herausgegeben von Ernst Friedlaender. Bd. I. (1506-1648)* (Leipzig 1887).

Friedmann, Robert: *Die Schriften der Huterischen Täufergemeinschaften. Gesamtskatalog ihrer Manuskriptbücher, ihrer Schreiber und ihrer Literatur 1529-1667. Mit 4 Tafeln* Zusammengestellt von Robert Friedmann unter Mitarbeit von Adolf Mais (Wien 1965).

Fritz, Friedrich: "Friedrich Gifftheil," *Bll. württ. KG* 44 (1940), 90-105.

———: "Konventikel in Württemberg von der Reformationszeit bis zum Edikt von 1743. (Erster Teil.)," *Bll. württ. KG* 49 (1949), 99-154.

Fuchtel, Paul: "Der Frankfurter Anstand vom Jahre 1539," *ARG* 28 (1931), 145-206.

Furcha, E.J.: "Key Concepts in Caspar von Schwenckfeld's Thought: Regeneration and the New Life," *ChH* 37 (1968), 160-173.

Fürst, Julius: *Bibliotheca Judaica. Bibliographisches Handbuch der gesammten jüdischen Literatur mit Einschluss der Schriften über Juden und Judenthum und einer Geschichte der jüdischen Bibliographie* (Hildesheim 1960).

Gansfort, Wessel: *Opera.* Facsimile of the Edition Groningen 1614. (Nieuwkoop 1966).

Gerber, Christian: *Historia derer Wiedergebohrnen in Sachsen* (Dresden 1726).

Gerhard, Elmer S.: "Balthasar Hoffmann (1687-1775). Scholar, Minister, Writer, Diplomat," *Schwenckfeldiana* 1 (1941), 2, 35-52.

Gerhard, Elmer S. and Schultz, Selina Gerhard: "The Schwenckfelders and the Moravians in Saxony, 1723-1734," *Schwenckfeldiana* 1 (1944), 4, 7-29.

Gichtel, Johann Georg: *Theosophia practica.* 3. Auflage. Bd. I (Leiden 1722).

Glombiowski, Karol: "Über die Verbreitung der Schriften des Erasmus von Rotterdam in Schlesien in der Zeit der Renaissance," *Kwartalnik historii nauki i techniki* 5 (1960).

Goeters, Gerhard: *Ludwig Hätzer (ca. 1500 bis 1529) Spiritualist und Antitrinitarier. Eine Randfigur der frühen Täuferbewegung* (Gütersloh 1957).

Goldmann, Eberhard: "Zur Geschichte der Kirchgemeinde Harpersdorf," (Liegnitz 1927/1928).

Goldmann, Karlheinz: *Verzeichnis der Hochschulen* (Neustadt an der Aisch 1967).

Gomolcke, Daniel (Schmied, Benjamin Gottlieb): *Der Heutigen Schlesischen Kirchenhistorie Dritter Theil, Worinnen alles dasjenige gezeigt wird, was sich währendem blutigem dreyssigjährigen Religions-Kriege in Schlesien sonderliches zugetragen hat* (1754).

Görlich, Franz Xaver: *Versuch einer Geschichte der Pfarrkirche zu Schweidnitz. Ein Beitrag zur schlesischen Kirchengeschichte. Zur 500 jährigen Jubelfeier* (Schweidnitz 1830).

Grünewald, Johannes: "Das älteste schlesische Gesangbuch," *JSchlKG NF* 43 (1964), 61-66.

———: *Predigergeschichte des Kirchendreises Goldberg* (Goldberg 1940).

———: *Predigergeschichte der Kirchenkreise Löwenberg I und II* (Liegnitz 1940).

———: *Predigergeschichte des Kirchendrieses Schönau. Bearbeitet von dem Primaner Grünewald, Goldberg. Druckfertig gemagt durch Pastor i.R Burkert, Hermsdorf Katzbach über Goldberg* (Glogau 1939).

Grünhagen, Colmar: *Geschichte des Ersten schlesischen Krieges nach archivalischen Quellen. Bd. II* (Gotha 1881).

———: *Geschichte Schlesiens. Bd. II* (Gotha 1886).

———: *Schlesien unter Friedrich dem Grossen* (Breslau 1890).

———: "Schlesien unter der Herrschaft König Ferdinands 1527-1564," *ZVG Schles.* 19 (1885), 63-139.

Grützmacher, Richard H.: "Schwenckfeld, Kaspar," in *RE* XVIII: 72-81.

———: *Wort und Geist. Eine historische und dogmatische Untersuchung zum Gnadenmittel des Wortes* (Leipzig 1902).

Guggisberg, Kurt: *Bernische Kirchengeschichte* (Bern 1958).

Hahn, Georg Ludwig: *Schwenckfeldii sententia de Christi persona et opere exposita. Commentatio historico—theologica* (Breslau 1847).

Hampe, O.: *Zur Biographie Kaspars v. Schwenckfeld* (Jauer 1882).

Hark, F.S.: "Der Konflikt der kursächsischen Regierung mit Herrnhut und dem Grafen von Zinzendorf. 1733-1738," *Neues Archiv für sächsische Geschichte* 3 (1882), 1-65.

Hartmann, Maximilian: *Die evangelische Kirche Schlesiens in geschichtlicher Entwickelung bis auf die Gegenwart* (Breslau 1928).

Hartranfft, Lorenz: *Ware, Christliche, vnd glimpffliche Widerlegung des Jrthumbs der Schwenckfelder* (Börlitz 1578).

Hasel, Gerhard F.: "Sabbatarian Anabaptists of the Sixteenth Century," *Andrews University Seminary Studies* 5 (1967), 101-121.

Heberle, Wilhelm: "W. Capito's Verhältniss zum Anabaptismus," ZHTh 27 (1857), 285-310.

Hege, Christian: "Baumhauer, Christoph," in *ME* I, 251.

———: "Baumhauer, Christoph," in *ML* I, 141.

Heinzelmann, Paul: "Beiträge zur Predigergeschichte der Grafschaft Glatz von 1524-1624," *Correspondenz-Blatt* 14 (1914), 1-62.

Helbling, Leo: *Dr. Johann Fabri. Generalvikar von Konstanz und Bischof von Wien 1478-1541. Beiträge zu seiner Lebensgeschichte* (Münster i. W. 1941).

Helden-, Staats- und Lebens-Geschichte . . . Friedrichs des Andern. Teil II (Frankfurt and Leipzig 1747).

Henel von Hennenfeld, Nikolaus: *Silesiographia renovata, necessariis scholiis, observationibus et indice aucta* (Breslau and Liepzig 1704).

Hensel, Johann Adam: *Protestantische Kirchen-Geschichte der Gemeinen in Schlesien* (Leipzig and Liegnitz 1768).

Hermelink, Heinrich: "Zu Luthers Gedanken über Idealgemeinden und von weltlicher Obrigkeit," *ZKG* 29 (1908), 267-322.

———: *Geschichte der evangelischen Kirche in Württemberg von der Reformation bis zur Gegenwart. Das Reich Gottes in Wirtemberg* (Stuttgart and Tübingen 1949).

Heubach, Joachim: "Die Aufgabe der christlichen Unterweisung bei den Böhmischen Brüdern," *ThZ* 14 (1958), 327-349.

Heumann, Johannes: *Documenta literaria varii argumenti in lucem prolata* (Altdorf 1758).

Heusler, Fritz: "Petrus Gynoraeus," *Zwingliana* 1 (1899), 120-122.

Heyne, Johann: *Dokumentirte Geschichte des Bisthums und Hochstifts Breslau. Aus Urkunden, Aktenstücken, älteren Chronisten und neueren Geschichtsschreibern. Bd. III. Denkwürdigkeiten aus der Geschichte der katholischen Kirche Schlesiens von der ersten Hälfte des 15. bis in die Mitte des 17. Jahrhunderts* (Breslau 1868).

———: *Urkundliche Geschichte der Stadt und des Fürstenthums Wohlau von den ältesten Zeiten bis auf die Gegenwart. (Nach authentischen Geschichtsquellen, Original-Urkunden und Aktenstücken.) Ein Beitrag zur kirchlichen und bürgerlichen Verfassungsgeschichte niederschlesischer Städte* (Wohlau 1867).

Hirsch, Emanuel: "Schwenckfeld und Luther," in Hirsch, Emanuel: *Lutherstudien. Bd. II* (Gütersloh 1954), pp. 35-67.

Hoffmann, Franz: *Caspar Schwenckfelds Leben und Lehren. Erster Teil* (Berlin 1897).

Hoffmann, Hermann and Engelbert, Kurt: "Aufzeichnungen des Breslauer Domherrn Stansilaus Sauer (gest. 1535) über den Bischof von Salza (1520 bis 1539) und seine Zeit. Ein Beitrag zur Vorgeschichte der Reformation in Schlesien,'' *ArSKG* 15 (1957), 124-170.

Höhne, Wolfgang: *Luthers Anschauungen über die Kontinuität der Kirche* (Berlin and Hamburg 1963).

Honecker, Martin ''Die Abendmahlslehre des Syngramma Seuvicum,'' *Bll.* *württ.* KG 65 (1965), 39-68.

Horawitz, Adalbert: ''Johann Heigerlin (genannt Fabri), Bischof von Wien, bis zum Regensburger Convent,'' *Sitzungsbericht der Philosophisch-Historischen Classe der Kaiserlichen Akademie der Wissenschaften* 107 (1884), 83-220.

Hruby, Frantisek: ''Die Wiedertäufer in Mähren,'' *ARG* 30 (1933), 1-36, 170-211; 31 (1934), 61-102; 32 (1935), 1-40.

Hubatsch, Walther: *Albrecht von Brandenburg-Ansbach Deutschordens-Hochmeister und Herzog in Preussen 1490-1568* (Heidelberg 1960).

Hubmaier, Balthasar: *Schriften* Herausgegeben von Gunnar Westin und Torsten Bergsten (Gütersloh 1962).

Jäck, Joachim Heinrich: *Pantheon der Literaten und Künstler Bambergs* (Erlangen 1812).

Jähne, Christoph Gottlob: *Dankbare Erinnerung an die Schwenckfelder in Nordamerika* (Görlitz 1816).

Jan, Johann Wilhelm: *Repetita demonstratio quod non hodiernae romanae sed evangelicae ecclesiae ministri habeant verum verbum Dei* (Wittenberg 1723).

———: *Verum Dei verbum ecclesiae evangelicae assertum. Dissertatio I. De methodo iesuitica convertendi Schwencfeldianos. 1721. Dissertatio II. Iterata et apodictica demonstratio quod non hodiernae romanae sed evangelicae ecclesiae ministri habeant verum verbum Dei. 1723* (Wittenberg 1726).

Jeremias, Joachim: *Die Kindertaufe in den ersten vier Jahrhunderten* (Göttingen 1958).

———: *Nochmals: Die Anfänge der Kindertaufe. Eine Replik auf Kurt Alands Schrift: ''Die Säuglingstaufe im Neuen Testament und in der alten Kirche''* (München 1962).

Jordan, Hermann: *Reformation und gelehrte Bildung in der Markgrafschaft Ansbach-Bayreuth. Eine Vorgeschichte der Universität Erlangen. I. Teil (bisgegen 1560)* (Leipzig 1917).

Jungnitz, Joseph: *Visitationsberichte der Diözese Breslau* (Breslau 1908).

Kadelbach, Oswald: *Geschichte des Dorfes Probsthayn, des Lehngutes und der Kirche vom Jahre 1200-1845 nebst zwei Anhängen* (Probsthayn 1846).

———: *Ausführliche Geschichte Kaspar v. Schwenkfelds und der Schwenkfelder in Schlesien, der Ober-Lausitz und Amerika, nebst ihren*

Glaubensschriften von 1524-1860, nach den vorhandenen Quellen bearbeitet (Lauban 1860).

Kahlo, Johann Gottlieb: *Denkwürdigkeiten der Königlichen Preussischen souverainen Grafschaft Glatz von ihrem ersten Ursprunge bis auf gegenwärtige Zeiten* (Berlin and Leipzig 1757).

Kantzenbach, Friedrich Wilhelm: "Johannes Brenz und der Kampf um das Abendmahl," *ThLZ* 89 (1964), 561-580.

Kastner, August: *Archiv für die Geschichte des Bisthums Breslau* (Neisse 1858/1866).

Kawerau, Gustav: *Der Briefwechsel des Justus Jonas* (Hildesheim 1964).

———: "Liturgische Studien zu Luthers Taufbüchlein von 1523," *ZWL* 10 (1889), 407-431, 466-477, 510-546, 578-599, 625-643.

Kawerau, Peter: *Melchior Hoffmann als religiöser Denker* (Haarlem 1954).

Kern, Karl: "Sebastianus Coccius, Rektor der Schwäbisch Haller Lateinschule (1525-1548). Ein Lebensbild," in *Württembergisch Franken NF* 8 (1903), 78-108.

Keseler, Caspar: "Catalogus pastorum ecclesiarum Lignicensium Petro-Paulinae et Marianae, ab initio reformationis usque ad annum 1653," in *Neue Beyträge von Alten und Neuen Theologischen Sachen* (Leipzig 1757), pp. 771-775.

Kessler, Johannes: *Sabbata mit kleineren Schriften und Briefen.* Unter Mitwirkung von Emil Egli und Rodolf Schoch herausgegeben vom Historischen Verein des Kantons St. Gallen (St. Gallen 1902).

Kihm, Engratis: "Die Drei-Wege-Lehre bei Tauler," in *Johannes Tauler. Ein deutscher Mystiker. Gedenkschrift zum 600. Todestag.* Herausgegeben von Ephrem Filthaut (Essen 1961), pp. 269-300.

Klampt, W.W.: *Urkundliche Chronik der Stadt und Herrschaft Neurode von ihrem Ursprunge bis auf die heutige Zeit, topographisch, statistisch und historisch dargestellt, nach den besten Quellen bearbeitet und mit den einschlagenden Urkunden belegt* (Neurode 1842).

Kliesch, Gottfried: *Der Einfluss der Universität Frankfurt (Oder) auf die schlesische Bildungsgeschichte dargestellt an den Breslauer Immatrikulierten von 1506-1648* (Würzburg 1961).

Klose, Konrad: Beiträge zur Geschichte der Stadt Lüben (Lüben 1924).

———: "Wer war der erste evangelische Pfarrer in Lüben?," *Correspondenz-Blatt* 12 (1911), 165-167.

———: "M. Franziskus Rosentritt. Ein Beitrag zur Lübener Kirchengeschichte aus der nachreformatorischen Zeit. *Correspondenz-Blatt* 10 (1907), 157-179.

———: "Schwenckfeld und die Schwenckfelder in Lüben. Ein Beitrag zur

Reformationsgeschichte der Stadt Lüben,'' *Correspondenz-Blatt* 11 (1909), 190-208.

Kluge, Gottlob: *Schlesischer Jubelpriester, worinnen das Leben Hundert Schlesischer Evangelisch-Lutherischer Jubelpriester beschrieben wird* (Breslau 1763).

Knörrlich, Siegfried: *Die Zufluchtskirche zu Harpersdorf in Schlesien* (Ulm 1963).

Knörrlich, Wolfgang: Kaspar von Schwenckfeld und die Reformation in Schlesien (Diss. phil. Bonn 1957).

Koch, Eduard Emil: *Geschichte des Kirchenlieds und Kirchengesangs der christlichen, insbesondere der deutschen evangelischen Kirche* (Stuttgart 1867).

Koffmane, Gustav: *Die religiöse Bewegungen in der evangelischen Kirche Schlesiens während des siebzehnten Jahrhunderts* (Breslau 1880).

———: ''Zu Luthers Briefen und Tischreden,'' *ThStKr* 58 (1885), 131-148.

———: ''Eine schlesische Universität in der Reformationszeit,'' *Correspondenz-Blatt* 2 (1883), 34-38.

———: ''Die Wiedertäufer in Schlesien,'' *Correspondenz-Blatt* 3 (1887), 37-55.

Kögler, Joseph: ''Historische und topographische Beschreibung der im Glatzer District gelegenen und zur Rengersdorfer Pfarreir gehörigen 5 Dörfer Rengersdorf, Eisersdorf, Märzdorf, Piltsch und Aspenau,'' *Vierteljahrsschrift für Geschichte und Heimatkunde der Grafschaft Glatz* 4 (1884/1885), 89-123; 213-232, 303-315.

———: ''Historische Nachrichten von der Pfarrkirche des hl. Erzengels Michael in der Königl. Preussischen Immediat-Stadt Habelschwerdt wie auch von allen übrigen Kirchen und Kapellen des gegenwärtigen Habelschwerdter Pfarrkirchensprengels,'' *Vierteljahrsschrift für Geschichte und Heimatkunde der Grafschaft Glatz* 1 (1881), 1-44, 97-108).

———: ''Kurzgefasste Regenten-Geschichte der Grafschaft Glatz,'' *Vierteljahrsschrift für Geschichte und Heimatkunde der Grafschaft Glatz* 4 (1884/1885), 1-26.

Köhler, Walther: *Bibliographia Brentiana. Bibliographisches Verzeichnis der gedruckten und ungedruckten Schriften und Briefe des Reformators Johannes Brenz. Nebst einem Verzeichnis der Literatur über Brenz, kurzen Erläuterungen und ungedruckten Akten* (Berlin 1904).

———: ''Kirchengeschichte vom Beginn der Reformation bis 1648,'' *Theologischer Jahresbericht* 28 (1909), 437-615.

———: *Zwingli und Luther. Ihr Streit über das Abendmahl nach seinen politischen und religiöse Beziehungen. Bd. I. Die religiöse und politische Entwicklung bis zum Marburger Religionsgespräch 1529* (Leipzig 1924). *Band*

II. Vom Beginn der Marburger Verhandlungen 1529 bis zum Abschluss der Wittenberger Kondordie von 1536 (Gütersloh 1953).

Kolb, Christoph: "Abraham und Ludwig Friedrich Giftheil," *Bll. württ. KG NF* 4 (1900), 75-82.

Kolde, Theodor: "Luthers Gedanke von der ecclesiola in ecclesia," *ZKG* 13 (1892), 552-555.

Köllner, Johann Christian: *Wolaviographia, oder accurate Beschreibung der Stadt Wolau in Schlesien* (Bautzen 1728).

Konrad, Paul: *Die Einführung der Reformation in Breslau und Schlesien. Ein Rückblick nach 400 Jahren* (Breslau 1917).

———: *Dr. Ambrosius Moibanus. Ein Beitrag zur Geschichte der Kirche und Schule Schlesiens im Reformationszeitalter* (Halle 1891).

Kopietz, J. Athanasius: "Wallensteins Armee in Schlesien im Jahre 1626 und im Frühjahr 1627," *ZVG Schles.* 12 (1874), 480-487.

Köpke, Adam: *Historische Nachricht von dem vor zweyhundert Jahren berühmten und verruffenen Schlesischen Edelmann, Herrn Caspar Schwenkfeld von Ossing, samt beygefügter Anzahl seiner Schrifften* (Prentzlau 1744).

Körner, Ferdinand: *Die kursächsische Staatsregierung dem Grafen Zinzendorf und Herrnhut bis 1760 gegenüber. Nach den Acten des Hauptstaatsarchiv zu Dresden dargestellt* (Leipzig 1878).

Krautwald, Valentin: *Ein nutzbar Edell Buchleinn von bereytunge zum sterben, mit underricht wie sich in den anfechtungen doselbst zu haldenn sey, auss dem latein, mit eyll und eynfeldig gedeutscht. Durch Valten krautwalt von der Neysse* (Breslau 1524).

Krebs, Julius: "Zur Geschichte der inneren Verhältnisse Schlesiens von der Schlacht am weissen Berge bis zum Einmarsche Waldsteins," *ZVG Schles.* 16 (1882), 33-62.

———: "Schlesien in den Jahren 1626 und 1627," *ZVG Schles.* 20 (1886), 1-32; 21 (1887), 116-148; 25 (1891), 124-184.

Krebs, Manfred: "Einleitung zu Martin Bucers 'Getrewe Warnung gegen Jacob Kautz' (1527)," in Bucer, Martin *Opera omnia. Series I. Deutsche Schriften.* (Gütersloh 1962), pp. 227-233.

Krentzheim, Leonhard: *Leichpredigt. Über der Begrebnis, der Gottseligen, Edlen, Ehr vnd Tugendtreichen Jungfrawen Sabina, Des Edlen, Wolehrnvesten Herrn Barthel von Logaw, von Olberssdorff, Weiland Fürstliches Lignitzisches Rath vnd Hoffmeisters, in Gottseligen, nachgelassenen Tochter. Darinnen zu gleich kürtzlich mit eingebracht, eine gründtliche verlegung des Schwenckfeldischen Jrthumbs von Wort Gottes. Gepredigt durch Leonhart Krentzheim von Jphofen, Pfarherr in vnser lieben Frawen Kirch zu Lignitz, den 17. Maij, des 1570* (Görlitz 1571).

Kretschmar, Georg: *Die Reformation in Breslau. I* (Ulm 1960).

Kriebel, Howard Wiegner: *The Schwenkfelders in Pennsylvania. A historical sketch* (Lancaster 1904).

Kriebel, Lester E. and Schultz, Selina Gerhard: "George Weiss (1687-1740). First Schwenkfelder Minister in Pennsylvania," *Schwenckfeldiana* 1 (1941), 2,5-33.

Kriebel, Martha: *Schwenckfeld and the Sacraments* (Pennsburg 1968).

Kriebel, Wilber C. and Hein, Gerhard: "Schwenckfelder," in *ML* IV, 139-140.

Krodel, Gottfried: *Die Abendmahlslehre des Erasmus von Rotterdam und seine Stellung am Anfang des Abendmahlsstreites der Reformatoren* (Diss. theol. Erlangen 1955).

Kruse, Martin: *Speners Kritik am landesherrlichen Kirchenregiment und ihre Vorgeschichte* (Witten 1971).

Laag, Heinrich: "Die Einführung der Reformation im Ordensland Preussen," *NKZlie 36* (1925), 845-873.

Lackner, Martin: *Geistesfrömmigkeit und Enderwartung. Studien zum preussischen und schlesischen Spiritualismus dargestellt an Christoph Barthut und Quirin Kuhlmann* (Stuttgart 1959).

Leemann van Elck, Paul: *Eie Offizin Froschauer. Zürichs berühmte Druckerei im 16. Jahrhundert. Ein Beitrag zur Geschichte der Buchdruckerkunst anlässlich der Halbjahrtausendfeier ihrer Erfindung* (Zürich and Leipzig 1940).

Leendertz, Willem Izaak: *Melchior Hofmann* (Haarlem 1883).

Leimbach, Carl Ludwig: *Beiträge zur Abendmahlslehre Tertullians* (Gotha 1874).

Lenfant, David: *Concordantiae Augustinianae, sive collectio omnium sententiarum quae sparsim reperiuntur in omnibus S. Augustini operibus. Ad instar concordantiarum Sacrae Scripturae* (Paris 1656-1665).

Levering, Joseph Mortimer: *A History of Bethlehem, Pennsylvania 1741-1892 with some account of its founders and their early activity in America* (Bethlehem, Pa. 1903).

Lichtstern, Friedrich: *Schlesische Fürsten-Krone, oder eigentliche, warhaffte Beschreibung Ober- und Nieder-Schlesiens* (Frankfurt am Main 1685).

Liefmann, Gottlieb: *Dissertatio historica de fanaticis Silesiorum et speciatim Quirino Kuhlmanno* (Wittenberg 1698).

Loetscher, Frederick William: "Schwenckfeld's Participation in the Eucharistic Controversry of the Sixteenth Century," *The Princeton Theological Review* 4 (1906), 352-386, 454-50

Löffler, Paul: "Die Trinitätslehre des Bischofs Hilarius von Poitiers zwischen Ost und West," *ZKG* 71 (1960), 26-36.

Löscher, Valentin Ernst: *Ausführliche Historia Motuum zwischen den Evangelisch-Lutherischen und Reformirten* (Frankfurt am Main and Leipzig 1707).

———: *Schvengfeldismum in Pietismo renatum praeside Val. Ernesto Loeschero. . . autor Samuel Zelenka* (Wittenberg 1708).

Loserth, Johann: "Oswald Glayt," *Zeitschrift des Vereins für die Geschichte Mährens und Schlesiens* 1 (1897), 70-73.

Lucae, Friedrich: *Schlesiens curieuse Denckwürdigkeiten, oder vollkommene Chronica von Ober- und Nieder-Schlesien* (Frankfurt am Main 1689).

Luschek, Fritz: *Notariatsurkunde und Notariat in Schlesien von den Anfängen (1282) bis zum Ende des 16. Jahrhunderts* (Weimar 1940).

Maier, Paul Luther: "Caspar Schwenckfeld—A quadricentennial evaluation," *ARG* 54 (1963), 89-97.

———: *Caspar Schwenckfeld on the Person and Work of Christ* (Assen 1959).

Maron, Gottfried: *Individualismus und Gemeinschaft bei Caspar von Schwenckfeld. Seine Theologie dargestellt mit besonderer Ausrichtung auf seinen Kirchenbegriff* (Stuttgart 1961).

———: "Schwenckfelder," in ibRGG V, 1622-1623.

Mathesius, Johannes: *Ausgewählte Werke. Bd. III. Luthers Leben in Predigten.* Herausgegeben, erläutert und eingeleitet von George Loesche (Prag 1898).

Maurer, Wilhelm: "Die Zeit der Reformation," in *Kirche und Synagoge. Handbuch zur Geschichte von Christen und Juden. Darstellung mit Quellen* (Stuttgart 1968), pp. 363-452.

Meckelburg, Adolf: "Chronik des Johannes Freiberg (für die Jahre von 1529 bis 1532)," *Neue Preussische Provinzial-Blätter* 4 (1847), 475-487.

Meiern, Johann Gottfried v.: *Acta pacis Westphalicae publica. Oder: Westphälische Friedens-Handlungen und Geschichte* (Hannover 1735).

Meisner, Heinrich and Röhricht, Reinhold: "Pilgerschriften I. Die Pilgerfahrt des Herzogs Friedrich II. von Liegnitz und Brieg nach dem heiligen Lande und die Descriptio templi Domini von Philippus de Aversa," *ZDPV* 1 (1878), 101-131, 171-215.

Melanchthon, Philipp: *Melanchthons Werke in Auswahl Unter Mitwirkung von Hans Engelland,* Gerhard Ebeling, Richard Nürnberger und Hans Volz (Gütersloh 1952).

Meyer, Christian: "Zur Geschichte der Wiedertäufer in Oberschwaben. I. Die Anfänge des Wiedertäuferthums in Augsburg," *Zeitschrift des Historischen Vereins für Schwaben und Neuburg* 1 (1874), 207-253.

Meynen, Emil: *Bibliographie des Deutschtums der kolonialzeitlichen Einwanderung in Nordamerika insbesondere der Pennsylvanien-Deutschen und ihrer Nachkommen 1683-1933* (Leipzig 1937).

Milan, Johann: *Examinator methodi jesuiticae convertendi Schwenckfeldianos* (Prag 1721).

———: *Lang geborgt, ist nicht geschenckt. Das ist: Die vorlängst schrifftlich verfasste, nun in offentlichen Druck gelegte Verthädigung dess Liechts in den Finsternussen, wider alle aus der Finsternuss anfliegende, und löschenwollende Mucken. Teil I-III* (Augsburg 1736-1737).

———: *Fünff kurtze und gründliche auss allgemeinen von jedem so nur den Christlichen Nahmen führen will zugestandenen Lehr-Sätzen gezogene Beweissthümer: Dass neimand bey gutem Gewissen der Schwenckfeldischen Sect beypflichten oder mit gesunder Vernunft in selbiger verbleiben könne* (Neisse 1720).

Moibanus, Ambrosius: *Catechismi capita decem, primum quibusdam thematis, deinde etiam colloquiis puerilibus illustrata, iuventuti Wratislaviensi proposita* (Wittenberg 1538).

———: *Ad magnificum ac generosum. Domin. Joannem Baronem a Bernstein, in Helfenstein. An communio infantium, quae apud quosdam servatur, probetur Ecclesiae. D. Ambrosius Moibanus parochus Vratislaviensis. Item libellus de officio principum. Phil. Melan.* (Vratislaviae 1541).

Müller, Nikolaus: *Die Wittenberger Bewegung 1521 und 1522. Die Vorgänge in und um Wittenberg während Luthers Wartburgaufenthalt. Briefe, Akten u. dgl. und Personalien* (Leipzig 1911).

Gesamlete Nachrichten und Documente den gegenwärtigen Zustand des Hertzogthums Schlesiens, Königreichs Böhmen, und Ertz-Hertzogthum Oesterreichs betreffend (1742).

Näf, Werner: *Vadian und seine Stadt St. Gallen* (St. Gallen 1957).

Neaetius, Christoph: "Liber Proventuum, Dotum ecclesiarum singularum, nec non et quarundam signaturarum ad Archidiaconi seu Decani Officium spectantium, propria manu conscriptus, in communem utilitatem Fratrum Comitatus Glacensis. Geschichtsquellen der Grafschaft Glatz. Bd. III (Habelschwerdt 1884), pp. 13-80.

Neustadt, Louis: "Aufenthaltsorte des Markgrafen Georg von Brandenburg," *Archiv für Geschichte und Alterthumskunde von Oberfranken* 15 (1883), 231-257.

Nicolovius, Alfred: *Die Bischöfliche Würde in Preussens evangelischer Kirche. Ein Beitrag zur Geschichte des evangelischen Kirchenrechtes* (Königsberg 1834).

Nova literaria Germaniae (Hamburg 1705).

Otto, Carl: "Über die Wahl Jacobs von Salza zum Bischof von Breslau und die derselben unmittelbar folgenden Ereignisse. (September 1520 bis September 1521)," *ZVG Schles.* 11 (1871), 303-327.

Palm, Hermann: "Der Dresdner Accord 1621," *ZVG Schles.* 13 (1876), 151-192.

———: "Schlesiens Antheil am dreissigjährigen Kriege vom Juli bis December 1620," *SVG Schles.* 12 (1874), 285-336.

———: "Die Conjunction der Herzöge von Liegnitz, Brieg und Oels sowie der Stadt und das Fürstentums Breslau mit den Kurfürsten von Sachsen und Brandenburg und der Krone Schweden in den Jahren 1633-1635," *ZVG Schles.* 3 (1861), 227-368.

Peschel, Carl Wilhelm: *Die Geschichte der Stadt Goldberg. 2. gekürzte Auflage* (Goldberg 1841).

Peschke, Erhard: *Die Böhmischen Brüder im Urteil ihrer Zeit. Zieglers, Dungersheims und Luthers Kritik an der Brüderunität* (Stuttgart 1964).

———: "Der Kirchenbegriff des Bruder Lukas von Prag," *Wissenschaftliche Zeitschrift der Universität Rostock* (Gesellschafts-und Sprachwissenschaftliche Reihe) 5, 273-288.

———: *Die Theologie der Böhmischen Brüder in ihrer Frühzeit* (Stuttgart 1935).

Peter Chelcickyu: "Von den Sakramenten," in Peschke, Erhard: *Die Theologie der Böhmischen Brüder in ihrer Frühzeit. Bd. I. Das Abendmahl. II. Texte aus alttschechischen Handschriften übersetzt* (Stuttgart 1940).

Peters, Johann: *Die Ehe nach der Lehre des hl. Augustinus* (Paderborn 1918).

Petersen, Johann Wilhelm: *Lebens-Beschreibung* (2nd ed., 1719).

Petrus Lombardus: *Libri IV Sententiarum, studio et cura PP. Collegii S. Bonaventurae in lucem editi. Liber III. et IV. Tomus II* (2nd ed., Claras Aquas 1916).

Pfaff, Christoph Matthäus: *Acta et scripta ecclesiae publica Wirtembergicae* (Tübingen 1720).

Pfeiffer, Gerhard: *Das Breslauer Patriziat im Mittelalter* (Breslau 1929).

Pfotenhauer, Paul: "Die Pförtner von Neumarkt und ihre Aufzeichnungen," *ZVG Schles.* 20 (1886), 260-296.

Pietz, Reinhold: *Der Mensch ohne Christus. Eine Untersuchung zur Anthropologie Caspar Schwenckfelds* (Diss. theol. Tübingen 1956).

Pol, Nikolaus: *Jahrbücher der Stadt Breslau. Zum erstenmale aus dessen eigener Handschrift herausgegeben von Johann Gustav Büsching. Bd. III* (Breslau 1819).

Pölnitz, Götz v.: *Jakob Fugger. Kaiser, Kirche und Kapital in der oberdeutschen Renaissance* (Tübingen 1949 and 1952).

Preger, Wilhelm: *Matthias Flacius Illyricus und seine Zeit. Erste Hälfte* (Erlangen 1859).

Erleutertes Preussen oder auserlesene Anmerckungen über verschiedene zur Preussischen Kirchen- Civil und Gelehrten-Historie gehörige besondere Dinge. Tomus I (Königsberg 1724).

Kayser- und Königl. das Erb-Hertzogthum Schlesien concernirende privilegia, statuta und sanctiones pragmaticae, mit allergnädigster Kayser- und Königl. Bewilligung, dem gemeinen Wesen zum besten zusammen getragen (Breslau 1731).

Radecker, Caspar: *Bericht ob weltlich Gewalt die Schrifften vnd Bücher der Schwermer frey zu zu lassen, oder aber weg zu nemen, schüldig sey, wider jtzige vnchristliche Rotten vnd Secten, gestellt* (Wittenberg 1556).

———: *Erklerung dreier Frage, zu notdürfftigem vnterricht der Kirchen zu Lewenberg, vnd ablenung falscher jrriger Lehr, der jenigen so meine Kirchen gern jrr machen, zustören vnd zurütten wolten* (Görlitz 1567).

Ratkos, Petr: "Die Anfänge des Widertäufertums in der Slowakei," in *Aus 500 Jahren deutsch-tschechoslowakischer Geschichte* herausgegeben von Karl Obermann und Josef Polisensky (Berlin 1958), pp. 41-59.

Regent, Karl Xaver: *Christliche Ablehnung derer Haupt-Unwahrheiten, welche die Schwenckfelder in einer Schrifft, (so genannte) Glaubens-Bekandtnuss der Neubekehrten Catholischen, höchst-sträfflich und vermessentlich auffgesetzet haben* (Neisse 1724).

———: *Der Neu-bekehrte Catholische Christ, oder ausserlesene Unterricht christlich, catholisch zu leben und zu sterben, denen Recht-Glaubigen zum Trost; denen Jrr-Glaubigen zur Nachricht vorgestellet* (Neisse 1723).

———: *Exempel der Schlesier, oder Vorstellung der fürnehmsten christlichen Tugenden, welche die vormahlen durchleuchtigste Hertzogin in Schlesien, anjetzo glorwürdigste Himmels-Fürstin, gnädigste Schutz-Frau und Landes-Mutter S. Hedwig zur Lebens-Zeit heylsam geübet, und nach dem Tod zur Nachübung hinterlassen. In eine trost-reiche Frucht bringende Andacht, besonders vor die nach Closter Trebnitz wallfahrtende Catholische Christen eingerichtet* (Neisse 1723).

———: *Der auss eigenem Gesang-Buch, und sonsten gebrauchlichen Büchern, dess Irrthums, überzeugte Schwenckfelder* (Neisse 1724).

———: *Gewissens-Scrupel, warumb es wider das Gewissen der Schwenckfelder seyn soll; ihre Lehr zu verlassen, hingegen den Catholischen Glauben anzunehmen, gewissenhafft auffgelöset. Zugleich: Dass die Schwenckfelder mit guten Gewissen den Röhmischen Glauben können annehmen, und sich zur Catholischen Kirchen bekennen; hingegen in ihrem Gewissen verbunden seynd, die Schwenckfeldische Lehr zu verlassen gewissenhafft bewiesen* (Neisse 1724).

———: *Heylsame Lehr-Stuck, für die Neu-bekehrte Recht-Glaubige Catholische Christen, wie auch für die Uncatholische, wie und auff was Weise selbste zum wahren Seeligmachenden Glauben gelangen mögen. Nebst den nothwen-*

digsten Glaubens-Puncten, besonders zum Nutzen für die zarte Jugend, der Neu-bekehrten Catholischen (Neisse 1723).

———: *Zusatz derer übrigen Jrrthümer welche die im Hertzogthum Schlesien befindliche Schwenckfelder in denen (so genannten) Glaubens-Bekandtnüssen arglistig verschwiegen. Teil I-V* (Neisse 1722-1724).

Reichel, Gerhard: *August Gottlieb Spangenberg, Bischof der Brüderkirche* (Tübingen 1906).

Reitzig, Hans: "Erste evang. Universität Deutschlands einst in Liegnitz. Zur 425. Wiederkehr ihres Begründungstages," *Der Schlesier* 4 (1952), 1, 6.

Reu, Johann Michael: *Quellen zur Geschichte des Katechismus-Unterrichts. Bd. II. Mittledeutsche Katechismen. Zweite Abteilung: Texte* (Gütersloh 1911).

Rican, Rudolf: *Die Böhmischen Brüder. Ihr Ursprung und ihre Geschichte* (Berlin 1961).

Richter, Aemilius Ludwig: *Die evangelischen Kirchenordnungen des sechzehnten Jahrhunderts. Urkunden und Regesten zur Geschichte des Rechts und der Verfassung der evangelischen Kirche in Deutschland* (Weimar 1846).

Roepell, Richard: "Das Verhalten Schlesiens zur Zeit der böhmischen Unruhen. März bis Juli 1618," *ZVG Schles.* 1 (1855), 1-32.

Rordorf, Willy: *Der Sonntag. Geschichte des Ruhe- und Gottesdiensttages im ältesten Christentum* (Zürich 1962).

Rosenberg, Abraham Gottlob: *Schlesische Reformations-Geschichte* (Breslau 1767).

Sammlung aller in dem sourverainen Herzogthum Schlesien und dessen incoporirten Grafschafft Glatz in Finanz-Justitz-Criminal-Geistlichen-Consistorial-Kirchen-Sachen etc. publicirten und ergangenen Ordnungen, Edicten, Mandaten, Rescripten etc. welche von der Zeit der glorwürdigsten Regierung Friedrichs Königes in Preussen als souverainen obersten Herzogs von Schlesien vom 1. Decembr. 1740. bis inclusive 1744. heraus gekommen und durch den Druck bekannt gemacht worden (Breslau).

Sartori, Paul: "Lätare," in *Handwörterbuch des deutschen Aberglauben 5 Bd. V.* (Berlin and Leipzig 1932/1933), pp. 918-922.

Scheibel, Johann Ephraim: *Geschichte der seit dreihundert Jahren in Breslau befindlichen Stadtbuchdruckerey als ein Beitrag zur allgemeinen Geschichte der Buchdruckerkunst* (Breslau 1804).

Schickfuss, Jakob: *New vermehrete Schlesische Chronica vnnd Landes Beschreibung* (Leipzig).

Schimmelpfennig, Adolf: "Herzog Karl I. von Münsterberg-Oels und seine Schwester Margaretha von Anhalt. Nach ungedruckten Briefen aus den Jahren 1503-1530," *ZVG Schles.* 18 (1884), 117-161.

Schleiff, Arnold: *Selbstkritik der lutherischen Kirchen im 17. Jahrhundert* (Berlin 1937).

Schmidt, Joseph: "Herzog Ernst von Bayern und die erste Glatzer Gegenreformation (1549-1560)," *Blätter für Geschichte und Heimatkunde der Grafschaft Glatz* 2 (1914), 22-50.

Schmidt, Martin: "Teilnahme an der göttlichen Natur. 2. Petrus 1,4 in der theologischen Exegese des Pietismus und der lutherischen Orthodoxie," in *Dank an Paul Althaus. Eine Festgabe zum 70. Geburtstag, dargebracht von Freunden, Kollegen und Schülern.* Herausgegeben von Walter Künneth und Wilfried Joest (Gütersloh 1958), pp. 171-201.

Schneider, August Friedrich Heinrich: *Zur Literatur der Schwenckfeldischen Liederdichter bis Daniel Sudermann* (Berlin 1857).

———: *Ueber den geschichtlichen Verlauf der Reformation in Liegnitz und ihren späteren Kampf gegen die kaiserliche Jesuiten-Mission in Harpersdorf. Abtheilung I. und II* (Berlin 1860/1862).

Schneider, Daniel: *Anonyme Rez.: Unpartheyische Prüfung des Caspar Schwengfelds und Gründliche Vertheydigung der Augspürgischen Confession. Giessen 1708. Unschuldige Nachrichten von Alten und Neuen Theologische Sachen* (Leipzig 1708), pp. 228-231.

Schnell, Heinrich: *Heinrich V., der Friedfertige, Herzog von Mecklenburg* (Halle 1902).

Schoeps, Hans Joachim: *Vom himmlischen Fleisch Christi. Eine dogmengeschichtliche Untersuchung* (Tübingen 1951).

Scholz, Paul: "Vertreibung der Bernhardiner aus Liegnitz im Jahre 1524," *ZVG Schles.* 12 (1874), 359-378.

Schornbaum, Karl: *Die Stellung des Markgrafen Kasimir von Brandenburg zur reformatorischen Bewegung in den Jahren 1524-1527 auf Grund archivalischer Forschungen* (Nürnberg 1900).

Schottenloher, Karl: "Der Pforzheimer Buckdrucker Georg Rab und die beschlagnahmte Postille des Schwenckfeldjüngers Johann Werner 1558," *Zeitschrift für die Geschichte des Oberrheins* 81 (1928), 400-411.

———: "Johann Fabri in Rom, nach einem Berichte Jakob Zieglers," *ARG* 5 (1907/1908), 31-47.

Schubart, Sebastian: "Vorrede wieder die Lehre der Schwenckfelder," in Bahlow, Ferdinand: *Die Reformation in Liegnitz* (Liegnitz 1918), pp. 149-154.

[Schultz, Christoph u.a.]: *Erläuterung für Herrn Caspar Schwenckfeld, und die Zugethanen, seiner Lehre, wegen vieler Stücke, beydes aus der Historie und Theologie, welche insgemein unrichtig vorgestellet, oder gar übergangen werden* (Jauer 1771).

Schultz, Selina Gerhard: "History of the 'Erläuterung,' " *Schwenckfeldiana* 1 (1940), 1,21-24.

———: *Caspar Schwenckfeld von Ossig (1489-1561). Spiritual Interpreter of Christianity, Apostle of the Middle Way, Pioneer in Modern Religious Thought* (Norristown, Pa. 1946).

Schultze, Otto: *Predigergeschichte des Kirchenkreises Schweidnitz-Reichenbach* (Glogau 1938).

Seckendorf, Veit Ludwig v.: *Commentarius historicus et apologeticus de Lutheranismo seu de Reformatione* (Frankfurt and Leipzig 1692).

Seebass, Gottfried: *Bibliographia Osiandrica. Bibliographie der gedruckten Schriften Andreas Osianders d. Ä. (1496-1592)* (Nieuwkoop 1971).

Seeberg, Erich: "Der Gegensatz zwischen Zwingli, Schwenckfeld und Luther," in *Reinhold-Seeberg-Festschrift. Bd. I* (Leipzig 1929), pp. 43-80.

Sippell, Theodor: "Caspar Schwenckfeld," *ChW* 25 (1911), 866-871, 897-900, 925-927, 955-957, 963-966.

Smulders, Pierre: *La doctrine trinitaire de S. Hilaire de Poitiers. Étude précédée d'une esquisse du mouvement dogmatique depuis le Concile de Nicée juspu'an règne de Julien (325-362)* (Rome 1944).

Soffner, Johannes: "Schlesische Fürstenbriefe aus der Reformationszeit," *ZVG Schles.* 21 (1887), 399-415.

———: *Geschichte der Reformation in Schlesien* (Breslau 1887).

Söhnel, Hermann: "Zur Kirchengeschichte des Fürstentums Wohlau," *Correspondenz-Blatt* 17 (1920), 51-63.

Sommersberg, Friedrich Wilhelm v.: *Silesiacarum rerum scriptores* (Leipzig 1729).

Spangenberg, August Gottlieb: *Leben des Herrn Nicolaus Ludwig Grafen und Herrn von Zinzendorf und Pottendorf. Teil I. und II* (between 1772 and 1775).

Spener, Philipp Jakob: *Theologische Bedencken und andere brieffliche Antworten. Teil I* (Halle 1700).

———: *Letzte Theologische Bedencken und andere brieffliche Antworten. Teil I II* (Halle 1711).

Staehelin, Ernst: *Briefe und Akten zum Leben Oekolampads. Zum vierhundertjährigen Jubiläum der Basler Reformation herausgegeben von der theologischen Fakultät der Universität Basel.* Bearbeitet von Ernst Staehelin. Bd. I: 1499-1526 (Leipzig 1927). Bd. II: 1527-1593 (Leipzig 1934).

———: *Oekolampad-Bibliographie* (Nieuwkoop 1963).

Staub, Ignaz: *Dr. Johann Fabri, Generalvikar von Konstanz (1518-1523), bis zum offenen Kampf gegen M. Luther (August 1522)* (Einsideln [Schweiz] 1911).

Steinberg, Michael: "Chronik Michael Steinbergs," in Schimmelpfennig, Adolf and Schönborn, Theodor: *Schweidnitzer Chronisten des XVI. Jahrhunderts* (Breslau 1878).

Stumpf, Margarete: *Beiträge zur Geschichte des Klosters Trebnitz bis zur Mitte des 15. Jahrhunderts* (Diss. phil. Breslau 1936).

Sturm, Ludwig: *Geschichte der Stadt Goldberg in Schlesien* (Goldberg 1888).

Sutorius, Benjamin Gottlieb: Die Geschichte von Löwenberg aus Urkunden und Handschriften. Zweiter Theil, welcher die Geschichte der Kirchen und Schulen dieser Königl. Preussl. Schlesischen Creiss-Stadt und der Landkirchen über welche die Stadt das Kirchlehn ausübet, enthält (Jauer 1787).

Tauler, Johannes: *Predigten, Vollständige Ausgabe* Übertragen und herausgegeben von Georg Hofmann (Freiburg, Basel, Wien 1961).

Teichmann, A.: *Chronik der Stadt Bolkenhain in Schlesien, von den ältesten Zeiten bis zum Jahre 1870* (Bolkenhain).

Thamm, Joseph: *Geschichte der Stadt Habelschwerdt, nebst einem Anhange über die Vesten des Habelschwerdter Kreises* (Habelschwerdt 1841).

Thebesius, Georg: *Liegnitzische Jahr-Bücher. Teil I-III* (Jauer 1733).

Tobolka, Zdenek Vaclav: *Michael Weisses Ein new Gesangbuchlein aus d. J. 1531 und sein Drucker Georg Styrsa* (Prag 1931).

Trotzendorf, Valentin: *Catechesis scholae Goltpergensis, scripta a Valentino Trocedorfio, cuius eximia fuit eruditio, et pietas. Cum praefatione Philip. Melanth.* (Wittenberg 1558).

———: *Precationes reverendi viri, Valentini Trocedorfii, Recitatae in schola Goltbergensi, pleraeque anno proximo ante mortem ex ore eius exeptae, et editae opera Laurentii Ludovici Leobergensi* (Wittenberg 1565).

Tschackert, Paul: "Friedrich von Heidek, Herr auf Johannisburg und Lötzen (died 1536)," *Sitzungsbericht der Altertumsgesellschaft Prussia* 17 (1892), 67-71.

———: Urkundenbuch zur Reformationsgeschichte des Herzogthums Preussen. Bd. I-III (Osnabrück 1965).

Urner, Hans: "Die Taufe bei Caspar Schwenckfeld," *ThLZ* 73 (1948), 329-342.

Usteri, Johann Martin: "Die Stellung der Strassburger Reformatoren Bucer und Capito zur Tauffrage," *ThStKr* 57 (1884), 456-525.

Velsen, Dorothee v.: *Die Gegenreformation in den Fürstentümern Liegnitz-Brieg-Wohlau. Ihre Vorgeschichte und ihre staatsrechtlichen Grundlagen* (Leipzig 1931).

Vogt, Otto: *Dr. Johannes Bugenhagens Briefwechsel* (Hildesheim 1966).

Voigt, Emil: "Die Burg Kynast und ihre Bestizer. II. Teil. Im 16. und 17. Jahrhundert," *ArSKG* 21 (1963), 215-254.

Völkel, Richard: *Die persönliche Zusammensetzung des Neisser Kollegiatkapitels während seiner Residenz in der Alstadt Neisse 1477-1650 an der Kollegiatkirche SS. Johannes Ev. und Nikolaus. 42. Bericht der Wissenschaftlichen Gesellschaft Philomathie in Neisse vom Oktober 1935 bis Februar 1938. 98. bis 100. Geschäftsjahr zugleich Festschrift zur Hundertjahr-Feier* (Neisse 1938).

Volkmer, Franz: "Auszüge aus einer Reihe Glatzer Chroniken. I. Aus der Chronik des lutherischen Schneiders Pankraz Scholz zu Glatz und seines Sohnes Nickel," *Vierteljahrsschrift für Geschichte und Heimatkunde der Grafschaft Glatz 10 (1890/91), 316-325.*

———: *Geschichte der Stadt Habelschwerdt in der Grafschaft Glatz (Habelschwerdt 1897).*

———: *"Geschichte der Stadt Habelschwerdt bis zum 30jährigen Kriege," Vierteljahrsschrift für Geschichte und Heimatkunde der Grafschaft Glatz* 10 (1890/91), 1-50.

———: "Denkwürdige Männer aus und in der Grafschaft Glatz (Gelehrte, Schriftsteller, Dichter, Würdenträger). Erster Nachtrag," *Vierteljahrsschrift ür Geschichte und Heimatkunde der Grafschaft Glatz* 8 (1888/89), 224-237.

Volz, Hans: "Die Breslauer Luther- und Reformationsdrucker Adam Dyon und Kaspar Libisch," *Gutenberg-Jahrbuch* 42 (1967), 104-117.

———: *Urkunden und Aktenstücke zur Geschichte von Martin Luthers Schmalkaldischen Artikeln (1536-1575)* (Berlin 1957).

Wach, Joachim: *Types of Religious Experience Christian and Non-christian* (London 1951).

Wachler, Albrecht: "Leben und Wirken Caspar Schwenckfeld's v. Ossig während seines Aufenthalts in Schlesien 1490-1528," *Schlesische Provinzialblätter* 97 (1833), 119-130, 209-221, 301-310, 381-389, 477-483; 98 (1833), 16-24, 118-127.

Walther, Anthon Balthasar: *Silesia diplomatica, oder Verzeichniss derer gedruckten Schlesischen Diplomaten, Privilegiorum...und andrer zur Schlesischen Historie und Rechtsgelehrsamkeit gehörigen Uhrkunden und Nachrichten* (Breslau 1741 and 1742).

Wappler, Paul: *Thomas Müntzer in Zwickau und die 'Zwickauer Propheten'* (Gütersloh 1966).

Weber, Franz Michael: *Kaspar Schwenckfeld und seine Anhänger in den freybergischen Herrschaften Justingen und Öpfingen. Ein Beitrag zur Reformationsgeschichte im Alb-Donau-Raum* (Stuttgart 1962).

Wedekind, Eduard Ludwig: *Geschichte der Grafschaft Glatz. Chronik der Städte, Flecken, Dörfer, Kolonien, Schlösser etc. dieser souverainen Grafschaft von der frühesten Vergangenheit bis auf die Gegenwart* (Neurode 1857).

Weichenhan, Erasmus: *Postilla, Das ist: Geistliche Hertzstärckung und Labsal, Wie auch Auslegung über die Evangelien, So man pfleget zu lesen an den Sonntagen und heiligen Festen. Christlich und einfältig geprediget und beschrieben, Durch ERASMUM Weichenhan, Pfarrern zu Langen-Bielau* (Sultzbach 1672).

Weigelt, Horst: *Sebastian Franck und die lutherische Reformation* (Gütersloh 1972).

———: "Sebastian Franck und Caspar Schwenckfeld in ihren Beziehungen zueinander," *ZBKG* 39 (1970), 3-19.

———: "Friedrich II. von Preussen und die Schwenckfelder in Schlesien. Ein Beitrag zum Toleranzverständnis Friedrichs II," *ZRGG* 22 (1970), 23 0-243.

Weissenborn, Johann Christian Hermann: *Acten der Erfurter Universität. Herausgegeben von der Historischen Commission der Provinz Sachsen. Bearbeitet von J.C. Hermann Weissenborn. II. Theil, 2 b—20. Allgemeine und Facultätsstatuten von 1390-1636. 3 b. Allgemeine Studentenmatrikel. 2. Hälfte.* (1492-1636) (Halle 1884).

Wernicke, Ewald: *Chronik der Stadt Bunzlau von den ältesten Zeiten bis zur Gegenwart* (Bunzlau 1884).

Wiedemann, Hans: "Das Sulzbacher Geistesleben unter Herzog Christian August," in Gerhard Pfeiffer and Hans Wiedemann: *Sulzbach in der deutschen Geschichte* (Sulzbach-Rosenberg 1965), pp. 17-35.

Windeck, Bernhard: *Die Anfänge der Brüder vom gemeinsamen Leben in Deutschland* (Diss. phil. Bonn 1951).

Wiswedel, Wilhelm: *Bilder und Führergestalten aus dem Täufertum. Ein Beitrag zur Reformationsgeschichte des 16. Jahrhunderts. Bd. III* (Kassel 1952).

———: "Oswald Glait von Jamnitz," *ZKG* 56 (1937), 550-564.

Wittich, Hieronymus: *Kurtze vnnd gründtliche widderlegung der vier Schlusreden die Johan Sigmund Werner, etwa Pfarherr zu Lignitz aus Schwenckfeldts Büchern gezogen, gestalt, vnd gericht hat wider die Christliche lehre vom dienst des Göttlichen worts vnd der hochwirdigen Sacrament Jesu Christi . . . . Item eine kurtze schrifft Matth. Flacij Illyrici* (Magdeburg 1555).

Wolfart, Karl: "Beiträge zur Augsburger Reformationsgeschichte. II. Zur Biographie des M. Bonifacius Wolfhart," *BBKG* 7 (1901), 167-180;

———: "III. Caspar Schwenkfeld und Bonifacius Wolfhart," *ibid.* 8 (1902), 97-114, 145-161.

Wotschke, Theodor: "Zur Reformation in Liegnitz," *Correspondenz-Blatt* 12 (1911), 155-164.

Wuttke, Heinrich: "Zwei Wallfahrten von Schlesiern nach dem gelobten

Lande im 16. Jahrhundert,'' *Schlesische Provinzial-Blätter* 121 (1845), 502-515.

Zimmermann, Elisabeth: *Schwenckfelder und Pietisten in Greiffenberg und Umgegend. Ein Beitrag zur Geschichte der Frömmigkeit im Riesen- und Isergebirge von 1670 bis 1730* (Görlitz 1939).

———: ''Über den Ursprung der Schwenckfelder im Iser- und Riesengebrige,'' *ZRGG* 1 (1948), 149-162.

Zimmermann, Franz: *Martikel der Martin-Luther-Universität Halle-Wittenberg* (Halle 1955).

Zinzendorf, Nikolaus Ludwig v.: *Büdingische Sammlung. Bd. III,* in Zinzendorf, Nikolaus Ludwig v.: *Ergänzungsbände zu den Hauptschriften herausgegeben von Erich Beyreuther und Gerhard Meyer. Bd. IX* (Hildesheim 1966).

———: ''Die Geschichte der verbundenen vier Brüder,'' *ZBG* 6 (1912), 7 2-108.

———: ''Kurze Relation von Herrnhut und Bertholsdorff seith der Abreise des Herrn Heitz,'' *ZBG* 6 (1912), 46-48.

Zobel, Alfred: ''Die Gegenreformation in der Grafschaft Glatz,'' *Evangelisches Kirchenblatt für Schlesien* 4 (1901), 131-132, 138-139, 146-148, 156-157.

———: ''Die Reformation in der Grafschaft Glatz,'' *Evangelisches Kirchenblatt für Schlesien* 4 (1901), 107-108, 113-114.

Index of Persons

Index of Persons

Index of Persons

Index of Persons

Index of Persons

Index of Persons

Index of Persons

Index of Persons

Index of Places

Index of Places

Index of Places

Index of Places

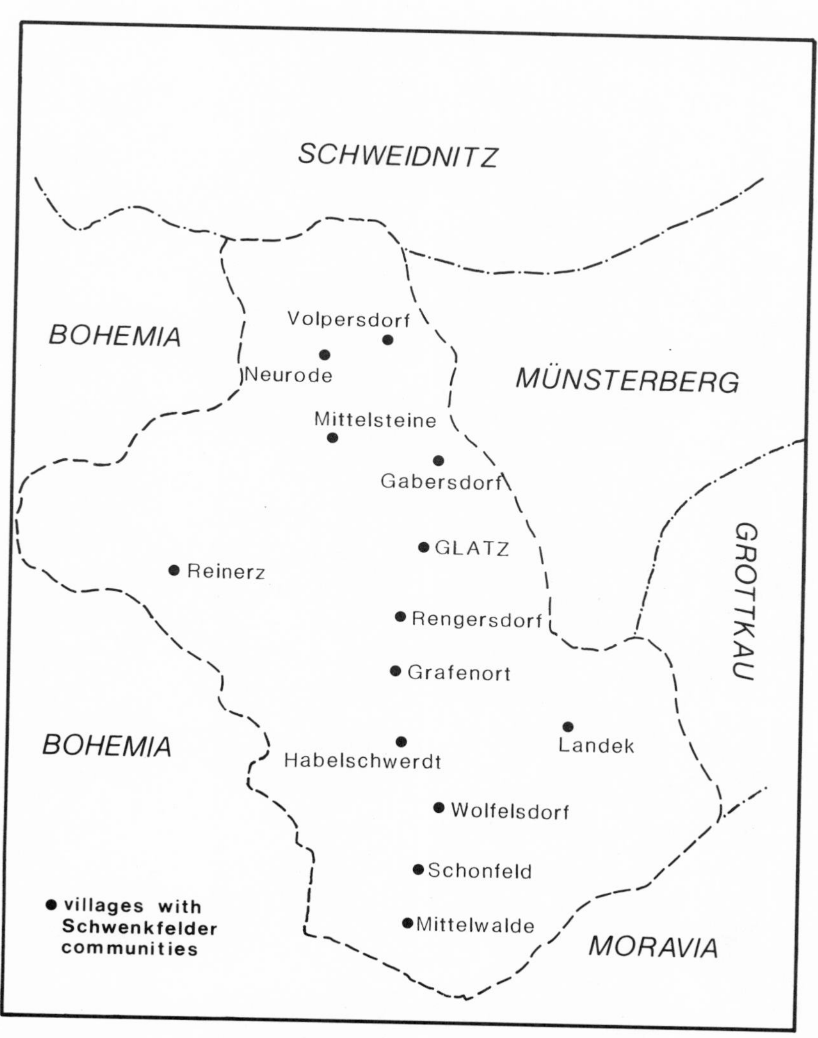
SCHWEIDNITZ
BOHEMIA
Volpersdorf
Neurode
MÜNSTERBERG
Mittelsteine
Gabersdorf
GLATZ
Reinerz
GROTTKAU
Rengersdorf
Grafenort
BOHEMIA
Landek
Habelschwerdt
Wolfelsdorf
Schonfeld
villages with Schwenkfelder communities
Mittelwalde
MORAVIA

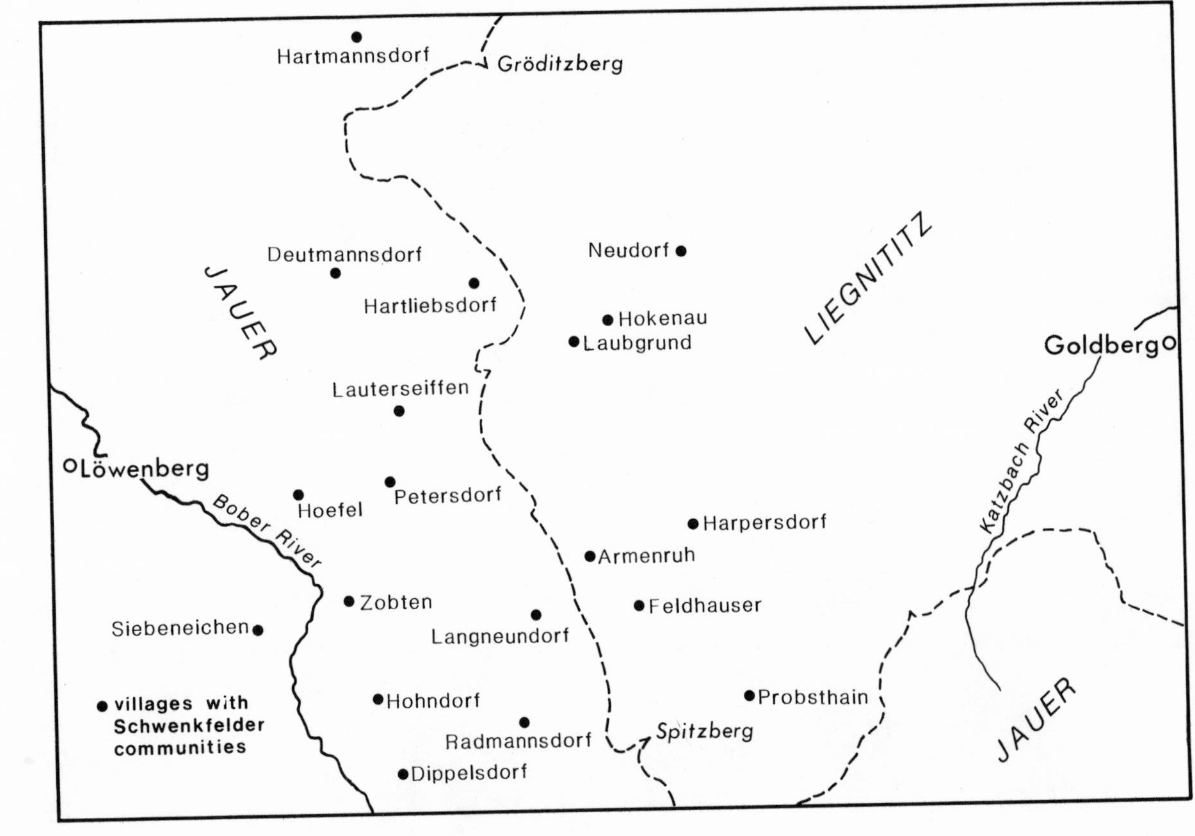
Hartmannsdorf
Gröditzberg
Deutmannsdorf
Neudorf
JAUER
Hartliebsdorf
Hokenau
Laubgrund
LIEGNITITZ
Goldberg
Lauterseiffen
Löwenberg
Petersdorf
Hoefel
Bober River
Katzbach River
Harpersdorf
Armenruh
Zobten
Feldhauser
Siebeneichen
Langneundorf
villages with
Schwenkfelder
communities
Hohndorf
Probsthain
Radmannsdorf
Spitzberg
JAUER
Dippelsdorf